Issues and Innovative Trends in Sustainable Growth – Strategy Challenges for Economic and Social Policies

Luminita Chivu / Constantin Ciutacu / Valeriu Ioan-Franc /
Jean-Vasile Andrei (eds.)

Issues and Innovative Trends in Sustainable Growth – Strategy Challenges for Economic and Social Policies

Proceedings ESPERA 2016
Part 1

PETER LANG

Bibliographic Information published by the Deutsche Nationalbibliothek
The Deutsche Nationalbibliothek lists this publication in the Deutsche Nationalbibliografie; detailed bibliographic data is available in the internet at http://dnb.d-nb.de.

Library of Congress Cataloging-in-Publication Data
A CIP catalog record for this book has been applied for at the Library of Congress.

Printed by CPI books GmbH, Leck.

ISBN 978-3-631-67331-7 (Print)
E-ISBN 978-3-653-06572-5 (E-PDF)
E-ISBN 978-3-653-70797-5 (EPUB)
E-ISBN 978-3-653-70798-2 (MOBI)
DOI 10.3726/978-3-653-06572-5

Peter Lang – Berlin · Bern · Bruxelles · New York · Oxford · Warszawa · Wien

This publication has been peer reviewed.

www.peterlang.com

Contents

Foreword

This edition is dedicated to Professor Constantin Ciutacu (June 3, 1946 – January 22, 2017), deputy general director of the "Costin C. Kirițescu" National Institute for Economic Research of the Romanian Academy (2007–2017) and one of the initiators and supporters of the ESPERA International Conference. Professor Constantin Ciutacu dedicated his scientific career of over 40 years to research and teaching activities that he successfully combined with practical experience in public service, in boards of directors of some companies and in consultancy to public institutions. His remarkable economic culture, his profound knowledge of the Romanian as well as European and world economic realities constituted the ground for his 55 books and over 300 papers published as author, co-ordinator or co-author in macroeconomics, economic restructuring, competition and state aid, labour market and industrial relations. This volume is opened by his remarkable speech delivered during the plenary session of the conference.

The present book contains the most valuable papers presented at the international conference "Economic Scientific Research: Theoretical, Empirical and Practical Approaches"–ESPERA 2016.

ESPERA, the fourth edition in 2016, is an annual event initiated by NIER in partnership with the National Bank of Romania, Centre for Economic Information and Documentation. In 2015, it was joined by the Romanian Cultural Institute, the Faculty of Economics and Business Administration, St. Kliment Ohridski University, Sofia, Bulgaria and the Institute of Agricultural Economics, Belgrade, Serbia.

The "Costin C. Kirițescu" National Institute for Economic Research (NIER) is an academic public institution for socio-economic fundamental scientific research. It also develops applied research financed by public or private internal and external sources, in accordance with the research strategy of the Romanian Academy and the National and European strategies and policies in the field of research and development.

The NIER network includes: a) five institutes with legal personality: Institute of National Economy; Institute of Agricultural Economics; Research Institute for the Quality of Life; Institute for Economic Forecasting; Institute of World Economy; b) four centres with legal personality: Centre for Industry and Services Economics; "Victor Slăvescu" Centre for Financial and Monetary Research; Centre for Studies and Researches on Agroforestry Biodiversity; Centre for Economic Information and Documentation; c) six centres without legal personality: Romanian Centre for Comparative Economics and Consensus; Centre for Macroeconomic Modelling; Centre for Demographic Research; Centre for IT Assistance of Decision; Centre for Promotion of Renewable Energy and Energy Effectiveness; Centre for Mountain Economy.

The aim of ESPERA is to present and evaluate the economic scientific research portfolio, to argue and substantiate development strategies, including European and global best practices. ESPERA intends to become a scientific support for the conceptualisation and establishment of policies and strategies and to provide a multi-sectional, systematic, permanent, wide and challenging dialogue within the European area of economic and social research.

The ESPERA 2016 edition attracted 375 participants in its plenary session and parallel workshops, which included over 50 foreign guests from Spain, Italy, the Republic of Moldova, Hungary, Bulgaria, Poland, Serbia, Egypt, India and Turkey.

This volume contains the researchers' scientific opinions and ideas focused on a diverse, sometimes divergent, sometimes convergent set of subjects: sustainable development; natural resources; smart development and human capital; migration, labour market; economic structures; trends and possible responses to globalisation and European integration challenges; models, scenarios, and evaluations.

A comprehensive analysis of the papers reveals that most converge to three core subjects: transition to market economy, accession to the European Union, financial-economic crises and globalisation.

Editors
Luminița Chivu
Valeriu Ioan-Franc
Jean-Vasile Andrei

Bucharest, June 2017

Constantin CIUTACU

Opinions of the NIER Researchers on Romania's Development Priorities

Although many warning signals were given by academic institutions, world and national elites, the technical and scientific discoveries and the globalist geopolitics regarding their use and practical implementation worsened the increasingly visible depletion—especially in the last two decades of the 20th century—of the resources of the growth model that led to prosperity and development after World War II.

Mankind and the states have undergone profound changes to their rules and institutions, new practices of economic restructuring were promoted, and commercial, military, cultural, social and political interactions and connections have moved to another level.

The role and the functions of the national states and of the public and private enterprises are changing and a "new management" with more "volatile objectives", especially in the short term, tends to be enshrined; budgets, programmes and prognoses are becoming increasingly fortuitous and medium- and long-term creations are becoming benchmarks of outdated thinking, growth linearity is being replaced with non-linearity, concepts for theorising and measuring the zero growth and negative growth are being formulated. We are now talking about crisis and post-crisis stages, economic recovery, management and optimisation of deficits and fiscal optimisation, stability and sustainability, sustainable development, security and safety (food, energy, military, environment), de-industrialisation and re-industrialisation, knowledge-based economy, robots and ICT, genetics revolution and renewable energy, climate change and greenhouse gas emissions.

In this context and to a different extent, actually in almost all countries we find mistrust in control and local institutions, dealing with interactions and relations between citizens and authorities (enterprises, public services, administration, state power institutions, school, church, media); local and national solidarity are being replaced with voluntary missions; centralisation is followed by decentralisation, NGOs and a civil society are being created to replace governments, etc.

Inequalities are worsening and economic growth is being "metropolised" and clustered, while the development poles compete against the poverty poles.

These developments seem to ignore the traditional opposition between the governing parties and the second-place parties.

In real life, there is an increasing opposition between: young and elderly, rich and poor, urban and rural, regional cultures, common good and individual good, public economy and private economy, public employees and private employees and self-employed individuals, centralisation and decentralisation, monarchy and republic, domestic capital and foreign capital, etc.

While living is worsening and the population is increasing in number, individualisation and self-employment are expanding; after the Church separation from the state many people are separating from the Church; while family has been a key institution of support and solidarity, it is becoming more fragile, and socialisation is mostly based on the internet.

Romania, a long-time European country and a member of the European Union in 2007, is influenced by all global economic and geopolitical phenomena and has to manage the 1990 system change that has caused disturbances to be felt in the near future as well.

In this domestic, European, regional and global context, the researchers of the "Costin C. Kiriţescu" National Institute for Economic Research were asked to comment on the identification of three issues considered to be essential for Romania's future development.

Our request received answers in writing from 87 researchers whose contribution adds scientific value that might provide support for policy makers and for the economic culture sorely needed for understanding and individual and social action in a very complex a complicated economic, social, political and geopolitical environment.

1. Considering the frequent mentioning of the issues concerning the population, the human capital, the workforce and training, education and health, these aspects may be ranked first among the researchers' opinions.

In this respect, we may cite opinions such as "population ageing and emigration endanger the future sustainability of the nation". Among others, this means recovering the human capital by offering incentives for returning home, motivating people with well-paid jobs, supporting birth rate increase, revival and the recovery of domestic labour.

Also, rhetoric formulations such as "who is to pay the bill for low wage policy?" were considered, since emigration is a short-term gain and a long-term loss.

Losses in the number of doctors, professors, engineers, researchers, high-skilled workers, youths, etc. represent a red line for the Romanian authorities and the top vulnerability for Romania's national safety and security.

2. The issues concerning the development and supporting of education and scientific research were mentioned (from various perspectives) by over 30 of the 87 researchers.

They refer to scarcity of resources and more funding for education and research or to paying higher wages to the educators and the educated; without the above actions any investment means a loss to the others.

The labour training for other markets means a huge budget cost to Romania and, consequently, state aid to other EU member or non-member countries. Similarly, the training of students in other universities is an engine for internalising the increasing cost of training and an engine of free externalisation of future gains and sources of economic growth for other enterprises, companies and economies in competition with Romania.

Moreover, Romania is confronted with chronic underfinancing of fundamental and applicative research. While other member states provide between 1.5 and 3% of their GDP for research, Romania has provided 0.4–0.5% for about 20 years, and the national RDI system has actually collapsed, as companies and the business environment do not invest in research.

Smart development is now only a topic for scientific meetings; it is not even discussed in election campaigns.

3. A total of 14 researchers mentioned the failure to draw up a country project, a consensus-based strategy for Romania's development and a programme for economic development.

Among others, they suggest creating a strategic planning body, formulating a strategy on the 2050 horizon, setting up an institution specialised in Romania's economic development—the Institute for Economic Studies and Strategies—and ensuring the coherence and correlation of sectoral policies, etc.

4. Another set of issues and proposals points out that the sustainability of economic growth is based on specialisation in unfavourable exports (low value added and low processed products requiring low skilled labour), as well as de-industrialisation; proposals are made for developing the capacities destined to capitalise the domestic resources, to support the market and to stimulate the consumption of Romanian products, for defining and identifying the national interest, for re-industrialisation and development of local industries, for promoting an industrial policy compatible with the EU policies, for sustainable utilisation of resources and taxation of the natural resources (there is a remarkable comparative study on the regime and way of collecting royalties), for finding opportunities to use the export potential of some regressing industries, etc.

5. The issues of agriculture and rural development have been approached by over 20 researchers.

The topics cover a wide range of problems from workforce ageing and the need for support for young farmers or the rural youths' access to education, to the subsistence farm, rural poverty, the need for professionalisation, association, cooperation, cadastral survey, the development of irrigation and infrastructures, technologies and agricultural equipment, etc.

They also cover the topics of food safety and security, trade balance improvement by means of agricultural products, regaining the national market, bio production and export of organic products, biodiversity management and support for rural development, rural area development and increasing the national budget resources to be added to the aid offered through the Common Agricultural Policy.

6. Infrastructure is approached by many researchers who explain the worsening quality of the national and local road networks, lack of highways, the low number of express roads, the collapse of railway infrastructure and the low railway speed, the poor condition of the equipment and the selling of over 110,000 goods, passenger wagons and engines as scrap iron, the disappearance of the national sea transport fleet, etc.

In this context, they mention the still unused capacities of modernisation of the road and railway transport infrastructures by means of European funds.

The quality of the transport infrastructure is a critical point of vulnerability that has a great impact on the economic growth by tourism (the contribution of tourism to GDP ranks Romania among the last EU member countries, although the country enjoys an exceptional landscape in Europe), agriculture, services and industries.

The third modernisation of Romania can be achieved only through a programme for the transport infrastructure (which remains as it did at the beginning of the 20th century).

7. The quality of the central and local administrations' overgrown bureaucracy and the functioning of the institutions of the state of law, poor absorption, bureaucracy and instability of the public procurement rules regarding the European funding, corruption among the policy makers and institutions profoundly influence economic growth and the market economy mechanisms.

Although there are hundreds of strategies at the national, regional, local, sectoral and institutional levels, they are not accompanied by rigorous action plans and correlated with the objectives to ensure coherence and the convergence and there is no institution for monitoring and assessing *ex ante* and *ex post* a set of indicators of the implementation, impact, efficiency and effectiveness of the outcome.

Many researchers deal with issues regarding the difficulty of the practical fulfilment of the wishes and suggest analysing what hinders the implementation of public policy or setting up a centre for managing, controlling and monitoring the fulfilment of the objectives of the national plans and strategies, or a permanent entity for strategic planning and risk assessment (e.g., in France, we find the Commissariat for Development Strategy).

8. Researchers have also expressed many important opinions and made proposals for economic growth.

For example, they deal with topics related to the domestic and foreign financial framework: dependence on deficits and on financial institutions, the diminution of the Romanian bank capital, non-sustainability and tax evasion, profit transfer through offshore centres, rising public debt and the increasing debt of private companies, exceeding the alert level to the foreign funding proportions (24% of the GDP in comparison to the 15% alert limit; the proportion of the public debt of non-residents: 51% in comparison to 45%; the deteriorations of the net investment position: from -29.4% of the GDP in 2005 to -70.4% in 2012 and -57.2% in 2014, when compared to -35%, etc.).

We should avoid changing the strategic objectives, the institutions in charge and the rules during the same election cycle.

The economic growth seems to be followed by more poverty, social polarisation and more inequalities, deterioration of the education and health care systems and of the social protection and assistance systems, which may affect what has remained from solidarity, social cohesion, equal opportunities, non-discrimination and fair distribution of the economic growth products.

The above opinions show that the economic, sociological and social research along with the research on justice and quality of life may have substantial, fundamental and founded contributions to rebalancing and recalibrating economic growth and access to welfare.

There are many other opinions of the NIER researchers that could be a real thinking treasure.

We intend to carry on these actions and further publish the outcome of every annual scientific conference of the "Costin C. Kiriţescu" National Institute for Economic Research.

Napoleon POP

Institute of World Economy, "Costin C. Kiriţescu"
National Institute for Economic Research, Romanian Academy;
Calea 13 September nr. 13, sector 5, Bucharest 050711, Romania;
iemnapoleon@gmail.com

Valeriu IOAN-FRANC

"Costin C. Kiriţescu" National Institute for Economic Research,
Romanian Academy; Calea 13 September nr. 13, sector 5,
Bucharest 050711, Romania; cide90@gmail.com

"Revenge" of the Globalization Losers

Abstract: The management of the globalisation challenges and opportunities by the European Union shows some weaknesses and the strength of the tools used does not match the social capacity to assimilate them. The quality of the EU governance is a reason why globalisation and belonging to the Euro Zone has caused damage not only to some social groups, but to whole nations (Greece, Spain, Portugal, and Italy). The cause is not the financial crisis, but the neglect of the structural reforms. There have been long debates on the effects of failure, but no solutions have been suggested (systems of education, health care, pensions, labour productivity stimulation, etc.). Our paper, presented on other occasions[1] as well, aims to explain the state of today's globalisation, considering international trade.

Keywords: globalisation; unemployment; financial crisis; technological progress; middle class; labour market; structural reforms; classic reform policies; isolation and populism; International Trade; European Union

1. Preliminaries

The two-decade stagnation of real income, high unemployment, effects with an (already) permanent impact produced by the financial crisis on economic growth in the long term as well as the mix of globalization (visible everywhere) and technological progress (limited) caused the de-structuring of the labour force consisting of workers, in a traditional sense, and now it affects the high-skilled labour force of the middle class. The labour market reforms are only related to job destruction (France) and wage freezing (Germany), and their application on a national scale

---

1 See also the paper on "Les conjonctures de la mondialisation", presented at the 11th Meeting of the Royal Spanish Academy of Economic and Financial Sciences of 10 November, 2016.

seems to have caused the Euro Area crisis. The successful reforms in Germany in the 2000s have brought about a cut in relative prices and export expansions, along with massive savings (budget and current account surplus) which (because of their individualism) caused a gap between the North and the South of the European Union.

If all countries had implemented structural reforms simultaneously (especially, national competitiveness improvement), there would not have been such different net gains among countries and not much of the present speech antagonising the EU countries would have occurred, and the social prevalence over the policies imposed by some countries on others (along with government changes) would have been lower.

The structural reforms of globalization (as some analysts say) produce much subtler effects than the handbook rules, and the correlation between the reform initiators and the implementation support for their parties have weakened. The result: globalisation has overwhelmed the classic reform policies and has been beyond the understanding capability of the existing establishment, and populism has expanded inside the western democracies (not only the younger ones). There is an increasing asymmetry among the EU countries involved in the integration ability of ensuring more compatibility, which requires other tools for re-routing the European integration project.

Isolation and populism caused by the political action of radicals in many countries are not solutions to the "unexpected effects"[2] of globalisation (of integration, for some). Poor management, caused by lack of knowledge, delay and palliatives, is the reason why many EU members are *de facto* losers of globalization, in a context showing a different distribution of the economic power in the world.

The decision-makers think in terms of political costs, i.e. longer time in power, unfortunately irrespective of results, but are unable to see what happens. Any social survey may signal what happens, and the present repositioning in relation to the Transatlantic Trade and Investment Partnership (TTIP) could—according to some analysts—diminish one of the anti-EU factors. It does not mean heightening the negative effects of globalisation on the Europeans, but we should understand that both European integration and globalisation are competition fields for winners and losers.

2. Globalisation and International Trade

For a long time, globalisation has supported the international trade liberalisation, and equally the international rules guiding the world trade have helped globalisation. But the positive synergy reached its effectiveness limit when the globalisation effects (as perception and reality) affected jobs, incomes, and the redistribution of

2 We discussed the matter on the occasion of the ESPERA 2015 Conference organised by the "Costin C. Kirițescu" National Institute for Economic Research of the Romanian Academy.

resources for social policies, especially in the developed countries confronted with the strongest global financial crisis.

Undoubtedly, the above opinions on social aspects have a quantitative relevance (statistical indicators) stemming from the economic mechanisms governing the global model: externalisation, liberalisation and deregulation at all levels of competence interaction; investors, shareholders, creditors, consumers, etc. As a result of the national and international institutional interactions, and the financial crisis and its effects—especially their management (for many people, their intensity and structure of the tools were inappropriate)—there was an attack against the way of living of the individuals/citizens and their voting option that influenced globalisation itself.

The international trade as a whole and the preferential zones created inside it in accordance with the World Trade Organisation (WTO, 2015) rules represent one of the main channels of transmission of the rejected effects of globalisation, such as Brexit and the election of the US President. The competition created or distorted by the excessive liberalisation of the international trade, due to the contradicting action of the WTC global agreement and the regional agreements, the negotiated (European Union (EU) Single Market, the North American Free Trade Agreement (NAFTA), the Association of Southeast Asian Nations (ASEAN)) or the under-negotiation (TTIP or TPP) have caused an increasing reaction from ordinary citizens to politicians against globalisation. Without ignoring that the political usually takes advantage of the citizens' dissatisfaction and strengthens emerging opinions (lack of trust, scepticism, search for alternatives, etc.), we notice that what stimulates the present confrontation between globalisation and international trade started long ago and now opposes the national to globalisation.

The new American administration seems to introduce an era of confrontation between bilateralism and multilateralism in relation to trade negotiations in a global economy, at a time of confrontation and plurilateralism. Some isolation of the United States of America (USA), revealed by some speeches critical of some important agreements on trade and investment in the Transatlantic and Pacific areas, shows that the USA opted for bilateralism to resolve its domestic economic problems.

Measures against Germany's commercial and financial aggressiveness were directed against Volkswagen and Deutsche Bank long ago and consisted of fines amounting to tens of billions of euro. A reason—sharply criticised by EU and non-EU countries—was the fact that Germany succeeded during the financial and economic crisis to achieve budget and current account surplus, while other countries were collapsing under the foreign debt burden.

The loss of jobs among the American middle class, usually employed in increasingly delocated industries confronted with unfair competition, helped to easily attack the TTP, which although finalised after seven years of negotiations (affecting about 40% of the American exports) is not yet ratified by the Congress. The president's order that the USA should break this agreement was an easy task, considering the criticism and the possible measures against the trade with Mexico (based on NAFTA) and the possible 35% increase in the customs duties on Chinese goods. Then the WTO was attacked, although 165 countries had succeeded to properly ensure the governance of international trade, following difficult and long negotiations, just under the American leadership.

So we come to sharply contest multilateralism in ordering and liberalising the international trade of the USA in goods and services, and the 2017 Commercial Policy Agenda, set by the United States Trade Representative (USTR), confirms the above-mentioned by the objective assumed: the USA will take future action so the trade expansion can be free and fair for all American citizens, focused mainly on: (1) bilateral negotiation (less on multilateral ones), and (2) on the efforts made by partners to open their markets. The USTR Agenda also mentions that the USA wants absolute control of the trade policy sovereignty, and any WTO decisions against the USA interests should be rejected. With regard to the USA's major trade deficits, tough anti-dumping measures should be taken (China is clearly mentioned, doubting that it is a market economy).

Following such actions, the TTIP seems unlikely to be finalised as it is already blocked because of some issues regarding the agricultural products (very high European subsidies that distort competitiveness), cultural products (less protected intellectual property in Europe) or the safeguarding measures. The US attack against the TTP seems to have affected the multilateral negotiations during the Doha Round, already delayed as regards the objectives; the two agreements are considered to speed up the negotiations. As the USA has doubts regarding the two "mega-partnerships", no other steps are taken to carry on the liberalisation of the foreign trade by tariffs (customs duties cut by 3.5% on average, following the General Agreement on Tariffs and Trade (GATT) liberalisation), along with the convergence of regulations for equal opportunities offered to foreign investors, to intellectual property, to the environment and to labour force.

While the international trade in goods is weakening, the international trade in services (more dynamic than the trade in goods) is also attacked, although it has greatly contributed to the gross domestic product (GDP) growth in the USA and many European countries.

3. The European Union in the present economic, political and social context

As for the EU, the challenges posed by a possible increasing protectionism worldwide should be viewed in relation to its status as a great exporter and importer of goods and services (one third of the EU's GDP consists of the trade in goods and services).

The challenge to the EU should be also viewed by the contents of reports on the evolutions and trends in commercial policies, beyond the commitments (G-20) not to impose new constraints. It is true that in 2015 the commercial protectionism intensified both within the G-20 and globally, as the number of new constraints was the highest since the beginning of the financial crisis, along with a slow-down (already a state policy) of the market liberalisation. Unfortunately, even the European Union, through countries pertaining to the G-20 (France, Germany, Italy and the United Kingdom), is responsible for the protectionism within the G-20 and worldwide. Agnes Ghibuțiu, the coordinator of several studies conducted by the Institute of World Economy of the Romanian Academy, found out that the openness of the foreign markets regressed. While the set of protectionist measures identified by the EU has increased since 2008 to 1,059, and only 20% of them have been eliminated, "the initiatives related to the protectionist commercial policy of the EU's trade partners exceed in number the liberalisation initiatives in a 3:1 proportion". Half of the total number of new restrictive commercial measures against EU products in 2014 and 2015 were taken by emerging economies, especially China, Russia, Indonesia and India.

According to the EU representatives, supporting the WTO's multilateral trade agenda is a basic aim of the EU commercial policy by adopting the trade liberalisation packages at the WTO's meetings in Bali (Indonesia) in 2013 and Nairobi (Kenya) in 2015. As regards the weakening of multilateralism, the EU itself initiates plurilateral negotiations, complementary to the multilateral initiatives for trade liberalisation even within the WTO.

As for the bilateral and regional agenda of the EU as a top commercial power in the world, we notice that it has reached preferential agreements with 52 countries and is negotiating free-trade agreements and economic partnerships with 80 countries, including strategic economic partners, with China on top. Owing to the free trade agreements, the weight of that trade has increased from less than a quarter of EU trade (a decade ago) to one third at present, and this proportion will reach two-thirds after the conclusion of the agreements.

4. Conclusion

The official withdrawal of the USA from the TPP has created an economic void in the Asia-Pacific area, supposed to be filled by China. This movement, promoted through the America First Strategy, is considered as a way to undermine the USA pole in the region, which is contrary to the rebalancing from the Middle East to Asia-Pacific, initiated by Hillary Clinton and Barack Obama in 2011. Therefore, the Regional Comprehensive Economic Partnership (including the ASEAN, Australia, New Zeeland, China, India, Japan, and South Korea) aims to fill this economic void hoping that China does not put more pressure on the American market. At the same time, China seems to strengthen the relations with traditional partners of the USA, such as the Philippines and Malaysia, supporters of free trade.

A "free trade" based on bilateral commercial agreements, tariff barriers and home relocation of American companies and profit repatriation (Daniel Dăianu, 2016) is not only a change in the vision of the liberalisation leader, but also a clear invitation to major structural changes in international trade flows as regards their structure and intensity. To these changes one should add the changes in the way the emerging economic powers respond to the protectionist measures, as they are co-authors of some of them.

The main question is how to compensate "the losers" of the free trade, as there is a consensus between the political and business elites that the anti-globalisation trend reflects the reality: it produced winners and losers, as well. Dani Rodrik (international political economy professor at Harvard University) says that the answer to this question is not "stop globalisation", but a way to compensate the losers and make them join the internationalisation trend. Nouriel Roubini writes: "the anti-globalisation struggle can be diminished and managed by compensating the labourers for losses and costs paid" (quotation from "Too Late to Compensate Free Trade's Losers"); thus, the losers' problem is brought to the individual level and not the state level. The states have "introverted" by the vote and/or support to the radical right-wing politicians; a nightmare hard to overcome after Brexit or the presidential elections in Austria and the parliamentary elections in the Netherlands. Losers must be brought back among the globalisation winners by redistribution policies for an equal increase in savings. Therefore, redistribution, having both economic and political reason, makes us conclude that from now on—as Rodrick says—trade partnerships are acceptable only if winners agree to share benefits with losers. We cannot envisage another policy able to maintain economies and open trade, unless it is supported by larger pro-globalisation agents.

The question is whether a compensation solution included in free trade partnerships is not too late. The answer seems to be "yes", as this solution was viable two decades ago during the globalisation boom. Unfortunately, the benefits promised to all were directed—by successive liberalisations—to the people in power; thus, the globalisation was perceived as an evil by many citizens. Rodrick says that now it is necessary to reconsider the rules of globalisation to remain together.

Daniel Dăianu reveals the "mermaids" favouring protectionism: "The erosion of the position of the USA and other developed countries as regards the economic power distribution in the world; New technologies that destroy jobs and economic/public policies responsible for social unrest and displacement; The financial crisis that fragmented and divided the society and caused withdrawals; The crisis that forced the countries and the central banks to take 'non-standard', interventionist measures; Bad corporate practices, tax evasion, which cause reactions against globalisation; A widespread feeling that external (financial) markets exercise an excessive power on national decision-making" (Dăianu, 2017).

The above issues may also affect the legitimacy of those in power to manage the public affairs. Therefore, it is obvious that safety, and the protection of the citizens and of the state are priorities on the public agenda of the developed countries.

References

1. Costa, R. (2012). Ultimul avertisment. A venit timpul să ne gândim la pericolul dispariției, Editura Trei.

2. Davos (2016). World Economic Forum, retrieve from: http://www.ft.com/indepth/davos, accessed on: 22.09.2016.
3. Dăianu, D. (2017). Protecţionism redivivus în lumea devoltată, retrieve from: www.ziare.com, accessed on: 06.02.2017.
4. Dăianu, D. (2017). The New Protectionism; Where does it come from and where does go, World Commerce Review, Spring Verlag.
5. De Montbrial, Th. (2016). *Discurs la Banca Naţională a României, cu prilejul aniversării a 150 de ani de la fondarea Academiei Române.*
6. European Commission (2005), European Economic Forecast – Autumn, Institutional Paper 11, https://ec.europa.eu/info/publications/economy-finance/european-economic-forecast-autumn-2015_en2015.
7. European Commission: – 22 June 2015 – Five Presidents' Report sets out plan for strengthening Europe's Economic and Monetary Union as of 1 July 2015, Brussels.
8. International Monetary Fund (October 2015). Adjusting to Low Commodity Prices.
9. International Monetary Fund (April 2015). World Economic Outlook – Uneven Growth, Short and Long-Term Factors.
10. Ioan-Franc, V., Pop, N. (2014). Repoziţionări ale actorilor economici", in Caiete Critice nr. 12, pp. 66–72.
11. Maxton, G. (2011). Sfârşitul progresului, Cum ne-a înşelat aşteptările gândirea econoică modernă, John Wiley & Sons Edition, Singapore Pte Ltd.
12. OECD. (November 2015). Economic Outlook.
13. Pop, N., Ioan-Franc, V. (2014). Globalizarea – o realitate a timpului nostru, in Caiete Critice nr. 1, pp. 70–76.
14. Pop, N., Ioan-Franc, V. (2015). O propunere de viziune strategică a Uniunii Europene (partea I), Institutul de Economie Mondială, Institutul Naţional de Cercetări Economice "Costin C. Kiriţescu", Academia Română.
15. Pop, N., Ioan-Franc, V. (2015). Resetarea viziunii strategice a UE în actualul context global şi european, in Caiete Critice nr. 4, pp. 69–80.
16. Pop, N., Ioan-Franc, V. (2016). L'Europenisation de la Roumanie – un acte de recherché academique, in Review of General Management, vol. 23, 1, pp. 16–25.
17. Popescu, D. (2015). Nation, Communitarism, Peace and Globalisation: A Vulnerable Relationship in ESPERA Conference, ed. 3, Institutul Naţional de Cercetări Economice "Costin C. Kiriţescu", Academia Română.
18. Rodrick, D. (2017). Too late to Compensate Free Trade's Losers, https://www.project-syndicate.org/commentary/free-trade-losers-compensation-too-late-by-dany-rodrick-2017-04.
19. WTO (April 2015). Modest Trade Recovery to Continue in 2015 and 2016.

Dan POPESCU

"Lucian Blaga" University of Sibiu, Bucharest University,
email: dan.popescu@ulbsibiu.ro

Migration between Blocking and Lasting Forever – A Component of the Way from Government to Governance and Back

*"Unfortunately, mankind causes new problems
faster than it can resolve the old ones"*

Abstract: Migration is not a recent phenomenon. Since ancient times it has been a dramatic challenge: pushed by hunger, famine, and scarcity people have migrated to other lands for a better life. Today they do the same. It is a migration for economic reasons. It has produced emigrants. But what about the migration caused by religious, national and racial persecution, by domestic, regional or world wars, by huge natural cataclysms or by racial hatred? This kind of migration has produced no-country people, outlaws, better called "refugees".

Keywords: globalisation, geopolitics, geoeconomics, emigration, immigration, economic and social governance

1. Introduction

One can hardly find a clear distinction between emigrants leaving for economic reasons and refugees determined to leave for the above reasons. In my opinion, persecutions of any kind—including those related to poverty—produce effects on the individual, family, national and global economic area. It is obvious that for centuries hundreds and hundreds of millions of people have migrated from one land to another, from one country to another.

It started in ancient times when Christians fled from the Roman Empire and Jews ran for their lives (Poutrin, 2016; Jacques Attali, 2011), etc. In modern times—but not only—religious migration is a major issue. Jews and Muslims alike have been forced out of Catholic Spain by tens of thousands or even more. Tens of thousands of Huguenots were expelled from France by Louis XIV following the cancellation of the Nantes Edict, which had reconciled the Catholics and the Protestants (issued by Henry IV about one century before) (See Popescu, 2015 b). During the early decades of the 20th century, hundreds of thousands of Russians, Jews and many others, deprived of their nationality or status, fled to other countries. That was the reason why the famous Norwegian explorer and diplomat Fridtjof Nanses conceived and issued—under the aegis of the newly established the League of Nations—the so-called Nansen Passport, granted to several nationalities (e.g., gipsies) (Kevonian, 2016). At the same time, Spanish republicans had to leave the country because of

Franco's terror; many Soviet people emigrated because of Stalin's dictatorship; and many Germans fled under the Nazi terror. And these movements went on after World War II.

Soon, the United Nations Organisation (ONU) adopted a more humanitarian management of the phenomenon and created the High Commissioner for Refugees, mostly inspired by Nansen. But the phenomenon exceeded expectations. Soon, millions of Israelis migrated to their ancient homeland. Many Palestinians fled in 1948 in search of a home. Many other people left the Soviet–Communist Bloc, from Central and Eastern Europe, Asia, even Africa. The wars among the emerging African states turned many people into refugees in search of a better world. The wars in former Yugoslavia caused a similar migration (Popescu, 2014). The camps for the refugees are now undersized and have evolved into "towns" facing serious problems (Marianne Amar, 2016). What about the 1990s and the 2000s? The phenomenon went on.

A brief statistical search shows that over 65 million refugees now live officially outside their countries, cities or villages; a world-scale challenge. The European Union (EU), the United States of America (USA) and other countries as well as world institutions are called to take proper measures; a way—as a component—from government to governance and possibly back. This is assuming that the nationless, the outlaws and the refugees are nationally taken on. Of course, the solution is not simple. It implies tolerance and education, civic spirit and national spirit, individual conscience and global conscience, individual gains and social gains. In any case, only few refugees return to their old homes.

Nansen himself said the refugees' problems should not last for ever, as any individual feels finally better at home than in exile. At the same time emigration had economic reasons; in both cases, Europe, the USA and Canada were "desired countries", and not only them. So, let us detail the question of demographic migration.

2. Questions, analyses and objectives in modern history

There are many examples. For an accurate approach, we consider the 19th century and some industrial revolutions. Let us confine our analysis to mutations in production and productivity in social structures, in families and individuals, in building and losing capital, especially in Europe, the two Americas, Asia and Africa. Of course, emigration and immigration are top issues. The long-term motivations behind emigration and immigration are hunger, poverty, exploitation, hope for a better life abroad, even if it is very far away. The wish of those people is generally determined by economic reasons (Popescu, 2010). We should add—by some calculations, the larger part in some moments—refugees and "forced" emigrations. Practically, they are forced by other people (see Popescu, 2011). Here we consider the military colonisations. Then, exiles to distant areas, the imprisonment of British convicts in Australia, as well as in Asia, Africa, in archipelagos (see Charriere, *Papillon*, 1991). Last but not least, there are emigrations based on the fear of death, crime and genocide. Fierce political persecutions play a leading role. We should remember the political deportations to Siberia (Stere, *În preajma revoluției*, 1998). Then the deportation of German prisoners in the USSR. What about racism and genocide, which besides death, caused the movement of millions of people (Le bilan, 1992)? Often history recorded them as being more spectacular and dramatic than the economic reasons, considered relatively "common". It is this last direction that is to be investigated in depth.

3. Other opinions

According to Kenneth Pommeranz, a history professor at the University of Chicago, the 19th century migration was mostly caused by quick and concrete changes in the structure of production and productivity. It was not forced migration, but rather "free migration" for certain freedoms and progress existing in some parts of the world. In other words, it was a migration freely accepted by those people (Pommeranz, 2016). But what caused such change and increased the migration size? And can we prevent it? Can we prevent refugees' movement?

In the early decades of the 19th century—even earlier in England—industrial revolutions took place, i.e. the transition from manual labour to mechanised labour (Popescu, 1981). Besides England, machinism succeeded in France, Belgium, the Netherlands, Italy, the United States, Germany and, later, Russia. Then it reached countries in Asia and Africa, and Australia (Popescu, 1981). But in many colonies, the industrial revolution influenced the railways, and to a lesser extent the processing industries. The impact was mainly in the extractive industry. The industrial revolution benefited the great maritime companies, which purchased steam liners, harbour equipment, etc. All of them aiming at easier and cheaper transportation of raw materials from colonies to the metropolis, and of processed goods from the metropolis to the colonies (Pommeranz, 2016)

Products were purchased from more distant areas and faster by countries that needed them. Usually they were raw materials and basic, especially exotic food from colonies exchanged for processed products from industrialised countries. Therefore, it is obvious how things evolved. Among the first ones who recounted this that we find Raul Prebisch who spoke about the Price Scissors (Popescu, 1981).

4. Reality between change and continuity

We notice a gradual change. Initially it occured in the United States—a colony becoming an industrialised country—caused by increasing integration of the western territories into the American economic circuit. A similar integration took place in Canada, Australia and in some Asian countries, which developed beyond the colonisation "borders". Transport became faster, cheaper, and machines were increasingly used in agriculture, usually dominated by huge properties. Of course, for northern America was the exception with its more mobile agriculture of the farmers (Hugues, 1987). On the other hand, we should consider the increasing globalisation of the capital market, merchandise market, labour market, etc. In these circumstances, prices of agricultural products are set by the world market, not by the producers. Since the classic exchange between metropolis and colonies, i.e. processed or highly processed products against raw material or early processed products, is less significant; this means wheat for wheat, wool for wool, cotton for cotton, fruits for fruits, as farmers from relatively advanced countries do not produce even their own food. Maybe not all, but many. Many farms from Italy, France, Germany, the United Kingdom, Ireland, and the Netherlands have become inefficient on the wheat market when competing with US products. Similarly, we can refer to wool from Australia and New Zealand, meat from Argentina. To say nothing of the distortions caused in colonies, dominions, dependencies, etc. The local traditional production of European advanced countries, besides the less developed ones, are facing such problems: lower productivity, higher costs, failing households (Pommeranz, 2016).

What do these people, many of them being Europeans, have to do? To emigrate in great number to America or other lands. Hundreds of millions of people. Of course, the picture presented by K. Pommeranz is more complex, but essentially things are like that. Only autarchic economies can oppose the market on limited areas. What has persisted—if it has—in some integrated economies as well as in increasingly globalised economies seems to be disastrous. Who could oppose—and why—the huge number of emigrants coming to promising America after the 18th century from the Netherlands, France, Germany, Ireland, Russia and even Romania? Shall we mention the African origin (albeit a distant one) of Barack Obama, the German origin of Donald Trump, the President in office, or the Irish origin of John Kennedy and others? Nobody could oppose that because the economic and social criteria of development were in action. And so, the present US population consists of 15% Germans, 5–6% Italians as well as Spanish, Asian, and African (Le Point, St., 2016). Who could oppose the huge wave of emigrants coming from poorly developed Italy to Argentina in the late 19th century and in the early 20th century? Nobody; and the Italians integrated into the new country. Who could oppose the people looking for a job in Germany—ruined after World War II but able to achieve a remarkable rebuilding of the country—coming first from Italy and then from Turkey? Again nobody, and the action was successful; the German economy has developed receiving that kind of support (Popescu, 2016).

5. Walls and borders. Evolution vs. involution

The present waves of emigrants from Asia and Africa to Europe have economic causes, besides the fear of death, persecutions, bloody wars, etc. They come from underdeveloped economies and lose basically from price. First, they emigrate to favelas or reservations on the outskirts of the cities, living in poor conditions, as nobody needs them. This is with or without documents, wanted or not by the host countries (Pommernaz, 2016; Popescu, 2016, a).

It is very difficult to prevent such evolutions or involutions. The border "walls", as fortified as they could be, are finally penetrated, bored or even jumped over by those looking for a better life. And this cannot be hindered as European economies with a population with a high life expectancy desperately need labour of a certain kind: unskilled or primary skilled accepting lower wages than the locals (Popescu, 2016a). Whether we agree on it or not is another question. The wave of emigrants and whatever it brings on, especially in the political context of breaking some restrictions concerning the family unification (included among the fundamental human rights), can be diminished only by global stimulation (in spite of the UNO's failure to implement "The Decades of Development") of development and progress in relatively or absolutely backward regions of the world. This is the only way. This has a price to be paid, but the expected efficiency is not sure. But if we do not pay this price, things will get worse (Popescu, 2016, a; Popescu, 2015 b).

Regarding the latest waves of Asian and African emigrants to Europe, to Germany but also to Romania, some policy-makers from some European countries—but not at the EU level—have protested vigorously. Borders have been consolidated, new walls have been built, and the small boats have been "hunted". Besides the hundreds of thousands of emigrants accepted by the EU in Germany, Italy, France, Romania, then in Turkey and Pakistan, there have been thousands and thousands who have died, especially women and children. Also, the "fortifications" and the restrictions cost a lot, but things seem to have calmed down, although the integration of newcomers has been difficult, because of other cultures, customs, educations and horizons. This is in spite of effective bureaucratic measures for integration (especially in Germany), first directed to emigrants useful for meeting specific labour needs. Angela Merkel was re-elected for the highest position in her party. But we shall see what happens after the elections in Germany, and not only there.

6. Conclusions

The issues are also complicated because of the fact that among the Asian and African newcomers (many of them Muslim) there have been potential terrorists. Finally, things seem to have calmed down, but only in part because many of these terrorists—living in France, Germany, Belgium, Spain, the United States, Russia and Turkey, etc. —have been citizens of those countries for decades, many were born there but preserved the spirit of Jihad, revenge and terror.

Without such crimes, caused by some marginalisation of the poor populations in Western Europe and in America, by lack of social insertion (Popescu, 2015; Popescu, 2014), the integration would have been smoother. But this should have implied the consideration of the world's economic history (hardly to be achieved because of lack of economic culture) since, in spite of the penalties inflicted, one cannot prevent emigration for a better life and integration (see *les émeutes de banlieues* in France) of those who have come in a limited number. The legislation of each country is important. Anyhow, there is no conquest of Europe by Asia or an Islamic return to the old European front—sometimes to Vienna's walls; in my opinion, it is the action of economic laws in a changing world (Popescu, 2016b).

The migration through refugees and emigrants provides a larger domain of European and global governance, even if it is later included in the governing process. But this is not alone. We should add pollution, climate change, natural disasters, nuclear energy and weapons, green permit exchange, etc. Many studies reveal the necessity (not implemented by the government so far) of a minimum global income, comparable to some extent. This is also a question of governance. Is it a mere exercise of imagination and reflection? I do not think so, even if such a global objective, which I have supported for about 15 years, needs a long contradictory way. And, of course, it undergoes appropriate, effective and far-reaching governing processes. But also processes of stimulating governance benefiting the individual and all partners. It is a better way.

References

1. Attali, J. (2011). Evreii, lumea şi banii (Istoria economică a poporului evreu), Edit. Univers, Bucureşti.
2. Charriere H. (1992). Papillon, Edit. Artemis, Bucureşti 1991.
3. Hugues J. (1983). American Economic History, Scott, Foresman and Company, Dallas, Texas, London, England.
4. Popescu, D. (1981). Civilizaţie şi industrie, Edit. Albatros, Bucureşti.
5. Popescu, D. (2010). Cataclismele economice care zguduie lumea, Edit. Continent, Sibiu-Bucureşti, pp. 11–112 etc.
6. Popescu, D. (2011). Amurgul lumilor paralele, Edit. Continent, Sibiu-Bucureşti, pp. 34–93.
7. Popescu D. (2014). Ameninţări pentru secolul XXI, Edit. Continent, Sibiu-Bucureşti, pp. 21–82; 147–197; 293–307.
8. Stere, C. (1998). În preajma revoluţiei, Edit. Cartea Românească.
9. (1997), Le bilan du XXeme siècle, Edit. Harenberg, Bruxelles, 1992.
10. Amar M. (2016). L'Histoire, nr.73, Collection, octobre.
11. Kevonian D. (2016). Un passeport pour les apatrides, L'Histoire, loc. cit., pp. 46–56.
12. Le Point (St.), nr. 2305, octobre.
13. Pommeranz K. (2016). La mondialisation du XIXeme siècle. Naissance du monde, L'Histoire, nr. 425–426, Juillet-aôut 2016.
14. Popescu, D. (2016, a). Confruntările muncitorilor cu patronatul, succintă privire în timp şi spaţiu, Transilvania, nr. 8/2016.
15. Popescu, D. (2015). Alungarea hughenoţilor. Toleranţă şi intoleranţă, în Studii de istorie economică şi istoria gândirii economice, coord. Acad. Iulian Văcărel, vol. 17, pp. 166–174.
16. Popescu, D. (2016, b). Amplificarea emigraţiei şi imigraţiei generată de integrare şi globalizare, în volumul Penser l'Europe, Edit. Academiei Române, Bucureşti.
17. Poutrin, I. (2016). Séfardes et morisques. Explosions massives, L'Histoire, La Collection de L'Histoire, L'Odyssée des refugies, octobre, pp. 22–24.

Caraiani PETRE

Institute for Economic Forecasting,
Romanian Academy, caraiani@ipe.ro

Does Forecasting the Oil with Nonlinear Models Produce Nonlinear Forecasts?

Abstract: The literature on forecasting energy prices with nonlinear models has produced general agreement that these nonlinear models can provide accurate forecasts. However, these forecasts have been analysed solely from the perspective of forecast accuracy. The literature has not addressed the question of whether these models generate energy prices forecasts that are themselves nonlinear. This paper provides a preliminary answer to this question, by performing a comparative test on the nonlinear properties of forecasts for oil prices generated by nonlinear models. The results provide clear evidence in favour of the hypothesis that nonlinear models can generate nonlinear forecasts for oil prices.

Keywords: nonlinear models, nonlinearity tests, forecasts

Introduction

The economic literature generally agrees that economic (and financial) time series are characterized by nonlinearity (see the widely cited paper by Barnett and Serletis (2000)). For the case of energy prices, the evidence is quite overwhelming, see Adrangi et al. (2001) or Kyrtsou et al. (2009).

This view has also influenced the field of forecasting, as can be seen in Teräsvirta's 2006 monograph on the most widely used nonlinear models in forecasting. However, while the forecasting literature agrees that nonlinear models perform well in terms of forecasting (see Teräsvirta (2006) or Franses and van Dijk (2005)), it has yet to answer the question of whether these models lead to forecasts that are themselves nonlinear, especially in the case of energy prices. The question of whether nonlinear models can generate nonlinear forecasts is of great interest, particularly since the recent dynamics of the energy markets have shown the need for models capable of generating forecasts for energy prices that behave in nonlinear ways.

The main interest of this paper is to test whether based on nonlinear models we can generate predictions for energy prices that are nonlinear themselves. In this sense, the paper uses several well-established nonlinear models based on which sufficiently large samples of forecasts are generated. Furthermore, the samples of forecasts are tested for nonlinearity based on a wide array of nonlinearity tests well known from the literature.

1. Literature Review on Nonlinear Models

I focus on several representative models from the literature on forecasting with nonlinear models, see Teräsvirta (2006) or Franses and van Dijk (2005). I discuss and apply univariate models on the grounds that using multivariate models would require the use of other series, for example gross domestic product (GDP) or industrial production, for which the number of available observations is much smaller. Moreover, it is much more debatable whether such series are nonlinear.

Picking several nonlinear models for comparison in a horse-race competition with respect to nonlinearity is also in the spirit of the much-cited paper by Barnett et al. (1995). As with the present paper, Barnett et al. concentrate on univariate models, but while they focus on the properties of series simulated by these models, this paper looks at the properties of forecasts reached with nonlinear estimated models.

I present the models used in this paper very succinctly; the reader will find more extensive presentations in the cited papers. Overall, the presentation loosely follows Franses and van Dijk (2000).

A first model used is the additive nonlinear autoregressive model (*AAR*, hereafter), which can be written as:

$$x_{t+s} = \mu + \sum_{i=1}^{m} s_i(x_t - (i-1)d) \tag{1}$$

Here, m stands for the embedding dimension, d for the number of steps, and μ stands for the mean, while s_i represents the univariate nonparametric functions of the lagged values of the time series.

The paper also applies two versions of the widely used threshold autoregressive model, namely the self-exciting threshold autoregressive model (*SETAR*, hereafter) and logistic smooth transition autoregressive model (*LSTAR*, hereafter).

A simple *SETAR* model with two regimes and one lag can be written as:

$$x_t = \begin{cases} \mu_{0,1} + \rho_{1,1}x_{t-1} + \varepsilon_t, x_{t-1} \le \theta \\ \mu_{0,2} + \rho_{1,2}x_{t-1} + \varepsilon_t, x_{t-1} > \theta \end{cases} \tag{2}$$

where θ stands for the threshold, the coefficients ρ represent the lags, and ε_t are the shocks.

The *SETAR* models can be slightly modified by assuming the presence of a smoother transition through a continuous logistic function *G( )*. This leads to the *LSTAR* model. Usually, one assumes the following specification for the transition function:

$$G(x_{t-1}, \gamma, \theta) = \frac{1}{1 + \exp(-\gamma[x_{t-1} - \theta])} \tag{3}$$

The function *G( )* is characterized by two coefficients: the location parameter θ, driving the transition, and the slope γ of the logistic function, characterizing how smoothly the transition occurs.

Finally, I also use a further widely-employed model, the neural network nonlinear autoregressive model (NNET, hereafter). A simple *NNET* model with one hidden layer can be formulated as:

$$x_{t+s} = \beta_0 + \sum_{j=1}^{d} \beta_j g\left(\gamma_{0j} + \sum_{i=1}^{m} \gamma_{ij} x_{t-(i-1)d} \right) \quad (4)$$

Here, d is the number of steps, m, the embedding dimension, and g a logistic function. The literature shows that the NNET model includes a regime-switching component which focuses on the nonlinear relationship between the independent and dependent variables—in our case, between the current values and lagged values of the same series x_t.

2. Data

For several reasons, this paper focuses on data relating to oil prices. First of all, there is general agreement about the inherent nonlinearity of such series, see for example the reference study by Kyrtsou et al. (2009). Secondly, these series provide a sufficient scale of observations, which is not the case of, for example, macroeconomic series. Lastly, but not least, given their recent history there is of late increased interest in the dynamics of energy prices.

Given these reasons, I have selected daily data from the Western Texas Intermediate oil prices and computed the daily change. The selected sample comprises more than 7500 observations from between January 2nd 1986 and May 4th 2015.

3. Results

3.1. Procedure

I follow a simple procedure to test for the nonlinearity of forecasts. Using information criteria, I estimate the optimal specification using the daily data from between January 2nd 1986 and May 4th 2015. I then use the estimated models to forecast oil prices for two different horizons, respectively 400 periods and 200 periods ahead. Using several methods, I then test for nonlinearity in the forecasts (that in the forecasted observations, i.e. in the series of 200 and 400 ahead forecasts).

The choice of forecasting horizon merits comment. From a forecasting perspective, the horizon is not only big enough, but larger than average for the sample forecasts chosen. This choice of a larger forecasting horizon is due to the fact that nonlinear tests are quite demanding in terms of number of observations. Series of 200 and 400 observations are comparable to the smaller of the sample sizes used in Barnett et al. (1995, 1997). While they also used a bigger sample of 2000 observations, it would be hard to think of a practical use for forecasts of 2000 periods ahead, and the option of doing so was therefore rejected.

3.2. Testing for Nonlinearity: The White and Teräsvirta Tests

I start by applying two widely used tests for nonlinearity to the two samples: the White test and the Teräsvirta test. The results for the White test are presented in Table 1 and Table 2, and those of the Teräsvirta test in Tables 3 and 4.

The results of the two tests essentially agree with each other. For each class of nonlinear model, and for both types of nonlinearity test, there is a clear rejection of the null hypothesis of linearity. The results are also robust to the dimension of the sample forecast.

Table 1: White test results: 400 periods ahead forecasts

Series	Test statistic	p-value
AAR	64.32	0.00
SETAR	1680.11	0.00
LSTAR	3706.89	0.00
NNET	1869.02	0.00

Source: Author's own computations

Table 2: White test results: 200 periods ahead forecasts

Series	Test statistic	p-value
AAR	31.82	0.00
SETAR	812.77	0.00
LSTAR	2110.77	0.00
NNET	938.03	0.00

Source: Author's own computations

Table 3: Teräsvirta test results: 400 periods ahead forecasts

Series	Test statistic	p-value
AAR	64.31	0.00
SETAR	3611.90	0.00
LSTAR	3705.46	0.00
NNET	187.99	0.00

Source: Author's own computations

Table 4: Teräsvirta test results: 200 periods ahead forecasts

Series	Test statistic	p-value
AAR	31.83	0.00
SETAR	1806.6	0.00
LSTAR	1852.55	0.00
NNET	936.85	0.00

Source: Author's own computations

3.3. Testing for Nonlinearity: Keenan and Tsay tests

I further consider two other widely-used tests for nonlinearity, the Keenan and the Tsay tests (the latter being a generalization of the first). The results are shown in Tables 5 and 6 respectively. I applied these tests at both one and two lags[1]. With the exception of the results of the Keenan test for the AAR forecasts, there is again a clear result which suggests that the forecasts are nonlinear across the models and forecast samples.

Table 5: Keenan test results at 1 lag

	400 periods ahead		200 periods ahead	
Series	**Test statistic**	**p-value**	**Test statistic**	**p-value**
AAR	0.0009	0.97	0.06	0.80
SETAR	532.36	0.00	265.03	0.00
LSTAR	62392	0.00	30964	0.00
NNET	242.72	0.00	120.59	0.00

Source: Author's own computations

Table 6: Tsay test results at 1 lag

	400 periods ahead		200 periods ahead	
Series	**Test statistic**	**p-value**	**Test statistic**	**p-value**
AAR	51.72	0.00	25.24	0.00
SETAR	22270	0.00	11000	0.00
LSTAR	4176000	0.00	2065000	0.00
NNET	1785	0.00	881.3	0.00

Source: Author's own computations

1 *I do not present the results for both lags; however, they are similar to the results for one lag.*

3.4. Testing for Nonlinearity: Delta test

I finally apply the so-called Delta test of linearity, which is based on conditional mutual information (see the study by Diks and Manzan (2002)). The results are presented in Tables 7 and 8. The results are generally in line with the other tests at an embedding dimension equal to 2; however, when a higher embedding dimension is used, the results are rather mixed.

Table 7: Delta test results at embedding dimension 2

	400 periods ahead		200 periods ahead	
Series	**Test statistic**	**p-value**	**Test statistic**	**p-value**
AAR	-0.13	0.72	-0.13	0.26
SETAR	-0.0025	0.14	-0.0058	0.06
LSTAR	-0.0025	0.04	-0.0051	0.04
NNET	-0.0030	0.02	-0.0399	0.04

Source: Author's own computations

Table 8: Delta test results at embedding dimension 3

	400 periods ahead		200 periods ahead	
Series	**Test statistic**	**p-value**	**Test statistic**	**p-value**
AAR	-0.09	0.30	-0.09	0.28
SETAR	-0.0025	0.06	-0.0051	0.46
LSTAR	-0.0025	0.22	-0.0050	0.18
NNET	-0.0025	0.16	-0.0051	0.18

Source: Author's own computations

Conclusion

This is the first paper to address the question of whether nonlinear models can generate nonlinear forecasts for oil. Using various nonlinear models, I generate sufficiently large forecast samples to test the proposition that they do, using various tests for nonlinearity. Most tests (White, Teraasvirta, Keenan, and Tsay) provide evidence strongly in favor of the nonlinearity of the oil forecasts. A fifth test, the Delta test for linearity, provides rather mixed results for higher embedding dimensions. Overall, however, the results suggest that nonlinear models can indeed generate oil forecasts that are nonlinear themselves.

Acknowledgement

This work was supported by CNCSIS–UEFISCSU, project number PNII–IDEI nr. 42/2.09.2013.

References

1. Adrangi, B., Chatrath, A., Dhanda, K.K., Raffiee, K. (2001). Chaos in oil prices? Evidence from futures markets, Energy Economics 23(4):405–425.
2. Barnett, W.A., Gallant, A.R., Hinich, M.J., Jungeilges, J.A., Kaplan, D.T., Jensen, M.J. (1995). Robustness of nonlinearity and chaos tests to measurement error, inference method, and sample size. Journal of Economic Behavior & Organization 27(2):301–320.
3. Barnett, W. A., Gallant, A.R., Hinich, M.J., Jungeilges, J. A., Kaplan, D. T., Jensen, M.J. (1997). Single-Blind Controlled Competition among Tests for Nonlinearity and Chaos. Journal of Econometrics 82, pp. 157–192.
4. Barnett, W.A., Serletis, A. (2000). Martingales, Nonlinearity and Chaos. Journal of Economic Dynamics and Control 24, pp. 703–724.
5. Diks, C., Manzan S. (2002). Tests for Serial Independence and Linearity Based on Correlation Integrals. Studies in Nonlinear Dynamics and Econometrics 6(2), 2002.
6. Franses, P.H., van Dijk, D. (2000). Non-linear time series models in empirical finance. Cambridge University Press.
7. Franses, P.H., van Dijk, D. (2005). The forecasting performance of various models for seasonality and nonlinearity for quarterly industrial production. International Journal of Forecasting 21(1):87–102.
8. Kyrtsou, K., Malliaris, A. Serletis, A. (2009). Energy sector pricing: On the role of neglected nonlinearity. Energy Economics 31, 492–502.
9. Teräsvirta, T. (2006). Forecasting economic variables with nonlinear models. In: Elliott, G., Timmermann A. (Eds), Handbook of Economic Forecasting, Elsevier.

Muhammad SHERAZ

Institute of Business Administration, Department of Mathematics and Department of Economics & Finance 75270, Karachi, Pakistan, msheraz@iba.edu.pk

Vasile PREDA

University of Bucharest, Faculty of Mathematics and Computer Science, 010014 Bucharest, Romania, vasilepreda0@gmail.com
Institute of Mathematical Statistics and Applied Mathematics of the Romanian Academy, 050711 Bucharest, Romania

Mathematical Models for the Assessment of Collapse in Oil Prices

Abstract: The methods addressing volatility in computational finance and econometrics have received considerable attention since the introduction of ARCH, first studied by Engle (Engle, 1982) and its generalization, the GARCH models by Bollerslev (Bollerslev, 1986). The Generalized hyperbolic distribution (Ghyp) was introduced into the literature by Barndorff-Nielsen (Barndorff, 1997). The application of this distribution in financial market price process have been used significantly. In this paper we consider European Brent Crude Oil returns from the period 1987–2008. We have implemented GARCH modeling and Ghyp distribution with its types for underlying return series.

Keywords: GARCH Models, Volatility, Generalized hyperbolic distribution, Time Series

Introduction

The standard autoregressive conditional heteroscedasticity model (GARCH model) has some drawbacks, and in order to capture the asymmetric volatility at the signs of the shocks many extensions have been introduced. The standard GARCH model assumes that both positive and negative shocks of equal magnitude have an identical effect on future volatility; however, the term leverage effect suggests that positive and negative shocks have an asymmetric impact on the conditional volatility of subsequent observations. The IGARCH models of Bollerslev (1982), EGARCH models of Nelson (1991) and many others have been used frequently in contemporary financial literature. Any distribution can be characterized by a number of features such as mean, variance, skewness and kurtosis. The measure of kurtosis is considered as whether the data are peaked or flat relative to normal distribution. The moments of distributions are functions of all the parameters. The generalized hyperbolic distribution (Ghyp) of Barndorff-Nielsen belongs to the family of distributions which allows returns series to be modelled almost completely. This distribution has the capacity to portray heavy-tailed and asymmetric behavior of underlying returns.

In this article we present methods of GARCH models implementation and Ghyp distribution to model European Brent Crude Oil returns series from 1987 to 2015. The time period has been divided in to two intervals, first from November 1987 to January 2008 and, second from January 2008 to January 2015, in order to study the variations in the statistical characteristics of the Crude oil return series after the occurrence of financial crises in 1987 and 2008 respectively. The paper is organized as follows.

In Section 1 we present a brief literature review of underlying models. Section 2 is comprised of mathematical definitions of GARCH models and Ghyp distributions and its classification. Section 3 contains the results of estimations, model selection and distributions implementation for the underlying returns. Section 4 concludes our findings.

1. Literature review

In many financial time series, empirical studies reveal some facts such as stock returns and foreign exchange rates that exhibit leptokurtosis and stochastic volatility. Any distribution can be characterized by a number of features such as mean, variance, skewness and kurtosis. The measure of kurtosis is considered as whether the data are peaked or flat relative to normal distribution. The empirical distributions of asset returns normally appear to be negatively skewed. In financial time series analysis, the asset returns often exhibit a property called "volatility clustering" that is squared returns, absolute returns and all measures of volatility exhibits strong serial correlation.

Observation of this type of property in financial time series has led to the use of conditional heteroskadasticity. Engle (1982) introduced Autoregressive Regressive Conditionally Heteroskadastic (ARCH) processes and their generalization, i.e. GARCH by Bollerslev (1986) (Engle, 1982) (Bollerslev, 1986). The use of heteroskadastic processes describes more precisely the term volatility clustering. Sheraz and Preda used Black-Scholes model with GARCH volatility to compute kurtosis and implied volatility (Sheraz, Preda, 2014; Sheraz, Preda, 2016). Some general properties—such as variance and kurtosis—of doubly stochastic models with asymmetric GARCH error and VaR and CTE measures can be found in Dedu, Ciumara, 2010 and Sheraz, 2014.

The generalized hyperbolic distribution (Ghd) was introduced into the literature by Barndorff-Nielsen (Barndorff, 1997). The work of Barndorff-Nielsen, Eberlein and Keller, Eberlein and Prause, and Prause presents the way for this distribution and its classes to become more widely known in the financial literature (Barndorff, 1998; Eberlein, Keller, 1995; Eberlein, Prause, 2000; Prause, 1997; Prause, 1999).

2. GARCH Models and Generalized Hyperbolic Distribution

If S_t is the price of an asset and $\in [0, T]$, R_i denotes log-return then mathematically and generally in financial econometrics we write:

$$R_t = \mu + \varepsilon_t,\ \varepsilon_t / F_{t-1} \sim N\left(\mu, \sigma^2\right)$$

The distribution of error term ε_t (residuals) is conditional on information set F_t and assumed to follow a standard Gaussain distribution with mean zero and variance 1. In the case of time varying second moment i.e. variance σ_t^2, following GARCH framework (Bollerslev, 1986) we write:

$$\varepsilon_t = \sigma_t z_t,\ z_t \sim N(0,1)$$

$$\sigma_t^2 = \omega + \sum_{i=1}^{p} \alpha_i \varepsilon_{t-i}^2 + \sum_{j=1}^{q} \beta_j \sigma_{t-j}^2,\ \omega > 0, \alpha_i \geq 0, \beta_j \geq 0$$

where $\omega, \alpha_i, \beta_j$ are real parameters.

Nelson (1991) introduced the EGARCH models given by

$$\log \sigma_t^2 = \omega + \sum_{i=1}^{p} \alpha_i g\left(z_{t-i}\right) + \sum_{j=1}^{q} \beta_j \log \sigma_{t-j}^2$$

$$g\left(z_{t-i}\right) = \theta z_{t-i} + \lambda\left(\left|z_{t-i}\right| - E\left|z_{t-i}\right|\right)$$

where $\omega, \alpha_i, \beta_j$, θ and λ are real parameters and both z_{i-1} and $z_{i-1} - E|z_{i-1}|$ are zero mean and identically independently distributed with continuous distributions. The coefficient α captures the sign effect and λ the size effect.

The generalized hyperbolic distribution (Ghyp) reveals the fact that the logarithm of the density function is of hyperbolic shape. On other hand, the logarithmic values of the normal distribution are parabolic. The density of the (Ghyp) is given by

$$Ghyp(x; \lambda, \alpha, \beta, \delta, \mu) = a(\lambda, \alpha, \beta, \delta)\left(\delta^2 + (x-\mu)^2\right)^{\frac{\lambda - \frac{1}{2}}{2}}$$
$$\times K_{\lambda - \frac{1}{2}}\left(\alpha \sqrt{\delta^2 + (x-\mu)^2}\right) e^{(\beta(x-\mu))}$$

where $\lambda, \mu \in \mathbb{R}, \delta > 0, 0 \leq |\beta| < \alpha$ and,

$$a(\lambda, \alpha, \beta, \delta) = \frac{\left(\alpha^2 - \beta^2\right)^{\lambda/2}}{\sqrt{2\pi}\alpha^{\lambda - \frac{1}{2}\delta^\lambda K_\lambda\left(\delta\sqrt{\alpha^2 - \beta^2}\right)}}$$

The parameter λ can be used to define further classes of Ghyp distribution, where δ and μ are location and scale parameters respectively.

For $\lambda = 1$ we get hyperbolic distribution (Hyp), a special case of Ghyp. In other words, the parameter λ can be described as a distribution class selection parameter.

If we select $\lambda = -\frac{1}{2}$ we get the normal inverse Gaussian distribution (Nig). The density function of Nig is given by

$$Nig(x;\alpha,\beta,\delta,\mu) = \frac{\alpha\delta}{\pi} e^{\left(\delta\sqrt{\alpha^2-\beta^2}+\beta(x-\mu)\right)} \frac{K_1\left(\alpha\sqrt{\delta^2+(x-\mu)^2}\right)}{\sqrt{\delta^2+(x-\mu)^2}}$$

where $x,\mu \in \mathbb{R}, 0 \le \delta, 0 \le |\beta| \le \alpha$.

Fig. 1: Histograms of Brent Crude Oil Returns series

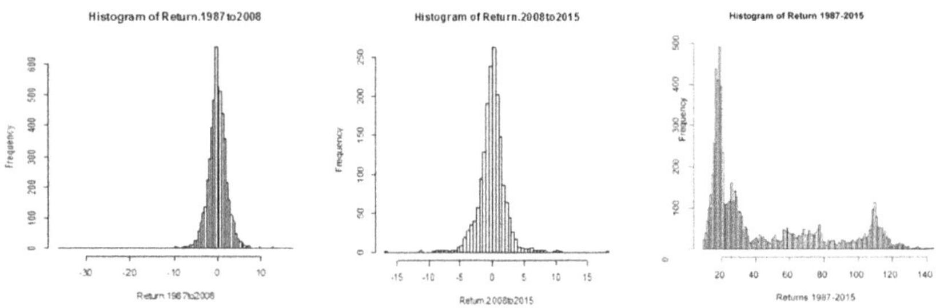

We divide time series of European Brent Crude Oil in to two periods. The first time-period is considered from the financial crises of 1987 until the financial crises of 2008. The second time-period consists of return series from 2008 to 2015. We used R package Quandl to download the daily prices of crude oil. In Table 1 we present the descriptive statistics for the daily returns of our selected oil prices.

Table 1: Descriptive statistics for daily returns

DATA	Min	Max	Mean	Var	Stdev	Skew	Kurt
1987–2008	-36.121	17.333	0.032	5.431	2.330	-0.846	16.708
2008–2015	16.832	18.129	-0.029	4.498	2.120	0.028	8.576

Fig. 2: Time series plot of Brent Crude Oil prices

3. Data Analysis

The first step is to examine the data for non-normality using Shapiro-Wiki test. In addition, the autocorrelation function and partial autocorrelation function of the return series conclude that the returns are essentially uncorrelated over time.

Model selection is always a crucial problem in any empirical study. The maximum value of likelihood functions (LH) could simply compare the two models when numbers of parameters are same, but for different numbers of parameters we can use Akaike Information Criterion (AIC), Bayesian Information Criterion (BIC), Schwarz Information Criterion (SIC) and Hannan-Quinn Information Criterion (HQIC) for "n" number of parameters of model "m" with N observations. In Table 2 we give our selection criteria results.

Table 2: Likelihood and information criterion results

Data	Model	Dist	AIC	BIC	SIC	HQIC	LH
1987–2008	GARCH	Ghyp	4.248	4.2603	4.2488	4.2528	10872.19
	GARCH	Nig	4.2490	4.2592	4.2490	4.2526	10873.76
	EGARCH	Ghyp	4.2455	4.2582	4.2454	4.2499	-10862.61
	EGARCH	Nig	4.2466	4.2581	4.2466	4.2506	-10866.49
2008–2015	GARCH	Ghyp	3.886	3.9149	3.8869	3.8973	-3409.54
	GARCH	Nig	3.8861	3.9110	3.8861	3.8953	-3409.82
	EGARCH	Ghyp	3.8748	3.9060	3.8747	3.8863	-3386.23
	EGARCH	Nig	3.8738	3.9019	3.8738	3.8842	-3386.41

For European Brent Crude Oil daily returns from 1987 to 2015, we consider AIC information criterion for the best fitted model EGARCH with conditional distribution generalized hyperbolic distribution (Ghyp). Similarly, for the returns from 2008 to 2015, EGARCH with normal inverse Gaussian distribution (Nig) is the best fitted model. We now turn toward characterization and modeling of the daily return process.

We want to estimate $\omega, \alpha, \beta, \gamma$ from the daily returns series. We fit the model to the data and investigate the output. It is evident that estimates of $\omega, \alpha, \beta, \gamma$ are all highly significant. The Jarque–Bera test suggests that the null hypothesis of joint zero skew and zero kurtosis is easily rejected. We also observe from the Box–Ljung test that the null hypothesis of independence of residuals is easily accepted. It is observed that variations in variance fall together with periods of greater uncertainty and movement in both the return series and the price series

Fig. 3: Empirical densities of standardized residuals of best fitted GARCH models

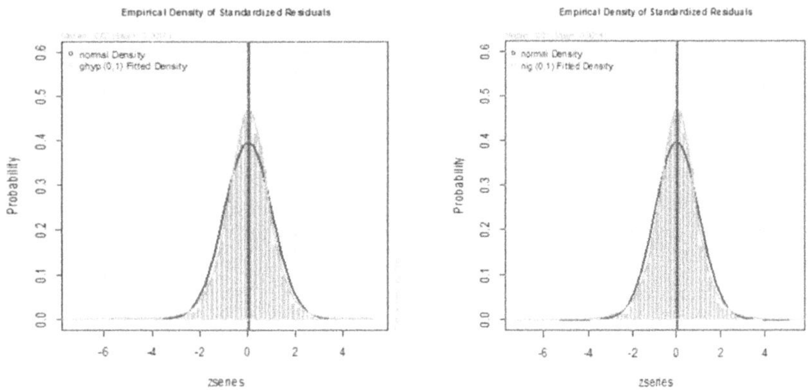

In Table 4 we present the results for parameter estimates of underlying GARCH models.

Table 4: Parametric estimation results of GARCH models

Model	**Data**	**Dist**	≠	!	→	↓	γ
sGARCH	1987–2008	Ghyp	0.0399	0.0633	0.0678	0.9216	
sGARCH		Nig	0.0400	0.0640	0.0695	0.9195	
EGARCH		Ghyp	0.032	0.020	-0.008	0.986	0.137
EGARCH		Nig	0.033	0.020	-0.006	0.985	0.144
sGARCH	2008–2015	Ghyp	-0.0447	0.0094	0.0452	0.9529	
sGARCH		Nig	-0.0458	0.0094	0.0446	0.9535	
EGARCH		Ghyp	-0.130	0.003	-0.060	0.997	0.085
EGARCH		Nig	-0.1316	0.0032	-0.0611	0.997	0.0834

Now we consider generalized hyperbolic distribution and its special cases, such as hyperbolic distribution, asymmetric hyperbolic distribution, normal inverse Gaussian distribution and its asymmetric form, for underlying daily return series. The poor description of the Gaussian empirical returns is strongly rejected. An example is given in Figure 4 below.

Fig. 4: Histograms of asymmetric hyperbolic returns and asymmetric normal Gaussian inverse distributions

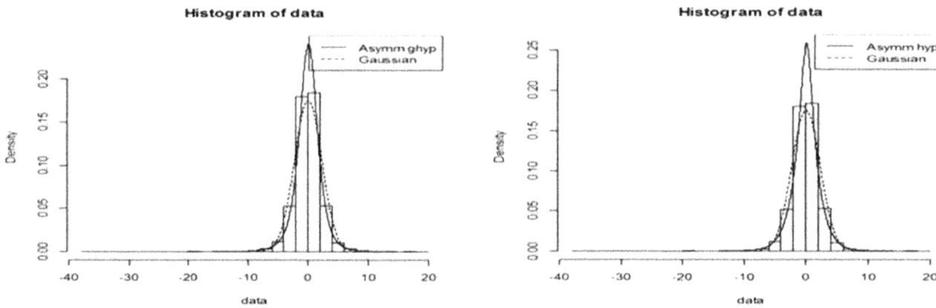

Table 5: Parameter estimates of underlying return distributions

Data	Dist	÷	→	≠	σ	õ	LH
1987–2008	Aghd	-2.037	0.007	0.1187	2.293	-0.085	-11113.44
	Ahd		0.621	0.144	2.223	-0.112	-11148.64
	Anig		0.876	0.134	2.256	-0.1022	-11128.66
2008–2015	Aghd	-0.696	0.456	0.062	2.103	-0.092	-3587.07
	Ahd		0.002	0.050	2.017	-0.079	-3591.554
	Anig		0.478	0.066	2.094	-0.097	-3587.151

The daily returns can be investigated better with the asymmetric generalized hyperbolic distribution (Aghd) than with the asymmetric hyperbolic distribution (Ahd) and asymmetric normal inverse Gaussian distribution (Anig) for the period 1987–2008. Similarly, for the period 2008–2015 Anig describes better than Aghd and Ahd. In addition it was not clear from the density plot of daily return series.

Table 6: Returns distributions and asymmetry for 1987–2008

Model	Symmetric	÷	⥲	≠	σ	õ	AIC
Ghyp	FALSE	-2.037	0.007	0.118	2.293	-0.085	22236.88
Hyp	FALSE	1.000	0.621	0.144	2.223	-0.112	22305.28
Nig	FALSE	-0.500	0.876	0.134	2.256	-0.1022	22265.32

Table 7: Returns distributions and asymmetry for 2008–2015

Model	Symmetric	÷	$\tilde{\rightarrow}$	≠	σ	õ	AIC
Ghyp	FALSE	-0.69	0.456	0.062	2.103	-0.092	7184.141
Hyp	FALSE	1.000	0.002	0.050	2.223	-0.112	7191.108
Nig	FALSE	-0.500	0.478	0.066	2.017	-0.079	7182.303

Table 8: Best fitted models of underlying returns

Data	Dist	÷	$\tilde{\rightarrow}$	≠	σ	õ	LH
1987–2008	Aghd	-2.037	0.007	0.1187	2.293	-0.085	-11113.44
2008–2015	Anig		0.478	0.066	2.094	-0.097	-3587.151

Our quantitative results based on AIC and Likelihood values suggest that Aghd and Anig are the best fitted models for the two data series 1987–2008 and 2008–2015 respectively.

Conclusions

In this paper we have studied the implementation of GARCH models and generalized hyperbolic distribution (Ghyp) with its types for European Brent crude oil daily return series. For the first time-period 1987–2008 the kurtosis of return series is found to be much higher than the return series of the 2008–2015 time period. The best fitted EGARCH model for both underlying series follow conditional distributions belong to the family of Ghyp distribution. This class of distribution is found best to capture the heavy tailed and asymmetric behavior of the returns.

Acknowledgements

"This work was partially supported by Ningbo Natural Science Foundation (No. 2016A610077) and K.C. Wong Magna Fund in Ningbo University."

References

1. Akaike, H. (1978). Information theory and an extension of maximum likelihood principle. Proceedings of 2nd international symposium on information theory, 1978, pp. 267–281.
2. Bollerslev, T. (1986). Generalized autoregressive conditional heteroscedasticity. Journal of Econometrics 31(3):307–327.
3. Barndorff, N.O. (1997). Normal inverse Gaussian distributions and stochastic volatility modelling. Scandinavian Journal of Statistics 24: 1–13.

4. Barndorff, N.O. (1998). Processes of normal inverse Gaussian type. Finance & Stochastics 2:41–68.
5. Dedu, S., Ciumara, R. (2010). Restricted optimal retention in Stop-Loss reinsurance under VaR and CTE risk measures. Proceedings of the Romanian Academy, 11(3: 213–217.
6. Eberlein, E., Keller, U. (1995). Hyperbolic distributions in finance. Bernoulli 1:281–299.
7. Eberlein, E., Prause, K. (2000). The generalized hyperbolic model: financial derivatives and risk measures. Mathematical Finance, pp. 245–260.
8. Engle, R.F. (1982). Autoregressive conditional heteroscedasticity with estimates of the variance of UK inflation. Econonometrica. 50: 987–1008.
9. Nelson, D.B. (1991). Conditional heteroscedasticity in asset pricing: a new approach. Econometrica, 59:347–370.
10. Prause, K. (1997). Modelling finacial data using generalized hyperbolic distributions FDM Preprint. 48, 1997, University of Freiburg.
11. Prause, K. (1999). How to use NIG laws to measure market risk FDM Preprint. 65, 1999, University of Freiburg.
12. Sheraz, M., Preda, V. (2014). Implied volatility in Black-Scholes model with GARCH volatility. Procedia Economics and Finance, 8: 658–663.
13. Sheraz, M., Preda, V. (2016). Kurtosis in Black-Scholes Model with GARCH volatility. Scientific Bulletin Series A: Applied Mathematics and Physics, 78(1):205–216.
14. Sheraz, M. (2014). Doubly stochastic models with asymmetric GARCH errors. Proceedings of the Romanian Academy, Series A, 15(2):107–114.

Adrian OTOIU

Bucharest University of Economic Studies, Department of Statistics and Econometrics, email: otoiu.adrian@gmail.com

Emilia TITAN

Bucharest University of Economic Studies, Department of Statistics and Econometrics, email: emilia_titan@yahoo.com

To What Extent are Country Rankings from Composite Indicators Relevant? Proposing an Alternative Method of Reporting Composite Indicators Results

Abstract: Much media and public policy attention is devoted to country rankings generated by composite indicators. However, annual rankings have limited relevance, not only because the relative position of some particular countries changes from year to year without any major impact for the countries in question, but also due to the fact that they do not account for the actual gaps in indicator performance. This paper addresses these flaws by proposing a change in current reporting methodologies for composite indicators, which makes results perfectly comparable with respect to relative performance gaps between countries, ensures complete comparability between annual performances, and makes time comparisons against relative peer performances feasible without further calculations. Results reported using the new methodology point out the relative size of the differences between countries with respect to HDI scores, and can be used to assess the actual gaps between countries, and determine whether score changes are truly significant over chosen periods of time. This approach makes a reality check of media claims, and, if used, will help in making a more objective interpretation of countries' performance as a guide for public policies.

Keywords: Human Development Index, indicator methodology, composite indicator

Introduction

Despite the fact that they have existed for over 30 years, composite indexes have become increasingly popular in recent years. Their numbers have increased dramatically in the past years (The Economist, 2015), tackling almost all aspects of human activity. Modern technology has also helped in the creation and maintenance of indexes, as now it is easy to automatically extract data from API interfaces, which makes their processing and dissemination quick and effective.

Their results elicit public policy comments and start media debates around the relative performance of a given country. Given the fact at least once a month there are news reports that comment on the relative standing of one country in a specific human or environmental area, it can be said that composite index releases have become a mainstream media product.

Despite this fact, many of the indexes, both established and new, suffer from two major shortcomings. The first one is that these indexes focus on the current, or more exactly the most recent known performance of countries, without providing a longer-term perspective of their evolution. To our knowledge, only the Canadian Index of Wellbeing has as a goal to track performance through time (Michalos et al., 2011), and only a handful publish tables with data that is consistent across different years, among which are the Environmental Performance Index (EPI) and the Human Development Index (HDI). While there are issues governing data availability of different input variables, which varies sharply between countries, the fact that index releases are fairly static and seldom make comparisons spanning over several years remains a weakness of composite indicators.

The second shortcoming lies with ranking as the favorite method of interpreting and disseminating results. Quite often index values are not analyzed; rather, they are considered a technical detail and completely overlooked when making comparisons between countries. Much importance is given to the relative changes of the countries at the top of a ranking, whereas the absolute differences in terms of actual index values is insignificant. This eventually leads to a misleading interpretation of ranks, which merely measure the order of the calculated index values instead of considering the size of the difference between countries, and trigger policy measures to diminish or even eliminate them.

Thus, we consider that the current situation is unacceptable, and we have found a solution that, if applied, would improve reporting of composite index results by making them relevant with respect to the actual between-country differences in index performance, comparable through time with respect to relative peer performance and its evolution, thus removing the need for backward recalculations. As our methodology is relatively straightforward, we consider this as a step forward in presenting results in a meaningful and objective way that ensures that an effective cross-sectional and longitudinal gap analysis can be done at any point in time, by using reported results that are straightforward to use and interpret.

1. Literature review

A review of several indexes reveals that most of them compare current performance with the performance of the previous years. This is true for the Legatum Prosperity Index (The Legatum Institute, 2015), HDI (UNDP, 2016), EPI (Hsu et al., 2016) as well as many other indexes.

Even methodological guides are biased towards construction of a one-time index rather than providing consistency across years. Perhaps the most comprehensive one is the OECD guide (OECD, 2008), which does not make any reference with respect to constructing index measures that are comparable through time.

The only index that addresses this longitudinal reporting bias is The Canadian Index of Wellbeing (Michalos et al., 2011), and its purpose is to explicitly track performance over several years. It uses 1994 as a base year and 2008 as the latest year for which full data was available. In trying to compensate for the one-year construction and reporting bias, some indexes, including the HDI and EPI, have recalculated previously reported values (Hsu et al., 2016, UNDP (a), 2015), which are not always compatible with the values that were computed at the time annual releases were disseminated.

The fact that there is a growing need to overcome this longitudinal reporting bias can be seen in the latest annual reports disseminating the latest index values and country rankings, such as the Human Development Report 2015 (UNDP (a), 2015), and the Legatum Prosperity Index 2015 (The Legatum Institute, 2015), which attempt to focus on long-term trends rather than on the annual rankings of countries.

Dissemination of results is done mostly using ranks, with index values reported merely as a technical detail used to derive them. As index values are not very meaningful as numbers between 0 and 1 (UNDP (b), 2015, Hsu et al., 2016), the fact that ranks are used to disseminate index results comes at no surprise.

Ranks are not a good measure when it comes to assessing the true size of differences, as they basically assume that all differences between items, no matter how large or small, are equal (Maniu et al., 2004). This has been pointed out by several authors. Thus, Lind (2004) argues that "[t]he HDI ranking of highly developed nations is so close and so uncertain that it is meaningless". This finding is consistent with Pribyla (2010) and Kovacevic (2010), who argue that the index is better at discriminating low and medium-income countries than developed ones. Thus, it seems that index values are much better positioned to explain the relative difference between countries than ranks because they are sensitive to dismal differences and annual changes.

While critics have addressed the issue of comparability over time and over countries with different levels of development, no major critique has addressed the question of whether reporting results "may send misleading policy messages if poorly constructed or misinterpreted" as per OECD (OECD 2008, p. 13). This paper will attempt to remedy this problem by proposing a new reporting methodology that, for the first time, tackles the way in which composite index results are presented, and may alter the way results are perceived.

2. A new methodology to compute and present final results

Based on the evidence concerning composite indicators and on the available statistical techniques, we have concluded that a better approach is needed in order to properly account for a country's relative status and to make it comparable through time.

First, we have considered the fact that final index scores convey the information concerning a country's relative performance in the most accurate and relevant manner. Therefore, they should be used as a standard point in computing a relevant final index measure that is easy to understand and interpret and can replace ranks. Among the choices available, we have chosen the normalized scores expressed in percentages, using the following formula:

$$Ix_c = \frac{x_c - \min(x)}{\max(x) - \min(x)} * 100 \qquad (1)$$

where Ix_c is the c element of the normalized (transformed) index value, x_c is the actual level of the initial index value, and max(x) and min(x) are the maximum and minimum observed index values.

The rationale for this is that, among the available measures proposed by the OECD Handbook of composite indicators (OECD, 2008), this is close to the Min-Max method with respect to not altering the distribution of the index scores. Also, the use of percentages is a standard practice used in statistics as it helps comprehension and interpretation of indexes for all audiences (Maniu et al., 2004).

We believe that this formula is a good candidate for replacing ranks, as it matches the level of complexity and methodological approaches presented in the OECD methodology guide (OECD, 2008). Therefore, using it will achieve the goal of easy interpretation and will gain both expert acceptance from the methodological point of view, and user friendliness needed for successful dissemination and interpretation.

Also, with respect to the longitudinal comparability dimension, this method helps to avoid establishing a reference period or country, which may be inappropriate or become irrelevant over time. The relative distance between the minimum and maximum performance helps showcase the year-by-year relative performance of a country in comparison with its peers in an unambiguous way. This is a step ahead of the current practices that mostly use ranks to compare performance over time (UNDP (a), 2015; The Legatum Institute, 2015; Hsu et al., 2016). While using ranks also takes into account the fact that, as shown in the latest HDI report (UNDP (a), 2015), countries tend to experience a general progress in their performance over time, it is not clear that this performance can hide the fact that a country outperforms or underperforms its peers, as shown by Lind (2004). Therefore, our measure allows the making of time comparisons while at the same time preserving the relative standing of a country against its peers at any time during the comparison period, without the need of reporting additional backcasted data (EPI, 2014), or providing recalculated data as HDI does.

3. Using the new index measure to improve HDI reporting

The HDI was chosen in order to test and validate our proposed index measure as it is one of the oldest and perhaps the most successful measures of human development and social progress, and has undergone major changes following critiques to improve it (Kovacevic, 2010). Availability of comparable index measures dating back to 1980 from HDI's website was another reason for choosing it, as the data was deemed to be comparable over time.

Our analysis started by choosing the years of analysis. Since differences between subsequent years were small, we chose to analyse differences between the years 2000, 2010 and 2014. We had to recompute the ranks as HDI was not calculated for some of the countries appearing in the 2014 data, a procedure that would be unnecessary if our proposed measure is used.

Table 1 shows whether differences between ranks and index measures in 2014 versus 2010 are significant using paired-sample t-tests. For ranks there are no significant differences, whereas index values exhibit significant differences over the same period (p-value is almost 0). However, it is not sure whether this is due to suppression of differences between the ranks, or due to a rising HDI trend as observed in the average HDI index values over the 1980–2014 period.

In order to remove the influence of progress and test our proposed final index measure, we have repeated the same analysis on normalized index values using formula 1. The same test performed on the 2000 vs. 2014 data showed again significant differences between index values, with p-values close to 0. The negative test value for the proposed index measure proves that it manages to remove the rising trend in original index values, and showcase some of the differences in relative performance experienced by some countries and groups of countries.

The fact that using ranks leads to significant information loss, and that our normalization method retains the features and variability of the original data to a good extent are thus proven by the results of Table 1.

Table 1: Significance of HDI differences for rank and index values

	Ranks		**Index Values**		**New Index Values**	
	r2014	***r2010***	***2014***	***2010***	***a2000***	***a2014***
Mean	94.3138	94.3298	0.69247	0.67975	56.0414	58.59242
Variance	2962.8	2966.17	0.02393	0.02477	666.932	675.3258
Observations	188	188	188	188	166	166
Pearson Correlation	0.99994		0.99941		0.98581	
Hypothesized Mean Difference	0		0		0	
Df	187		187		165	
t Stat	-0.3552		29.1634		-7.5261	
P(T<=t) one-tail	0.36142		8.5E-72		1.6E-12	
t Critical one-tail	1.65304		1.65304		1.65414	
P(T<=t) two-tail	0.72284		1.7E-71		3.2E-12	
t Critical two-tail	1.97273		1.97273		1.97445	

Source: Authors' calculations based on www.undp.org

While the results obtained were encouraging and confirmed our initial intuition about using normalized index measures expressed in percentages, we furthered our analysis to see whether the new method is capable of overcoming the HDI weakness in discriminating amongst different groups of countries.

Thus, we performed t-tests on the four quartiles on the normalized index values to see whether our method can lead to improvements in the discrimination power of HDI. They correspond to the HDI classification of countries into four categories: Very High Human Development (Q1), High Human Development (Q2), Medium Human Development (Q3), and Low Human Development (Q4).

Table 2: Significance of HDI differences for normalized index values by quartile

	Q1		Q2		Q3		Q4	
	a2000	*a2014*	*a2000*	*a2014*	*a2000*	*a2014*	*a2000*	*a2014*
Mean	86.68	89.53	66.19	70.24	51.20	52.63	20.21	22.09
Variance	47.25	31.84	48.97	22.12	99.94	58.93	87.89	90.48
Observations	42	42	41	41	41	41	42	42
Hypothesized Mean Difference	0		0		0		0	
Df	41		40		40		41	
t Stat	-6.334		-5.940		-1.909		-2.541	
P(T<=t) one-tail	7E-08		3E-07		0.031		0.007	
t Critical one-tail	1.682		1.683		1.683		1.682	
P(T<=t) two-tail	1E-07		6E-07		0.063		0.014	
t Critical two-tail	2.019		2.021		2.021		2.019	

Source: Authors' calculations based on www.undp.org

Results in Table 2 were different than those obtained by authors that observed a higher discrimination power of HDI for medium and less developed countries (see literature review section). It appears that, with the newly computed final indexes, there are significant differences in scores among all levels of human development. The only exception is not for the top-ranked countries, but by those classified as having medium development.

Here, the two-tailed test on the difference between the means fails at a 5% level of confidence, however the one-tailed test passes at the same level of confidence. This essentially proves the fact that the relative final index values are better at showing the actual relative progress of countries through time, which is concealed by the use of ranks, and not directly shown by raw index values, which need to be recomputed to make them comparable with subsequent issues of composite indicators.

Fig. 1: Kernel density plot of HDI normalized index values

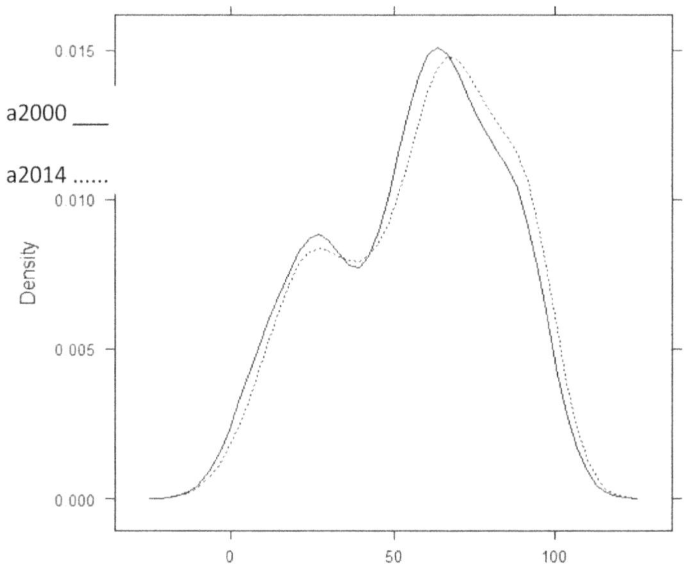

Source: Authors' data calculations based on UNDP data www.unpd.org

We can also see that most of the relative progress is seen in countries with high and very high human development, as shown in the values of the t statistics. This is an important development showing that, while all country groups have improved, a fact shown by the negative values of the t statistic, there is in fact no catching up of the less developed countries with the more developed countries. This would not be apparent if ranks were used, since the widening difference would be hidden by the levelling done by using just ranks. The only instance of catching up happens between medium developed countries and least developed countries. However, the catching-up rate is well below the advances made by the developed countries, among which there is no evidence of catching up as both normalized differences appear to be very close. The kernel density plot in Figure 1 reinforces these findings, with the density curve for 2014 normalized index values moving leftward, with larger gaps between it and the 2000 curve, starting from the middle of the distribution.

Another significant development is the increase in variability across normalized index scores for all development levels but the least developed countries. The highest increase was for high development countries, with comparable but smaller increases for those with very high development and medium development. However, this has not affected a clustering of the normalized index scores and a reduction in disparities between countries belonging to the same group, as density plots exhibit similar shapes. The changes observed for the least developed countries appear to break the patterns observed for the other country groups. They have preserved the variability of normalized index results.

These developments may actually signal a potential weakness, and pose challenges to the interpretation of results, as it seems that the relatively low performance of the bottom least developed countries may present the performance of the rest of the countries in a much better light, especially the developed ones. While it shows that there are still countries lagging more and more behind most others, it also helps overstate progress and clustering of developed countries.

A review of the individual cases that show the largest differences in both rank and proposed index values shows that, in 12 out of 25 cases, there are significant mismatches between rank differences and proposed index value differences. Countries with a decrease in performance show inconsistent results with either large rank differences for relatively small index changes (Belize, Dominica), or relatively small rank differences for rather large index changes (Syria, Central African Republic). It is striking to see that Syria and Libya, both affected by devastating civil wars, show similar decreases in human performance as shown by the index, while the rank decrease for the first is 12 and for the second is 35. At the other end of the changes, we see Belarus, Kazakhstan, Azerbaijan show rank increases of 19, and 18 respectively, while Rwanda and Ethiopia, with stronger increases in both HDI and newly proposed index values, increase by only ten and nine ranks.

Conclusions

Based on the recalculations of HDI country scores using normalized index scores and the subsequent analysis, we can conclude that the proposed technique is a viable alternative for presenting and disseminating composite index results.

Because of the use of relative ranks for single years, the new method is able to show the relative country performance against its peers, and to which extent one country surpasses, or falls behind, its peers. It also allows a finer analysis done separately for each of the four country groups, and is able to show the evolution of relative performance over time. It also helps spot whether there is a possible clusterization of countries, and track whether there is convergence/catching up of countries with medium and low development. Using normalization helps achieve the objectives of objectivity and neutrality in reporting human development levels, in stark contrast with the current techniques that emphasize ranks rather than distances/gaps in human development levels among countries, which, in many cases, are rather disconnected from actual changes in scores and new index values.

Thus, the proposed technique can send correct policy signals of the relative performance of countries. It is almost impossible to directly assess the way in which indexes by themselves contribute to active policy measures as, to our knowledge, only four countries have as a policy goal to improve human development index scores or ranks (Bryant, 2015). Rather, these measures act as broad awareness tools that eventually lead to measures targeting the improvement of specific indicators, e.g. Millennium Development Goals (Soares et al., 2015), after lengthy policy and funding processes which are hard, if at all possible, to match to single, all-encompassing annual index measures.

A possible caveat in using our method is the choice of the reference level. Using the performance of the worst performing country may potentially overstate the performance of countries with medium to very high human development. However, a better choice of a reference point in computing normalized index scores is beyond the scope of this paper, as it should be a public policy issue involving consultations and expert consensus rather than a technical, statistics-based issue.

Application of the newly proposed method is staightforward, however, it should be taken into account that it could involve more calculations for indexes that use a different normalization technique. This may also impact the methodology of the indexes that may choose to switch to this new method, so that sub-index data can be properly aggregated into the final index and yield objective results of relative country performance.

References

1. Bryane, M. (2015). What Does Brunei Teach Us About Using Human Development Index Rankings as a Policy Tool?, 2015, EconStor Preprints 10740.
2. EPI (2014). 'EPI Indicator Scores and Backcasted Data' http://www.epi.yale.edu/resource-category/2014-epi-data-files, accessed on January 5, 2016.
3. Hsu, A. (2016). Environmental Performance Index. New Haven, CT, 2016, Yale University. Available: www.epi.yale.edu, accessed on January 9th, 2017.
4. The Legatum Institute: The Legatum Prosperity Index 2015, available at http://www.prosperity.com/download_file/view_inline/2833, accessed on January 9th, 2017.
5. Lind, N. (2004). Values reflected in the Human Development Index. Social Indicators Research, 66 (3):283–293.
6. Kovacevic, M. (2010). Review of HDI Critiques and Potential Improvements. United Nations Development Programme, Human Development Reports, Research Paper 2010/33.
7. Maniu, I., Mitrut, C., Voineagu, V. (2004) Statistica, Ed. Universitară, Bucureşti, Romania.
8. Michalos, A.C., Smale, B., Labonté, R., Muharjarine, N., Scott, K., Moore, K., Swystun, L., Holden, B., Bernardin, H., Dunning, B., Graham, P., Guhn, M., Gadermann, A.M., Zumbo, B.D., Morgan, A., Brooker, A.-S., Hyman, I. (2017). The Canadian Index of Wellbeing. Technical Report 1.0. Waterloo, 2011, Canadian Index of Wellbeing and University of Waterloo, Retrieved from https://uwaterloo.ca/canadian-index-wellbeing/sites/ca.canadian-index-wellbeing/files/uploads/files/Canadian_Index_of_Wellbeing-TechnicalPaper-FINAL_0.pdf on January 9th, 2017.
9. OECD (2008). Handbook on Constructing Composite Indicators: Methodology and User Guide, 2008.

10. Pribyla, P. (2001). Human Development Index: How to cope with its limitations?, Global Affairs, 1st of April 2010, available at http://www.globalpolitics.cz/clanky/human-development-index-how-to-cope-with-its-limitations?en=1, accessed on January 20, 2017.
11. Soares, S. S. D., Osório, R. G. (2015). Sustainable Development Goals (SDGs):Less is More!, 2015, The International Policy Centre for Inclusive Growth, available at http://www.ipc-undp.org/pub/eng/OP277_Sustainable_Development_Goals_Less_is_More.pdf, accessed on June 3, 2017.
12. The Economist: "Ranking the rankings" November 8th print edition 2014, accessed on November 2, 2015 at www.economist.com.
13. UNDP. (2015, a). Human Development report 2015: Work for Human Development available at http://hdr.undp.org/sites/default/files/2015_human_develop ment_report.pdf.
14. UNDP. (2015, b). Human Development Index Technical Notes. http://hdr.undp.org/sites/default/files/hdr2015_technical_notes.pdf, Accessed Nov 30, 2016.

Appendix 1. Countries showing top rank and proposed index value differences

	2000			2014			Differences	
Country	**Rank**	**Score**	**Proposed**	**Rank**	**Score**	**Proposed**	**Proposed**	**Rank**
China	108	0.588	50.15	81	0.728	63.76	13.61	-27
Mongolia	107	0.589	50.30	82	0.727	63.59	13.29	-25
Belarus	66	0.683	64.55	47	0.798	75.50	10.96	-19
Kazakhstan	70	0.679	63.94	52	0.788	73.83	9.89	-18
Azerbaijan	90	0.64	58.03	72	0.751	67.62	9.59	-18
Botswana	113	0.561	46.06	96	0.698	58.72	12.66	-17
Iran (Islamic Republic of)	**81**	**0.665**	**61.82**	**64**	**0.766**	**70.13**	**8.32**	**-17**
Singapore	27	0.819	85.15	11	0.912	94.63	9.48	-16
Mauritius	**74**	**0.674**	**63.18**	**58**	**0.777**	**71.98**	**8.80**	**-16**
Angola	149	0.39	20.15	134	0.532	30.87	10.72	-15
Cambodia	143	0.419	24.55	128	0.555	34.73	10.19	-15
Algeria	**90**	**0.64**	**58.03**	**75**	**0.736**	**65.10**	**7.07**	**-15**
Zambia	138	0.433	26.67	124	0.586	39.93	13.27	-14
Rwanda	**156**	**0.333**	**11.52**	**146**	**0.483**	**22.65**	**11.14**	**-10**
Ethiopia	**165**	**0.284**	**4.09**	**156**	**0.442**	**15.77**	**11.68**	**-9**
Timor-Leste	**125**	**0.469**	**32.12**	**120**	**0.595**	**41.44**	**9.32**	**-5**
Central African Republic	**161**	**0.31**	**8.03**	**166**	**0.35**	**0.34**	**-7.69**	**5**
Haiti	**134**	**0.442**	**28.03**	**146**	**0.483**	**22.65**	**-5.38**	**12**
Syrian Arab Republic	**109**	**0.586**	**49.85**	**121**	**0.594**	**41.28**	**-8.57**	**12**
Swaziland	120	0.496	36.21	135	0.531	30.70	-5.51	15
Kuwait	**30**	**0.804**	**82.88**	**46**	**0.816**	**78.52**	**-4.36**	**16**
Dominica	**64**	**0.694**	**66.21**	**85**	**0.724**	**63.09**	**-3.12**	**21**
Belize	**66**	**0.683**	**64.55**	**92**	**0.715**	**61.58**	**-2.97**	**26**
Jamaica	62	0.7	67.12	90	0.719	62.25	-4.87	28
Libya	50	0.731	71.82	85	0.724	63.09	-8.73	35

Note: Table compiled by merging top 20 rank changes and 20 top new index scores. Bold stands for countries which belong to only one list.

Source: Authors' data calculations based on UNDP data www.unpd.org

Pradeep KUMAR

University of Applied Sciences in Nysa, Nysa, Poland;
email: pradeep.kumar@pwsz.nysa.pl

Economic Development Based on Higher Education: Indian Growth and Global Norms

Abstract: Economics is known as a method of fulfilling unlimited desires with limited resources, which is directly connected with human development and our approaches in order to get basic needs and expected desires. It is education that is contributing not only to increases in an individual's income but also to the national income. Globally, it has been noticed that higher education and skilled human capital becomes the main driver of economic growth for many developed and developing economies.

In the recent years, emerging economies have made fantastic progress by focusing on 'skills education' in their higher education for economic growth. India is a relevant example of education based economy, beeing the fastest growing economy in the world. With a GDP growth rate of 7.9%, a population of 1.29 billion people, occupying the second place in the world (after the USA) from the point of view of the number of English speakers, with the highest number in the world of young population aged between 16 and 35 years, with the largest number of service providers, and a growing middle-class, India has important economic growth potential for the next 30 years. This paper will address how education and educational institutions are essential for the long-run economic development of India, and how Poland and Romania can be complementary and supplementary for eachother's need for sustainable growth.

Keywords: Economic Development, Education, India, Poland, Romania

1. Introduction

Today, the global economy is reshaping and nations are getting recognition through economic and social development based on skills and human capital. New advances in technologies have become driving forces for individual and societal progress for the contemporary world, from traditional practices to a research-based knowledge economy.

In order to maintain economic prosperity and social well-being, nations are required to bring changes in their strategies to develop skill labour forces as the backbone of their sustainable growth. In this regard, higher education plays a very important role in innovation, human capital development, and knowledge economy. Considering the importance of education and skilled labour forces, education has become an important part of the agenda of many developed and developing nations going through various reforms. In past years, traditional universities were known for their long traditional practices of research and higher education for the elite, without accessibility to the general people.

Today the picture is totally different. Higher education has become a basic need of society and gives accessibility to the larger communities. On the one hand, many developed nations are facing demographic problems and their traditional universities are struggling to maintain their branding by getting less and less applicants; on the other hand, many developing nations are getting overcrowded and are not in the position to fulfil the demands of higher education. The different level of demands from developed and developing countries has changed the entire profile of higher education from traditional institutions to knowledge-based institutions; from research centres to innovative technological hubs; from elite to large segments of population, and from costs pressure to new forms of financing with accountability.

2. Global Norms and Changing Demands of Higher Education

For many developing countries, education has been seen as an important tool for the economic growth and as playing the role of a cultivator for social and political development. The benefits of education for development and social changes have long been contemplated, from the colonial era to the contemporary world, and emerged as a method for the modernisation of societies, where people believe that "better education creates a better world". Education plays a key role in the ability of emerging economies to absorb modern technology and to develop their capacity for self-sustaining growth and development.

So, it is very important for local/national governments to create policies for economic development by utilising the education system in order to educate people with the necessary skills for economic growth.

Nobel Laureate Amartya Sen's word (Development as Freedom, 1999): *"education can add the value of production in the economy and also to the income of the person who has been educated. But even with the same level of income, a person may benefit from education-in reading, communication, arguing, in being able to choose in a more informed way, in being taken more seriously by others and so on".* Thus, education plays a crucial role in creating productive societies and generating sustainable economic growth for the nations.

A. Short Analysis of Changing Educational Demands

Higher education has crossed many boundaries and changed in the past five decades. In the late 1960s and 70s, the scope of higher education was very limited and not accessible to everyone. Educational universities were only accessible to society's elite. Universities were based on purely academic endeavour, not necessarily relevant to the local communities' demands. Universities were known as a place for "true education", and vocational training programs were not considered as up to the university level. So, all vocational training programs came under the government policies to train people by developing their skills and utilise them for the economic development of the nation.

In the 1980s and 90s, the importance of higher education received less attention for economic growth and social changes. Academic institutions and systems faced pressure from the communities' requirements. Traditional universities started to get less attention and face financial constrain due to the following reasons:[1]

1. Insufficient results: universities failed to produce the results that were expected of them in much of the developing world.
2. Failure to address local issues: many higher educational institutes were not concerned with local, regional, or national issues and problems. The content and style of education was often divorced from the reality that surrounded them and sometimes exacerbated inequalities.
3. Low rate of return: due to a highly economic view of development and the resulting methods of measuring the impact of higher education institutes they were considered to have a "low rate of return".

In recent years, the relations between higher education and the norm for social-economic development have changed. The role of higher education has been reconsidered for the social and economic changes. The expectations from the academic institutions have increased but the system and institutions are facing pressure to increase their numbers of students under demographic changes. The demands for practical/vocational courses has become a part of regional and global requirements, which also increased the accountability of students and institutions. The changing traditional classrooms and the impact of new technologies are creating new environments at educational institutions and connecting regional supply for global demands.

B. Global Higher Education Sector Today

Today, the higher education sector is much broader and open towards internationalisation. Over the last decade, the number of students traveling to another country in pursuit of higher education increased from 2.1 million students in 2000 to over 4.1 million students globally in 2013 (UNESCO, 2016).[2] In the year 2009, global tertiary enrolments reached 170 million (UNESCO Institute for Statistics, referred to hereafter as UIS). Only four countries—China, India, the US and Russia—have a combined share of 45% of total global tertiary enrolments. Other emerging economies with

1 Andrew Thomson, "Exploring the Relationship Between Higher Education and Development: A Review and Report", Guerrand-Hermes Foundation for Peace, September 2008, http://www.ghfp.org/Portals/ghfp/publications/thomson_hei_role_dev.pdf.

2 Pradeep Kumar, "A New Roadmap for Higher Education in Poland and India: Opportunities and Challenges", Indo-European Education Foundation, A Bridge Between India, Poland and EU, 2017, http://www.iie.org/Research-and-Publications/Project-Atlas/About#.WJ-nPBiZOuU.

significant numbers of tertiary enrolments include: Brazil (6.2 million), Indonesia (4.9 million), Iran (3.4 million), South Korea (3.3 million) and Turkey (3.0 million).[3]

Going abroad for higher education is not new occurrence, but the increasing number of students in recent years is very significant, which has been seen as an impact of globalisation and a global economy. The fast-paced growth in the global education sector has also affected world trade growth and helped to increase the national income of many countries who act as host countries. As students' mobility is increasing and bringing direct capital flow to the host country, education becomes a priority for many countries in order to bring new strategies for attracting international students, scholars and investors. Recently, Poland launched new rules and regulations in order to make the Polish education system and educational institutions more internationalised in order to attract foreign students and scholars to Poland. Polish universities used to receive 10,000 PLN (approximately) per Polish students' enrolment for a full study program (bachelor/master) as a grant from the government. Now, according to a new law, every Polish university will receive 30,000 PLN (approximately)[4] for one international student's enrolment, which is three times higher than a Polish student's grant. The government is also supporting short- and long-term mobility of students, scholars and staffs. New regulations are applicable from 1st January 2017[5].

3. Demand of Higher Education by 2020

The changing world scenario indicates that the global economy is going to be influenced by a combination of demographic drivers and tertiary skill education. Rapid expansion of tertiary education capacity will reshape the global higher education landscape by 2020. Based on demographic statistics India, China, the USA and Indonesia will account for over half of the world's 18-22-year-old population by 2020, and Pakistan, Nigeria, Brazil, Bangladesh, Ethiopia, the Philippines, Mexico, Egypt and Vietnam will be rapidly growing into populated countries.

The rapid growth of population indicates the importance of economic growth and the future of tertiary education demand, which is establishing a strong relationship between GDP per capita at purchasing power parity (PPP) and gross tertiary enrolment ratios. Also, the correlation statistical ratio is very positive and significant for these emerging economies, especially for India.

3 "The shape of things to come: higher education global trends and emerging opportunities to 2020" Going Global 2012, British Council https://www.britishcouncil.org/sites/default/files/the_shape_of_things_to_come_-_higher_education_global_trends_and_emerging_opportunities_to_2020.pdf.

4 Gazeta Prawna, Urszula Mirowska-Łoskot, 22.12.2016, available at: http://serwisy.gazetaprawna.pl/edukacja/artykuly/1004732,finansowanie-uczelni-studenci-zagraniczni.html.

5 POLSKA Thursday, 22 December 2016 (06:45), available at: http://fakty.interia.pl/polska/news-dgp-student-z-azji-wart-wiecej-niz-ten-z-polski,nId,2326758.

China and India used to be dominant countries globally for tertiary enrolments (2002–2009), accounting for 26 million of the overall increase of 55 million. But the forecast for combined growth for the period 2011–2020 declines to 12 million, with growth in tertiary enrolments in China falling from 17 million (2002–2009) to five million (2011–2020). India's tertiary enrolment growth (in absolute terms) is forecast to outpace China's growth between now and 2020. Following China and India, other emerging economies with significant forecast growth in tertiary enrolments over the next decade will include Brazil (+2.6 million), Indonesia (+2.3 million), Nigeria (+1.4 million), Philippines (+0.7 million), Bangladesh (+0.7 million), Turkey (+0.7 million) and Ethiopia (+0.6 million)[6].

4. Poland, India, Romania - Education Perspective

In the current scenario, Poland is facing a huge demographic problem and not getting enough qualified students for their well-established educational institutions; India has the largest youngest population in the world who are looking to go abroad for higher education due to the lack of well qualified universities in India. In the case of Romania and India, their situation is quite similar to Poland's and opportunities for future cooperation between Romania and India are huge.

A. Polish Perspective

Poland is a country of 38.5 million people (as per 12th February 2017)[7] and day by day this number is decreasing (demographic problems). About 501 universities are in Poland, including 131 government-funded and 326 privately-owned, all of which accommodate about 1,500,000 students. Out of this total number of students, about 57,119 international students are studying in Poland, which is 10,000 more than a year ago. Currently, international students make up 4.1% of the total student body in the country (ten years ago the figure was only 0.6%, in 2015 - 3.1%)[8]. The increasing number of international students at the Polish universities is not an accident but it is an effect of Poland becoming more global and internationalised.

By launching more English medium courses, Polish universities are trying to attract more foreign students, which can be supplementary to the vacant places left by insufficient numbers of Polish students. In the academic year 2015/16, a total of 1,405,133 people were studying at the Polish universities—over 64,254 students

---

6 The goal of Project Atlas is to collect and report accurate, timely and comprehensive data on global student mobility. More details are available at: www.iie.org/Research-and-Publications/Project-Atlas/About.

7 http://www.worldometers.info/world-population/poland-population/.

8 Perspektywy Education Foundation 2016, available: http://www.studyinpoland.pl/en/index.php/news/43-over-57-119-international-students-in-poland.

fewer than in the previous year, and over 200,000 fewer than three years ago.[9] It means in coming years Polish universities need to attract more and more foreign students otherwise they will not be able to run many classes, faculties, departments or even universities.

Many private schools/universities are facing such problems and getting closed due to insufficient numbers of students and lack of funds. Public universities started to encounter similar problems and in order to avoid them they became more willing to be more internationalised by accommodating more foreign students[10]. But the problem is that the majority of Polish universities run programs only in the Polish language, and very few academic institutions and universities run programs in English. Many private and public universities are willing to receive international students but not able to make internal institutional changes.

The bilateral trade figures for the last few years are below

Table 1: Three years of bilateral trade between India and Poland

Trade data	2013	2014	2015
India's exports	1470	1806	1742
India's imports	491	624	464
Trade turnover	1961	2430	2206

Source: *Central Statistical Office of Poland (GUS)*[11].

B. Romanian Perspective

Romania has 19.9 million[12] inhabitants as of 12th February 2017. Education in Romania is made up of public and private institutions and is organized in levels for the coherence and continuity of education. Currently, in Romania there are more than 56 higher education institutions accredited (49 civilian institutions of higher education in state universities and seven military), 26 private institutions of higher

9 http://www.studyinpoland.pl/en/index.php/news/43-over-57-119-international-students-in-poland.

10 Pradeep Kumar, *ASM Business Review*, the Bi-annual Refereed Journal, *Business Strategies Practices and Innovations*, Vol. 6, No. 1, January 2017, ISSN No. 0974–9136, Pune, India, pp. 7–19.

11 "India-Poland Relations Political Relations", Embassy of India, Warsaw, May 30, 2016, https://www.mea.gov.in/Portal/ForeignRelation/India_Poland_Relation_31_5_2016.pdf, last accesed February 2017.

12 "Romania Population 1960–2017", http://www.tradingeconomics.com/romania/population, last accesed February 2017.

education accredited, and six graduate schools[13]. In cooperation with India a Hindi Chair was established by ICCR at the University of Bucharest in 1998.

The Indian community in Romania numbers around 950. The majority are students (nearly 250 Indian students[14] attend courses in Romanian institutions, mainly pursuing medicine on a self-financing basis at Timisoara, Oradea, Bucharest, Constanta and Iasi). Others are businessmen, professionals and technical specialists.

India-Romania trade statistics over the last three years are as follows

Table 2: Indian-Romanian trade data

Trade data	2013–2014	2014–2015	2015–2016
Exports from India	286.10	416.79	259.32
Imports by India	375.65	296.45	208.85
Total	661.75	713.24	468.17 (March 16)

(Department of Commerce, Government of India statistics in million US$)[15].

C. India Education Sector

India is the home country of 1.34 billion[16] people (second highest in the world), and has the largest education system in the world in terms of the number of institutions and the number of students. With a median age of 25 years, India has over 550 million people below the age of 25[17]. According to Census figures, over 32% of the 1.34 billion-strong population is between the age group of 0–14 years of age. This means that the number of people in India needing primary and secondary education alone exceeds the entire population of the USA[18].

Since these students will be seeking higher education in India over the next decade this illustrates the sheer size of the Indian education market. Based on available data for 2014 (MHRD - Government of India Ministry of Human Resource Development), the number of higher education institutions is very limited; 760 universities and 50,774 institutions offering degree and diploma courses offer education for

---

13 http://www.studyinginromania.com/education-romania.html, last accesed February 2017.

14 "India – Romania Relations", Embassy of India, Bucharest, December 2016, https://www.mea.gov.in/Portal/ForeignRelation/Romania_Dec_2016.pdf.

15 "India – Romania Relations", Embassy of India, Bucharest, December 2016, https://www.mea.gov.in/Portal/ForeignRelation/Romania_Dec_2016.pdf.

16 http://www.indiaonlinepages.com/population/india-current-population.html, last accesed February 2017.

17 "India-Higher Education Sector, Opportunities for Private Participation", 2012. Available: https://www.pwc.in/assets/pdfs/industries/education-services.pdf.

18 "India-Higher Education Sector, Opportunities for Private Participation", 2012, https://www.pwc.in/assets/pdfs/industries/education-services.pdf.

millions of students[19]. As of today, India has 26 million students enrolled in tertiary education, by illustration it would need another 800 universities and over 40,000 colleges in the next eight years to provide the planned additional 14 million places. The indicators show that by 2020, India will need 40 million university places[20] (an increases of 14 million), and 500 million skilled workers.

5. Why do Indian students go abroad for higher education?

As the second-most populated and fastest economy in the world, India is also recognized as the fastest-growing middle-class in the word. About 25 million households in next five years will be in the position to pay $15,000 as fees for their higher education.[21] Financial strength allows middle class people to get better education. Indian society has a good appetite for higher education and looks forward to getting admission to well-recognized universities around the globe. This is because for general and average students, gaining admission to pioneering Indian universities/institutes is not so easy due to limited availability of places and low numbers of such universities and institutes in India.

The successful selection ratio is 1:250 students at IIMs (Indian Institute of Management) and IITs (Indian Institute of Technology), which is much tougher than MIT, Oxford or Cambridge, whose selection ratios are 1:10, 1:2 or 1:1. As an option foreign universities are much more favourable due to low-expense degree programs and high quality education, e.g. low tuition fees and low leaving costs in comparison to the local private/government universities persuade students to abroad for higher education.

19 "Educational Statistics at a Glance", Government of India, Ministry of Human Resources Development, New Delhi, 2016, http://mhrd.gov.in/sites/upload_files/mhrd/files/statistics/ESG2016_0.pdf.

20 "40 million by 2020: preparing for a new paradigm in Indian higher education", Ernst & Young (2011).

21 "Rivers of Innovation: NESTA (2012). available: https://www.britishcouncil.org/sites/default/files/understanding_india_report.pdf.

6. Income Factor of Indian Higher Education

Table 3: The number of households within the top three income brackets (2011 vs 2022)[22]

Household Income	No. of Households (2012)	No. of Households (2022)
Over $20K	2.5m	7m
$10k to 20k	4m	19m
$5k to $10k	34m	81m

Source: *McKinsey & Company 2012*[23]

It is not only about the growth of the population but also tge changing dynamism of household incomes in Indian society. Table 3 shows that by 2022, about 40–45 million Indian households will be in the position to spend $5,000–$15,000 on their higher education, when more than 50% of India's population is under the age of 25.[24] By 2020, India will have one of the youngest populations in the world, with an average age of 29.[25]

Table 4: Expected Expenditure on Higher Education

Source of Investment	2012	2022 Estimate
Public	$7bn	$50bn
Private	$13bn	$50bn
Total	$20bn	$65bn

Source: *McKinsey & Company 2012.*

Table 4 shows the picture of estimated expenditure from public and private sectors. In the year 2012 public investment was lower than private investment and predictions show that the government is taking the initiative to increase public investment up to $50 billion by 2022, which will be equal to private investment. It means private sectors are participating more actively in the higher education system than the public sector.

22 McKinsey & Company 2012.
23 "Estimates and projections of the economically active population: 1990–2020", International Labour Organisation (2011).
24 "Rivers of Innovation": NESTA (2012).
25 "Estimates and projections of the economically active population: 1990–2020", International Labour Organisation (2011).

7. Demand-Supply Chain Model

The entire economic development is based on *demand-supply* policy. In the case of India–Poland and India–Romania *demand-supply* policy is very much applicable. Poland is going through the process of internationalisation of higher education and demanding a number of qualified students from foreign countries, and India has the largest skilled human capital ready to go abroad for higher education, and is lacking in number of universities.

In recent years, the interest of Indian students in Polish universities has increased. And the total number of Indian students studying in Poland rose to 896 in 2016 from 227 in 2014[26]. As the number of students is increasing between India and Poland, bilateral trade is also growing; from the 2014 level of USD 2.3 billion it surpassed three billion in 2016 and is expected to reach over USD five billion by the year 2018.[27]

A similar development model can be used for Romania. The increasing number of Indian students to Romanian universities and the presence of Indian-Romanian companies may create new road maps for others. The current total of Indian students studying in Romania is about 250 and also the decreasing data on bilateral trade between India and Romania is a matter of concern for new strategies in order to create new business relations between the two entities, and policymakers must consider these factors in order to increase trade flows.

Conclusion

Despite an average growth rate of over 7.5% in the last decade, India's GER in higher education is very low. By some estimates, even if India succeeds in its target of 30% GER by 2020, 100 million qualified students will still not have places at university. India needs to drastically increase the number of places at universities and enrolment through distance learning programmes.

Therefore, it is much easier for Indian students to go overseas for higher education than stay in India. According to the data presented by the industry chamber, 450,000 Indian students spend over USD 13 billion each year in acquiring higher education overseas. Thus, this huge potential market is open for foreign cooperation with unlimited opportunities and Poland and Romania can play a wider role to fillip the gap of demand and supply left in the education sector in both countries.

26 Perspektywy Education Foundation, 2016, Study in Poland.
27 A. Bisaria, Ambassador of India in Poland and Lithuania, "We Plan to Double Indo-Polish Trade & Investment, for Economic Magazine "Polish Market" Special Edition, No. 252/2016, p. 8.

References

1. Kumar, P. (2017). ASM Business Review, the Bi-annual Refereed Journal, *Business Strategies Practices and Innovations*, Vol. 6, No. 1: 7–19.
2. Wozniak, T., Krystyna, P. Market. Warsaw, Poland special edition No. 252/2016, p8.
3. Andrew Thomson, "Exploring the Relationship between Higher Education and Development: A Review and Report", Guerrand-Hermes Foundation for Peace, September 2008, http://www.ghfp.org/Portals/ghfp/publications/thomson_hei_role_dev.pdf.
4. http://www.iie.org/Research-and-Publications/Project-Atlas/About#.WJ-nPBiZOuU, Last accessed February 2017.
5. "The shape of things to come: higher education global trends and emerging opportunities to 2020", Going Global 2012, British Council, https://www.britishcouncil.org/sites/default/files/the_shape_of_things_to_come_-_higher_education_global_trends_and_emerging_opportunities_to_2020.pdf.
6. *Gazeta Prawna*, Urszula Mirowska-Łoskot, 22.12.2016, available at: http://serwisy.gazetaprawna.pl/edukacja/artykuly/1004732,finansowanie-uczelni-studenci-zagraniczni.html.
7. POLSKA Thursday, 22 December 2016 (06:45), available at: http://fakty.interia.pl/polska/news-dgp-student-z-azji-wart-wiecej-niz-ten-z-polski,nId,2326758.
8. Pradeep Kumar, "A New Roadmap for Higher Education in Poland and India: Opportunities and Challenges", Indo-European Education Foundation, A Bridge Between India, Poland and EU, 2017, http://www.iie.org/Research-and-Publications/Project-Atlas/About#.WJ-nPBiZOuU.
9. http://www.worldometers.info/world-population/poland-population/, Last accessed February 2017.
10. Perspektywy Education Foundation 2016, available at: http://www.studyinpoland.pl/en/index.php/news/43-over-57-119-international-students-in-poland.
11. "India – Romania Relations", Embassy of India, Bucharest, December 2016, https://www.mea.gov.in/Portal/ForeignRelation/Romania_Dec_2016.pdf.
12. "Romania Population 1960–2017", http://www.tradingeconomics.com/romania/population, last accessed February 2017.
13. http://www.studyinginromania.com/education-romania.html, last accessed February 2017.
14. "India-Poland Relations Political Relations", Embassy of India, Warsaw, May 30, 2016, https://www.mea.gov.in/Portal/ForeignRelation/India_Poland_Relation_31_5_2016.pdf, last accessed February 2017.
15. http://www.indiaonlinepages.com/population/india-current-population.html, last accessed February 2017.
16. "India-Higher Education Sector, Opportunities for Private Participation", 2012, available at: https://www.pwc.in/assets/pdfs/industries/education-services.pdf.

17. "Educational Statistics at a Glance", Government of India, Ministry of Human Resources Development, New Delhi, 2016, http://mhrd.gov.in/sites/upload_files/mhrd/files/statistics/ESG2016_0.pdf.
18. "Rivers of Innovation": NESTA (2012), available at: https://www.britishcouncil.org/sites/default/files/understanding_india_report.pdf.

George-Cornel DUMITRESCU

Institute for World Economy, email: george.cornel@gmail.com

Simona MOAGĂR-POLADIAN

Institute for World Economy, email: smpoladian@yahoo.com

Ion-Alexandru TĂNASE

Institute for World Economy, email: ialexandrutanase@gmail.com

The Relations Between the USA and the Main Actors in East Asia from the Perspective of the New American Leadership

Abstract: Donald Trump's election as president of the United States of America has caused a moment of suspense, the major global actors waiting to see to what extent his declared intentions as a candidate will coincide with the concrete actions dictated by the president. Our work aims to assess the priorities on the presidential agenda towards East Asia, and the reactions of America's key allies and competitors in the region to it, in order to identify the new trends in the relations among the world's greatest powers. The analysis is based primarily on the published literature, the official positions of the main stakeholders and relevant databases of international institutions.

Keywords: Trump, Asia, China, India, TPP

1. Introduction

Donald Trump's election as president of the United States (US) represents an inflexion point in the dynamics of the American politics and economics, home and abroad. His campaign represented a change of paradigm, through the novelty of the debated issues, the magnitude of the potential implications and the uncertainty of the effects in the long run.

In his "Contract with the American Voter" the candidate Donald Trump pledged, among other things: "to clean up the corruption and special interest collusion in Washington, DC; to protect American workers (renegotiate North American Free Trade Agreement (NAFTA) or withdraw from the deal under Article 2205, withdraw from the Trans-Pacific Partnership, label China a currency manipulator; to identify all foreign trading abuses that unfairly impact American workers and to end those abuses immediately; establish tariffs to discourage companies from laying off their workers in order to relocate in other countries and ship their products back to the U.S. tax-free; cancel billions in payments to United Nations (U.N.) climate change programs and use the money to fix America's water and environmental infrastructure) etc." (Donald Trump, 2016a).

During his campaign, Donald J. Trump also stated that, as president, he would withdraw U.S. military forces from allied countries such as Japan and South Korea if these countries would not "significantly" increase their defence contributions: "At some point we have to say, you know what, we're better off if Japan protects itself against this maniac in North Korea, we're better off, frankly, if South Korea is going to start to protect itself or they have to protect themselves or they have to pay us" (Donald Trump, 2016b).

2. TPP

Through TPP and TTIP the U.S. aimed at writing the world trade rules for the years to come, setting the standards that other players had to meet in order to keep themselves in the global trade game. Griffith et al. (2015) underlined that for around 50 years, America focused its commercial policies on multilateral agreements within GATT. Once the World Trade Organisation (WTO) was created, the U.S. focused more on bilateral agreements in which they had better leverage than within the WTO where Brazil, Russia, India, China and South Africa (BRICS) gained more and more influence.

At the beginning of 2015, president Obama pleaded that "[t]he United States and not China must write trade rules for Asia", asking for more flexibility to negotiate trade deals for the U.S. Ford (2017) emphasised that the previous republican president, George W. Bush, concluded free trade agreements with Australia, South Korea, and Singapore and began talks on what became the Trans-Pacific Partnership (TPP). From this standpoint, the previous republican president practised a combination of bilateral and plurilateral agreements from which Donald Trump favours the first approach.

Obama's pivot in Asia, argues Ford (2017), made China believe that the U.S. was practising a form of complex military containment and reacted in a more assertive way. Ford argues that should TPP's door have remained opened for China, and America had been more favourable towards AIIB, Beijing would have assessed the "Pivot" as "an effort to take full advantage of the economic opportunities presented by Asia's dynamic economic growth, instead of appearing to be a strategy to undermine China". Hence, Trump's strong opposition to the TPP (that materialized by its cancellation in the first days of his term) and to other American trade agreements (such as the one with South Korea), underline Sutter and Limaye (2016, p. 7) was at odds with the free trade policies favoured by Republican congressional leaders, and, as we mentioned, with the views of George W. Bush, "but had a strong appeal among both Republican and Democratic voters". Asad (2016, p. 1) underlined that "America's anaemic support for the TPP is disconcerting to Southeast Asia, but it is the groundswell of anti-free trade sentiment that is more worrisome. It is shocking to hear one of the strongest advocates of free trade indulge in an anti-globalization tirade." Trump's stance against TPP is related to the fact that the Partnership would have hurt the American workers who already lost jobs in favour of labourers from China, and other countries in the analysed region. In Choong's (2017, p. 2) interpretation, TPP was meant to be an American economic commitment towards the countries in Asia-Pacific that turned into a lost opportunity for Trump to continue projecting American influence in the region.

The Chinese president, Xi Jinping, reacted to Trump's phobia of plurilateral agreements pledging recently in Davos to lead the world in a return to free trade (Graceffo, 2017). This is a change of paradigm!

3. American Alliances

Donald Trump considers that the cost of these alliances is too high for the American taxpayers and from this perspective, new beneficial agreements have to be signed. The president is not against alliances, but he is rather concerned about the costs. In Asia, Trump's "verbal stick" aims at preparing the Asian partners and allies, mainly Japan and South Korea, that he sees as "free riders", to make more concessions in the future negotiations with the U.S.

Donald Trump emphasised two important facts regarding the military cooperation with Japan, one of the USA's most important allies in the region. First, that America is paying far too much to protect Japan. However, for the 50,000 US soldiers based in Japan, the local government pays annually about $1.7 billion to offset the cost of their basing and supply. Second, he does not agree on the nature of this commitment, namely if Japan is attacked, the U.S. has to use full force on its enemies but when America is attacked, Japan does not have to do anything (Johnson, 2016). South Korea covers about 40% of the total costs of the U.S. troops stationed in the peninsula, under a five-year cost-sharing agreement. The mentioned agreement is coming up for renegotiation in 2017 and Trump's foreign policy adviser Pete Hoekstra suggested that the current Korean contribution might not be sufficient (Hu, 2016). This possible renegotiation is a matter of concern for the policymakers in Seoul, as South Korean exports have not yet embarked on a firm recovery after falling for most of the past two years.

Table 1: Military Expenditure in Japan and South Korea, 2013–2017 (USD billions)

Country	Classification	2013	2014	2015	2016	2017
Japan	Growth rate (%)	0.8	2.2	0.8	0.8	2.3
	Value	41.1	42	42.4	42.7	43.7
	% in GDP	0.8	0.9	1	0.9	0.8
South Korea	Growth rate	4.2	4	4.9	3.6	4
	Value	30.4	31.9	36.4	34	35.1
	% of GDP	2.4	2.4	2.4	2.39	2.4

Source: Japan Ministry of Defense, South Korea Ministry of National Defense.

Table 1 reveals that both American allies increased their defence budgets for the current year as compared to the budgets of previous years. The idea of withdrawing or diminishing the military presence close to its main economic competitor is counterproductive for the American interests. The created void will be very inviting for the American adversaries and a reversal is very costly. The U.S. should consider, and we think they do not disregard, that having allies in strategic areas gives them negotiation power with potential adversaries such as China or the Russian Federation. Allies, in general, enhance the military capabilities by providing troops, logistics, strategic advantages and local know-how.

Kagan (2017, p. 2) considers that "[a]s long as the United States were perceived as a dependable ally, Chinese and Russian leaders feared that aggressive moves would backfire and possibly bring their regimes down." But now, "the uncertainty might be a good ally for China and the Russian Federation to get their revenge over the U.S. as world dominant power", since "granting the revisionist powers spheres of influence is not a recipe for peace and tranquillity but rather an invitation to inevitable conflict". During the first unofficial meeting with the president-elect, Donald Trump, the Japanese Prime Minister, Shinzo Abe, said that "the Japan-U.S. alliance is the axis of Japan's diplomacy and security. The alliance becomes alive only when there is trust between us" (Hunt, Ogura, Wakatsuki, 2016).

In light of the last developments, namely, the visit of the secretary of defence, James Mattis, in South Korea and Japan, and the official visit of premier Abe in America the trust between America and their Asia allies seems to be restored. James Mattis made it clear that if South Korea is to be attacked with nuclear weapons by North Korea the reaction will be "overwhelming" and he reassured the deployment of the THAAD system, which would be used to intercept medium-range missiles from North Korea.

During the last official meeting of Shinzo Abe in the U.S., Donald Trump affirmed that "the United States of America stand behind Japan, its great ally, 100 percent" (Kong, Reynolds, 2017) and he thanked Japan for hosting the U.S. military and described the Abe administration by calling the bilateral alliance "the cornerstone of peace and stability" in the Asia-Pacific region.

American political elite won't allow the new administration to weaken the military presence abroad, thus losing the global hegemony of over seven decades. That means that all the tough positions expressed during the campaign and after being elected by the president and his staff members might represent just bargain chips for better leverage on negotiating the real deals to come (Dingli, 2017, p. 2). The extra compensations expected from the American allies and the acceptance of a possible nuclear proliferation in South Korea and Japan contradict the general view in the Republican Party as per Sutter and Limaye (2016, p. 7). Again, President Trump had a different position than the one of his party.

On the other hand, Kagan (2017, p. 2) argues that "the tough talk with China will likely lead Beijing to test the new administration's resolve militarily."

As a reaction to the phone call between Donald Trump and the Taiwanese president, and the "One China" policy issue, which Trump considered as open to negotiations, China reacted by seizing an underwater U.S. Navy drone, deployed its aircraft carrier to the Taiwan Strait, piled diplomatic pressure on Taipei and issued veiled threats against U.S. automakers and made it clear that it is not ready to offer any concessions under pressure, suggesting that the U.S. *respect the facts* and speak and act cautiously to avoid harming the peace and stability in the South China Sea (De Luce, 2017).

According to a study by PEW Research Center (2014, p. 10), China considers the U.S. as a chief threat, while the U.S. considers the Russian Federation (China's main ally) as the major enemy. The same study emphasises that the global perception of the world's leading economy changed from in China's favour from 19% in 2008 to 31% in 2014, the U.S. dropping from 49% to 40% in the same period. Across the nations surveyed, a median of 50% shows that China will eventually replace/has replaced U.S. as a superpower.

From an economic standpoint, the relations between the U.S. and their two Asian allies are also subject to negotiations, as the U.S. register trade deficits with both countries and Donald Trump dislikes an unbalanced trade. Japan and South Korea are among the top ten trading partners of the USA, with a total trade value of almost 615 billion dollars in 2015 and 2016.

Table 2: U.S. deficits with Japan and South Korea, 2008–2016 (in billions of dollars)

Country	2016	2015	2014	2013	2012	2011	2010	2009	2008	2007
Japan	68	68	67	73	76	62	59	44	72	82
South Korea	27	28	25	20	16	13	10	10	13	13

Source: U.S. Census Bureau

Table 3: U.S. total trade in goods with Japan and South Korea, 2008–2016 (in billions of dollars)

Country	2016	2015	2014	2013	2012	2011	2010	2009	2008	2007
Japan	195	193	201	203	216	195	181	147	205	208
South Korea	112	115	114	103	101	100	87	68	82	82

During his visit to the U.S. in February 2017, Prime Minister Shinzo Abe discussed with President Trump the economic cooperation between the two countries. Takumi Sakuyama, a former TPP negotiator for the Japanese government declared that "bilateral discussions are going to give an advantage to the larger economy, and Mr. Trump's record of complaints about Japan's automotive trade, beef tariffs and currency manipulation indicates he will drive a hard bargain" (The Japan News, 2017).

Trump has called the free trade agreement with South Korea (signed in 2010) a "disaster" underlining that it has destroyed almost 100,000 American jobs and that he is against such agreements in general. As in the case of the North American Free

Trade Agreement, he declared that his administration either renegotiates it or breaks it, because "they were poorly negotiated and resulted in millions of Americans losing jobs" (Council on Foreign Relations, 2016).

4. Staff's opinion

According to Boot (2017), Trump's republican supporters suggested that the new president does not really mean all of his campaign rhetoric and he is going to delegate governing to Mike Pence, and other trusted officials while playing a lot of golf, as he recently did with the Japanese premier.

On the other hand, the presidential staff members have a history of "unorthodox" opinions on international issues, such as the "One China" policy, the extremist Muslims, South China Sea etc.

Steve Bannon (2016), Trump's chief strategist, senior adviser and a member of the National Security Council declared last March that the U.S. would go to war in the South China Sea in five to ten years. On the same topic, during the confirmation hearing, Rex Tillerson, the State Secretary, argued that "America should deny China access to the bases it had built on disputed reefs and islands in the South China Sea" (The Economist, 2017b). His position was reconfirmed by the president's spokesman who at a briefing replied that "[i]t's a question of if those islands are in fact in international waters and not part of China proper, then, yeah, we're going to make sure that we defend international territories from being taken over by one country." There are some moderates in the presidential team. Panda (2017, p. 1), notices that after taking over the office, the position of the defence secretary Jim Mattis on the subject was "remarkably conciliatory", an attitude "warmly received in Beijing." Stashwick (2017, p. 1) suggests that it "is too late to dislodge China from its bases in the South China Sea without a clash". According to Reilly and Heath (2017), the United States have a main interest in the South China Sea, "an important trade channel" of the world. Around 70% of the world trade, approximately $4.5tn, crosses the Sea every year in all directions (Africa, Europe, and the Americas).

The visit to Japan of the defence secretary Mattis aimed to seize the opportunity to balance the relations between the two countries, since, during the campaign, President Trump argued that the U.S. will walk away from the mutual defence pact. Mattis declared that: "One thing is certain, the alliance between the United States and Japan is enduring and will remain as the cornerstone of peace and security in the Asia-Pacific region" (Cronk, 2017), pointing out that the American commitment also extends to the disputed islands in the East China Sea. Secretary Mattis described Japan as "a model of cost sharing" and praised the administration of Prime Minister Shinzo Abe for increasing spending on the military (Gordon, Hun, 2017).

Stone Fish (2017, p. 1) argues that Peter Navarro, the director of the National Trade Council, considers that China's currency manipulation "is threatening to tear asunder the entire global economic fabric and free trade framework" and the appointment of Peter Navarro in that important position "is an economic in-their-face challenge to the Chinese dragon". Trump's nominee for the United States trade representative, Robert Lighthizer, has called for a "much more aggressive approach in dealing with China."

5. China

From the economic standpoint, there are several asymmetries between the U.S. and China that Trump dislikes. Trade wise, as we show in Table 4 the trade in goods deficit of the U.S. with China increased constantly from $10.4 billion in 1990 to $367 billion in 2015, only to decrease slightly in 2016 (by 5.44%).

Table 4: U.S. trade in goods balance with China (millions of US dollars)

1990	1995	2000	2005	2010	2015	2016
-10,431.0	-33,789.5	-83,833.0	-202,278.1	-273,041.6	-367,172.9	-347,037.9

Source: United States Census Bureau, 2017

According to Dingli (2017, p. 2), "the difference in import prices between the two countries in recent years varied between 1:3 and 1:4. The United States levy an import tax of 2–3 percent, while China's import tax is 3–9 percent." While the U.S. markets are still essentially open, the Chinese companies are able to invest in almost every sector and own 100% of their American subsidiaries, in China there are rules restricting the U.S. companies as to where, how much and how to invest. Foreign companies cannot own land in China, while in the U.S. it is possible (Graceffo, 2017).

Robert Lighthizer, Trump's chief trade negotiator considers that: "Years of passivity and drift among U.S. policymakers have allowed the U.S.-China trade deficit to grow to the point where it is widely recognised as a major threat to our economy" (Lawder, 2017, p. 1).

To counter that, Donald Trump threatened to impose a 45% tariff on the imports from China. But as *The Economist* (2017, p. 59) analysts argue "a big blanket tariff would slice through supply chains, hurt American consumers and fly in the face of the global system of trade rules overseen by the World Trade Organisation."

Trump also vowed, during the elections, that he would label China as a currency manipulator. Still, many analysts argue that China indeed manipulates its currency so that the renminbi does not devaluate too quickly rather than weakening it to help exporters.

These trade discrepancies could be solved using the framework of the World Trade Organisation through targeted complaints submitted by the U.S. since Donald Trump did not mention anything about America quitting the WTO (Dingli, 2017, p. 2.). Thus, America will still have a legal forum to settle the disputes with China and other trade rivals using the arbitration mechanism of the WTO. Unfortunately for the new president, the WTO does not define state-owned enterprises and "it is hard to identify and oppose subsidies from state-owned banks", another issue of discontent on the American behalf. TPP included several definitions; a section on currency manipulation and other regulations that would have protected American workers from unfair competition, but this was scrapped by Trump at the beginning of his term (The Economist, 2017, p. 59).

To all these issues, the Chinese Foreign Affairs Ministry declared through its spokesperson that "China will work with the U.S., in the principle of non-conflict, non-confrontation, mutual respect and win-win cooperation, to expand cooperation, manage differences, and strive for greater achievements in our bilateral relationship by ensuring its healthy and sound growth."

China has leverage in a potential trade war with the U.S. Large American companies such as Apple, Boeing, General Motors etc. are dependent on the Chinese market. In the case that Trump imposes the tariff of 45% on the imports from China, Beijing could import American airplanes, mobiles and agricultural products. A blanket tariff of 45% on imports from China could be balanced by retaliatory measures by Beijing as it happened before when America imposed tariffs on Chinese tyres and China chose to buy chicken legs from Brazil (*The Economist*, 2017, p. 59).

6. Perspectives

To put a more realistic emphasis on the statements made by the presidential candidates during the elections, the Chinese ambassador to the U.K. declared: "I think I understand the American election politics. We listen to what they are saying today, but we must pay more attention to what they are going to do after the election." This is also our opinion since the practice proved that candidates promise "the world" to the people during the campaigns and deliver almost nothing afterwards. But, at least concerning China, so far, the American president has not put the facts where his campaign words were (*The Economist*, 2017, p. 59).

After the recognition of "our" One China policy by Donald Trump, it seems that his administration will continue the American approach to China, namely a mix of engagement and balancing. To support this assertion, it is worth mentioning the fact that before the phone call between Donald Trump and Xi Jinping, the Americans had unofficial contacts with their Chinese counterparts. Panda (2017, p. 2) mentions the meeting between Stephan Schwartzman, a billionaire with close ties to Trump, with Xi Jinping during the last World Economic Forum in Davos, the meeting of Henry Kissinger with the Chinese leader in last December and Ivanka Trump's attendance at the celebrations of the Chinese New Year at the Chinese Embassy in Washington. But "[i]f the United States truly wishes a cooperative partnership with Beijing", Washington must dispel Chinese doubts "and publicly support China's peaceful reunification." (Hathaway and Wilson, 2005).

The uncertainty regarding the American alliance policy in the analysed region could be easily speculated by China, a country that can provide certainty to some "confused" actors in the area.

The resurrection of bilateralism as a way to conduct trade deals, as president Trump agrees and an increased American and local support to developing compatible, stronger and modern allied armies might represent a balanced approach that can reinsure the American commitment to this strategic part of the Asian continent and preserve the current status quo.

Increased assertiveness in the field of trade and a more acute arms race might be the vectors of the following years if we take into account the fact that regional powers will place more emphasis on increasing their self-defence capabilities.

According to Tao (2016), Trump is expected to bring "pragmatism and flexibility – two crucial qualities in the business world – into his foreign policy-making". He also mentions the Chinese elite propensity to the republicans because they are "straightforward and practical" while the democrats are "hypocritical and ideological".

Conclusions

Foreign leaders are adjusting, however haltingly, to the Trump Era. An adviser to Japan's prime minister said that "we don't have to take each word that Mr. Trump said publicly literally". This perspective could be a sign that Trump is going to approach relations with countries such as China, Japan, or South Korea more as a transactional businessman than a traditional American president, changing the paradigm from multilateralism to bilateralism.

Our first conclusion is that, so far, some of the positions advocated by candidate Trump did not materialise in the case of Asian countries, either allies or competitors. It is true that the analysed period was very short, but in some relevant cases, we could identify nuances suggesting the direction of some policies.

Concerning China, Trump still has not labelled China as a currency manipulator, though he was right, but in the wrong way. On the "One China policy", a subject debated after his election, there was another change of heart, but about this, we consider that we do not have all the data to come up with the right conclusion. Still, the general opinion on this topic is that Trump lost some points.

On the TPP, the American president kept his promise and from the reactions of Shinzo Abe, it seems that his campaign position on trade worked, as the Japanese prime minister is willing to give an advantage to the larger economy, namely the U.S.

The second conclusion is that even the American president is a tough negotiator; in the field of international relations the dynamics are a bit different and the decision-making process takes into consideration additional parameters that can influence the initial opinion on a subject. Continuing some of the previous policies is not wrong as long as the results are beneficial for America first and then for its allies.

Regarding the contributions of the allies in Asia, the presidential position is not very clear. On the one hand, James Mattis conveyed a message of reassurance to South Korea and Japan, which contradicts candidate Trump's initial position, but on the other hand, we still do not know the costs of this reassurance.

The third conclusion did not result from our analysis, but the general perception is that Donald Trump seems to be very kind with most of his counterparts.

And that leads us to the conclusion that the new leader of the free world has not shown all his cards yet.

References

1. Asad, L. (2016). The high stakes for Southeast Asia of the 2016 US presidential election.
2. Bannon, S. (2016). Breitbart News Daily – Lee Edwards, 2016, March 10.
3. Choong, W. (2017). Trump and the Asia-Pacific: Managing Contradictions, Survival 59.1.
4. De Luce, D. (2017). Trump's China Policy: 'This Is How You Stumble Into Crisis', Foreign Policy, 2017, January 26.
5. Dingli, S. (2017). The Future of China-US Relations in the Trump Era. How will the Trump administration influence US-China ties in the political, economic, and security spheres? The Diplomat, 2017, February 4.
6. Ford, J. (2017). The Pivot to Asia Was Obama's Biggest Mistake, The Diplomat, 2017, January 21.
7. Gerzhoy, G., Miller, N. (2016). Donald Trump thinks more countries should have nuclear weapons. Here's what the research says, The Washington Post, April.
8. Gordon, M., Sang-Hun C. (2016). Jim Mattis Seeks to Soothe Tensions in Japan and South Korea, The New York Times, February.
9. Griffith, M., K., Richard S., John, Z. (2015). Great Power Politics in a Global Economy: Origins and Consequences of the TPP and TTIP. The University of California, Berkeley.
10. Hathaway, R.M., Wilson, L. (2005). George W. Bush and East Asia: A First Term Assessment. Woodrow Wilson International Center for Scholars.
11. Hu, E. (2016). Japan and South Korea Rattled By Trump's Talk of Closing U.S. Bases, NPR, November.
12. Hunt, K., Ogura, J., Wakatsuki, Y. (2016). Japan's Abe on US mission to 'build trust' with Donald Trump, CNN Politics, November.
13. Johnson, J. (2016). Trump rips U.S. defence of Japan as one-sided, too expensive, The Japan Times, August.
14. Kagan, R. (2017). Backing Into World War III. America must check the assertive, rising powers of Russia and China before it's too late. Accepting spheres of influence is a recipe for disaster, Foreign Policy, February 6.
15. Kim, C., Park, Y. (2016). South Korea FX official expects Trump to strengthen Treasury's currency reporting scheme, Reuters, November.
16. Kim, S. (2016). Trump Says '100%' With Park on Need to Deter North Korea Threat. Bloomberg, November.
17. Kong, K., Reynolds, I. (2017). Abe, Trump Show Unity in Condemning North Korea Missile Test, Bloomberg, February.
18. Lawder, D. (2017). Trump names China critic Lighthizer as U.S. trade representative, Reuters, 2017, January 3.
19. Ministry of Defense: "Defense Programs and Budget of Japan", (2016) August.

20. Ministry of Foreign Affairs of the People's Republic of China, Ambassador Liu Xiaoming's.
21. Q&A after his speech on the South China Sea at the Chatham House (2016), July 30.
22. Ministry of National Defense: Defense Budget, 2016.
23. Parameswaran, P. (2016). What Will Donald Trump's Asia Policy Look Like? The Diplomat, November 10.
24. Pew Research Center: Global Opposition to U.S. Surveillance and Drones, but Limited Harm to America's Image – Many in Asia Worry about a Conflict with China (2014), July 14.
25. Sieg, L. (2016). Trump candidacy stirs alliance angst in Japan, Reuters, March 2016.
26. Stashwick, S. (2017). Perpetual Stalemate: China Can Neither Be Dislodged From the the South China Sea Nor Control It. The Diplomat, February 06.
27. Stone F.I. (2017). Confronting Chairman Trump, Slate.com, January 30.
28. Sutter, R., Satu, P.L. (2016). America's 2016 election debate on Asia policy and Asian reactions".
29. Tao, X. (2016). How Will President Trump Deal With China?, The Diplomat, November 29.
30. The Economist: Rules of engagement. Even without a trade war, there is plenty of scope for trade tensions between America and China (2017), January 28, pp. 59–60.
31. The Economist: Own shoal, 2017, January 28, pp. 19–20.
32. The Japan News: Abe, Trump take baby steps on trade, February (2017).
33. Trump, D. (2016). Donald Trump's Contract with the American Voter, assets. donaldjtrump.com, October 23.
34. Trump, D. (2016, b). Japan and South Korea hit back at Trump's nuclear comments. CNN, 2016b, March 31.

Anton S. KOSTADINOV

Economic Research Institute, Bulgarian Academy of Sciences, Sofia, Bulgaria, tonykostadinov@abv.bg

EU–China Food Trade Perspectives

Abstract: At present, one of the main concerns of decidents form China is to ensure food security for its large population. About one fifth of the global population is living in China, on 1/15 of rural land and using only 8% of the fresh water resources. At the same time, the degree of urbanization and the disposable incomes are increasing with a high speed. This all means that the food consuming pattern in China is also changing, and food consumption in the country will grow in both quantity and quality. EU-China trade relations are complicated and protectionism can be seen on both sides. The EU have large trade deficits with China. Most member states also have large deficits, but not Germany and Finland. EU member states have very different positions about trade relations with China. In the food sector the EU experiences overproduction, closed markets in the Russian Federation, and internal market tensions. Furthermore, the EU has placed a strong emphasis on speeding up free trade agreements with Asian countries, including China, but there are no plausible results yet.

Keywords: China, EU food trade, food security

1. Introduction

European Union (EU)–China trade relations could be described as very delicate. Trade is fast growing but there are several important issues. First, the EU recorded trade deficit in goods with China in 2015, but recorded surplus for trade with services, while trade with services is only a fraction of total trade, approximately 10%. After 2012, the EU reported surplus with China in food trade. Second, trade rules are reflecting the tensions in the EU–China trade relations. Third, China is penetrating the EU market through separate market agreements with EU member states. Of course, the lack of cohesive EU position eases that. Furthermore, China is rebalancing its economy, and the country is reporting a shrinking total trade surplus from USD 60b in 2015 to USD 40.5b in 2016. This tendency is in unison with the Chinese road to the "New Normal". Yang Yao (2016) argues that there are strong signs that the Chinese economy is entering a stage of a "New Normal". Penetration of the EU market and shrinking total trade surplus are clear indicators of the willingness of China to further open its economy and to trade more. However, this is a slow process.

2. Recent developments in China's food trade

Fast industrialization in China in the past 40 years opened the way to global leadership. From the second poorest, China became the second richest country in the world, and in 2018 is expected to surpass the USA. During that period China experienced economic growth between 7–10%. The role of new global power means China is seeking the new state of its political, economic and social systems. Zhang (2014) argues that over the last two years, the new development model has been articulated with increasing force and clarity at the highest levels of China's government (CCCPC, 2013; State Council, 2013; Anon., 2015b). The seeking of "New Normal" also means that China is preparing to jump up in the global value chain, to rebalance its economy as an innovation-based one. There are three main factors influencing Chinese food trade relations. The first is urbanization, which is the largest movement of people ever. Di Chengfeng (2013) argues that more than 300 million people are moving to urban areas. The second factor is the growing disposable incomes of Chinese households (Figure 1). The third factor is the soaring demand for foods in both dimensions—quality and quantity.

Fig. 1: Disposable incomes in China

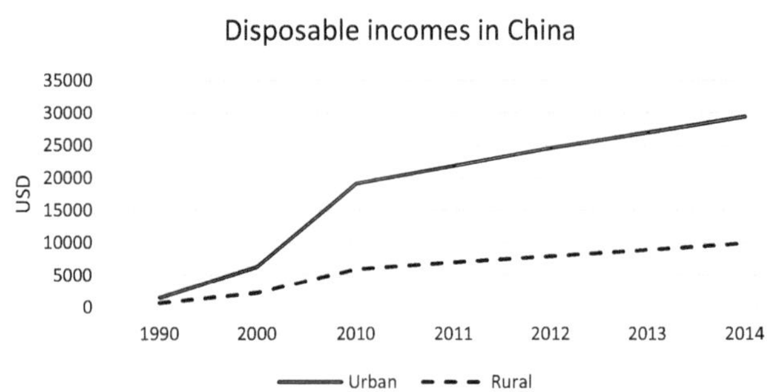

Source: World Bank statistics

Impressive changes in agricultural production in China allowed the country to gain self-sufficiency in grain and as a net exporter of many agricultural products. At the same time, disposable incomes of the Chinese population are growing, faster in urban areas and slower in rural areas (Kate Stratford and Arianna Cowling). Higher disposable incomes mean that the food consumption pattern is changing. Food consumption patterns in urban rural areas are different, but there is a clear tendency revealing China's population's diet change. People in urban areas consume more processed food, also better quality foods with more protein.

Furthermore, there is a change in the meat consumption pattern—a move to the consumption of better quality meat. To feed its 1.4 billion-strong population, China is facing a big challenge; the country is losing arable land, per capita fresh water is only 31% of the world's average and approximately 20% of the arable land in the country is poisoned with heavy metals. In 1995 China announced a White Paper on its grain issues, which declared the need to achieve a 95% grain self-sufficiency rate.

Even later, in 2008, China announced its Long-Term Grain Security plan. In the past, there was a volatility in China's food trade. During the 50s, China was a net food exporter, and in the 60s food imports were minimal. In 1995 grain imports reached 20 million tons. China's socioeconomic development, combined with the largest urbanization ever, have sped up the demand for food in terms of both quality and quantity, and have resulted in the decline of the self-sufficiency rate. One of the possible paths for China is to import more land-intensive foods in order to release the pressure on its own resources. But China's long-term dependence on foreign imports may worsen the food security problem in the country. China is now near the top of developing countries and is approaching the income levels of high-income countries.

Fast and large-scale urbanization was a major factor influencing food consumption in the country. China is now the largest pork meat, rice and wheat producer in the world, but it still needs imports in order to balance internal consumption. China is importing not only raw agricultural materials, but also processed food. In both categories China has large deficits (Figure 2).

Fig. 2: Raw agricultural and food imports and exports

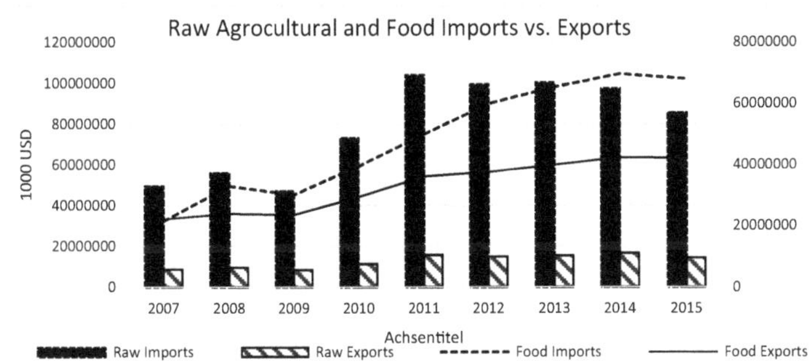

Source: World Bank statistics

China is making a lot of efforts to rebalance and consequently to open its economy. This active position reveals the necessity to develop its trade relations, in particular with key food suppliers, such as the EU. China's government is forced by its rapidly growing urban population with growing disposable incomes, scarcity of arable land and fresh water to develop trade relations with key global market players. The EU seems an appropriate supplier because it is producing high quality land-intensive foods.

3. Obstacles to EU–China food trade

The approach of the EU to China is controversial. Now China is the second largest global power, but the role of the EU is diminishing as a global player. This also concerns trade relations between the two. Since 2006 the EU has been laying stress on the Free Trade Agreement (FTA) with China, but at the same time it does not recognize China as a market economy.

Fig. 3: EU Member states' attitudes towards China

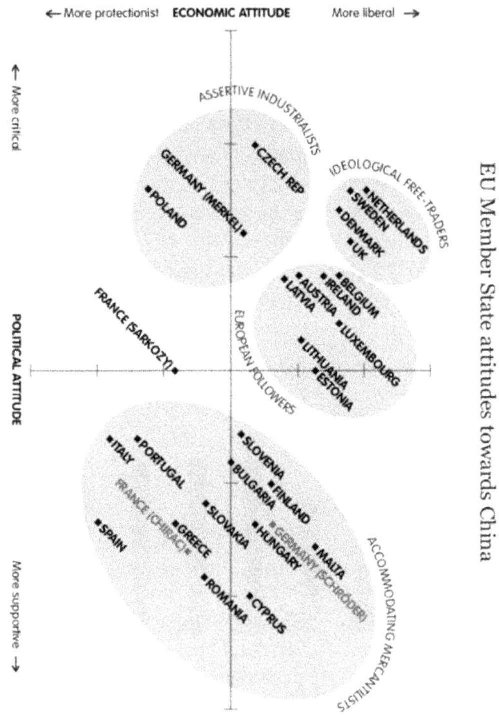

Source: A power audit of EU–China relations

So far, there is no EU–China FTA, and there are still many tariff and non-tariff trade barriers. Trade disputes occur very seldom. John Fox and François Godement (2009) argue that at the bottom of that problem there are some differences between EU member states and the anachronistic beliefs that China will reform and liberalize its economy under pressure. The EU established diplomatic relations with China back in 1975, but China's economy, foreign policy and society have evolved. Now China is a global power and decisions taken in Beijing concern the EU in every aspect. Differences in EU member states are decisive for relations with China. The analysis of John Fox and François Godement categorizes the Member States into the four groups shown on the chart: Assertive Industrialists, Ideological Free-Traders, Accommodating Mercantilists and European Followers (Figure 3).

The lack of consistent approach of the EU towards China is based on deep differences between member states economies, and makes trade issues even more complicated. The group of Assertive Industrialists may not allow market forces to shape the EU–China trade relationship. Strong industry in these countries cause them to support anti-dumping measures against subsidized goods coming from China. Yu Chen (2015) argues that the solar panel dispute was the biggest trade controversy between the EU and China. In 2013 China launched the investigation a day after the EU imposed anti-dumping levies on Chinese solar panel imports. Countries from this group tend to pressure China with sector-specific demands and to support protective "anti-dumping" measures against unfairly subsidized Chinese goods.

The countries in the group of Ideological Free-Traders are mostly innovative countries, and they are not willing to restrict trade with China. The actions of this group make it very difficult for the EU to give a coherent response to China's very carefully prepared trade policy.

The group of Accommodating Mercantilists tends to be the largest and here the belief that political relations will lead to economic benefits is valid.

The last country group of European Followers does not consider the relationship with China as important for their economies. They rely on EU support to hedge their economies of being harmed by China.

The agricultural sector in the EU and China is very strongly protected. Furthermore, both sides are also using non-tariff barriers, which additionally complicates food trade. China has long been pushing self-sufficiency policy, but the EU spends nearly €50 billion per year on its Common Agricultural Policy. Agricultural markets on both sides are highly sensitive areas of interests, and bound by consistent policies, and with tariff and non-tariff barriers. Furthermore, China is following a policy of government-controlled agricultural sector, and controlled prices and quantities in order to sustain food self-sufficiency. What is important here is what agro-products the Chinese tariff and non-tariff protection is stopping the potential export of from the EU. The EU is interested in China's market because of internal market pressure and the export ban of the Russian Federation.

Tariffs in agriculture are higher than in most industries, because of the abovementioned reasons. Jaques Pelkmans and Joseph Francois (2016) argue that European tariffs are centred mostly on relatively low thresholds, but the EU's non-tariff barriers are much more complicated and impenetrable than the Chinese ones. There are product groups that are sensitive to both sides, and we can observe tariff peaks. In the most impacted product group for the EU, prepared fruits and vegetables, there are a lot of tariff peaks. This is also valid for China. Even though there are complicated trade barriers, the tendency of food trade growth after 2009 is clear. China is gradually scaling down its self-sufficiency policy, which is proven by rapid import growth, and the signing of several FTAs. Further EU–China food trade growth will depend mostly on the EU's coherent approach to China, because the reality is that China is now a skilful and pragmatic global power.

4. Developments in EU–China food trade

Only 14 years after China's accession to the World Trade Organization (WTO) in 2001, the country ranks as the second largest economy. In 2014 China was the biggest exporting economy with a share of 12.4% of the world's total. In 2014 Chinese imports amounted to 1.97 trillion USD, accounting for 10.45% of the global total. Chinese food trade also boomed (Figure 4).

After 2007 China has experienced trade deficits with foods, and this gap is widening. The reasons for the surging demand for foods, in terms of quality and quantity, have been discussed above.

China's tightly controlled economic and industrial policies resulted in increasing food production in the country, but it is still not enough to equal constantly increasing demand. China is strengthening its food security program, but is still relying on large scale imports from abroad. Powder milk, imported from New Zealand and Algeria, is an example. Local powder milk production is not able to provide food for more than 16 million births per year. Polluted environment concerns already influence food trade policy and trade. The most important trading partners in food trade for China are the USA, the EU, Brazil, Japan, S. Korea, New Zealand and Australia.

The food trade between the EU and China is approximately 3% of total trade volume. The soaring food demand in China can also be found in the positive food trade balance that the EU enjoys after 2012. This figure is not only valid for the EU, but also for other countries: Brazil and the USA, for example. The EU exports steadily grew until 2009, then the tempo seriously increased. For China, the EU is the third largest import partner after the USA and Brazil.

In 2007, US food imports to China accounted for 28% of total food imports, Brazilian for 20%, but European only 8.2%; while in 2015 the US accounted for 27% of food imports, Brazil for 24%, and Europe only 13.4%. The EU share of food imports in China is growing in spite of the record trade deficits the EU experiences in other sectors. The largest export food market for China in 2015 was Japan with a 29% share of total food exports, the EU with 20.5% and the USA with 20.26%.

Fig. 4: China's global food exports and imports

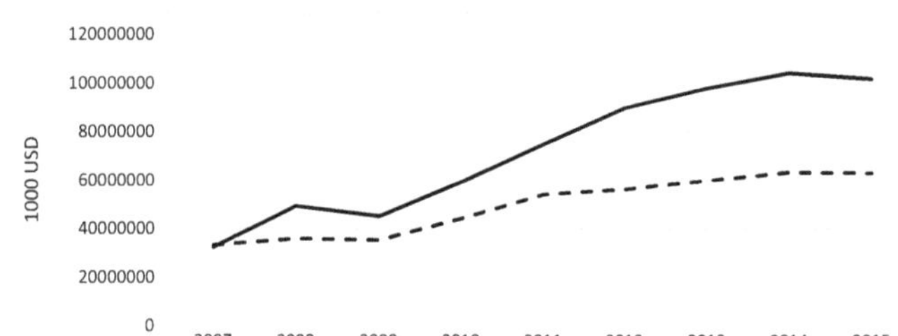

	2007	2008	2009	2010	2011	2012	2013	2014	2015
Imports	32264538	49304191	45075272	59246206	74882188	89851231	97896642	104321652	101897644
Export	33152847	35866134	35295837	44116767	54119905	56274773	59932952	63436277	63186196

Source: World Bank statistics

The leading export market for the EU food is the USA with a share of 4.11% of total EU food exports. China's market share is 1.88%, Japan's 1.2%, and the Russian Federation 1%. The largest food imports in the EU arrive from Brazil (10.7%), the USA (9.56%), Argentina (4.8%), and China, which has a 4.32% share of total food imports.

Fig. 5: EU–China imports and exports

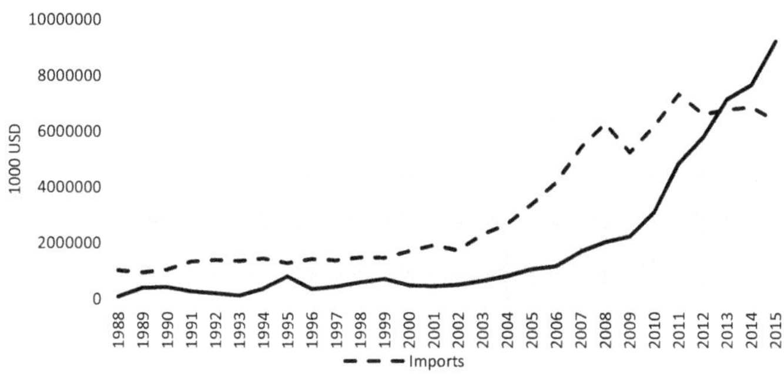

Source: World Bank

After 2012 the EU enjoyed a positive trade balance with China (Figure 5). EU agri-food exports to China grew by 39% from 2014 to 2015, but the imports by only 10.6%. The main export commodity going to China is the group of infant food and other cereals. Judith Banister, David E. Bloom, and Larry Rosenberg (2010) argue that there are difficulties in keeping the food supply growing. The explanation for that is the aging of the Chinese population. That is why the Chinese government abolished its one-child policy, and now we have approximately 16.5 million births per year. Furthermore, in 2010 senior citizens accounted for 13.26% of the population, with 8.87% aged 65 or above. In 2025, the elderly population will account for more than 20% of the total with about 12% aged 65 or above (Li Jiabao).

5. Perspectives of the EU–China food trade

The EU is China's number one trading partner, and a valuable supplier of high-value-added products. Because of high demand, the importance of the EU as a food supplier to China is growing. Nevertheless, EU political influence is shrinking, with Germany, France and the UK being more important to China than the EU as a whole. China's pragmatic and aggressive approach to the EU shows that the EU needs new and better approaches to China. In order for China and the EU to further open their markets to each other, the divisions between member states need to be diminished. China's strategy of separate trade agreements means weakening the EU position. Food security for both sides is a strategic issue. Acceleration of food demand in a growing economy like China's means that it will continue to be vulnerable to food insecurity. China will probably sustain self-sufficiency in some product groups like rice and wheat, but in others like meat, dairy products, and some processed food will continue to be import dependent. Urbanization in China means that a smaller proportion of people will produce food, so the urban population will consume more processed food. Soil, water and air pollution mean that there are serious risks to food security in the country.

Exhausted natural resources are forcing the Chinese government to diversify food suppliers in order to meet the soaring demand in the country. Trade relations between the EU and China are also shaped by some perception gaps. Both China and the EU impose legal, financial, and administrative blockages. Furthermore, most of the EU member states have significant deficits with China, but others like Germany and Finland are running surpluses.

As shown in Figure 6, the EU is the third largest food importer in China. A greater share of EU exports to China are mostly based on beverages, the group of miscellaneous foods, cereals, and dairy products. The Chinese food market will continue to grow and it means it would be a destination for more European food. The significance of the EU as a food supplier to China will grow because more disposable income means increased demand for more quality processed food, such as food produced in the EU.

Fig. 6: Biggest food importers in China

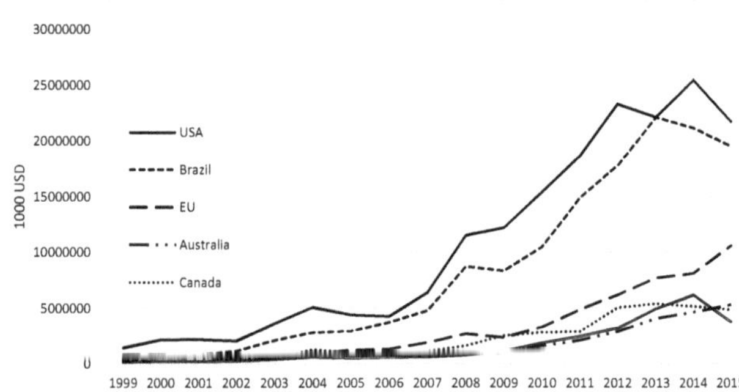

Source: *World Bank*

6. Conclusion

Maybe the EU is in decline because of economic sluggishness, demographic lethargy, military weakness, political disunity, etc. But the EU will continue to be a global superpower during the 21st century, and it has resources for regional and global influence. The relations with China will be the test point of the EU's ability to adapt to a new global power like China. Trade and investments are supposed to be the main driver for a bilateral relationship. Food trade is an essential part of that relationship, and that is why it will grow. Whether China will become an even more attractive market for EU food depends on domestic developments. As a destination for EU goods, including food, China has to maintain its economic growth rate and productivity, create jobs and continue to increase the living standards of its citizens. The challenge for the EU is to regain economic dynamism and keep the protectionist pressure at bay, while the challenge for China is to develop its domestic market, to make it more competitive and open.

References

1. Anonymous, (2015a). Coming down to earth. The Economist, [Online] Available at: http://www.economist.com/news/briefng/21648567-chinese-growth-losing-altitude-will-it-be-soft-or-hard-landing-comingdown-earth. [Accessed: 19th Dec 2016].
2. Central Committee of the Communist Party of China (CCCPC). (2013). Decision on Major Issues Concerning Comprehensively Deepening Reforms. [Online] 15 November 2013. Available at: http://news.xinhuanet.com/politics/2013-11/15/c_118164235.htm. English Version available at: http://english.people.com.cn/90785/8525422.html. [Accessed: 19th Dec 2016].
3. David, S., M. Gordon, and T. Cecilia. (2010) Urbanization and its implications for food and farming. Phil. Trans. R. Soc. 365:2809–2820.
4. Di Chengfeng. (2013). Urbanization in China: Population and Land. [Online] Available from: econ.core.hu/file/download/seba/di.ppt. [Accessed: 19th Dec 2016].
5. Popescu, Gh.H. (2016). The Role of Multinational Corporations in Global Environmental Politics, Economics, Management, and Financial Markets 11(3):72–78.
6. Nica, E., Ioan H. (2016). The State-led System of Global Environmental Governance, *Economics, Management, and Financial Markets* 11(3):79–85.
7. Zaga, S.D. (2016). The Impact of Nutritional Programs in Mexico, American Journal of Medical Research 3(1):7–38.
8. Nica, E. (2016). Employee Voluntary Turnover as a Negative Indicator of Organizational Effectiveness, Psychosociological Issues in Human Resource Management 4(2):220–226.
9. Machan, T.R. (2016). Commerce and Its Normative Dimensions, Psychosociological Issues in Human Resource Management 4(1):7–40.
10. Fleming, C. (2009) Food security, urbanization and social stability in China. J. Agrar. Change 9:548–575. Wiley Online Library.
11. Fox, J., Francois, G. (2009). A power audit of EU-China relations. Brussels: European Council on Foreign Relations.

12. Ghose, B. (2014) Food security and food self-sufficiency in China: from past to 2050. [Online] Available from: http://onlinelibrary.wiley.com/doi/10.1002/fes3.48/full. [Accessed: 26th Nov 2016].
13. Judith, B., David, E. B., Larry, R. (2012). "Population Aging and Economic Growth in China." in *The Chinese Economy: A New Transition*, eds. Masahiko Aoki and Jinglian Wu, 114–49. London: Palgrave Macmillan.
14. Li, J. (2014). Aging nation means challenges and opportunities. China Daily, USA. [Online] Available from: http://usa.chinadaily.com.cn/epaper/2014-01/30/content_17266338.htm.
15. Pelkmans, J., Hu, W., Mustilli, F., Di Salvo, M., Francois, J., Bekkers, E. Manchin, M., Tomberger, P. (2016). Tomorrow's Silk Road: Assessing an EU-China Free Trade Agreement. Series. Centre for European Policy Studies (Brussels). CEPS Paperbacks. UNSPECIFIED.
16. Stratford, K., Arianna, C. (2016). Chinese Household Income, Consumption and Savings. [Online] Available from: https://www.rba.gov.au/publications/bulletin/2016/sep/pdf/rba-bulletin-2016-09-chinese-household-income-consumption-and-savings.pdf. [Accessed: 21th Oct 2016].
17. Yang, Y. (2016). A New Normal, but with Robust Growth: China's. Growth Prospects in the Next 10 Years. [Online] Available from: https://www.brookings.edu/wp-content/uploads/2016/07/tt20-china-growth-prospects-yao.pdf. [Accessed: 21th Jan 2017].
18. Yu, C. (2015). EU-China Solar Panel's Trade Dispute: Settlement and challenges to the EU. [Online] Available from: http://www.eias.org/wp-content/uploads/2016/02/EU-Asia-at-a-glance-EU-China-Solar-Panels-Dispute-Yu-Chen.pdf. [Accessed: 21th Jan 2017].
19. Zhang, G. (2014). Comprehensively deepen reforms to promote sustainable and healthy development of the economy and society. [online] Speech at the 15th China Development Forum. 23 March 2014. Available at: http://cpc.people.com.cn/n/2014/0324/c6409424714056.html].

Vasili EROKHIN

School of Economics and Management, Harbin Engineering University, P.R. China, basilic@list.ru

Food Security: A Challenge for China and Russia to Resolve in Northeast Asia

Abstract: Food security concerns in the region of Northeast Asia are among the most critical. For the countries in the region, providing the growing population with food in sufficient quantity and variety is a challenge, which includes a range of issues of food production, import dependence and export orientation of the food market, solvency and dietary patterns. Despite the rapid growth of agricultural production complexes and long traditions of the rural way of life, domestic food production in the region of Northeast Asia fails to meet demand. Even big and completive agricultural producers such as China and Russia have, to some extent, to rely on agricultural imports, suffering from price fluctuations on the global market, which threaten their food security. This paper includes an overview of the current state of agricultural production and food consumption trade in the region of Northeast Asia, primarily China's Northeast and Russia's Far East, with particular attention to the development of rural territories. Influences of the interregional collaboration between China and Russia on food security in the macro region of Northeast Asia are discussed. This paper is concluded with an overview of expected influences of the development of rural territories on domestic food markets, sustainability of agricultural production, and food security.

Keywords: Food Security, Northeast Asia, Regional Integration, Food Sovereignty, Far East

Introduction

In the region of Northeast Asia, the demand for food and agricultural products is rising. From the 1980s to the 2010s, rapid economic growth and urbanization in China caused a substantial shift in the structure of food consumption. Zhou (2010) and Zhou, Liu, Cao, Tian, and Wang (2014) record growth of consumption of food products of higher quality, nutrient value, and price in China (meat and meat products, milk and dairy products, and seafood) to the prejudice of cheaper and lower crops. Consequently, Chinese meat and dairy producers demand more crops as fodder for agricultural animals, which increases the load on agricultural lands and accelerates their degradation (Liu and Diamond, 2005). According to Nath, Luan, Yang, Yang, Chen, Li, and Cui (2015), by 2030, China will need to increase agricultural lands under crops by 21% to be able to meet the increasing internal demand for food. Obviously, in the years ahead, China will face new challenges in the sphere of food security.

Russia, which borders China in the region of Northeast Asia, is abundant in agricultural land. However, the eastern parts of the country experience food security problems of different origin. In 2014 and 2015, because of Western sanctions, collapsing oil prices, and ensuing ruble depreciation, Russian agricultural producers were hurt by the rise in prices for imported inputs. While retaining sanctions and countersanctions, high-interest rates and low state support in the longer term, Russian agricultural production will suffer from the drop in investment and, accordingly, in production.

Against the backdrop of different sources of food security problems, both countries have to search for effective solutions in the region of Northeast Asia. Regardless of the concrete mechanisms selected in China and Russia, the basis for the ensurance of food security is the development of domestic agricultural production, sustainable to economic shocks and international market fluctuations and responsive to shifts in consumption patterns (Erokhin, 2018).

1. Literature review

In Russia, the understanding of food security differs from the internationally accepted one of the Food and Agricultural Organization of the United Nations (FAO). Thus, in some governmental documents and the works by Nechaev (2008), Ushachev (2013), and Shagaida and Uzun (2015) food security is treated as increasing of domestic food production up to the certain threshold set by the government. Spoor and Robbins (2012) point out the high political background of food security issues in Russia and countries of Central and Northeast Asia. Many researchers from China, including Luan, Cui, and Ferrat (2013), Ghose (2014), and Jianhua (2011) understand food security as food independence or food self-sufficiency. More attention is paid to such dimensions of food security as the ensurance of physical and economic access to food products of high quality and the sustainability of this access in the long term. While the FAO considers food security as access by people to enough food on the domestic market by means of both domestic production and imports, some Chinese experts argue that the increasing scale of international trade threatens the food security of China (Zhu, 2016; Yu, Elleby, and Zobbe, 2015; Yu, Feng, Hubacek, and Sun, 2016; Zhou, 2010).

Taking into account the abundant land resources and scarce population in Northeast Asia, one of the key solutions to the food security problem in this region is sustainable development of those territories which provide a supply of agricultural products and food. Over the transition period of the 1990s to the 2000s, there were certain reforms implemented in agricultural production and land relations. According to Ivolga (2014), in Russia those reforms led to the stabilizing of the situation in rural areas during the transition period. In the case of China, rural areas lag behind urban ones in terms of living standards and quality of life because of their low level of industrial development and urbanization (Long, Liu, Li, and Chen, 2010). As Heilig (2003) details, the economic boom in China during the 2000s and 2010s was mainly generated by urbanized coastal provinces in southern and eastern parts of China. Rural areas in the northern and northeastern parts of the country experienced little economic growth after the first wave of development in the early 1980s when family farming was re-introduced after decades of centrally planned agricultural communes (Chen and Fleisher, 1996).

Countries of Northeast Asia have much in common in the sphere of agricultural production and food security issues. In this region, the issues of food security shifted from agriculture itself to a broader spectrum, which included the social and economic situation in rural territories, development of rural infrastructure, employment and involvement of rural households in economic activities, environmental and recreational issues, etc. (Erokhin, 2014). The effectiveness of such policies directly affects food security through the social and demographic situation in rural areas, living standards of rural people, and development of traditional cultures and rural way of life.

For the purposes of the current research, we have primarily addressed the works related to the analysis of local specifics of food security and economic conditions of certain regions (Merzlov, Ovchintseva, and Popova, 2012; Zhou, Wu, Chen, and Chen, 2007). Regional specifics of sustainable development of rural areas in the northern and eastern parts of China are obtained from the works of Ma (2011), Chen and Fleisher (1996), Chen, Xiangzheng, Jianing, and Peiying (2016), and Liu, Heijman, Zhu, Dries, and Huang (2016), while an overview of contemporary issues of sustainable rural development in Russia in terms of existing differences between regions is made based on the works of Ivolga (2014) and Zhuplei (2015). Impacts of international markets, international trade, and international cooperation on food security in relation to the region of Northeast Asia are addressed in the works of Stiglitz and Greenwald (2006), Taranov and Panasyuk (2010), Taranov and Panasyuk (2012), and Zhu (2016).

2. Results and Discussion

Development of agricultural production is crucially important for the stabilization of the social and economic situation and the establishment of comfortable living and working environments in the rural areas of China's North and Russia's Far East (hereinafter, CNRFE region). The revival of the agricultural sector is key to the retention of the workforce in rural areas and the sustainable development of rural areas in this region of the world (Erokhin and Ivolga, 2012).

The major strategic goal of the agri-industrial complex is the provision of agricultural products and food. However, for the CNRFE region, this overall goal has specific implications: sustainable development of rural territories which are vast, sparsely inhabited, and underdeveloped; increase of competitiveness of agricultural products; ensurance of financial viability and modernization of agricultural production; accelerated development of traditional agricultural industries (animal husbandry, hunting, etc.); preservation and recovery of agricultural lands and natural resources involved in agricultural production (Li, Ali, and Zhang, 2007).

Both the overall macroeconomic conditions and specific features of the region condition development of rural territories of the CNRFE region. Objective features include natural and climatic conditions for agricultural production; existing infrastructure in the agricultural sector, including production, storage, transportation, and distribution of agricultural products; and the specific dietary habits of rural people in the region. Subjective features that affect the agricultural sector and rural territories in the CNRFE region include continuing migration of people from rural areas to cities or to other regions of Russia and China; worsening social and demographic conditions in rural areas; lack of qualified labour force; degradation of rural territories in the light of China's growing expansion; relatively weak entrepreneurial behavior of rural people; low effectiveness of state support programs in the sphere of small and medium entrepreneurship; low competitiveness of Russian agricultural and food products in comparison with Chinese ones; low effective demand in the region, especially in Russia.

One of the most influential factors constraining the effective development of agricultural production in the CNRFE region is the low labour potential of rural areas. Rural population in both Russia and China is decreasing. During the decade of 2004–2014, the number of rural dwellers in Russia decreased by 1.7%, and in China by 18.3%. Unemployment along with poor standards of living caused a rapid increase of migration outflow from rural areas. Between 2002 and 2010 (2010 is the year of the most recent census in Russia), the rural population of Russia's Far East decreased by 14.3%. The decline of the rural population happens in parallel with the liquidation of rural settlements, particularly in the northern areas of the Far East. Between 2002 and 2010, 104 rural settlements were liquidated, including 91 in the northern part of the region.

Just like Russia, China is now experiencing the "rural flight", when fewer people are needed to bring the same amount of agricultural output to market, and related agricultural services and industries are consolidated. Until 1983, the Chinese government, through the hukou system, restricted the ability of the citizens to internally migrate. A hukou is a record in a government system of household registration required by law in mainland China and Taiwan and determines where citizens are allowed to live. Since 1983, the Chinese government has slowly lifted the restrictions on internal migration leading to a great increase in the number of internal migrants, especially from rural areas towards the urbanized regions. Currently, a huge surplus of the labour force in rural areas of China form the labour market for crop production. In the very first years of economic reforms, the number of rural migrants reached 100 million people. The problem of excessive labour supply is quite pressing for China. One hundred to two hundred million people migrate within the country seeking income opportunities. Their major field of employment is the agricultural sector, or so-called rural settlement enterprises. State regulation in China is targeted at the redistribution of migration flows, determination of the hosting districts, and facilitation of easy migration of rural people from the northern provinces of China to neighboring regions of Russia (primarily Primorsky Krai, Khabarovsky Krai, and Amurskaya Oblast) for employment in agricultural production, farming, entrepreneurial, intermediary, and other types of business activities.

Despite the easier regime, even today, the hukou system limits the ability of rural migrants. The share of rural population in the total population in China is much higher in comparison to Russia (Table 1). Over 42% of the population of Heilongjiang Province lives in rural areas, while in neighboring regions of Russia this figure is only 24.64% (Far Eastern Federal District in total, average).

Table 1: Share of rural population in total population in the selected regions of China and Russia in 2015, %

Country / region	**2014**
China, total	45.23
Heilongjiang Province	42.60
Russia, total	26.03
Far Eastern Federal District of Russia, total	24.64
Republic of Sakha (Yakutia)	34.71
Kamchatsky Krai	22.45
Primorsky Krai	23.11
Khabarovsky Krai	18.17
Amurskaya Oblast	32.70
Magadanskaya Oblast	4.58
Sakhalinskaya Oblast	18.63
Jewish Autonomous Oblast	31.73
Chukotsky Autonomous District	31.45
Siberian Federal District of Russia, total	27.39
Zabaykalsky Krai	32.61

Source: State Council of the Russian Federation, 2016; National Bureau of Statistics of the People's Republic of China, n.d.

One of the most recent measures to fight depopulation in rural areas and develop agricultural production in Russia's Far East is the program of free-of-charge distribution of one hectare of land per person to everyone interested. The initiative suggests a solution to several problems: involvement of underutilized land into the turnover, establishment of new employment (and self-employment) opportunities, and attraction (or return) of the employable population to the rural areas of Russia's Far East. Land plots are assumed to be leased for a period of five years, upon the expiration of which the decision on future use of the plot should be taken. If the land is used in a proper manner, the plot is transferred to the property of the land user. In the case of improper use, or no use, the land plot is confiscated.

The author argues that the initiative will not cause a mass migration of Russian people to the Far East. In such a vast region access to land is not a problem, hence the distribution of land is not an incentive. People in rural areas in the Far East have excessive access to land–it is doubtful that new land plots may retain them in rural areas. During the 1990s and 2000s, cultivated agricultural lands in the Far East decreased by 40%. These are abandoned lands in the areas where agricultural production is not economically viable due to climatic conditions. Such regions are predominantly urban, except Amurskaya Oblast, where the share of rural population in the total population of the region is relatively high.

In China, on the contrary, much attention is paid to the problem of decreasing areas under cultivation. The country loses agricultural lands because of their removal from turnover in favour of the construction of industrial enterprises, roads, mining sites, and other objects. China's land policy assumes stabilization of arable lands and increase of areas under cultivation by means of tilling wild land in the northern regions. In recent years, the Chinese government concentrates on the protection of agricultural lands from erosion and bogging, their melioration and drainage.

The author believes that the problem of depopulation of rural territories in the Far East cannot be solved by the provision of land plots only. Such an idea can be productive only in the case that the people moving to the Far East are provided with substantial support from the state, including financial (interest-free loans, resettlement benefits, etc.) and infrastructural (access of allotted land plots to infrastructure in terms of power, transportation, and water supply) measures.

Summarising the results of the analysis of agricultural production in the Far East, the author emphasizes the following negative impacting factors: low rates of economic growth; low effectiveness of reproduction processes; absence of strategic vision of sustainable development of the region; uncertainty of strategic and tactic tasks of agricultural development; low effectiveness of the existing system of state regulation of agricultural production and food market; irregularity of relations between the the federal government and regional administrations; and lack of financial support for research and development in the sphere of agricultural production.

Merzlov et al. (2012) developed the classification of Russia's regions, which included four types and nine subtypes of regions depending on the character of rural development, utilization of available agricultural and environmental resources, and the level of social and demographic development. Far Eastern regions of Russia are included in the Subtype 3c ("poor social and natural conditions") and are characterized by a combination of unfavorable social and environmental conditions. Republic of Sakha (Yakutia), Kamchatsky Krai, Chukotsky Autonomous District, Magadanskaya Oblast and Sakhalinskaya Oblast are related to Type 4 ("low level of territorial development"). Those are northeastern parts of Russia with an area of 62% of Russia's territory and a population of only 6% of the total population. According to this classification, northern-eastern provinces of China can also be referred to as Type 3 ("relatively unfavourable conditions"), just like Russia's Far East regions. According to Zhou et al. (2007) and Ma (2011), the land infertility is a severe issue and plenty of land in the northern parts of China is in arid, semiarid or desert regions. Moreover, the environment in northern China is vulnerable due to serious soil erosion, soil desertification, shortages of agricultural water resources and lowering of groundwater levels. Based on this kind of natural environment, agricultural productivity is comparatively low in comparison to than that of southern China (Ma, 2011).

The Chinese government pays attention to the development of market mechanisms in rural areas and their control. In China, an increase of farmers' income by 1% adds 0.51% to GDP growth (Beloglazov, 2007). That is why the increase of prosperity in rural areas is so important for the government. The positive experience of development of rural territories in China should be adopted by Russia. Implementation of those measures that have been effective in China may cause an essential positive influence on the development of the neighboring regions of Russia's Far East. The most important lesson to be studied from the Chinese experience is the model of gradual transition from an administrative economy to a market environment with effective state regulation, without declines in production and standards of living in rural areas. Due to the unfavourable climatic conditions and related difficulties in agricultural production in the majority of the administrative regions of Russia's Far East, it is necessary to provide support for domestic agricultural organizations (by means of subsidies) and rural households (through agricultural consumer cooperatives) that focus on production of the most competitive and value-added products, or ensure sustenance of the rural population.

Support has to be provided to the common implementation of innovative agritechnical decisions, the introduction of high-productive breeds of agricultural animals and high-yielding crops, and the involvement of new resources in agricultural production for the purpose of output increase.

The development of agricultural production in the eastern parts of Russia and northern parts of China should be facilitated by the measures focused on the improvement of soil fertility, an increase in cultivated lands with high-quality varieties of crops, and the development of forage resources for animal husbandry. It is necessary to create economic conditions for equipping crop production organizations with modern resource-saving machinery, for the modernization of animal husbandry farms, the development of the genetic potential of animals in meat and dairy production, the attraction of investments into the agricultural sector, and research and development of innovation technologies.

Rural territories require a substantial breakthrough in the development of social infrastructure and engineering facilities, housing construction and improvement of the living environment in rural areas, the creation of new employment opportunities in rural areas, and the education of rural people in the agricultural colleges and universities of the region.

An important task is the elimination of disparities in the agricultural sector by means of support for those industries that have potential advantages on both domestic and international markets but are not able to unlock this potential without state support and regulation (Anderson, Jha, Nelgen, and Strutt, 2013). In particular, state support has to be focused on the stabilization of the population of agricultural animals, and including the sectors of animal husbandry which are traditional for indigenous communities (primarily, deer, horses, and sheep). Development of these sectors will help to increase production of meat and ensure the preservation of a traditional way of living and employment in rural areas of the CNRFE region.

Development of crop production and an increase in productivity of grain crops have strategic importance for the fulfilment of potential advantages of the region on domestic and international markets. In some subsectors of agricultural production, state policy should be focused on support for small entities: rural households and farmers. They have to be provided with equal rights on the distribution of agricultural products and access to production and transport infrastructure.

Nowadays, due to the degradation of traditional large-scale agricultural production of the Soviet-type, rural households remain the only form of employment in many rural settlements in Russia's Far East. In the light of ensurance of sustainable development of rural territories and food security of the region, support for rural households and retention of people in their traditional places of habitation have to be among the top priorities for the government. In Russia, the effectiveness of support for small entrepreneurship (farmers, rural households, and agricultural consumer cooperatives) is low. Between 2000 and 2015, the share of rural households in the gross production of agricultural products declined (from 75% in 2000 down to 45% in 2015). The increase in productivity of small economic entities can not be achieved without substantial changes in state regulations. The major portion of rural households produces agricultural products for self-consumption only (Trukhachev, Ivolga, and Lescheva, 2015). Rural people are not ready to become entrepreneurs and do not feel strong support on the part of the state. One of the prospective ways to increase the involvement of rural households in the commercial production of agricultural products is the promotion of cooperatives in rural areas. The most productive ones may become those cooperatives that unite households on the basis of the family contract.

Conclusions

In the region of Northeast Asia, both Russia and China will definitely benefit from studying each other's practices in the sphere of ensurance of food self-sufficiency and food security. Experiencing unfavourable environmental conditions of agricultural production, suffering from a rural flight and high unemployment rates, facing a lot of internal structural problems, both countries in this region have to make every possible effort to develop diversification of the rural economy and support farmers and alternative forms of employment and self-employment. The set of measures has to include the implementation of rural development issues into the national and regional development strategies; consideration of sustainable rural development in the rural area planning schemes; improvement of rural infrastructure, including transport and communications; analysis of environmental problems and existing threats to sustainable environmental development; elaboration of measures to secure biodiversity; expansion of special support measures, such as for young people and families, in order to retain them in rural areas; increase of investment attractiveness of rural areas in general and rural settlements in particular as local centres of rural development.

The increase of food security in both Russia's Far East and the Chinese North East is only possible if the regional diversity is taken into account in development concepts (Heilig, 2003). Like Russia, China has all possible extremes in climate, population, and infrastructure availability. It is, therefore, essential, that detailed regionalized analyses are undertaken to understand the specific development constraints and options of various regions, their similarities, and differences, and those social and economic conditions that determine the development potential of rural areas in those regions.

References

1. Anderson, K., Jha, S., Nelgen, S., Strutt, A. (2013). Re-examining Policies for Food Security in Asia. Food Security 5(2):195–215.
2. Beloglazov, G. (2007). Food Security of the People's Republic of China and its Russian Vector. Russia and Pacific RIM 3, 2007, pp. 75–83.
3. Chen, J., Fleisher, B.M. (1996). Regional Income Inequality and Economic Growth in China. Journal of Comparative Economics 22(2):141–164.
4. Chen, Z., Xiangzheng, D., Jianing, D., Peiying, H. (2016). Urbanization and Sustainability: Comparison of the Processes in "BIC" Countries. Sustainability 400(8):1–18.
5. Erokhin, V. "Establishing Food Security and Alternatives to International Trade in Emerging Economies", IGI Global Diseminator of Knowledge, https://www.igi-global.com/book/establishing-food-security-alternatives-international/178540, available in 2018.
6. Erokhin, V. (2014). Approaches to Sustainable Rural Development in a Predominantly Non-Rural Region. Economics of Agriculture 2: 291–306.
7. Erokhin, V., Ivolga, A. (2012). How to Ensure Sustainable Development of Agribusiness in the Conditions of Trade Integration: Russian Approach. International Journal of Sustainable Economies Management (IJSEM) 2(1):12–23.
8. Ghose, B. (2014). Food Security and Food Self-Sufficiency in China: From Past to 2050. Food and Energy Security 3(2):86–95.
9. Heilig, G.K. (2003). Sustainable Regional and Rural Development in China: Where Do We Stand? Laxenburg: IIASA. 2003.
10. Ivolga, A. (2014). Overview of Contemporary Issues of Sustainable Rural Development in Russia in Terms of Existing Differences between Regions. Economics of Agriculture 2:331–345.
11. Jianhua, Z. (2011). China's Success in Increasing Per Capita Food Production. Journal of Experimental Botany 32:1–5.
12. Li, W.J., Ali, S.H., Zhang, Q. (2007). Property Rights and Grassland Degradation: A Study of the Xilingol Pasture, Inner Mongolia, China. Journal of Environmental Management 85: 461–470.

13. Liu, J., Diamond, J. (2005). China's Environment in a Globalizing World. Nature 435: 1179–1186.
14. Liu, M., Heijman, W., Zhu, X., Dries, L., Huang, J. (2016). Individual and Social Optima of Rural Land Allocation by Stakeholders: A Case Study on Eco-Fragile Areas of Northern China. The Rangeland Journal 38: 57–72.
15. Long, H., Liu, Y., Li, X., Chen, Y. (2010). Building New Countryside in China: A Geographical Perspective. Land Use Policy 27:457–470.
16. Luan, Y., Cui, X., Ferrat, M. (2013). Historical Trends of Food Self-Sufficiency in Africa. Food Security 5(3):393–405.
17. Ma, L. (2011). Sustainable Development of Rural Household Energy in Northern China. Journal of Sustainable Development 5(4):115–124.
18. Merzlov, A., Ovchintseva, L., Popova, O. (2012). Regional Experience of Elaboration of Programs of Sustainable Rural Development. Moscow: Rosinformagrotekh. 2012.
19. Nath, R., Luan, Y., Yang, W., Yang, C., Chen, W., Li, Q., Cui, X. (2015). Changes in Arable Land Demand for Food in India and China: A Potential Threat to Food Security. Sustainability 7(5):5371–5397.
20. National Bureau of Statistics of the People's Republic of China: Database. Available from http://www.stats.gov.cn/.
21. Nechaev, V. (2008). Conceptual Foundations of Ensurance of Food Security in Russia. Moscow: All-Russian Research Institute of Agricultural Economics. 2008.
22. Shagaida, N., Uzun, V. (2015). Food Security in Russia: Monitoring, Tendencies, and Threats. Moscow: Russian Academy of National Economy and Public Administration under the President of the Russian Federation. 2015.
23. Spoor, M., Robbins, M.J. (2012). Agriculture, Food Security, and Inclusive Growth. The Hague: Institute of Social Sciences. 2012.
24. State Council of the Russian Federation: Report on Sustainable Development of Rural Territories of the Russian Federation. Moscow: Council under the President of the Russian Federation on Implementation of Priority National Projects and Demographic Policy. 2016.
25. Stiglitz, J., Greenwald, B. (2006). Helping Infant Economies Grow: Foundations of Trade Policies for Developing Countries. The American Economic Review 96(2), 2006, pp. 141–146.
26. Taranov, P., Panasyuk, A. (2010). Food Dependence of Russia in the Light of Joining the World Trade Organization (WTO). Bulletin of Orenburg State Agrarian University 26:106–109.
27. Taranov, P., Panasyuk, A. (2012). Competitiveness of Agri-food System of Russia in the Light of Eurasian Economic Integration. National Interests: Priorities and Security 40(181):56–60.
28. Trukhachev, V., Ivolga, A., Lescheva, M. (2015). Enhancement of Land Tenure Relations as a Factor of Sustainable Agricultural Development: Case of Stavropol Krai, Russia. Sustainability 7:164–179.

29. Ushachev, I. (2013). Food Security of Russia in View of the Global Partnership. Moscow: Russian Academy of Agricultural Sciences, All-Russian Research Institute of Agricultural Economics. 2013.
30. Yu, W., Elleby, C., Zobbe, H. (2015). Food Security Policies in India and China: Implications for National and Global Food Security. Food Security 7(2):405–414.
31. Yu, Y., Feng, K., Hubacek, K., Sun, L. (2016). Global Implications of China's Future Food Consumption. Journal of Industrial Ecology 20(3):593–602.
32. Zhou, Z. (2010). Achieving Food Security in China: Past Three Decades and Beyond. China Agricultural Economic Review 2(3):251–275.
33. Zhou, Z., Liu, H., Cao, L., Tian, W.M., Wang, J.M. (2014). Food Consumption in China: The Revolution Continues. Cheltenham: Edward Elgar Publishing. 2014.
34. Zhou, Z., Wu, W., Chen, Q., Chen, S. (2007). Study on Sustainable Development of Rural Household Energy in Northern China. Renewable and Sustainable Energy Reviews 12(8):2237–2239.
35. Zhu, Y. (2016). International Trade and Food Security: Conceptual Discussion, WTO and the Case of China. China Agricultural Economic Review 8(3), 2016, pp. 399–411.
36. Zhuplei, I. (2015). Sustainable Development of Agriculture: Regional and Applied Aspect. Almanac of Modern Science and Education 99(9):64–67.
37. Anderson, K., Jha, S., Nelgen, S., Strutt, A. (2013). Re-examining Policies for Food Security in Asia. Food Security 5(2):195–215.
38. Beloglazov, G. (2007). Food Security of the People's Republic of China and its Russian Vector. Russia and Pacific RIM 3, 2007, pp. 75–83.
39. Chen, J., Fleisher, B.M. (1996). Regional Income Inequality and Economic Growth in China. Journal of Comparative Economics 22(2):141–164.
40. Chen, Z., Xiangzheng, D., Jianing, D., Peiying, H. (2016). Urbanization and Sustainability: Comparison of the Processes in "BIC" Countries. Sustainability 400(8):1–18.
41. Erokhin, V. (2014). Approaches to Sustainable Rural Development in a Predominantly Non-Rural Region. Economics of Agriculture 2: 291–306.
42. Erokhin, V., Ivolga, A. (2012). How to Ensure Sustainable Development of Agribusiness in the Conditions of Trade Integration: Russian Approach. International Journal of Sustainable Economies Management (IJSEM) 2(1):12–23.
43. Ghose, B. (2014). Food Security and Food Self-Sufficiency in China: From Past to 2050. Food and Energy Security 3(2):86–95.
44. Heilig, G.K. (2003). Sustainable Regional and Rural Development in China: Where Do We Stand? Laxenburg: IIASA. 2003.
45. Ivolga, A. (2014). Overview of Contemporary Issues of Sustainable Rural Development in Russia in Terms of Existing Differences between Regions. Economics of Agriculture 2:331–345.
46. Jianhua, Z. (2011). China's Success in Increasing Per Capita Food Production. Journal of Experimental Botany 32:1–5.

47. Li, W.J., Ali, S.H., Zhang, Q. (2007). Property Rights and Grassland Degradation: A Study of the Xilingol Pasture, Inner Mongolia, China. Journal of Environmental Management 85: 461–470.
48. Liu, J., Diamond, J. (2005). China's Environment in a Globalizing World. Nature 435: 1179–1186.
49. Liu, M., Heijman, W., Zhu, X., Dries, L., Huang, J. (2016). Individual and Social Optima of Rural Land Allocation by Stakeholders: A Case Study on Eco-Fragile Areas of Northern China. The Rangeland Journal 38: 57–72.
50. Long, H., Liu, Y., Li, X., Chen, Y. (2010). Building New Countryside in China: A Geographical Perspective. Land Use Policy 27:457–470.
51. Luan, Y., Cui, X., Ferrat, M. (2013). Historical Trends of Food Self-Sufficiency in Africa. Food Security 5(3):393–405.
52. Ma, L. (2011). Sustainable Development of Rural Household Energy in Northern China. Journal of Sustainable Development 5(4):115–124.
53. Machan, T. R. (2016). Commerce and Its Normative Dimensions, Psychosociological Issues in Human Resource Management 4(1):7–40.
54. Popescu, Gh.H. (2016). The Role of Multinational Corporations in Global Environmental Politics, Economics, Management, and Financial Markets 11(3):72–78.
55. Merzlov, A., Ovchintseva, L., Popova, O. (2012). Regional Experience of Elaboration of Programs of Sustainable Rural Development. Moscow: Rosinformagrotekh. 2012.
56. Nath, R., Luan, Y., Yang, W., Yang, C., Chen, W., Li, Q., Cui, X. (2015). Changes in Arable Land Demand for Food in India and China: A Potential Threat to Food Security. Sustainability 7(5):5371–5397.
57. National Bureau of Statistics of the People's Republic of China: Database. Available from http://www.stats.gov.cn/.
58. Nechaev, V. (2008). Conceptual Foundations of Ensurance of Food Security in Russia. Moscow: All-Russian Research Institute of Agricultural Economics. 2008.
59. Nica, E., Ioan, H. (2016). The State-led System of Global Environmental Governance, Economics, Management, and Financial Markets 11(3):79–85.
60. Nica, E., Cristina, M., Ana Madalina P. (2016). Competition in the Worldwide Workplace: Economic Globalization and Labor Rights, Journal of Self-Governance and Management Economics 4(3):73–79.
61. Nica, E. (2016). The Effect of Perceived Organizational Support on Organizational Commitment and Employee Performance, Journal of Self-Governance and Management Economics 4(4):34–40.
62. Nica, E. (2016). Employee Voluntary Turnover as a Negative Indicator of Organizational Effectiveness, Psychosociological Issues in Human Resource Management 4(2):220–226.
63. Popescu, Gh.H. (2016). The Role of Multinational Corporations in Global Environmental Politics, Economics, Management, and Financial Markets 11(3):72–78.

64. Popescu, Gh. H., Florin, C.C., Teodora, I.B. (2016). Environmental Consequences of Liberalized and Expanding Global Trade, Journal of Self-Governance and Management Economics 4(3):66–72.
65. Popescu, Gh. H., Mihaela, C., Oana, M. S. (2016). The Role of Human Capital in the Knowledge-networked Economy, Psychosociological Issues in Human Resource Management 4(1):168–174.
66. Shagaida, N., Uzun, V. (2015). Food Security in Russia: Monitoring, Tendencies, and Threats. Moscow: Russian Academy of National Economy and Public Administration under the President of the Russian Federation. 2015.
67. Spoor, M., Robbins, M.J. (2012). Agriculture, Food Security, and Inclusive Growth. The Hague: Institute of Social Sciences. 2012.
68. State Council of the Russian Federation: Report on Sustainable Development of Rural Territories of the Russian Federation. Moscow: Council under the President of the Russian Federation on Implementation of Priority National Projects and Demographic Policy. 2016.
69. Stiglitz, J., Greenwald, B. (2006). Helping Infant Economies Grow: Foundations of Trade Policies for Developing Countries. The American Economic Review 96(2), 2006, pp. 141–146.
70. Taranov, P., Panasyuk, A. (2010). Food Dependence of Russia in the Light of Joining the World Trade Organization (WTO). Bulletin of Orenburg State Agrarian University 26:106–109.
71. Taranov, P., Panasyuk, A. (2012). Competitiveness of Agri-food System of Russia in the Light of Eurasian Economic Integration. National Interests: Priorities and Security 40(181):56–60.
72. Trukhachev, V., Ivolga, A., Lescheva, M. (2015). Enhancement of Land Tenure Relations as a Factor of Sustainable Agricultural Development: Case of Stavropol Krai, Russia. Sustainability 7:164–179.
73. Ushachev, I. (2013). Food Security of Russia in View of the Global Partnership. Moscow: Russian Academy of Agricultural Sciences, All-Russian Research Institute of Agricultural Economics. 2013.
74. Yu, W., Elleby, C., Zobbe, H. (2015). Food Security Policies in India and China: Implications for National and Global Food Security. Food Security 7(2):405–414.
75. Yu, Y., Feng, K., Hubacek, K., Sun, L. (2016). Global Implications of China's Future Food Consumption. Journal of Industrial Ecology 20(3):593–602.
76. Zaga, S.D. (2016). The Impact of Nutritional Programs in Mexico, American Journal of Medical Research 3(1):7–38.
77. Zhou, Z. (2010). Achieving Food Security in China: Past Three Decades and Beyond. China Agricultural Economic Review 2(3):251–275.
78. Zhou, Z., Liu, H., Cao, L., Tian, W.M., Wang, J.M. (2014). Food Consumption in China: The Revolution Continues. Cheltenham: Edward Elgar Publishing. 2014.
79. Zhou, Z., Wu, W., Chen, Q., Chen, S. (2007). Study on Sustainable Development of Rural Household Energy in Northern China. Renewable and Sustainable Energy Reviews 12(8):2237–2239.

80. Zhu, Y. (2016). International Trade and Food Security: Conceptual Discussion, WTO and the Case of China. China Agricultural Economic Review 8(3), 2016, pp. 399–411.
81. Zhuplei, I. (2015). Sustainable Development of Agriculture: Regional and Applied Aspect. Almanac of Modern Science and Education 99(9):64–67.

Valeriu IOAN-FRANC

Costin C. Kiriţescu National Institute for Economic Research, Romanian Academy; Calea 13 Septembrie nr. 13, sector 5, Bucharest 050711, Romania; cide90@gmail.com

Napoleon POP

Institute of World Economy, Costin C. Kiriţescu National Institute for Economic Research, Romanian Academy; Calea 13 Septembrie nr. 13, sector 5, Bucharest 050711, Romania; iemnapoleon@gmail.com

One Decade from Romania's Accession to the European Union. A National Strategic Project Is Required

Abstract: For a national project or for the national interest to be promoted, we should consider the realities of our world and an appropriate assessment of our power within the external forces. Romania has gained much by adapting to the world, and now it is a member of the Euro-Atlantic family, with a good macroeconomic status following a political adoption of good economic discipline/practice that should go on. Romania seems to enjoy the strongest strategic partnership with NATO and the USA (considering the realities of the Ukrainian crisis) and an increasing geopolitical visibility. At the same time, Romania may become more credible and able to involve the citizens in a medium or long-term national strategic project in order to take advantage of the above opportunities.

Keywords: Romania; European Union; national interests; sustainable economic growth; globalisation challenges; modernisation of Romania; national strategic project; global network of multiple national interests; real convergence; structural reforms; civic education; professional education; governance; economic policies

1. Introduction. Statality as a pillar of national interest's promotion

Taking into consideration the new commitments of Romania in a wide-scale exercise—the presidency of the European Union (EU) Council in 2019—it is necessary to rethink the national strategic development project. Recent events show us that all political and intellectual forces should join a comprehensive national project, and the EU presidency is a good opportunity. A key problem is whether in the present, internal and external, contradictory context that confuses the elites involved in the systemic changes in the 1990s, we can "afford" to promote a credible and effective national project. Why? Because that elite still considers that an essential foundation, consisting of state's prerogatives, represent a major factor for a successful national project.

Of course, a national project for mobilization is necessary considering the opportunity to be included in a European area of interests. It has two connotations, both important, although they are contradictory. The first one (positive) is that, unlike the 1990s, we now have a clear anchor for a functional state, more than a model to be followed. The second one is revealed by the fact that a link of the national project to our EU membership—as values, principles, community acquis—may provide some validation "in fashion", especially through interferences—not to call them obligations—that spring surprise on us and cause anger. By that we should not understand that an uncompleted state is opposed to a national project, but we want to understand the criteria for judging us regarding the uncompleted state in the sense of a real state of law. Moreover, we should look for a solution in a very short term, resulting from a historical necessity—if we miss a strategy—which is compulsory.

A national project should be based on a correct identification of the national interests, and the definition, the domestic support, the external promotion and the implementation depend on the state power, a notion of great concern now, even if we represent it by governance, i.e. an action for a strong state. If we agree with the concept of individual freedom, especially in a globalized world, then the national interests are truly national until they reach other national interests.

First, the delay in formulating and promoting our interests leaves a small room among the interests of the others, and so we could understand some urges, but up to where we feel our state is affected. What surprises us is a change in the role played by some foreign representatives, causing a change in the traditional political-diplomatic culture that has inspired us for centuries. Second, while the state of the others is a model of fundamental values; looking at their interests, it seems that a young state of a western type could be inappropriately consolidated because of an internal outburst of totalitarianism and some "national interests" of the others. It is not something new but we see other moments of our history when our state depended on the interests of the European powers.

2. National interests and a strategic national project

The integration into a structure with a long-term dynamic renders the interest credible to our citizens and acceptable to the partners through transparency and predictability. We speak about the absence of private and institutionalized investors. Even if the present economic statistical performance is favourable, we should remember that it does not follow an adequate dynamic of investment and crediting, as the short-term consumption cannot cope with the benefits of productive investments based on long-term employment.

As for the state of law, three fundamental elements should be harmonized: human rights, including the rights of the minorities, private ownership and entrepreneurship. They are requirements for our state relationships with our western partners;

based on them we have been recognized as a state of law with a functional market economy. Also, they are principles for our international agreements on equal bases. At the same time, they ensure the link between the dynamics of a western societal life, on the one hand, and democracy and market economy on the other.

Any lack of rights or congruence between the rights and the material basis—guarantees for licit ownership—affects the vectors of the societal progress: entrepreneurship, competition, optimum allocation of resources, and factors of attraction of any kind of investors. As for the rules, there are objections regarding the law content and enforcement: laws without sanctions, laws enforced up to sanctioning and wrong sanctions, which, on another plane, means an amalgamation of other principles such as presumption of innocence, future action of the law, justice should be fair, and the institutions should have resources to be strong but not too big. Corruption is the outcome of ambiguity, of the shift from the rule accuracy to voluntarism in enforcement, finally affecting the national security, i.e. the national interests.

The present context shows the constraints determined by the direction and strength of the European integration, the compliance of the European governance with the political project, and the response to present challenges and the actions to prevent them becoming permanent. We should take into account the new challenges at the eastern border of the EU and NATO, the political assimilation of sustainable economic growth as a factor of social and political stability (which means that the political should be based on rules of the public policies to eliminate voluntarism, following the election cycles, even to our long-term interest), the link between sustainable economic growth and sustainable development, the global risks, even the globalization challenges.

Our relationship with the Euro-Atlantic community should produce a new type of relation between the political elite and the academic elite for a quality government, without electoral populism and promises that cannot be covered by multiannual resources. The instruments used to attract the voters for a consensus-based project usually for one mandate, seem to cause a huge gap between the citizen's well-being and the real role of the political, even missing the protective national interests.

3. The third modernization of Romania. A proposal for restructuring the national strategic project

We first point out that the project only seems to be a traditional one, although under this name it has marked development and progress stages, and, cyclically, it must be resumed as a better interpreted part. It is Romania's modernization project updated to the opportunities and challenges of the 21st century.

There is a risk of repeating some terms, but what we want to express has always been linked to modernization and the main European actors who were examples for the Romanian countries, the United Principalities, post-war Romania, etc. (1884, 1859, 1866, 1913, 1930 and 1947). Now, we talk about a country returning to the family of European democracies, a member of two elite clubs that mark the advance of economic development (integration-globalization) in conditions of collective security (NATO, ESP), along with the most advanced form of partnership in history. The last aspect does not mean perfect international relations as long as we know that human action at different decision stages is unpredictable, but we are now at a qualitative level of international order that is more qualified and able to express itself in a more acceptable way than before, although we notice an almost cyclical emergence of imperial behavior of older powers and possible new ones.

What may distinguish a new modernization project from other more or less completed projects is the context in which it is conceived, promoted and implemented, the standard required and especially the political consensus for validating it over election cycles and making it credible to our citizens and foreign partners. In the complex global network of multiple national interests, a first chance of a country is the credibility and the predictability of a strategic national project (especially in the case of small and medium countries), which enable more resourceful actors to use this flexibility, possibly to our advantage as well.

To know what the political class wants for the nation and how it would act (on an orderly and fluid basis and in the medium or long term) is now (for all partners sharing the same values—note, please, this condition) a guarantee for a stronger partnership, which is equal to assuming responsibilities in accordance with the "burden sharing" concept. We should remember that it is valid for countries that do not show loyalty to the same values, thus causing antagonism in several areas (economic, military, security, etc.).

Of course, Romania must modernize in relation to the new realities. This project has become urgent for 25 years of fragmentary and fragmented search. The arguments for a compulsory strategic project of modernization of the country are many and require debating, but they should not be contrary to finality. We present below the fundamental arguments for such action.

The systemic transformation initiated in 1990 has not been finalized from an institutional and legislative point of view, aiming at building a modern democracy and market economy.

The recognition of Romania as a state of law with a market economy is not very clear if we take into account the Cooperation and Verification Mechanism (CVM) and the attractiveness fluctuation because of the failure to consolidate the factors that can stimulate it in the long term (lack of predictability and stability of the business rules, no commercial courts based on quick procedures).

The small number of investments, even big ones (car industry, cement industry, oil processing, etc.), their concentration on some branches, but mainly the unbalanced development of the counties (a very important aspect for the euro adoption), are often considered ways of "invasion" of foreign capital. Or, this cannot be an invitation to increase investments as a whole and the number of jobs.

The EU and NATO memberships still need a pro-active structured involvement, but, it seems, only in the area functioning "on request" is the political will more coherent and reactive, while in other areas the Community decisions look like foreign intervention. There is no continuity of the great policy of integration, which means that the possible keepers of the new rules of international cooperation at the institutional level are often replaced for political reasons, unable to acquire skills. We forget in key moments that we agreed on the principle of transferring some competences from the national level to the Community level, the fact that Community rules take on various forms—treaties, regulation, directives and decisions—and the failure to observe them hinders our integration into various unions, which could mean the use of structural funds as a lever of national developments for achieving real convergence.

Real convergence—a permanent support for stability and sustainability of the nominal convergence criteria—requires continuous political action for a national long-term development program, using the experience (too criticized) acquired through economic policies imposed by international financial partners (IMF, World Bank, IFC) that placed macrostability under the firm control of the budget and external deficit (of the sovereign debt). Instead of understanding this "teaching" (that is not imposed on us), which we are now asking for in the name of the seriousness we have to show due to our belonging to the EU and NATO, we are trying to be relieved of the constraints meant to prepare us for a development less exposed to external contamination.

International experience with international financial partners, which caused a diminution in the costs of financing from private sources in the capital markets, is the best guarantee of a partner ready to assume additional responsibilities (such as an increase in the defense required by the accession to NATO, now even more urgent because of the geostrategic situation in Eastern Europe) for long-term economic security, provided that the acquired macroeconomic discipline goes on. The new structures of macroprudential stability form the instrument for a continuous politico-professional training. Instead of being angry with no reason about the bureaucratic multiplication (already obsolete, according to the lessons of the last financial crisis), we would agree that the global economy undergoes a paradigm change and we must give up the old bureaucratic institutions and accept their replacement with new ones. Maybe this way we understand the meaning of the structural resources and take measures to reduce the bureaucracy of the requirements of the new economic paradigm: preventing the shocks caused by globalization and absorbing them without shattering social stability, in a world of inequalities and uncontrolled development (disappearance of the middle class, unbalanced income distribution, inequality globalization, etc.).

Structural reforms are due around the world. The states eager to start such reforms should be supported by other states, and Romania's "duty" to assume structural reforms is required through the option of an economic club (the EU) based on equal rights. We think it is simple to understand that a union cannot be strong unless each member is strong. Being aware of Romania's economic and political power in our region and in Europe helps us to understand that our national interests (if properly promoted inside the EU) in relation to our capacity to amplify that economic and political power can be included—through the EU—in the matrix of the world powers structure, and the EU is expected to be an active and contributive actor by restoring its economic and political power.

A strategic national project can be based only on a real and firm partnership between citizen and state, and this moment seems to favor it provided that the state adopts better marketing of the two advantages: macrostability and EU and NATO membership. The synergy with the citizen within the above partnership is a prerequisite for a new successful long-term project, since only the involvement of the citizen in a national project based on concrete objectives turns him into an active participant.

A national project for the lead-up to the euro adoption by 2019 has been launched. We say it is a target since the euro adoption is not unilateral and even the euro governance might be changed after the Euro Zone crisis (see Greece's sovereign debt crisis). At the same time, the above lead-up is now more complicated, as the Maastricht criteria are not enough to ensure the single currency sustainability after the acceptance of a new member of some importance regarding some characteristics of its membership.

We are aware that efforts have been made to improve the euro governance and that this political project needs to be improved as regards the technical pillars, but, unfortunately, without dealing with the real matter (Fiscal Union). The evolution of the euro governance is an aspect to be considered in the national project for the single currency adoption, requiring a complex approach to an enlarged union that is facing a new challenge.

For Romania, the euro adoption project is only a vehicle and not the very purpose, but quite useful for the discipline of implementing the strategic modernization project. Now we try to present only the structure of a national strategic project for our country's modernization. In our opinion, we should consider the fundamental objectives of the project in relation to many of the already presented requirements and their quality of vectors or vector support vehicles. They are not many, but only they can be the starting point for the citizen's option to become real partners in the project.

Institutional capacity modernization, essential for implementing policies in every field, requires a body of experts trained in the spirit of the state of law and the market economy. This modernization implies a wide-scale structural reform for the final institutional adaptation to the commitments as a member of NATO and the EU. This objective also implies the completion of the country's systemic transformation, i.e. a European and trans-Atlantic state, credible and predictable.

The modernization of the institutional capacities concerns the parties, parliament, the government, the presidential administration, the judiciary system, the civil society, which are able to serve society—the community and the individual—in areas where the state has traditional prerogatives. The reform in this field requires the clarification of some ambiguities of the constitution and the correction of all legislation, which included a voluntary behavior and way of action in institutions to the detriment of the society and the individual. The elimination of excessive exceptions, the restricted advantages and the generalization and uniformization of the legislation can substantially diminish bureaucracy, help to improve the legislation knowledge, cut costs and improve effectiveness.

Modernization of civic education and professional education is an essential medium and long-term objective for ensuring societal governance, since now many citizens—who become politicians and executive officers in institutions—do not actually know in what society they live. There is evidence that many of their actions and decisions are not consistent with society's requirements and Romania's international institutional commitments.

Civic education should help people quickly acquire the values of their society and the values and principles specific to the public domain or the private area where they intend to work: education, economy, finance, banking, academic research, justice, defence, and security.

Education's effects on the two development areas of the society—the public system and the private sector—and on the state-market relation are very important. There cannot be a competitive society without competences equal to those of the international partners. For the time being, there are only competitive youths and professionals who leave our country. In these conditions become harder to support a strong state through competent services to the population and to develop a national private sector that should not be based mostly on the persons with working life experience, on one hand, and on a quarter of million of illiterates, on the other hand. Moreover, there is a propensity for certificates and diplomas for professions that are not consistent with the market needs.

The labor market needs potential employees with competences but the curricula are not consistent with the structural demand for labor. In this respect, the objective of education depends primarily on the modernization of the institutional capacities and knowledge acquisition, while in the medium and long terms, the same objective aims at the consolidation of the institutional capacity and the proper operation of the labor market as essential elements for increasing the societal value added through labor.

Modernization of the governance of the economic policies mix implies professionalism and continuity of the institutions of special importance in the real economy governance, especially the Ministry of Finance and the Central Bank. The top positions of the institutions that establish, enforce and monitor the economic and monetary policies, irrespective of the political support and promotion, shall be filled with persons with competences certified by a diploma and broad experience in order to maintain the macroeconomic stability. Only this, besides the market mechanisms, guarantees the correct implementation of the policies in relation to the economic cycle and the optimum allocation of private and public resources for development.

The optimum allocation of national development resources implies their capacity to ensure broad recovery through consolidated revenues to the budget and to maintain the balance in accordance with standards of financial discipline, predictability and stability, as defined after the financial crises. These characteristics of public policies are not only economic theory rules, they are now a public good and the responsibility for their security is absolutely necessary.

Achieving economic governance in accordance with the Stability and Growth Pact—as assumed by Romania as an EU member—allows us to allocate continuous resources for keeping economic growth in line with the potential GDP, i.e. non-inflationary growth, free of accidental "heating" accompanied by the already known risks, full capacity to prevent and manage crises, a resilience mechanism able to withstand asymmetric shocks through contagion caused by globalization.

Understanding the importance of the governance of the public policies mix and of the regulation has a positive impact on the governing programs in relation to the people's expectation. It means ensuring the continuity of the resources for the public expenditure on the infrastructure of education, health care, public order, defence and development through public investment in accordance with real convergence. This way, we can carry out the euro adoption project and the funding of the physical infrastructure for linking Romania to the European area, in the best form of integration—the Economic and Monetary Union.

The preventive character of the objective and the early creation of resources on a national and/or mutual European or global basis aims to consolidate the national resilience mechanism that could prevent austerity programs. It should be understood as helping us to achieve the normal state through stimulation of economic growth by productive public investment and creation of jobs. It is the only way to talk in proper terms about smart, green, sustainable, competitive development that can only be ensured by means of proper resources provided by a balanced real economy.

Regional geopolitical realities as well as global challenges, such as climate change, show us the main directions of the public policies. We urgently need measures for prevention and intervention for the safety of the air we breathe and our drinking water, for food security, social security (related to the contributive means that have reached maturity and have been a potential burden: the pension, insurance and health systems), the citizen's safety, the national defence, the security of the physical links with the rest of the continent. Listing is an easy task, but we need another approach to the immobilism caused by misinterpreted external pressure in order to take firm political action for development that is to the benefit of all citizens, and strongly supports our national interests before the partners looking for equal co-workers.

Opinions are exchanged in the public space, which is normal. But they are not based on good knowledge of the economic culture, of the normal set of economic policies in relation to the economic cycle (the latter is even rejected by some people) but they show aspirations based on criticism and arguments that often annoy the real specialists. The number of so-called specialists exchanging opinions in the public area has increased very much if compared to the specialists who are ready to make decisions; but the worst thing is that they do not understand in what economic system we chose to live.

The public is overwhelmed with opinions against everything, implying that any economic measure has a hidden purpose and is populistic. A governance free of any suspicion should be eliminated, and this depends on true credibility, and on the process of turning the professional into a politician and the politician into a professional. It is a reform that the political should carry out to its own benefit, i.e.

parties providing stability in the real sense of the political democracy to the benefit of the economic democracy.

A recent example of comment on the national macroprudentiality committees, which tells us about the European effort to understand the change of paradigm in the economic thought on equilibrium and macroeconmic stability, reveals the lack of communication regarding how Romania assumes an agenda of capital importance for the EU institutions. A significant technical instrument, able to cope with potential asymmetric risks to an economy under globalization which needs first a preventive management and then a crisis management, almost distorted the democratic system and the power equilibrium because of lack of communication.

Equally, proper parliamentary control is required along with consultations regarding a public country position, with all pros and cons. It is a useful exchange of opinions on official documents, implying an economic and social committee eager to discuss themes on institutional changes at the European level. We need a real cooperation among the Romanian parliamentarians regarding issues of national interest, and not an internal party fight inside a forum that decides the fate of the European citizens; Romanian specialists, supported at home, should be more present and take positions of international officers in European institutions—the European Commission, the European Central Bank—which set the details of the economic policies affecting Romania, as well.

4. Conclusions

It is not the lack of intelligence that make us perceive a typically Romanian laziness, but the failure to share that intelligence when and where is absolutely necessary. We have to make this intelligence work for a national strategic project, not to use it for hindering or even destroying what is a national public good. The Romanian history shows that it is possible on one condition: to give up the irreducible opposition among parliamentary parties because of the failure to understand the role of multiparty democracy. The party competition does not seem to promote the national interests, but becomes a totalitarian party.

Therefore, we need more civic and professional education to meet the present challenges and to carry out a national project. The EU and NATO are no longer absolute shields for Romania, but a team to enable us to respond to new challenges and cope with a new global order.

References

1. Ioan-Franc, V., Pop, N. (2015). Oui il y a deux Europes, in *Caiete Critice*, nr. 2, pp. 76–80, FNSA, Bucharest, Romania.
2. Ioan-Franc, V., Pop, N. (2016). L'Europeanisation de la Roumanie, un act de recherche academique, in Penser l'Europe, ed. 14, pp. 165–171, FNSA, Bucharest, Romania.

3. Isărescu, M., Postolache, T. (2000). An open project: Romania's medium term national strategy of economic development, The Romanian Center for Compared and Consensual Economy, Romanian Academy, Bucharest, Romania.
4. Postolache, T. (2006). Un projet ouvert. Discours sur l'integration européenne, Expert Publishing House, Bucharest, Romania.
5. Pop, N., Ioan-Franc, V. (2015). The reset of the EU's strategic vision in the Nowadays Global and European Context, in Caiete Critice, nr. 4, pp. 69–80, FNSA, Bucharest, Romania.

Mihaela-Nona CHILIAN

Institute for Economic Forecasting, Bucharest, Romania, cnona@ipe.ro

Marioara IORDAN

Institute for Economic Forecasting, Bucharest, Romania, miordan@ipe.ro

Convergence and Divergence Patterns in the EU and Romanian Regions

Abstract: In the current context of increased pressure on the process of European Union integration, one of the primary goals is the convergence of the regional income per capita and, hence, how to generate a process of convergence not only conducive to benefits to all EU citizens, but also perceived and valued as such. In the economic literature, theories of convergence and divergence examine the reasons for diminishing or increasing the disparities between rich and the poor regions, and in the case of divergence, explain the persistence of such disparities. Based on the concept of real convergence, the paper presents an analysis of such a process in the EU and Romanian regions, based on specific indicators (GDP per capita, gross speed of convergence).

The results show different convergence speeds and patterns both in the EU and in Romania, the economies of the regions adapting differently to the challenging economic environment of the EU single market, generally dependent on their pre-accession development level. The results are in line with the findings of other studies on the economic convergence of the member states and/or their regions, but also reveal some peculiarities of the catching up and development processes going on in the EU and Romanian regional economies, especially calling for increased attention to be paid to the implementation of the national general and development policies at all levels, as well as of the EU regional policy.

Keywords: real convergence, convergence indicators, EU and Romanian regions, regional policy

Introduction

The economic and social cohesion at the regional level is a fundamental objective of the European Union (EU), being considered as a key driving force for the integration of people and territory. It was especially reinforced in the Treaty of the European Union (1992), which called for balanced development, as well as economic and social cohesion, but the need for policies to promote both regional development and a reduction in economic disparities across regions has increased remarkably since the enlargements of 2004 and 2007 (Peiro-Palomino, 2016). Therefore, delivering it at territorial level lies at the heart of the Europe 2020 strategy, being also a key theme of "inclusive growth" (European Commission 2010a, Rodriguez-Pose and Tselios, 2015). In particular, the objective of regional convergence aims at reducing regional disparities by helping those regions with an income per capita below 90% of the EU-27(28) average, but the intention of the EU national and regional policies is not only to reduce the disparities between the levels of economic development of the various regions and the backwardness of the least favoured regions, but also to cap the disparities in social welfare and ultimately to improve the EU citizens' quality of life (Rodriguez-Pose and Tselios, 2015; Peiro-Palomino, 2016).

However, a large body of devoted literature has suggested the presence of a polarization pattern in Europe, including two differentiated groups of regions (or convergence clubs): one of relatively poor regions, and the other of regions evolving around the mean income. Moreover, such studies have also revealed that such a polarization pattern has been a persistent trend especially in Western Europe over the last three decades (e.g. Quah, 1996), achieving a successful implementation of policies aimed at reducing these disparities essential for achieving the targets of cohesion policies (Peiro-Palomino, 2016). To make things more complicated, the EU as a whole is accommodating the integration of the New Member States and their regions, which at the moment of accession were (and many still are) economies in transition with levels of income per capita far below the EU average (Chilian, 2013; Peiro-Palomino, 2016). Last but not least, to all these we add the effects of the global financial and economic crisis, which might be of interest from the convergence point of view, since the recession has disrupted the growth mechanisms and has had an uneven impact across regions, affecting countries and regions differently depending on their responsiveness and reaction (Iordan and Chilian, 2015; Peiro-Palomino, 2016).

The paper aims at contributing to the literature by presenting an analysis of such a process in the NUTS-2 EU and Romanian regions based on the concept of *real convergence* by using specific indicators (GDP per capita, gross speed of convergence, variation coefficient, gross labor productivity, gross productivity growth rate), and also convergence indicators pertaining to business and income statistics.

Literature review and methodological issues

In accordance with the significance of the national and regional development policies in the EU and worldwide, the regional convergence issues have been highly debated in the economic literature, especially since the beginning of the 1990s, when a sharp increase in the scholarly interest occurred in the area of regional income convergence (Lim, 2016). However, regional inequality has been the subject of intensive academic debate since the 1950s, but it has gained increasing attention more recently mainly because of developments in the fields of economic integration, economic geography, and endogenous growth and development (Artelaris and Petrakos, 2016). In literature, *theories of convergence and divergence* examine the reasons for diminishing or increasing the disparities between rich and the poor regions, and in the case of divergence, explain the persistence of such disparities. As stated by Barro and Sala-i-Martin (1991), regional income convergence applies if a poor region tends to grow faster than a rich one, so that the poor region catches up with the rich region in terms of per capita income (Lim, 2016). Different definitions of convergence can be found, corresponding to different concepts related to convergence, based on *economic growth theories* (neoclassical growth model and endogenous growth theory – Lucas (1988); Romer (1986); Solow (1956); Swan (1956)) or on *economic integration theories* (neoclassical or endogenous growth bases – e.g., Quineti et al., 2011). Since the 1990s, the most prominent theoretical and empirical models of regional economic growth convergence have been those established by Barro and Sala-i-Martin (1991, 1992) and Mankiw, Romer, and Weil (1992).

By and large, two types of convergence are identified in the neoclassical growth theories: the *absolute convergence* (also known as the *beta convergence*), which implies that poorer countries or regions tend to grow faster per capita than the rich ones and the *conditional convergence* (the *sigma convergence*), which implies that an economy grows faster the farther it is from its steady state value, either it is poor or rich (Quineti et al., 2011). The beta convergence appears to be a necessary, but not sufficient prerequisite for the sigma convergence, because random shocks can disrupt the convergence of countries/regions, they evolve towards different stable states (Neagu, 2013). The literature on economic growth also identified and analyzed the groups of economies (countries or regions) that present homogeneous economic growth patterns and converge towards a common steady state, called the *convergence clubs*, which in the case of the EU were separate spatial convergence clubs formed by regions that belong to cohesion and non-cohesion countries (e.g., Quah, 1996; Lopez-Bazo et al., 1999; Ertur et al., 2006; Mora, 2008; Dall'erba et al., 2008; Lim, 2016).

Real convergence is a process endogenous to each national entity, and it was one of the major objectives of the EU cohesion policy in the 2007–2013 period, when it covered the poorest EU regions, defined as convergence regions (Chilian et al., 2016). The key objective in these regions, eligible for the cohesion policy, implied the stimulation of growth potential to maintain and achieve high growth rates in such regions (Jozwik and Ponikowski, 2014). In literature, the *real convergence approaches* are connected to the study of long-term economic growth, economic development and the dynamics of complex economic sectors with high economic and social impacts, and also to the supporting/unsporting institutions and economic mechanisms (market structure, distribution of economic results).

The main indicators used to analyze real convergence refer to the differences in *GDP per capita at purchasing power parity* and in *income per capita, differences in labor productivity* and in the *price level* (e.g., Tselios 2009; Miron, Tatomir and Alexe, 2013; Iordan, Ghizdeanu and Tapu, 2014; Chilian et al., 2016). The literature highlights several indicators that can be used to assess the real convergence process, from *broader indicators* (GDP growth rate, GDP per capita, the ratio of exports to GDP, the intensity of foreign investment, stock market capitalization, unemployment rates, labor costs and R&D expenditures, etc.) to *specific indicators and modelling methods* used to assess the beta and sigma convergence, the convergence clubs, and the concentration and entropy of the process (coefficient of variation, Lorenz curve, Gini index, Atkinson index, Theil index, average logarithmic deviation, Robin Hood index, Markov chains, panel regressions, non-parametric methods, etc. See Albu, 2013; Iancu, 2009; Răileanu Szeles and Marinescu, 2010; Miron, Tatomir and Alexe, 2013; Neagu, 2013; Simionescu, 2014; Chilian *et al.*, 2016).

There is a vast empirical literature on economic cohesion in the European context, but the results provide mixed evidence regarding convergence. Although several studies report decreasing regional inequalities and convergence, supporting the presence of *absolute convergence* between the EU member states and/or their regions (however, with the pattern and speed of convergence varying sharply across different sub-periods and regional subsets, with peculiarities for the EU15 countries and the New Member States, and also within these groups of countries—*e.g.* Landesmann and Romisch, 2006; Ezcurra et al., 2007a; Melchior, 2008; Enflo, 2010, Jozwik and Ponikowski, 2014; Dobrinsky and Havlik, 2014), other studies showed that across the EU the *conditional convergence* was less pronounced, supporting the existence of selective tendencies, convergence clubs, and asymmetric shocks, including the uneven impact of the crisis upon the NMS and EU15 countries (Petrakos and Artelaris, 2009, 2014; Rozmahel et al., 2013). At the same time, across the EU the *conditional convergence* was less pronounced, signaling increasing disparities among the regions (Landesmann and Romisch, 2006; Carrington, 2006; Quineti et al., 2011), especially in the EU15 countries but also in the NMS, revealing the existence of selective tendencies, convergence clubs, and asymmetric shocks (Petrakos and Artelaris, 2009, 2014). Moreover, the European Commission's successive Periodical Reports show that real economic convergence is in many respects "a goal too far" and in some countries the regional economic disparities have even worsened (European Commission 2004, 2007, 2010c; Rodriguez-Pose and Tselios, 2015).

The evidence is also mixed regarding the relationship of convergence in income per capita and the social convergence. Some studies (Tselios, 2009) suggested the presence of a conditional convergence in income per capita and that of an unconditional convergence in income inequality in many regions of the EU, while other studies indicated that the weak or even the lack of economic convergence is not matched by a similar absence of social convergence, as the welfare levels have converged significantly across European regions, although the regions with high social welfare levels may remain advantaged in welfare terms while the low social welfare regions may continue to lag behind (Rodriguez-Pose and Tselios, 2015).

As regards the Romanian economy, most studies have addressed the *convergence towards an "average" level* of the entire European Union economy or groups of member states (Albu, 2012; Miron, Dima and Păun, 2009; Răileanu Szeles and Marinescu, 2010; Simionescu, 2014), while the studies on the economic convergence of the regions/counties of Romania were based both on *specific indicators and approaches in the broader context of the cohesion process* (Antonescu, 2012; Neagu, 2013, Iordan, Ghizdeanu and Tapu, 2014; Iordan et al., 2014; Chilian, 2013; Ghizdeanu et al., 2015; Iordan and Chilian, 2015, Iordan et al., 2015), or addressing *specific issues*, but related to the process of cohesion, such as the economic resilience and the impact of the 2008 global economic crisis (Iordan and Chilian, 2014; Zaman and Goschin, 2015) and the modelling of spatial structures in Europe (Koczisky et al., 2015). The key findings of such studies were that, generally, during the pre-accession period Romania experienced a process of *economic convergence*, while during the post-accession period a *divergence/economic differentiation process* was noticed, accompanied by *growth in the inter and intra-regional disparities, deepened by the economic and financial crisis*. However, during the crisis Romania was among the few countries that have improved the real convergence as compared to the EU average (Iordan, Ghizdeanu and Tapu, 2014), developments that are not specific only to Romania, but may be also found in other newer or older EU member states (Antonescu, 2012; Chilian, 2013; Ghizdeanu et al., 2015).

Real convergence dynamics and speed in the EU regions

As previously mentioned, the paper presents an analysis of *real convergence* in the NUTS-1 and NUTS-2 EU and Romanian regions, based on specific indicators, over a longer time span (2000–2013/2014), which includes the ante-crisis, crisis and post-crisis periods. In order to analyze the process of *real convergence*, the following indicators were used:

- *GDP per capita at PPP*, in percentage of the EU-28 average;
- *"Gross speed" of convergence/divergence*, computed as a ratio of the difference between the absolute levels of the above-mentioned indicator at the beginning and the end of the period to the length in years of the analyzed period (see Zaman and Goschin, 2015), for the entire analyzed period, namely 2000/2003–2013/14 and for *sub-periods*, namely ante-crisis, 2000/2003–2007, economic crisis, 2008–2010 and post-crisis, 2011–2013/14.
- *Percentage change* in the GDP per capita over the entire analyzed period and over sub-periods defined as above.

The results[1] reveal mixed evidence regarding the real convergence in the EU regions, with both peculiarities and similarities for the regions of the EU15 and NMS13 countries. Thus, in most EU countries we may find a single highly developed region, usually the region where the capital of the country is located, which recorded the best performance in terms of real convergence over the entire analyzed period and/or the analyzed sub-periods. The only exceptions are Italy, the Netherlands, Spain and Finland, suggesting the presence of several well-performing "regional growth engines", although the convergence performances varied over the sub-periods. None of the NMS13 countries revealed a similar pattern, at least at this level of territorial analysis.

While the "regional growth engines" recorded, indeed, the best real convergence performance nationwide, the things were different by sub-periods. In both the EU15 countries and the NMS13 countries we may find such regions that had their best real

1 Due to text limitations, the results could not be included and are available upon request.

convergence performances during all or almost all the analyzed periods (the most notable exception being the post-crisis period, especially in the case of the NMS13 regions): Hovestaden in Denmark (except for the ante-crisis period), Hamburg in Germany, Attiki in Greece, Comunidad de Madrid in Spain, Île-de-France in France, Provincia Autonoma di Bolzano in Italy, Southern and Eastern Ireland (except for the ante-crisis and post-crisis period), Noord-Holland in the Netherlands, Stockholm in Sweden, London in the United Kingdom (except for the post-crisis period), Yugozapaden in Bulgaria (except for the post-crisis period), Praha in the Czech Republic (except for the post-crisis period), Kozep-Magyarosag (also except for the post-crisis period), Mazowieckie in Poland, Bucuresti-Ilfov in Romania (except for the crisis and post-crisis periods) and Bratislavsky Kraj in Slovakia. We may also find EU15 "growth engines", regions that witnessed rather divergence during the analyzed periods (except for the crisis period, when their performances generally improved): Region de Bruxelles in Belgium, Pais Vasco in Spain, Piemonte, Valle d'Aosta, Lombardia and Lazio in Italy, Groningen and Utrecht in the Netherlands, Wien in Austria, Area Metropolitana de Lisboa in Portugal, Helsinki-Uusimaa in Finland. However, in the case of the most developed regions of the EU15 countries (but also in some NMS13 countries) we mention their very high level of GDP per capita and its growth trend up and away from the EU average, which makes the "weak" performance in terms of real convergence as usually defined in literature (as catching-up towards the average) a logical consequence. We may, therefore, attempt to redefine the real convergence as, for instance, catching-up not towards the average, but towards the highest regional GDP per capita level, which may dramatically expand the growth gaps and redraw the map of convergence/divergence clubs identified so far among the EU regions, but this calls for another analysis.

With very few exceptions (Austria and Romania), in all the EU countries we may find at least two less developed regions that showed weak performances nationwide in terms of real convergence over the entire analyzed period and/or by sub-periods. Similar to other studies, this suggests the presence of larger divergence clubs of laggard regions, with the levels of the gaps against the EU regional GDP per capita average and the speed of the catching-up process differing between the EU15 regions and the NMS13 regions. Thus, whether in almost all the laggard NMS13 regions the convergence speeds, though modest, were generally positive over all the analyzed periods, in the case of the laggard EU15 regions they were mostly negative, revealing growth stagnation and higher "atomisation" of the regional growth process. There were, however, exceptions: either laggard regions that recorded best performances nationwide in terms of real convergence advancement, at least during certain sub-periods, (Moravskoslezsko in the Czech Republic, Sjaelland and Nordjylland in Denmark, Thessalia and Voreio-Aigaio in Greece, Extremadura in Spain, Corse in France, Calabria in Italy, Drenthe in the Netherlands, Burgenland in Austria, Podkarpackie in Poland, Norte in Portugal, Pohjois-ja Ita Suomi in Finland, Smaland med oarna in Sweden and Cornwall and Isles of Scilly in the United Kindgdom) or laggard regions that recorded positive convergence performances over the entire period or by certain sub-periods, but not enough as to significantly diminish their development gaps nationwide (Province Luxembourg in Belgium, Mecklenburg-Vorpommern, Luneburg, Chemnitz, Sachsen-Anhalt and Thuringen in Germany, Centro in Portugal, Lansi-Suomi in Finland, Mellersta Norrland in Sweden, Highlands and Islands in the United Kingdom). Again, a possible redefinition of the catching-up process as towards the highest regional GDP per capita level may dramatically change the composition of the divergence and/or laggard clubs and increase the "pixelisation" of the EU regional growth maps.

Finally, the impact of the 2008 global crisis on the real convergence process in the EU regions may be quite clearly revealed: convergence generally slowed down considerably and divergence increased during the crisis period, with the "growth engine" regions mostly performing better than the laggard regions, but for different reasons in the EU15 and NMS13 countries, in connection with their previous levels of development. While in the EU15 countries developed regions such as Region de Bruxelles in Belgium, Hovestaden in Denmark, Hamburg in Germany, Île-de-France in France, Provincia Autonoma di Bolzano in Italy, Wien in Austria, Area Metropolitana de Lisboa in Portugal, Aland in Finland, Stockholm in Sweden and London in the United Kingdom showed best or near-best performances in terms of real convergence due to the decline in the absolute levels of GDP per capita and in the EU average as a whole. In the NMS13 countries the most developed regions had generally slowed down convergence during the crisis period, although the "speed" levels were still mostly high and positive. Such developments must be also followed over a longer post-crisis period, the analyzed one showing again mixed evidence regarding levels, trends and changes in both the EU15 and NMS13 regions. Once more, maybe that redefining of real convergence in terms of catching-up towards the (ever-moving) absolute level of regional GDP per capita may bring new insights regarding how much and for how long the global crisis influenced the process of convergence or/and divergence of the overall regional income per capita in the EU. Future ideas for deepening research also refer to a greater territorial detailing (NUTS-3 level), inclusion of additional indicators, econometric modelling to identify key factors, etc.

Concluding remarks

The issues of convergence or divergence among the European regions have generated huge academic debates over the past decades, of particular interest after the recent EU enlargements. This paper attempted to assess the dynamics of GDP per capita for the NUTS-1 and NUTS-2 European Union regions, contributing to literature in two different ways. First, it analyzed a longer time span, by focusing on the period 2000–2013/2014 and on three different sub-periods determined by the global economic crisis that started in 2008: ante-crisis, crisis and post-crisis. Second, besides the usual dynamics of the process an attempt was also made to analyze its "speed", overall and by sub-periods, in order to draw conclusions on certain country-group peculiarities (if any) also during periods of time defined by real socio-economic events and not in a merely statistical manner.

Though the indicators were basic, the results suggest mixed evidence, in favor of both convergence and divergence, with both peculiarities and similarities for the regions of the EU15 and NMS13 countries. Moreover, beside the "usual" convergence/divergence clubs of engine/laggard regions in the EU15 and NMS13 countries separately, we may eventually identify new ones across all the EU regions, based on similar behavior during certain periods and/or in response to certain real-life global or European events (the "capital regions" club, for instance). New research ideas such as redefining the catching-up process, increased territorial detailing of indicators and subsequent analysis, adding new indicators and econometric modelling will certainly provide new valuable insights regarding the very dynamic, continuous and "live" regional growth processes and patterns in the European Union and its countries and the necessary policy actions to be done.

References

1. Albu, L.L. (2012). The Convergence Process in the EU Estimated by Gini Coefficients, Romanian Journal of Economic Forecasting, 4, 5–16.
2. Albu, L.L. (2013). Trends in Real Convergence and Structural Changes in EU, Project "Increasing the contribution of foreign trade to achieving real convergence", Strengthening the institutional capacity for evaluation and formulation of macroeconomic policies for economic convergence with the EU within the National Commission for Prognosis - SMIS code 27153 - project co-financed by the European Social Fund through PODCA - Operational Programme for Administrative Capacity Development.
3. Antonescu, D. (2012). Measuring regional convergence – An application to the European Union and Romania, Revista Economică. 2012, vol. Supplement, issue 1, 46–59.
4. Artelaris, P., Petrakos, G. (2016). Intraregional Spatial Inequalities and Regional Income Level in the European Union: Beyond the Inverted-U Hypothesis, International Regional Science Review 2016, Vol. 39(3) 291–317.
5. Barro, R. J. (1991). Economic Growth in a Cross-section of Countries. Quarterly Journal of Economics 106:407–43.
6. Barro, R. J., Sala-i-Martin, X. (1991). Convergence across States and Regions. Brookings Papers on Economic Activity 1:107–82.
7. Barro, R. J., Sala-i-Martin, X. (1992). 'Convergence'. Journal of Political Economy 100:223–51.
8. Capello R. (2007). Regional Economics, Routledge, London and New York.
9. Carrington, A. (2006). Regional Convergence in the European Union: A Stochastic Dominance Approach, International Regional Science Review 29, 1: 64–80, January.
10. Chilian, M.N. (2013). Coeziunea economico-socială la nivel regional – Elemente de fundamentare a unei strategii regionale, Editura Expert, Bucureşti.

11. Chilian, M.N., Iordan, M., Pauan, C.B. (2016). Real and Structural Convergence in the Romanian Counties in the Pre-accession and Post-accession Periods, ERSA Congress 2016, Wien, Austria.
12. Dall'erba, S., M. Percoco, and G. Piras (2008). The European Regional Growth Process Revisited, Spatial Economic Analysis, 3:7–25.
13. Dobrinsky, R., Havlik, P. (2014). Economic Convergence and Structural Change: the Role of Transition and EU Accession, WIIW Research Report 395, July.
14. Enflo, K.S. (2010). Productivity and employment—Is there a trade-off? Comparing Western European regions and American states 1950–2000, Annals of Regional Science, 45: 401–421.
15. Ertur, C., Le Gallo, J., Baumont, C. (2006). The European Regional Convergence Process, 1980–1995: Do Spatial Regimes and Spatial Dependence Matter? International Regional Science Review 29, 1: 3–34, January.
16. European Commission, (2004). A New Partnership for Cohesion: Convergence, Competitiveness, Cooperation, Third Report on Economic and Social Cohesion, Office for Official Publications of the European Communities, Luxembourg.
17. European Commission, (2007). Growing Regions, Growing Europe, Fourth Report on Economic and Social Cohesion, Official Publication Office; Office for Official Publications of the European Communities, Luxembourg.
18. European Commission. (2010a). Europe 2020: A European Strategy for Smart, Sustainable and Inclusive Growth. Brussels, Belgium, March 3, 2010: COM (2010) 2020.
19. European Commission (2010b), DG regional – Social mobility and intra-regional income distribution across EU countries, N° 2008CE160AT054/2008CE16CAT017, Final Report, July 2010.
20. European Commission, (2010c), Investing in Europe's Future, Fifth Report on Economic, Social and Territorial Cohesion, Official Publication Office; Office for Official Publications of the European Communities, Luxembourg.
21. European Commission (2012), Inclusive growth: a high-employment economy delivering economic, social and territorial cohesion. Europe 2020 [online], http://ec.europa.eu/europe2020/europe-2020-in-a-nutshell/priorities/inclusive-growth/index_en.htm.
22. Ezcurra, R., Pascual, P. (2005). Is There Convergence in Income Inequality Levels among the European Regions? Applied Economics Letters, 12:763–67.
23. Ezcurra, R., Pascual, P., Rapun, M. (2007a). Spatial disparities in the European Union: an analysis of regional polarization, Annals of Regional Science, 41: 401–429.
24. Ezcurra, R., Pascual, P., Rapun, M. (2007b). Spatial Inequality in Productivity in the European Union: Sectoral and Regional Factors, International Regional Science Review 30, 4: 384–407, October.
25. Firgo, M., Huber, P. (2013). Unconditional Convergence in Currency Unions: An Analysis of European Regions from 1991 to 2009, WWW for Europe Policy Paper No. 4, June.

26. Fischer, M., Stirbock, C. (2006). Pan-European Regional Income Growth and Club Convergence: Insights from a Spatial Econometric Perspective, Annals of Regional Science, 40:693–721.
27. Ghizdeanu, I., Iordan, M., Chilian, M.N., Tapu, D. (2015). Real Convergence in the Romanian Regions in the Period of Post-Accession to the European Union, The Tenth Edition of the International Conference on Theoretical and Applied Economic Practices Economic Growth in Conditions of Globalization, National Institute for Economic Research, Chisinau, Republic of Moldova October 15–16.
28. Halmai, P., Vasary, V. (2011). Nominal and Real Convergence in the New Member States (Longer-Term Perspective), Bulletin of the Transilvania University of Braşov, Series V: Economic Sciences, Vol. 4 (53), No. 1, pp. 193–220.
29. Havlik, P. (2014). Patterns of Structural Change in the New EU Member States, WIIW Research Report 394, April.
30. Iancu A. (coordinator) (2008). Convergenţă economică, Academia Română, Institutul de Cercetări Economice, Editura Academiei Române, Bucureşti.
31. Iancu, A. (2009). Real Convergence and Integration, Working Papers of National Institute of Economic Research, 090102, National Institute of Economic Research.
32. Iordan, M., Ghizdeanu, I., Tapu, D. (2014). Romania – Between the Real Convergence Aim and the Reality of Territorial Concentration of the Economic Development, Strategii Manageriale / Management Strategies, Universitatea "Constantin Brâncoveanu", Piteşti, Anul VII, nr. 1/2014, Editura Independenţa Economică, ISSN 1844-668X, pp. 50–63.
33. Iordan, M., Chilian, M.N. (2014). The sectoral structures in Romania, its regions and the EU countries – Key features of economic and social cohesion, Procedia Economic and Finance, Elsevier, 2014, Vol 8, 8 pp.
34. Iordan, M. (coordinator) et al., (2014). Coeziunea economico-sociala a Romaniei in perspectiva Strategiei Europa 2020, IPE, INCE, 2013–2014.
35. Iordan, M., Chilian, M.N. (2015). Dynamics of Real and Structural Convergence at Sub-regional Level in Romania, Proceedings of the 3rd International Conference 'Economic Scientific Research – Theoretical, Empirical and Practical Approaches', ESPERA 2015, 3–4 December 2015, Bucharest, Romania, Peter Lang Publishing House, forthcoming.
36. Jozwik, B., Ponikowski, H. (2014). Real convergence, economic crises and EU cohesion policy, Cambridge Conferences Business & Economics, July 1–2, Cambridge, UK.
37. Landesmann, M., Römisch, R. (2006). Economic Growth, Regional Disparities and Employment in the EU-27, Vienna: WIIW Research Report 333.
38. Le Gallo, J., Dall'erba, S. (2006). Evaluating the Temporal and Spatial Heterogeneity of the European Convergence Process: 1980–1999, Journal of Regional Science 46:269–88.
39. Le Gallo, J., Ertur, C. (2003). Exploratory Spatial Data Analysis of the Distribution of Regional Per Capita GDP in Europe, 1980–1995, Papers in Regional Science 82:175–201.

40. López-Bazo, E., Vayá, E., Mora, T., Suriñach, J. (1999). Regional dynamics and convergence in the European Union. Annals of Regional Science, 33(3):343–370.
41. Li, G., Fang, C. (2016). Spatial Econometric Analysis of Urban and County-level Economic Growth Convergence in China, International Regional Science Review 1–38, DOI: 10.1177/0160017616653446.
42. Lim, U. (2016). Regional income club convergence in US BEA economic areas: a spatial switching regression approach, Annals of Regional Science (2016) 56:273–294.
43. Mora, T. (2008). Factors conditioning the formation of European regional convergence clubs, Annals of Regional Science, 42:911–927.
44. Melchior, A. (2008). Regional Inequality and Convergence in Europe, 1995–2005, CASE Network Studies and Analyses No. 374.
45. Miron, D., Tatomir, F., Alexe, I. (2013). Do Central and Eastern European countries become more similar in terms of sectoral structures as their real convergence with the Euro Area increases? Analysis on the last decade, Economic Computation & Economic Cybernetics Studies & Research, Vol. 47 Issue 1, pp. 5–26.
46. Miron, D., Dima, A., Păun, C. (2009). A Model for Assessing Romania's Real Convergence Based on Distances and Clusters Method. Munich Personal RePEc Archive MPRA, paper no. 31410.
47. Neagu, O. (2013). Measurement of Territorial Convergence. An Analysis in the Case of Romania, Annals of the "Constantin Brâncuşi" University of Târgu Jiu, Economy Series, Issue 3/2013, pp. 117–125.
48. Quah, D. T. (1993). Galton's Fallacy and the Convergence Hypothesis, Scandinavian Journal of Economics, 95, pp. 427–443.
49. Quah, D. T. (1996). Regional Convergence Clusters across Europe, European Economic Review 40:951–58.
50. Quineti, A., Matejkova, E., Pietrikova, M., Serences, R., Toth, M., Dvorak, M. (2011). Looking for the evidence of socio-economic convergence within the European Union, Agricultural Economy - Czech, 57 (8), 384–393.
51. Peiro-Palomino, J. (2016). European regional convergence revisited: the role of intangible assets, Annals of Regional Science (2016) 57:165–194.
52. Petrakos, G., Artelaris, P. (2014). Intraregional Spatial Inequalities and Regional Income Level in the European Union: Beyond the Inverted-U Hypothesis, International Regional Science Review, 1–27, irx.sagepub.com.
53. Petrakos, G., Artelaris, P. (2009). European Regional Convergence Revisited: A Weighted Least Squares Approach, Growth and Change, 40:319–31.
54. Petrakos, G., Kallioras, D., Anagnostou, A. (2011). Regional Convergence and Growth in Europe: Understanding Patterns and Determinants, European Urban and Regional Studies, 18:375–91.
55. Petrakos, G., Rodriguez-Pose, A., Rovolis, A. (2005). Growth, Integration and Regional Disparities in the European Union, Environment and Planning A, 37:1837–55.

56. Răileanu Szeles, M., Marinescu N. (2010). Real convergence in the CEECs, euro area accession and the Role of Romania, The European Journal of Comparative Economics, Vol. 7, No. 1, pp. 181–202.
57. Rey, S., Janikas, M. (2005). Regional Convergence, Inequality, and Space, Journal of Economic Geography 5:155–76.
58. Rodriguez-Pose, A., Tselios, V. (2015). Toward Inclusive Growth: Is There Regional Convergence in Social Welfare? International Regional Science Review, Vol. 38(1) 30–60.
59. Rodrıiguez-Pose, A., Tselios, V. (2010). Inequalities in Income and Education and Regional Economic Growth in Western Europe, The Annals of Regional Science, 44:349–75.
60. Rozmahel, P., Kouba, L., Grochova, L., Najman, N. (2013). Integration of Central and Eastern European Countries: Increasing EU Heterogeneity? WWW for Europe Policy Paper No. 9, June.
61. Sala-i-Martin, X. X. (1996). Regional Cohesion: Evidence and Theories of Regional Growth and convergence, European Economic Review 40, 1325–1352, 1996.
62. Simionescu, M. (2014). The Assessment of Income Convergence Hypothesis in Romanian Counties Using the Panel Root Approach, Studia Universitatis Babes Bolyai-Oeconomica, No. 2, pp. 57–67.
63. Sala-I-Martin, X. X. (1996). Regional Cohesion: Evidence and Theories of Regional Growth and Convergence, European Economic Review, 40:1325–52.
64. Stehrer, R., Ward, T., et al. (2012). Sectoral Employment Effects of Economic Downturns, WIIW Research Report 379, August.
65. Tselios, V., Rodrıguez-Pose, A. Pike, A., Tomaney, J., Torrisi, G. (2012). Income Inequality, Decentralisation, and Regional Development in Western Europe, Environment and Planning A 44:1278–301. doi:10.1068/a44334.
66. Tselios, V. (2009). Growth and Convergence in Income Per Capita and Income Inequality in the Regions of the EU, Spatial Economic Analysis, 4:347–70.
67. Zaman, G., Goschin, Z. (2015). Economic Downfall and Speed of Recovery in Romanian Counties. A Spatial Autoregressive Model, Economic Computation and Economic Cybernetics Studies and Research, Volume 49, No. 3, pp. 21–40.

Alina Georgeta AILINCĂ

"Victor Slăvescu" Centre for Financial and Monetary Research, Bucharest, Casa Academiei, Calea 13 Septembrie no. 13, Romania, email: alina.glod@gmail.com

Towards a European Youth Well-being Index

Abstract: Becoming more aware of the serious demographic problems, researchers, experts, media and national and international institutions focus on finding and minimizing the short-comings in the lives of specific categories of individuals. There are global indexes regarding old age and youth, but the EU has not yet built such specific indexes. At present, Europe is still going through an important social, political and economic crisis and the young people from Europe are affected by high levels of unemployment, poverty and social exclusion. Though the EU programs, initiatives and financing schemes seem to outline the general framework of action and the EU has some specific targets for young people, the major positive results are not very evident. At the worldwide level, there is a Global Youth Wellbeing Index and a Global Youth Development Index and, at the European level, there are numerous indicators to highlight the situation and well-being of young people but there is no general index to synthesize these indicators. Therefore, this article tries to emphasize the necessity of such an index at the European Level and to offer some suggestions regarding its construction.

Keywords: young people, life quality, European Union

Introduction

Though it is a usual term, there is no recognized global definition of "youth". According to the Global Youth Development Index and Report 2016, the youth are defined as persons aged between 15 to 29 years.

Regarding EU member states, the EU Work Plan for Youth (2016–2018) seeks to tackle more efficiently the problem of high youth unemployment rates, the social inclusion issue and the transition from youth to adulthood, the health and the well-being of young people, the participation of EU youth in democratic and civic life and the challenges posed by the increasing number of young refugees and migrants in the EU.

Despite European plans on youth welfare, according to Schraad-Tischler and Schiller (2016, pp. 9–17), high youth unemployment is a structural problem, being above the pre-crisis levels (20.4% in 2015 compared to 15.6% in 2008 for EU average) and the opportunities for young people's participation in the labor market has seen no improvement since 2008. At the same time, the authors highlight that there are big differences between the EU countries: Nordic states (Finland, Sweden, Denmark and the Netherlands) are doing much better than the southern and southeast European states (Spain, Italy, Greece, Romania and Bulgaria) regarding what they define Social Justice Index. The mentioned authors also point out that, during the crisis and even now, poverty risk among young people and severe material deprivation of young people are much higher than that of older persons partly because of the fact that benefits and pensions for older people have not been negatively affected as much as incomes for younger people.

At the same time, for the young people, the problems regarding the transition from education to the labor market are reflected in a high rate of NEET (Not in Education, Employment, or Training). According to Eurostat, this NEET rate is also very high regarding the southern European countries, while in the Czech Republic, Germany, Denmark, Luxembourg, the Netherlands, Austria, Sweden, Iceland, Norway and Switzerland the NEET rate is well below 10% and close to 5%. The high NEET rate usually translates into a high unemployment rate on the labor market but also into severe restrictions and deprivations for young people in the present and the future. Also, easier access to education (disregarding the social background) or an effective vocational education can provide higher levels of school performance and/or professional performance of young people. At the same time, fair and equal opportunities for young people attending the education system will decrease the number of early school-leavers and improve the number of students in higher education.

According to the OECD (2015) and Ostry et al. (2014) the increase in inequalities has a negative impact on long-term economic growth. Also, the stagnation of the income (of young people), in the context of accelerated economic growth, increases the inequalities in the society (Dobb et al. 2016). So, the link between economic growth and social performance should no longer be ignored by the policy makers. If the EU member states reinforce their youth support policies through an efficient tax and transfer system (e.g. allowances and benefits for children, low fees for day care centres, preschool and school for young parents, rent control laws and correlation of the rent with the minimum income, housing benefits for young people, social housing programs, transport facilities for students, offering targeted support for socially disadvantaged families, easy access of young people to (preventive) healthcare system, etc.) and through ambitious policies to keep the young people in education and support them to enter the labor market, then the issues of sustainability of the public and private economic systems would be insured at least for the near future. Thus, releasing the young people from the long-term unemployment trap could be a good hope for taking them out of the poverty trap. In this sense, in order to identify the best solutions for young people we need to see their most important problems. In Europe, this panoramic image can be offered by an index like the Global Youth Wellbeing Index and the Global Youth Development Index, at the European level, or like the Social Justice Index in the EU, exclusively for young people.

1. Literature review

If we look at the Global Youth Wellbeing Index (GYWI) (Goldin et al. 2014), a composite index, it analyzes 40 indicators divided into six main domains. The data are collected from 30 countries, all around the world. The period analyzed is 1997–2013 and data are collected mainly from the World Bank, the International Telecommunications Union, the UNESCO, etc. The multiple sources of data cannot be avoided in the case of a global index such as GYWI, but at the European level this can be avoided, with Eurostat providing a similar methodology for all the 28 member countries. According to the GYWI methodology the domains analyzed are: citizen participation, economic opportunity, education, health, information and communication technology (ICT), safety and security. In the GYWI five of the six domains are weighted evenly with 18 percent, while ICT has only 12 percent. Knowing that the youth's access to information is vital for acquiring knowledge, training and getting a good job, it is somewhat difficult to understand why this area (ICT) has a much smaller share in this index. Thus, I propose a more balanced share between all six domains of this index, taking into account that even in the GYWI methodology it is mentioned that five domains (less citizen participation) are directly or indirectly related. For the aggregation of indicators which cannot be commensurate, a normalization process is carried out, and each indicator is scaled between a score of 0 to 1 relative to a set of global data, the maximum being assigned with a value of 1.

In the Global Youth Development Index (GYDI) there are 18 indicators covering five main domains such as: education, health and well-being, employment and opportunity, political participation and civic participation (Commonwealth 2016). The data are collected from 183 countries, nearly a quarter of the countries belonging to the Commonwealth. Although data sources are also extremely varied in the GYDI case (e.g. the World Bank, the UNESCO, the International Telecommunications Union, the OECD, the International Labor Organization, the Gallup World Poll, etc.), according to the methodology, all indicators receive the same importance in this composite index. It must be said that in the GYDI, the 18 indicators are divided asymmetrically among all five areas. For example, they are two indicators for the civic participation domain, while there are six indicators for the health and well-being domain.

Another issue of the GYDI could be that the methodology is constantly improved, and the index is not comparable with the previous version of the GYDI. Also, the definitions of "youth" used by various institutions was a significant challenge for the GYDI evolution. The GYDI scores a value between 0 and 1, 1 meaning the highest possible youth development level. It should be noted that the GYDI can hide the differences at the sub-national level, the index collecting data and focusing only on the national level.

In spite of all the imperfections of the GYWI and the GYDI, these indexes are a good starting point in conceiving a genuine youth index at the European level.

2. Motivation for a European youth index

Usually, there is a lot of debate and many studies about global old-age problems and there are several indexes to cover the issue of old people. But a look into the future can be more useful than a glimpse into the past. Thus, focusing on youth issues can provide real solutions to the future because the young people do not know how to "lie socially", do not have the age and the experience to adapt to a shady world and to compromise. The need to cut the Gordian knot by change and innovation is the central piece of the existence of the young people. In this sense, the enthusiasm of the young people should be doubled by education, by very good qualifications and should be assisted by an experienced workforce.

In Europe, although some progress has been made, national and European policies should be better directed towards the reiteration of the apprenticeship. In this respect, companies should be offered an attractive tax relief package for those who hire and keep a young person simultaneously coupled with an elderly worker. But before conceiving the necessary policies, youth problems should be much better known. In this respect, a European index regarding young people is expected.

Also, it should be mentioned that a youth index might be divided into two indices: one that might surprise the disadvantages or issues of youth and the other to uncover and capitalize the strengths, positive aspects and opportunities of the young people. However, an overall complete index, which should encompass all aspects relating to the young people (positive and negative), might give important solutions to the human society. In Europe, some of the young people issues might start from a much higher level than the rest of the world; therefore, a special Europe index is more than desirable.

3. The need for a design of European youth index

Interesting for comparison with the GYWI and the GYDI is the EU Social Justice Index (EUSJI). This index is a composite one that transcends the limits of the youth index, but is provided for the European Union countries. It contains six areas weighted as follows: poverty prevention (triple weight), equitable education (double weight), labor market access (double weight), social cohesion and non-discrimination (normal weight), health (normal weight), intergenerational justice (normal weight) (Schraad-Tischler and Schiller 2016, pp. 9–17). While we may debate the weights allocated to the six areas it is important to note that statistics used in this index are more uniform than the one used at the global level (GYWI and GYDI), as data are collected locally by Eurostat. The EU Social Justice Index contains no more than 40 indicators, some domains having only five indicators while the others have eleven indicators. A more balanced distribution of the indicators in this index might offer a better perspective of the social realities, including of the young people.

Although they aren't similar, the indices mentioned (GYWI, GIDI and EUSJI) could be interpreted as having some correspondences between the areas or the analyzed domains (see Table 1). At the European level (more concretely at the European Union level), the designing of an index with only five main domains but more consistent should not be excluded. Also, if the European Union has a different opinion on youth, being concerned about the functionality and efficiency of certain youth policies, it should design an index that could better reveal those realities.

Table 1: Comparison between the analyzed indexes and their domains

Global Youth Wellbeing Index	Global Youth Development Index	EU Social Justice Index
Citizen participation	Civic participation	Intergenerational justice
Economic opportunity	Employment and opportunity	Labor market access
Education	Education	Equitable education
Health	Health and well-being	Health
Information and communication technology	Political participation	Social cohesion and non-discrimination
Safety and security		Poverty prevention

Source: Goldin et al. (2014), Commonwealth (2016), Schraad-Tischler and Schiller (2016, pp. 9–17).

Basically, according to Table 1, all the analyzed indexes (including the EU Social Justice Index, which is not a specific index for the youth) cover almost the same main domains, but their compositions have important specific indicators, which are hardly comparable.

If we look at the European Countries by the GYWI the ranking is: Sweden (2), the United Kingdom (4), Germany (5) and Spain (8). Practically, the index has almost no representation at the European Union level.

When we look at GYDI (Commonwealth 2016), the European Union countries have very high and high scores and are ranked as follows: Germany (Rank (R): 1, GYDI overall score (GYDIOS): 0.894), Denmark (R: 2, GYDIOS: 0.865), United Kingdom (R: 5, GYDIOS: 0.837), the Netherlands (R: 6, GYDIOS: 0.836), Austria (R: 7, GYDIOS: 0.826), Luxembourg (R: 8, GYDIOS: 0.825), Portugal (R: 9, GYDIOS: 0.816), Slovenia (R: 12, GYDIOS: 0.811), Sweden (R: 13, GYDIOS: 0.810), Ireland (R: 15, GYDIOS: 0.806), Belgium (R: 17, GYDIOS: 0.802), France (R: 19, GYDIOS: 0.795), Malta (R: 20, GYDIOS: 0.794), Spain (R: 22, GYDIOS: 0.776), Finland (R: 25, GYDIOS: 0.773), Hungary (R: 29, GYDIOS: 0.740), Latvia (R: 30, GYDIOS: 0.737), Romania (R: 35, GYDIOS: 0.728), Italy (R: 37, GYDIOS: 0.726), Cyprus (R: 38, GYDIOS: 0.722), the Czech Republic (R: 39, GYDIOS: 0.719), Croatia (R: 44, GYDIOS: 0.709), Slovakia (R: 45, GYDIOS: 0.708), Estonia (R: 47, GYDIOS: 0.697), Poland (R: 54, GYDIOS: 0.681), Greece (R: 66, GYDIOS: 0.662), Bulgaria (R: 68, GYDIOS: 0.659), Lithuania (R: 78, GYDIOS: 0.646). Thus, according to this index all European Union countries have a very high (GYDIOS: 0.607–1) or a high (GYDIOS: 0.607–0.671) level if compared with the rest of the 183 world countries.

The realities are much different if we analyze the EU Social Justice Index (EUSJI) (Schraad-Tischler and Schiller 2016). The Social Justice Index is much more than a youth index, addressing a wide range of social issues (including the elderly), but reveals realities that are usually hidden in other youth indexes. According to the EUSJI, in 2016, the ranking (R) and overall scores (OS) are: Sweden (R: 1, EUSJIOS: 7.51), Finland (R: 2, EUSJIOS: 7.17), Denmark (R: 3, EUSJIOS: 7.16), the Czech Republic (R: 4, EUSJIOS: 6.85), the Netherlands (R: 5, EUSJIOS: 6.80), Austria (R: 6, EUSJIOS: 7.17), Germany (R: 7, EUSJIOS: 6.66), Luxembourg (R: 8, EUSJIOS: 6.57), Slovenia (R: 9, EUSJIOS: 6.51), France (R: 10, EUSJIOS: 6.27), Belgium (R: 11, EUSJIOS: 6.18), United Kingdom (R: 12, EUSJIOS: 6.16), Estonia (R: 13, EUSJIOS: 6.15), Poland (R: 14, EUSJIOS: 5.81), Lithuania (R: 15, EUSJIOS: 5.69), Malta (R: 16, EUSJIOS: 5.57), Slovakia (R: 17, EUSJIOS: 5.55), Ireland (R: 18, EUSJIOS: 5.40), Croatia (R: 19, EUSJIOS: 5.07), Cyprus (R: 20, EUSJIOS: 5.04), Latvia (R: 20, EUSJIOS: 5.04), Portugal (R: 22, EUSJIOS: 4.97), Hungary (R: 23, EUSJIOS: 4.96), Italy (R: 24, EUSJIOS: 4.78), Spain (R: 25, EUSJIOS: 4.76), Bulgaria (R: 26, EUSJIOS: 4.03), Romania (R: 27, EUSJIOS: 3.91), Greece (R: 28, EUSJIOS: 3.66). Analyzing the above information, it is clear that there is a huge gap between the North-West and South-East of the European Union countries concerning the social status of their citizens, including the youth, details which are seen less in the GYDI and even less in the GYWI.

If we imagine an index, let's call it the European Union Youth Wellbeing Index (EUYWI) with five main domains with an equal domain weight of 20% or 0.2, its construction could be as presented below (see Table 2):

Table 2: Design of a possible EUYWI, possible domains, indicators and weights

Domain	**Indicator**	**Weight**	**Domain weight**
Citizen participation	Frequency of contacts with relatives or friends by sex and age (yth_part_020)	20%	20%
	Participation of young people in activities of churches or other religious organizations by sex and age (yth_part_030)	20%	
	Persons participating in cultural activities in the last 12 months by sex and educational attainment level (cult_pcs_cae)	20%	
	Participation of young people in informal voluntary activities by sex and age (yth_volunt_010)	20%	
	Persons attending live sport events in the last 12 months by sex and educational attainment level (sprt_pcs_see)	20%	

Domain	**Indicator**	**Weight**	**Domain weight**
Employment and economic opportunity	GDP per capita in PPS	12.5%	20%
	Youth employment by sex, age and educational attainment level (yth_empl_010)	12.5%	
	Young temporary employees as a percentage of the total number of employees, by sex, age and country of birth (yth_empl_050)	12.5%	
	Part-time employment as a percentage of the total employment for young people by sex, age and country of birth (yth_empl_060)	12.5%	
	Youth unemployment rate by sex, age and country of birth (yth_empl_100)	12.5%	
	Youth long-term unemployment rate (12 months or longer) by sex and age (yth_empl_120)	12.5%	
	Young people neither in employment nor in education and training by sex, age and labor status (NEET rates) (yth_empl_150)	12.5%	
	Young people neither in employment nor in education and training by sex, age and educational attainment level (NEET rates) (yth_empl_160)	12.5%	
Education	General government expenditure by function (COFOG) recreation, culture and religion (gov_10a_exp)	20%	20%
	Early leavers from education and training by sex and labor status (edat_lfse_14)	20%	
	Young people by educational attainment level, sex and age (yth_demo_040)	20%	
	Young people learning at least two foreign languages (yth_educ_040)	20%	
	Participation rate in non-formal education and training (last four weeks) by sex and age (yth_educ_060)	20%	

Domain	Indicator	Weight	Domain weight
Health	Young daily smokers by sex and age—collection round 2008 (yth_hlth_010)	20%	20%
	Obesity of young people by sex and age—collection round 2008 (yth_hlth_020)	20%	
	Crude death rate by suicide of young people by sex and age (yth_hlth_030)	20%	
	Psychological distress of young people (average score) by sex and age—collection round 2008 (yth_hlth_040)	20%	
	Young people having a long-standing illness or health problem by sex, age and income quintile (yth_hlth_080)	20%	
Safety and security (including social security)	Injuries of young people following road accidents by sex and age (yth_hlth_050)	20%	20%
	Young people's at-risk-of-poverty rate by sex, age and living/not living with parents (yth_incl_060)	20%	
	Severe material deprivation rate of young people by sex, age and living/not living with parents (yth_incl_090)	20%	
	Young people living in households with very low work intensity by sex and age [yth_incl_100]	20%	
	In-work at-risk-of-poverty rate for young people by sex and age (yth_incl_130)	20%	

Source: Author's work, Eurostat database.

Considering the above table, comments must be made in order to explain the limits of the calculations of the proposed index. First, it should be mentioned that many indicators capture only part of the period of youth's general definition of 15–29 years (for example 15–24 or 16–24 years). Another important problem is that the data are not comparable in time; for example, many indicators are dated 2006, 2008, 2010, 2012 or 2013. Also, there are problems regarding the countries analyzed, many of them having no data for some indicators. However, there are no insurmountable problems, once European institutions, including Eurostat, understand the need to develop such an index for young people. After successive developments, this index could be divided or particularized in order to capture only male or female problems or only positive or negative issues or particular domains of the index that require special attention from the social point of view.

Conclusions

A youth index can be an important tool to promote young people's agenda and a powerful guide for the design of an adequate youth policy. This sort of index can highlight specific limitations but also the positive elements that can be included both in research papers and especially in the public policy for young people. More integrated data and youth-specific surveys can offer more sophistication for this index. Thus, a specific index for the well-being of youth in the European Union can much better tackle the youth issues from this part of the world.

In order to improve the scoring of the European youth index the public and private organizations should:

- See and not ignore the problems of youth in terms of employment; the lack of a (stable) job could affect the possibility of integration into society and could generate numerous mental and social problems for young people;
- Reduce the impact of youth lay-off policy, old workers usually being preferred to the new, younger employees; the problem of youth discrimination could also be seen in wage policies;
- Conceive more friendly state and private policies for the young people who have children, so that their income is higher and more attentively distributed for education and child nutrition;
- Conceive a conjugated (state and private) policy for young people over 18 who want a job (and can prove to have looked in the past 12 months for a job but not obtained one) to get a job even at the minimum wage in the economy; at the EU level through a unified legislation this sort of thing could be faster and better resolved than at the global level;
- Increase the degree of participation and time spent doing activities: playing, working, elderly, children, health care; basically all volunteer activities could develop or improve the emotional and social intelligence of young people;
- Create centres for the elderly and disabled people, assist with employees representing previously unemployed young people, retrained through courses for care for elderly or disabled persons;
- Increase the degree of literacy and education level of young people, including through public or private free access to museums, concerts, degrees, training courses, mind sports, social and competitive activities, etc.; the NEET people should be specifically targeted by these policies; in the public educational system, in order to restore the civic and moral spirit, children and young people should be taught to be independent, enterprisers, courageous and with moral, religious and civic sense; reinforcing the family values is a necessity; also, although increasing the number of years of study is not a grant for higher wages for that person, this may be a prerequisite for better lifetime earnings for that individual;
- Increase the team sport activities for young people at all stages of the education system, etc.

A European youth index could improve the knowledge about the young people and could validate young people's positions in local governments, parliaments, communities and policymaking institutions and public and private agencies and companies.

References

1. Commonwealth Secretariat Marlborough (2016). Global Youth Development Index and Report 2016, House Pall Mall London SW1Y 5HX United Kingdom, ISBN (e-book):978-1-84859-053-6, 2016, pp. 3, online at: http://cmydiprod.uksouth.cloudapp.azure.com/sites/default/files/2016-10/2016%20Global%20Youth%20Development%20Index%20and%20Report.pdf.
2. Dobbs, R., Madgavkar, A., Manyika, J., Woetzel, J., Bughin, J., Labaye, E., Huisman, L., Kashyap, P. (2016). Poorer Than Their Parents? Flat or Falling Incomes in Advanced Economies, McKinsey Global Institute, McKinsey & Company, 2016, July.
3. Goldin, N., Patel, P., Perry, K. (2014). The Global Youth Wellbeing Index, report of the Centre for Strategic et International Studies (CSIS) Youth, Prosperity and Security Initiative and the International Youth Foundation, 2014, April. Online at: http://www.youthindex.org/full-report/.
4. Schraad-Tischler, D., Schiller, C. (2016). Social Justice in the EU – Index Report 2016 Social Inclusion Monitor Europe, Bertelsmann Stiftung, 2016, pp. 9–17, online at: http://www. social-inclusion-monitor.eu/uploads/tx_itao_download/Social_Justice_Index_2016.pdf.
5. OECD. (2015). In It Together: Why Less Inequality Benefits All Paris, 2015, online at: https://www.oecd.org/els/soc/OECD2015-In-It-Together-Chapter1-Overview-Inequality.pdf.
6. Ostry, J., D., Berg, A., Tsangarides, C.G. (2014). Redistribution, Inequality, and Growth, IMF Staff Discussion Note, SDN/14/02, 2014, online at: http://www.imf.org/external/pubs/ft/sdn/2014/ sdn1402.pdf.

Andreea-Emanuela DRĂGOI

Institute for World Economy, andreeadragoi@iem.ro

Prisecaru PETRE

Institute for World Economy, petreprisecaru@gmail.com

State Aid Policy in the Post-Crisis Period: Implications for the Stability of the European Financial Sector

Abstract: The State Aid Policy has undergone a major reform process during the post-crisis period, a series of new rules (BRRD Directive, The Temporary Framework for State Aid for the Banking System) being enforced at the European level in order to support and ensure the stability of the EU's financial sector. Our paper aims to assess the effectiveness of the reformed state aid policy in preserving the stability of European banks in particular and of the financial system in general. For this objective, our research will use both a quantitative assessment, based on the latest State Aid Scoreboard Data, but also a qualitative analysis based the most relevant theoretical approaches. The final part of our article presents the authors' conclusions regarding State Aid Policy as a tool of preserving the stability of the European Financial sector in the post-crisis period.

Keywords: State Aid Policy, financial sector, BRRD Directive

Introduction

State aid policy is undoubtedly an important pillar in the context of the implementation of competition rules on the European internal market. In the last decades, this policy has undergone a major reform (SAM Communication, 2012) in order to both modernize the European rules in the field and achieve the State Action Plan objective (State Aid Action Plan, 2005). While the State Aid Action Plan aimed to guide the Member States to grant "less and better targeted[1] state aid", the SAM Communication had three main objectives: to foster growth on the internal market, to focus the enforcement on state aid measures with a significant impact on the economy and to streamline regulations that increase the speed of the decision process both at national and European levels.

1 Better targeted state aid should, according to the State Aid Action Plan guidelines, be granted for horizontal objectives such as: R&D, innovation, SMEs, environmental protection.

This was the global environment regarding European regulations in the field of state aid control when the international economic crisis started and suddenly the rules of the game were changed. Our research aimes to assess, through a quantitative and qualitative analysis, the changes caused by the crisis in the field of state aid regulation. The qualitative analysis will base its assumptions on the most relevant theoretical studies and articles regarding the efficiency of this new legislative framework in sustaining the stability of the European financial sector. The quantitative analysis is based on the latest data from the European State Aid Scoreboard and our target is to asses which were the member states that granted the largest amount of state aid to the banks, also highlighting the most utilized tools (guarantees, aids for rescue and recovery, capital injections, depreciated assets relief, grants).

1. Literature review

According to the current regulations, state aid is defined as a form of subsidy based on specific selection criteria offered by the member states to a national enterprise. Some studies (Kurcz, Vallindas, 2008) show that in terms of the selective nature of the measures or state aid schemes, the objective is to prevent the distortion of free competition by granting various discriminatory financial forms of support (subsidies, tax exemptions, guarantees, loans, capital injections, support for recapitalization, rescue and restructuring) to national companies. Kurcz and Vallindas (2008) also stress that the advantage granted to legal persons that are not companies cannot be considered state aid according to Article 107 (paragraph 1) of the TFEU.

Some analyses (Drăgoi, 2009) have highlighted that after 2005 the state aid policy has undergone a comprehensive process of reform and modernization focused, on the one hand, on granting aids for horizontal objectives (R&D, innovation, SMEs, environmental protection and support for renewable energies), and, on the other, on decreasing the amount of state aid with distorting potential for the free competition (especially aids for rescue and restructuring of large enterprises, as well as aids granted to the energy sector).

Other authors (Câmpeanu, 2012) pointed to the negative impact of the international financial and economic crisis on the European financial sector, particularly on the banking sector, which required an adequate support including state aid measures and schemes in order "to increase confidence in this sector and to allow banks to lend to the real economy". The same analyses point out that "the political control of state aid by the European Commission was one of the main factors that have ensured the implementation of unprecedented measures to rescue the European financial sector in a coordinated manner, without distorting the competition in the EU internal market." In the following sections we present some of those measures involving the member states that used the largest amounts of the state aid for supporting their banking systems.

Recent analyses (Adamczyk, Windisch, 2015) have highlighted the immense impact of state aid policy on the banking sector in the post-crisis period, underlying that "around 25% of the entire European banking sector has been restructured under EU state aid rules, while the Commission reviewed the aid granted to some of Europe's biggest financial institutions"[2].

2. State aid reform implications for the European financial system

The state aid reform aims to restrain the amount of state aid granted to large companies (banks and credit institutions included) in order to limit the negative effects that such subsidies could have on the free competition on the internal market. However, the international financial and economic crisis severely affected the banking system of the EU, hence new exceptional regulations were necessary in order to sustain the European financial sector. By the new regulations member states could support their banks using a variety of tools (loans, guarantees, rescue aids). Eight years after the peak of the crisis (2009), according to the latest European Scoreboard, the state aid granted in the Member States shows that the aid for the financial system holds an important share in the total state aid granted at EU level (see Figure 1).

Fig. 1: Types of state aid granted in the EU during 2009–2016

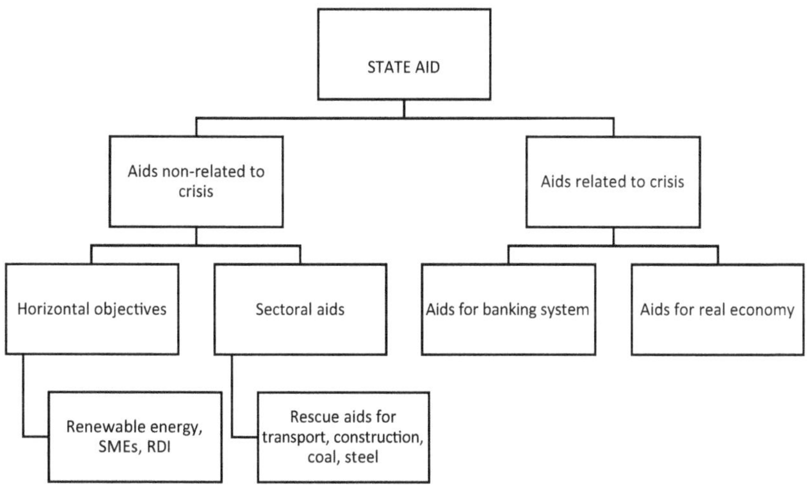

Source: *Authors, based on the EU State Aid Scoreboard (2016).*

According to the DG Competition statistics, since the beginning of the financial crisis, 112 banks in the EU, representing around 30% of the EU banking system by

2 According to the State Aid Scoreboard Data, out of the top 20 European banks, the Commission approved aid to 12 banks, of which six were subsequently restructured, five received aid through approved aid schemes, and one was orderly liquidated.

assets, have received state aid.[3] The aid provided in cash expenditure represents 5.4% of the EU GDP in 2008 (or 671 billion euro in capital and loans injected into banks) and 10.3% in contingent exposure (or 288 billion euro of liquidity and asset guarantees provided to banks). To overcome the risks to financial stability, almost all member states have made state aid available. In fact, in quite a few countries, more than half of the banking sector received state support.[4] After the crisis, the Commission approved restructuring plans for 56 banks, agreed on plans for the orderly wind-down for 33 banks, and reviewed the viability of 14 other banks without further need for a restructuring plan. As some studies (Drăgoi, 2013) showed after starting the reform, a series of new regulations were adopted (for rescue and restructuring aids, regional aids, aids for the financial sector, aids for growth, aids for agriculture and forestry).

All these regulations had as their major objective to increase transparency in granting state aid, while reducing the administrative burden for national authorities and cutting the red tape at the European level. Taking into account these changes in the field of EU legislative framework regarding the state aid control, it should be noticed that a series of procedural acts[5] have also been enforced in order to achieve a better targeted policy in the field while addressing the imbalances brought by the crisis in the European economy. The state aid reform has been shaped by the impact of the international financial and economic crisis, which imposed the granting of numerous state aids for the financial and banking sector of the member states. The most utilized types of state aid were: loans, tax exemption, capital injection, and aid for rescuing and restructuring the banking sector. As regards to the tools used for granting aids to the financial sector for the whole EU-28, the biggest share was held by state aid in the form of grants (see fig.1).

3 In total, 112 banks were examined individually with respect to the state aids received. This excludes cases receiving state aid under a governmental scheme but in amounts smaller than the relevant thresholds above which a separate notification would have been required. The specific conditions for notification evolved during the crisis.

4 Overall, 22 Member States provided aid to the financial sector. In Belgium, Cyprus, Greece, Ireland, the Netherlands, Portugal and Slovenia, over 50% of the financial system (by assets) received state support.

5 General Block Exemption Regulation (17 June 2014), Procedural Regulation with regard to complaint-handling and market information tools and sector inquiries in state aid (Council Regulation No 734/2013 of 22 July 2013), Communication to increase transparency of state aid awards (21 May 2014), Commission Staff Working Document on a common methodology for state aid evaluation (January 2014) and Provisional Supplementary Information Sheet for the notification of an evaluation plan (2014).

Fig. 1: Types of state aid granted in the EU to the financial and banking system during the crisis (% of total)

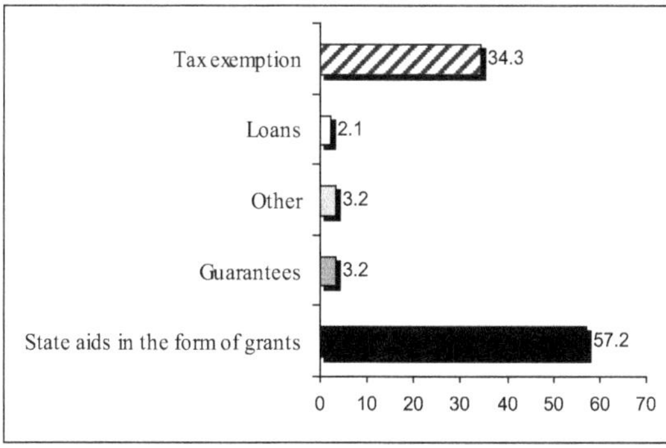

Source: Authors based on the State Aid Scoreboard data.

In the first years after the crisis (2010–2013) regarding the situation of the state aid linked to the crisis, the "champion" of this type of aid at the EU level was Ireland (crisis-related state aid totalling 285.2 billion euro), followed by the UK (191.5 billion) and Denmark (146.9 billion euro) an important part of this aid being granted in the form of recapitalization. In the same period, a number of the member states, including Romania, did not grant crisis-related aid: Bulgaria, Croatia, the Czech Republic, Estonia, Finland, Lithuania, Malta, Poland and Slovakia. We notice that the member states affected by the sovereign debt crisis have given a high volume of crisis-related aid to the financial sector: Spain (91.3 billion euro), Italy (85.7 billion euro) and Greece (69.2 billion euro). For Greece, the year 2013 represented the peak in terms of granting such aid (50.1 billion euro to recapitalize the banking system).

Fig. 2: Member states with the highest amount of crisis-related aids (billions of euro)

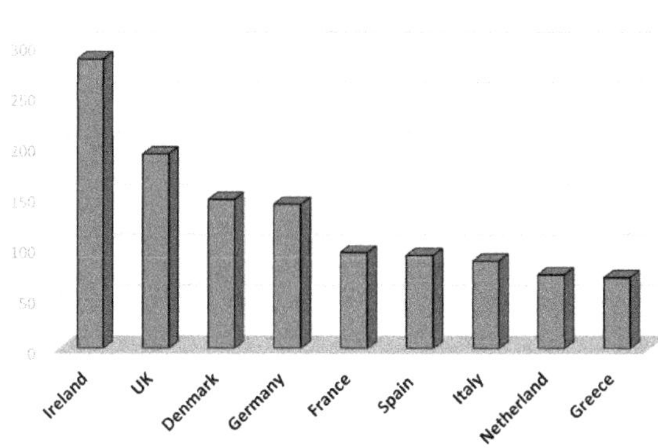

Source: Authors, based on the State Aid Scoreboard data.

During 2008–2014, the amount of crisis-related state aid granted in the form of guarantees (for the banking system) went upwards, as we may see in fig. 3.

Fig. 3: Guarantee aids granted to the banking system (billions of euro)

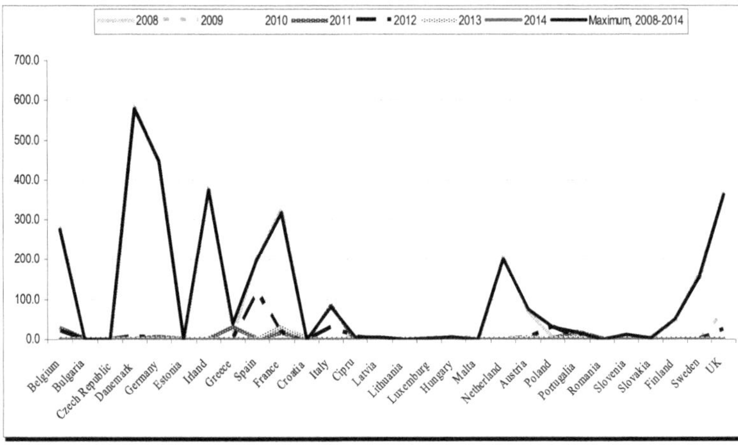

Source: Authors, based on the State Aid Scoreboard data.

Although the guarantees represented an important form of state aid and held a large share in crisis-related aids (2008–2015) they were granted as rescue and restructuring aids (see Table 1).

Table 1: Types of crisis-related aid to the European banking system

Type	Amount (billions of euro)	% of EU GDP
Rescue and restructuring	802.1	5.7
Damage assets	603.3	4.3
Guarantees	3 249	23.3
Capital injection	229.7	1.6

Source: Authors, based on the State Aid Scoreboard data.

Since the rescue and restructuring aid became a "popular" tool in the member states, more rules were necessary to ensure that such instruments were not used in a manner that could negatively distort the free competition, hence the BRRD

Directive was adopted. Below we discuss the BRRD[6] adoption and implication for the state aid regime.

3. Key changes caused by BRRD and consequences for the financial sector

Seven years after the peak of crisis, the EU banking system is still plagued by widespread fragilities. In view of this reality, the BRRD has provided the tools and legal provisions to address moral hazard issues in the field of state aid. It may be argued that the BRRD provides the new discipline for restructuring state aid granted to the banks along with a solid framework for aggregate policy in the European financial system.

The BRRD adoption was an important success on the path to the Banking Union. While this regulation has established the framework for granting rescue and restructuring aids in the European financial system, some analysts (Micossi et al., 2016) have highlighted the fact that BRRD was necessary in order to prevent an abusive use of the state aid tool by the member states and to preserve the free competition in the European financial sector.

We should note that the project of a Banking Union in the Eurozone, defined at the 13 December 2012 European Council Summit, is based on three pillars: the Single Supervisory Mechanism (SSM), the Single Resolution Mechanism (SRM), and the European guarantee scheme. The first pillar, SSM, started on 4th November 2014 with a Supervisory Board within the European Central Bank, based on the Council Regulation of 2012, and it functions in correlation with the second pillar, SRM, based on the Single Resolution Board (SRB), the Single Resolution Fund (SRF) and the BRRD provisions. The aim of BRRD is to replace the bailout procedure (using public money for rescuing ailing banks) with bail in procedure (using the funds of shareholders, bondholders and large depositors for bank recovery).

BRRD rules on the recovery and resolution of failing banks and established the Single Resolution Mechanism. The new rules defined by BRRD established some key elements in the field of aids for rescue and restructuring granted to banks: a binding 3% leverage ratio (LR) which prevents institutions from excessively increasing lending when they do not have enough capital, a binding detailed net stable funding ratio (NSFR) which requires credit institutions and systemic investment firms to finance their long-term activities (assets and off-balance sheet items) with stable sources of funding (liabilities) and a requirement to have more risk-sensitive own funds (i.e. capital requirements) for institutions that trade in securities and derivatives, following Basel's work on the fundamental review of the trading book (FRTB). Micossi et al. (2016) show that NSFR requirements will increase banks' resilience to funding constraints, while LR (the leverage ratio) is an essential prudential measure

6 BRRD represents the acronym for the EU *Bank Recovery and Resolution Directive*, adopted by the European Commission in 2014 (**Directive** 2014/59/EU).

that will enhance the stability of the financial sector by determining the capital requirements on the basis of non-risk weighted assets.

In should be mentioned that the BRRD adoption highlighted some vulnerabilities in the European banking system, e.g. Italy. In Italy, the financial situation is a critical one, the public debt is 2,000 billion euro (135% of GDP), banks have debts of 350 billion euro and a desperate need to increase their capital, hence the former prime minister, Matteo Renzi, tried unsuccessfully to persuade Brussels and Angela Merkel that the Italian government must apply the bailout solution instead of BRRD provisions. Subsequently, an Italian private equity fund, Atlante, was set up, and it was meant to recapitalize some Italian banks and it functions under the EU Alternative Investment Fund Managers Directive. It collected around 4.25 billion euro from 67 investors (banks and insurers) but it spent over half of the funds to recapitalize regional banks such as Popolare di Vicenza and Veneto Banca. A spin-off fund—Atlante II—was set up to buy bad bank debts with the goal to raise a further 3.5 billion euro from investors, but it could only raise 750 million euro and the first Atlante fund was forced to transfer it another 900 million euro. Atlante II already spent 1.6 billion euro on buying up Banca Monte dei Paschi's bad loans (Valentina Za and Andrea Mantala, 2016).

It is worth mentioning that many state aid cases for the Italian banks have already been subjected to the BRRD provisions, as shown in Box 1.

Box 1: BRRD and state aid measures – The case of the Italian banking system

In 2015 and 2016 the Italian banking system has been confronted with severe difficulties. One of the banks that was confronted with such imbalances was Monti Bank (Monte dei Paschi). While the Italian government was seeking a solution even through a state aid guarantee scheme (GACS), the new BRRD requirements made the whole process more difficult. The negotiations with the European Commission regarding the Italian guarantees scheme (GACS) highlighted some of the BRRD regulation weaknesses.
It this respect, we point out that the Bank Romagna Cooperativa (BRC) case (in 2015) revealed some inequities caused by the BRRD. In July 2015, the authorities started the liquidation of BRC. Although this went largely unnoticed abroad, the resolution of the BRC was the first bail-in in Italy. As it was carried out before 2016, the operation only required a "minimum" bail-in, limited to shareholders and subordinated bondholders. Such a bail-in should have been retrospectively reimbursed by the Italian sectoral guarantee fund.
The subordinated bonds of BRC were wholly owned by small investors. The BRC case brought to light a problem that is very widespread in the Italian system, where about a third of all bonds issued by banks are held by families: these small investors have little awareness of the risks they take.

This liability became even clearer after the enforcement of the new European rules on the bail-in (BRRD), when the government announced it would save four regional banks. While depositors and senior bondholders were protected, the shareholders lost about four billion euros. Then a significant share of these subordinated bonds was sold to retail investors and in order to limit the bail-in to a minimum and keep the state formally outside the operation, the resolution fund contributed 3.6 billion euros.

Under the new BRRD framework, the bail-in should include at least the 8% of the liabilities and can affect shareholders, bondholders (subordinated and, perhaps, senior) and corporate deposits. While the BRRD allows for some possible exceptions (national authorities may decide to exclude specific categories of liabilities from the bail-in, if there is a tangible risk of systemic crisis) for the cases when the bank bonds are in the hands of families, even a limited bail-in could have painful effects (as in the Italian case). But the most dangerous effect is the flow of capital from the South to the North of Europe and even outside the European Community (an excess liquidity has already moved from Europe to the USA). Authors like Charles Gave (2017) believe that there is not a liquidity crisis in the EU, but a solvency crisis, as half of Eurozone economies are facing a widening credit spread (lowering debtors' reliability). Anyhow, Europe faces the consequences of a liquidity trap, a deflation trap and a debt trap as a result of the financial crisis caused by an obsessive inflation targeting leading to some speculative bubbles (real estate, derivatives) and also by neglecting the long-term financial stability. Quantitative easing is the only unconventional monetary tool used with good results to counteract the negative effects of these traps and to support a robust economic recovery.

4. Conclusions

The financial crisis of 2008–2009 and the crises stemming from it, i.e. sovereign debt and banking crises within the Eurozone, made national governments support several banks through extensive state aids. While in the first years after the crisis, such subsidies were granted at the tax-payers' expense, after the BRRD adoption, the new provisions regarding bank resolution established a credible promise that shareholders and creditors would no longer carry the full burden of bank losses, mainly through the new sharing and bail-in instruments. Ensuring an efficient resolution of the financial institutions is, in our opinion, an essential element for the proper functioning of the European banking system, given that the lack of financial stability may have negative domino effects on the EU economy. While the state aid policy has become essential in order to ensure a fair and prudential support for the banking sector, BRRD requirements are the core of the new Banking Union and aim to preserve the stability and growth in the European banking sector.

Concerning the BRRD importance, some analyses (Freshfields, Bruckhaus, Derringer, 2015) stated that its adoption ends the lack of a harmonized regime between the different individual member state insolvency procedures within the EU for the banks.

The overall evolution of the state aid granted by member states in the post-crisis period indicates that the modernization reform was a success since the share of state aid for horizontal objectives is constantly increasing while the sectorial aid is diminishing. According to the European statistics (although after the crisis a large number of state aid for the financial sector was awarded, once the "peak" of imbalances was exceeded), the share of this type of aid decreased in the 2012–2013 period. In conclusion, we may say that in the post-crisis era, state aid policy has been effective in sustaining the financial sector stability, contributing at the same time to the recovery of the EU economy. In answer to the question of whether the state aid policy was effective for ensuring the European financial sector stability we say "yes". National and European analyses have proved that after receiving aid the backed up and restructured banks are showing significant improvement in operational and risk indicators, and in funding and solvency positions. Our finding, based not only on State Aid Scoreboard Data, but also on a recent asset quality review and stress test conducted by the European Central Bank on the main European banks, is that most banks under state aid control successfully passed the test confirming their solvency.

References

1. Adamczyk, G., Windisch, B. (2015). State aid to European banks: returning to viability, in Competition State Aid Brief, Issue 2015–01, available at: http://ec.europa.eu/competition/publications/csb/csb2015_001_en.pdf.
2. Câmpeanu, V. (2012). Ajutoare de stat în UE în contextul crizei economice. Eurolex nr. 2/2012, available at: http://www.iem.ro/ro/articole-eurolex/170-scoreboard-ul-de-toamn-2011-al-ajutoarelor-de-stat.
3. Drăgoi, A. - E. (2013). Implications of International Economic and Financial Crisis on the State Aid granted in the EU Member States. The Journal of Global Economics, Volume 5, Issue 4.
4. Drăgoi, A. - E. (2014). Consideraţii asupra succesului modernizării politicii ajutoarelor de stat în UE. Eurolex nr. 4/2014, available online at: http://www.iem.ro/ro/articole-eurolex/808-consideraii-asupra-succesului-modernizrii-politicii-ajutoarelor-de-stat-in-ue.
5. European Commission (2012). State Aid Modernisation Communication (SAM), available at: http://ec.europa.eu/competition/state_aid/modernisation/index_en.html.
6. European Commission (2005). State Aid Action Plan, available at: http://ec.europa.eu/competition/state_aid/reform/saap_en.pdf.
7. Freshfields Bruckhaus Derringer (2015). Key points about BRRD Directive, available at: http://www.freshfields.com/uploadedFiles/SiteWide/News_Room/Insight/RRP/EU%20Directive%20key%20points.pdf.
8. Gave Ch. (2017), The End Of The European Dream, Amos News, 10 February.
9. Kurcz, B., Vallindas, D. (2008). Can general measures be selective? Some thoughts on the interpretation of a state aid definition. Common Market Law

review 45: 159–182, available at: http://www.kluwerlawonline.com/abstract.php?area=Journals&id=COLA2008007.
10. European Commission (2014). BRRD Directive, available at: http://eur-lex.europa.eu/legal-content/EN/ALL/?uri=CELEX:32014L0059.
11. European Commission (2015). State Aid Scoreboard, available at: http://ec.europa.eu/competition/state_aid/scoreboard/index_en.html.
12. Micossi, S., Bruzzone, G., Cassella, M. (2016). State aid, bail-in, and systemic financial stability in the EU. CEPR's Policy Portal, available at: http://voxeu.org/article/state-aid-bail-and-systemic-financial-stability-eu.
13. Za, V., Mantala A., (2016), UPDATE 1-Italian bank rescue fund Atlante to buy more bad loans, Reuters, Financials, November 22.

Julia S. STEFANOVA

Economic Research Institute at the Bulgarian Academy of Sciences, Sofia, Bulgaria, stefanovajs@abv.bg

Zachary K. WENNER

Academic Research Fellow at Fulbright Commission, Sofia, Bulgaria, z.k.wenner@gmail.com

Bulgaria's Capital Market Integration into the European Union

Abstract: The Bulgarian capital market remains limited in size and insufficiently developed relative to Eurozone countries and Central and Eastern European (CEE) member states. To redress an array of market deficiencies and structural shortfalls, the European Union (EU) and Bulgarian government entities have collaboratively sought to catalyze market development through enhanced capital market integration. The research evaluates the scope of EU and Bulgarian market interventions, the factors related to the nascence of Bulgaria's capital market and the extent of capital market integration. Through statistical evaluation of price-based indicators for financial integration, the research analyzes alignment between Bulgaria's capital market and those of the Eurozone and regional countries. These findings are based on correlation analysis and parametric hypothesis testing with respect to the existence of integration dependencies. Through empirical analysis, the report evaluates the integration of the government securities market, the stock market and the banking market and indicates the determinants with the greatest influence on the development of the Bulgarian stock market.

Keywords: capital market integration, stock exchange

1. Introduction

The integration of the Bulgarian capital market into the European Union (EU) is intended to promote efficient capital allocation and economic growth. The process of integration materialized as a result of the joint efforts of both institutional entities and local market participants. As of 2016, the Bulgarian capital market remains nascent and incompletely integrated into EU capital markets due, among other aspects, to the incomplete consolidation of EU stock exchanges. An efficient consolidation process will require an array of government-led interventions and structural shifts, such as the diversification of stock exchange incomes as a risk mitigation strategy.

2. The Development of the Capital Market in Bulgaria

In 2014, the EU introduced new European regulations and directives in areas such as short selling, OTC derivatives, central counterparties and trade repositories—all of which are priorities for the Bulgarian regulatory authority in alignment with the Financial Supervision Commission. According to a World Bank report (World Bank, 2011), Bulgarian legislation is characterized by a high degree of harmonization with EU directives.

The new regulatory framework for the EU capital markets addresses all stages of trade, including trade on regulated and OTC markets, and the clearing and settlement of securities. The framework also expands the scope of financial instruments subject to regulation and disclosure. A primary objective of the new regulatory framework is to increase capital access for Bulgarian companies through enhanced alignment between the Bulgarian capital market and others throughout the EU. Due to the small size of Bulgaria's public companies as well as its investment intermediaries, the country's pan-European counterparts have demonstrated limited interest in the Bulgarian market. The regulatory framework for the single passport and alternative trading systems has therefore had limited effect on Bulgaria's small-scale capital market.

As of 2016, the Bulgarian capital market was underdeveloped relative to both Eurozone countries and other Central Eastern European EU member states. Accordingly, an IMF Working Paper (IMF, 2012) highlighted the need to further develop Bulgaria's capital market in pursuit of heightened economic growth and productivity through structural reforms. While Central and Eastern European countries (especially Hungary, the Czech Republic and Poland) have rapidly converged with the economic structure of the EU, Bulgaria has not replicated such near-term integration. Instead, divergence with average EU indicators remains significant (Institute for Economic Research BAS, 2012). The obstacles to rapid integration include high levels of corruption, inefficient institutional systems and limited access to financing. Addressing these deficiencies and doing so in adherence to the "Strategic Framework of the National Programme for the Development of the Republic of Bulgaria: Bulgaria 2020" (Council for Development at the Council of Ministers, 2012) will require optimization of institutional capacities, effective use of financial instruments for small and medium-sized enterprise (SME) growth and the promotion of sustainable development.

Following the global financial crisis, market capitalization as a proportion of GDP continued to decline in Bulgaria. By the end of 2015, it reached 9.94% of GDP (Bulgarian Stock Exchange, 2015) (see Table 1 in Appendix 1)—a low figure relative to Bulgaria's Euro area counterparts, which maintained an average of 60.4% in 2015 (Convergence Report, 2016, ECB). Moreover, Bulgaria's capital market faces low liquidity due to the limited volume of shares freely traded on the stock exchange. This liquidity issue was exacerbated by the outflow of foreign investors following the crisis.

Bulgaria's 2015 market capitalization was BGN 8.5 billion—a decrease of 11.98% from 2014. All indices trended downward in 2015, a reversal of 2014's modest upward trend. In 2015, reductions were 11.72% for Sofix, 11.27% for BGBX40, 1.74% for BGREIT and 5.81% for BGTR30. In 2015, the turnover of the annual base reached BGN 411 million, BGN 759 million in 2014, and BGN 1,521 million in 2013. The most significant absolute reduction was in the turnover of shares, an approximate decrease of 54%, which was in line with a 55% decrease in 2014. Similarly, the turnover in exchange traded products decreased to almost zero, while the turnover of compensatory instruments decreased by 51.76% from BGN 23 million to BGN 11 million.

In 2012, modifications to the rules of the Bulgarian stock exchange (BSE) resulted in the following market segmentation: Premium shares (with five issues in 2015, a decrease of two issues from 2014); standard shares (with 90 issues in 2015, no change from 2014); Equity Real Estate Investment Trusts (with 14 shares in 2015, no change from 2014); Collective Investment Units/ ETFs (with one issue in 2015, no change from 2014); Compensatory Instruments (with three issues in 2015, no change from 2014), Bonds (with 56 issues in 2015, a decrease of four issues from 2014); and Subscription Rights (with one issue in 2015, no change from 2014).

The Bulgarian stock exchange is designed to facilitate the trade of less liquid issues by maintenance of a separate market segment for that purpose: Equities (with 215 issues in 2015, a decrease of two from 2014) and REITs (with 47 issues in 2015, a decrease of two from 2014). The stock exchange includes 55 members, two fewer than 2014 membership, while the number of financial instruments admitted to trading in 2015 was 434, a decrease of ten from 2014.

According to Table 2 in Appendix 1, shares realized the largest turnover (82% of total turnover), followed by bonds (12%) and shares of ETFs (3%). In sectoral terms, 55.37% of the turnover was realized by the financial sector (banks and insurance companies), 21.43% by the manufacturing industry and 7.71% by real estate activities.

As a result of changes to the National Code of Corporate Governance (Bulgarian Stock Exchange Sofia AD, 2012), the Bulgarian capital market corporate practices reached a greater degree of harmonization with those of other EU countries due principally to the application of the requirement to "comply or explain". The principle stipulates that if listed companies fail to comply with any of the recommendations of the Code, the company is to formally justify such aberration. This requirement promotes transparency, accountability and improved business ethics, as well as the equal treatment of all shareholders. In 2016, the Code was extended and amended in conformity with the requirements of the corporate governance principles of the OECD. The increased scope includes heightened protections for minority shareholders, the adoption of best practices in internal and external auditing as well as in custodian services, avoidance of conflicts of interest, portfolio management and related rights with respect to corporate events. The Bulgarian stock exchange continues to support and actively participate in the activities of the National Corporate Governance Committee.

The priorities of the Bulgarian stock exchange for 2016 include a) a separate segment for trading in government securities as part of the regulated market operated by the stock exchange and b) the establishment of a segment for spot trading in foreign financial instruments, which would enable settlement of such transactions in the central depositary and in the the SEE Link system (see below) for routing orders to the regional stock markets (including Bulgaria, Macedonia, Croatia and Slovenia).

Despite the high degree of alignment between the legal framework and market practices of the EU and Bulgaria, limitations to the effective functioning of Bulgaria's capital market persist. These include:

Micro level challenges:

- Low quality of publicly listed companies, resulting in limited volume of freely traded shares;
- Low capitalization of listed companies with limited appeal for national and foreign institutional investors;
- Low liquidity, resulting in increased transaction costs and price volatility.

Institutional level challenges:

- Lack of infrastructure for central counterparty clearing, which hinders the development of the derivatives market in Bulgaria;
- Slow process of integration of the Central Depository to the European settlement infrastructures;
- Difference between the Bulgarian capital market and developed European markets;
- Lack of political capital mobilized toward redressing these issues.

Addressing the above deficiencies will require leveraging existing market forces and properly aligning incentives. Institutional restructuring is intended to mitigate remaining legal, tax, regulatory and business environment barriers while also minimizing systemic risks.

3. Integration of the Bulgarian Capital Market to the EU

From a methodological perspective, the extent of alignment between the Bulgarian capital market and the Eurozone is based on statistical evaluation of price-based indicators for financial integration (Stefanova, 2013). The evaluation compares returns on assets. The statistical research is based on correlation analysis and parametric hypothesis testing with respect to the existence of integration dependencies between the Bulgarian capital market and the Eurozone for the 2003–2013 period. The empirical research addresses the integration of the government securities market, the stock market and the banking market.

According to Syllignakis and Kouretas (2006), CEE stock markets are characterized by high levels of information asymmetries and volatility. The CEE markets also display a relationship between their stock markets and those of Germany and the United States. In the near term, the influence of country-specific factors has more influence on the stock markets than EU-level factors. Through analysis of the Capital Asset Pricing Model (CAPM) in emerging markets, Kostenarov (2012) established that modifications to the CAPM are applicable to neither Bulgaria, Romania nor Turkey due to the low coefficient of determination and the excessive modification error. These results indicate the insufficient degree of development among emerging capital markets such as Bulgaria's.

Analysis of the process of Bulgaria's capital market integration includes the following **assumptions** (Stefanova, 2013):

- Increased post-2007 alignment between Bulgaria and the EU with respect to the basic criteria for membership in the Economic and Monetary Union (Convergence Report, ECB, 2014), which would serve to promote competition and improve market mechanisms.
- Convergence of Bulgaria's average long-term interest rates with those of the Eurozone proves the law on one price in the course of gradual removal of various legal, regulatory, institutional and other barriers that investors face in portfolio restructuring.
- Increased opportunities for economic agents to access Bulgaria's capital markets as a result of regulatory harmonization with the EU along with the application of the single passport principle. This process conforms to the definition of financial integration delineated by Baele et al.

The empirical analysis of Bulgaria's capital market integration to the EU (Stefanova, 2013) indicates the following **results**:

- The integration of government securities markets has produced mixed results. With respect to Bulgarian and German government bonds, there was moderate correlation in yield spreads. For two-year maturities, Bulgarian and French government bonds exhibited weak correlations due to the insufficiently long statistical series. Contributing factors to these results include the relatively high risk of Bulgarian government securities—as indicated by the discrepancy between credit ratings in Bulgaria, Germany and France—and differences in perceived credit risk and liquidity. Finally, Bulgaria's immature secondary market for government securities is a barrier to liquidity along with Bulgaria's underdeveloped repurchase market.
- The integration of Bulgaria's stock markets (stock index SOFIX) with those of Germany (stock index DAX) demonstrated a high degree of correlation in the post-crisis period. This correlation is due, among other aspects, to a) the Bulgarian stock market's use of the Deutsche Boerse XETRA platform, which, in its unification of standards, facilitates the listing of issues in the cross-border context; b) Bulgaria's small size; c) Bulgaria's economic openness; and d) the increasing influence of common data variables from international capital markets during the global financial and economic crisis.
- The integration of the banking market for medium- and long-term assets and liabilities exhibits moderate correlation. This trend indicates that retail banking

remains a localized activity in Bulgaria, in which banks leverage their comparative regional advantages in order to maximize benefits. The increase in banking concentration leads to less competitive pricing on loans and deposits for consumers. The fragmentation of these markets is due to the presence of asymmetric information and the significant costs of service bank changes in Bulgaria.

Particular aspects related to the integration of the Bulgarian equity market with those of the European Monetary Union (EMU) help to contextualize the above results. Stoyanov (2011) offers two hypotheses: a) the Bulgarian equity market is underdeveloped relative to equity markets in the Euro area, providing higher returns in combination with increased systemic risk and b) the Bulgarian equity market is inadequately integrated with the equity markets of the Eurozone. The participation of a country in the EMU circumscribes the systemic risk of its equity markets, but does not eliminate such risk entirely. In particular, EMU participation does not remove national risk factors such as internal and external indebtedness.

The opening of a country's financial sector increases the prevalence and activity of foreign financial intermediaries within the domestic capital market. According to the general indicator for financial openness, IFIGDP[1], Bulgaria's equity market is moderately integrated with those of Europe. In 2009, Bulgaria's IFIGDP was 106.2%, while those of the Eurozone-13 were 209%. Stoyanov (2011) followed the development of the indices of the Bulgarian stock market and the Eurozone between 2003 and 2010. Prior to 2008, the Bulgarian and Eurozone equity markets were weakly correlated, with their correlation coefficients extending between 0.10 and 0.20. Following 2010, the coefficients ranged from 0.56–0.81, indicating a high degree of correlation resulting from the capital market decline of the global financial crisis.

The financial openness indicator confirms that Bulgaria's equity market is shifting due to European integration. And while Bulgarian equities investment is increasing, participation in international and European equity markets is still limited. With the onset of the financial crisis in combination with the withdrawal of foreign investors, Bulgarian market capitalization and turnover decreased significantly, with the main stock index SOFIX reflecting the downward trend of regional stock market indices.

According to IESE Business School (IESE Business School, 2010), the key determinants of a country's capital market attractiveness relate to the following factors (particularly with reference to venture capital markets):

1) Economic activity: Economic activity indicators include levels of economic growth and GDP, inflation and net flows of foreign direct investments. In Bulgaria, the currency regime introduced in 1997 seeks to bolster these areas while preserving financial stability. In 2015, Bulgaria's budget deficit approached 2.1% of GDP, an increase from 0.8% in 2013—a period during which the Bulgarian

1 $IFIGDP_{it}$ = (financial assets from the international investment position – financial liabilities from the international financial position)/GDP.

government introduced a liquidity scheme following the 2014 collapse of one of Bulgaria's largest banks. The European Commission 2016 Alert Mechanism Report concluded that Bulgaria maintains macroeconomic imbalances requiring large-scale structural reforms in support of the business and institutional environments. For example, Bulgaria's government aims to reduce the deficit by 1.9% of GDP in 2016. According to the Regional Competitiveness Index of the European Commission, Bulgaria is among the leading EU countries in terms of macroeconomic stability, along with Germany, Finland, Austria and the Netherlands. However, this indicator cannot compensate for the weaknesses of the country per the other elements of the index, thus placing Bulgaria among the least competitive economies in the EU (Marinov, E., 2015).

- Gross Debt Domestic Ratio: In 2013, gross domestic debt to GDP was 18.9% followed by an increase to 26.7% in 2016. According to the Maastricht criteria, this ratio is still below the 60% benchmark but has risen steeply due to financing of the budget deficit and the provision of liquidity to the banking sector.
- Inflation: Between 2011 and 2013, inflation dropped from 3.4% to 0.4%. In 2015, Bulgaria experienced a deflationary trend (inflation of -0.4%) driven by declining commodity prices and a drop in energy prices.
- GDP Growth Rate: The real GDP growth rate turned the negative tendency of -5.5% in 2009 and gradually rose from 0.6% in 2012 to 0.9% in 2013. By 2015, the GDP growth rate had reached 3%, while FDI decreased from 89% to 81% of GDP in the same year.

2) Entrepreneurial culture: Entrepreneurial culture relates to factors such as a country's level of innovation, R&D expenditures and the availability of appropriately structured risk capital. In 2015, Bulgaria's R&D expenditures were 0.80% of GDP, less than the average EC-28 value of 2%. The National Framework Programme Europe 2020 expects this indicator to reach 1.5% of GDP. In 2015, Bulgaria's angel investment network formed to provide support for start-up SMEs; however, many of these companies continue to depend on public financial support (via EU programme funding). Venture capital investments in Bulgaria were 0.002% of GDP in 2015—the second lowest in the EU, which averaged 0.62% of GDP. The Bulgarian research, development and innovation systems remain fragmented with limited connectivity among public and private research centers and businesses.
3) Depth of the capital market: This category relates to the establishment of robust capital markets, as measured by market capitalization or the number of listed public companies. The predominance of bank-centric financing indicates an underdeveloped capital market, which restricts entrepreneurial activities due to the conservative nature of bank finance. The market capitalization of the Bulgarian stock market declined from 48.2% of GDP in 2007 to 9.94% at the end of 2015. Credit extended to companies and households was 58.1% of GDP in 2015—a reduction from over 70% in 2012 and 2013.
4) Protection for investors and corporate governance: This category relates to the presence of a stable legal framework that safeguards the rights of investors and

reinforces the development of a highly-functioning corporate culture. Bulgaria's stock market corporate governance code seeks to foster this type of environment, an initiative that has helped to bolster the competitiveness of the market. According to the World Bank Doing Business Report (2015), some new EU member-states have small capital markets but are nonetheless well-positioned with respect to legal determinants of capital market development. For example, Bulgaria, Cyprus and Slovenia rank among the global top 20 countries on the index for minority investors protections. However, Bulgaria's protracted and weak insolvency procedures and frequently changing legal framework reduce overall investor interest.

5) Taxation: This category relates to levels of corporate tax and tax preferences. Bulgaria's capital gains tax is 10% accrued to non-resident entities, while a 5% withholding tax on distribution of dividends is applied to both residents and non-residents (with the exception of EU/EEA entities). The overall tax burden in Bulgaria (27.8%) is the second lowest in the EU (European Commission, 2016).
6) Social environment: This category encompasses areas such as prevalence of corruption and the scope of the unregulated ("gray") economy. The Global Perception Index 2015 measures the perceived level of public sector corruption on a scale of 0–100 (where 0 indicates a country is perceived as highly corrupt and 100 indicates a perceived lack of corruption). According to this index, Bulgaria scores 41. For context, CEE counties with more favorable levels of perceived corruption include Poland (62), Slovenia (60), the Czech Republic (56) and Hungary (51).

According to the European Commission (2016), over 60% of private sector companies consider bureaucracy and corruption to be a significant barrier to business in Bulgaria. The World Economic Forum (2015) reports that Bulgaria is one of the EU's lowest performers with respect to government effectiveness, regulatory quality, rule of law and prevention of corruption. According to the World Bank (2015), Bulgaria is the EU's lowest ranked country in terms of redressing corruption. Moreover, Visa Europe indicated that in 2013 Bulgaria had the greatest share of gray economy among 31 surveyed countries at over 30% of GDP. In terms of regional context, Romania reported a gray economy of 28% of GDP (similar to that of Slovenia, Turkey, Lithuania, Estonia and Croatia). The countries with the lowest share of gray economy in CEE are Slovakia at 15% and the Czech Republic at 16%, while the European average is 18.2%.

The combination of institutional deficiencies and capacity gaps within Bulgaria's domestic social and business environment has impelled a number of Bulgarian companies to list their shares abroad, predominately on the Warsaw stock exchange (WSE). Currently, at least four Bulgarian companies trade their shares on WSE, the first of which was Sopharma JSC. This trend became viable as a result of an agreement between one of Bulgaria's banks and the central depositary of Poland, KDPW. These Bulgarian companies seek to boost their liquidity and visibility, as WSE remains a regional leader in CEE in terms of capital raised and IPOs (ahead of both the Vienna Stock Exchange and CEESEG AG)

Recently, funds from the Operational Programme "Innovations and Competitiveness" were earmarked to support the listing of SMEs on the Bulgarian stock exchange. The total budget of the Operational Programme 2014–2020 is EUR 30 million, of which 25% will support SME listings. Under this measure, each SME is eligible for up to BGN 70,000. The subsidy will absorb the costs of investment intermediary, the preparation of a prospectus and listing fees. Receipt of the subsidy will be dependent on the success of an SME's IPO. The fund stipulates that participating SMEs must remain public entities for at least a three year period.

For an overview of the political, economic, social and technological (PEST) factors influencing the Bulgarian capital market, see Table 1 in Appendix 3.

4. Analysis of Integration Indicators of the Bulgarian and Regional Capital Markets

Correlation analysis of the Bulgarian and the Romanian capital markets indicates that the correlation coefficient between the SOFIX and BET indices for the period 2000–2013 is 0.78, indicating a substantial relationship. The coefficient of determination, r^2, is 0.608, which indicates that over 61% of the changes in SOFIX may be attributed to changes in the variation of BET. The empirical results confirm significant correlation between the Bulgarian and the Romanian stock exchange indices, SOFIX and BET. Utilizing Granger tests, Todur (2011) established that the correlation coefficient between SOFIX and BET reached $r = 0.94$ following 2009.

The applied correlation analysis for the Slovak and the Bulgarian stock indices (SAX and SOFIX) for the period 2000–2013 results in $r = 0.75$ and $r^2 = 0.56$. This value indicates a higher than average correlation between the two stock exchange indices.

The correlation analysis of the Bulgarian and the Croatian stock indices (SOFIX and CROBEX) for 2000–2013 yields a correlation coefficient of $r = 0.92$ and a coefficient of determination of $r^2 = 0.85$[2], which indicates a marked relationship between SOFIX and CROBEX. These results are in line with a study by Visek et al. (2006), which analyzed the daily closing price indices for the Slovenian, Hungarian, Czech, Polish, German and Croatian stock markets between 1997 and 2006. The study demonstrated the substantial level of multilateral integration between the Croatian equity market and the analyzed CEE markets and the German market.

Empirical analysis (Stefanova, 2014) of the integration links between Bulgaria and Central and Southeastern Europe indicates significant correlation between the capital markets of Serbia (correlation coefficient of 0.993), Montenegro (correlation coefficient of 0.966) and Austria (correlation coefficient of 0.915). Twelve percent of the changes in SOFIX are due to fluctuations in the Serbian index BELEX 15, while

2 Value of the coefficient b_1 = 0,3306 indicates that for each increase of 1% of the value of CROBEX the expected value of Y (SOFIX) is to rise by about 33%. The Durbin–Watson statistic stands at 1.603, which means that the residuals are not auto-correlated and that the least-squares method used in the regression analysis is valid.

approximately 16% are due to variations in the Austrian and the Montenegrin stock indices. The Macedonian capital market is the only one in the Southern and Eastern Europe region for which there are weak correlation links with the Bulgarian, Serbian, Montenegrin and Austrian markets.

In 2014, the stock exchanges of Bulgaria, Macedonia and Croatia signed an agreement for the creation of a single regional securities trading platform, SEE Link—a joint stock company in which the three stock exchanges contribute 33.3% of total capital (each contributing EUR 80,000). The EBRD provided EUR 540,000 of grant funding to develop the platform. The regional trading platform is expected to increase the liquidity of the three stock exchanges through the establishment of standardized financial services and increased visibility of the three stock markets. The trading platform provides investors with access to the listed securities of the member stock exchanges and to two blue chip indices, SEE Linx and SEE Linx EWI. The settlement of all transactions is conducted in the accounts of the three local central depositaries. The EBRD is currently developing a regional central counterparty to service the regional stock market. Moreover, there is interest for the stock exchanges of Bosnia and Herzegovina, Serbia, Greece and Romania to join the SEE Link trading platform.

5. Methodology and Results from Empirical Analysis of Economic Factors Influencing the Bulgaria's Capital Market

The application of multiple regression analysis indicates the determinants with the greatest influence on the development of the Bulgarian stock market. The formula is as follows:

$$Y = \beta + \beta_1.X_1 + \beta_2.X_2 + \ldots \beta_p.X_p + \varepsilon \quad (1)$$

where:

Y is the dependent variable representing the value of the market capitalization of the stock exchange

$X_1, X_2 \ldots X_p$ are the included independent variables

β_i are the regression coefficients

ε is the standard error of the model

The empirical analysis tests the necessary assumptions for regression: linearity, independence and normality of errors. The variables included in the model and the source of information can be seen in Table 3 (Appendix 1). The regression analysis is based on value of $\alpha = 0.05$.

We determine simultaneously the influence of the included independent variables—FDI, GDP, Interest Rate, R&D expenditures, Legal Rights Index on the respective dependent variable, the market capitalization. In Appendix 2 (Table 1) the correlation matrix shows that only the correlation coefficient r = 0.590, expressing the relation between FDI and LRI, is statistically significant, as indicated by *Sig.* $t = 0.002 < \alpha = 0.05$.

As demonstrated in Table 4: ANOVA in Appendix 1, the calculations are conducted in two steps. The multiple regression model is applicable since in the second step *Sig.* $F = 0.003 < \alpha = 0.05$. The application of the stepwise multiple regressions starts by including all factor variables and by excluding the independent variable, which has a correlation coefficient greater than the statistical error (i.e. greater than 0.05) until reaching a factor variable which can determine the lowest possible deviation of Fisher's coefficient.

From Table 5: Coefficients in Appendix 1, it is obvious that the coefficients indicate that the analysis included the variables Legal Rights Index and GDP, while the other three variables (R&D, Interest Rate and FDI) are excluded. The coefficients $b_1 = 37{,}948$ and $b_2 = 28{,}605$ are statistically significant because for them *Sig.* $t = 0.003 < \alpha = 0.05$ and *Sig.* $t = 0.008 < \alpha = 0.05$. According to the empirical results a 100-unit increase in GDP leads to an increase in market capitalization on the Bulgarian stock exchange of 28,605 units. Alternatively, an increase of one unit of Legal Rights Index leads to an increase of market capitalization of 37,948 units.

According to the World Bank, Bulgaria's Legal Rights Index for the period 2004–2014 shows a constant score of nine, indicating higher than average protection of the rights of borrowers and lenders during the period.

The real GDP growth rate began increasing from 4.7% in 2002 to a peak of 6.7% in 2007, followed by a downtrend. Beginning in 2003, Bulgaria's market capitalization increased from approximately 1.7 billion USD to a peak of 21.7 billion USD in 2007.

Table 6: Model Summary in Appendix 1 indicates that the correlation coefficient expressing the influence of Legal Rights Index and GDP on the capitalization of the Bulgarian stock exchange is $r = 0.643 < 0.9$. This result indicates moderate correlation between the Bulgarian stock exchange market capitalization, Legal Rights Index and GDP. The determination coefficient $r^2 = 0.414$ indicates that only 41% of the changes in the variation of Bulgarian stock exchange market capitalization depends on variations in Legal Rights Index and GDP, while the remaining 59% is affected by other factors.

An extensive body of research (La Porta et al., 1999) confirms that investor protection is a key determinate due to the principle agency problem, influencing the scale and scope of a country's debt and equity markets. These studies indicate a link between legal systems and economic development. According to Komijani et al. (2012), protection of shareholders has a positive and significant effect on the development of the stock market, with a 1% increase on the index of investor protections leading to an increase in market capitalization to GDP of 9.542%.

The Bulgarian stock exchange has adopted and implemented a National Corporate Governance Code, which supports standards of corporate culture for listed companies. Due to this initiative and complementary measures, Bulgaria has maintained a legal rights index value of nine out of a possible twelve. Alternatively, Bulgaria continues to perform poorly on the corruption index, with a Global Perception Index value of 41 according to the Transparency International Report (Transparency

International, 2015) and the highest share of the gray economy in Europe (Visa Europe, 2013).

Furthermore, a number of studies (Demirguc-Kunt and Levine (1996a), Singh (1997), Levine & Zervos (1998)) confirm a positive, two-way relationship between GDP growth and capital market development. Supporting this finding, the Bulgarian stock exchange reported the highest levels of market capitalization during the years in which real GDP increased. Policy makers and economic actors should foster this relationship, particularly through measures intended to attract local and foreign investors.

The Bulgarian capital market is currently without a central counterparty clearing institution, which has forestalled the development of a derivatives market. To address this infrastructure gap, the Central Depository seeks to integrate with the European financial markets and to establish links with other depository institutions. For example, an outcome of this effort may be the prospective integration of Bulgaria's Central Depository with Clearstream and/or Euroclear. Such integration may enhance the ability of the Central Depository to attract foreign investors while also enabling a more efficient operational cost structure. As of 2010, the Bulgarian Central Depository had a BIC for SWIFT, which allows direct connection with other depositaries. For example, the Bulgaria Central Depository established a direct link with the Central Depository of Romania in 2013. Given this latitude, the Central Depository will likely increase its connectivity to other participants of the European and regional capital markets.

6. Conclusions

In the context of increasing globalization, the Bulgarian capital market risks remaining in the "periphery" with absent substantial intervention at the micro and institutional levels. These efforts should enhance connectivity of the Bulgarian stock exchange and help to facilitate a merger with leading regional and/or European stock exchange operators. Moreover, a strategic alliance or other forms of horizontal integration for Bulgaria's stock exchange will foster greater transparency among Bulgarian listed companies and increase the investor base due to heightened competition from alternative EU trading systems.

The improved functioning of Bulgaria's capital market will depend on increased levels of liquidity, reduction of transaction costs, promotion of internet trading and the attraction of retail investors. The introduction of competition from alternative trading systems will be a key factor in improving liquidity levels. Preservation of the zero capital gains tax on stock exchange transactions is also critical.

The lack of a derivatives market and innovative financial products such as futures, options, and structured financial products is another factor that limits market liquidity and discourages investors due to the inability to hedge risks. The Bulgarian capital market has only recently started to offer a mechanism for dual listings of securities. Dual listings stimulate the liquidity of small capital markets and facilitate the increase in price transparency and disclosure requirements. Many publicly listed companies on the Bulgarian stock exchange are still characterized by low levels of transparency in their corporate governance and a disregard for small shareholders. Expanding the scope of information subject to disclosure, coupled with the removal of barriers for minority shareholders to take effective legal action, may serve to renew investor confidence.

Prerequisite to the increased inflow of foreign investment to the Bulgarian capital market is the general improvement of the country's business environment. These improvements include reducing administrative burdens and easing conditions for the acquisition of public companies. Levels of corruption will similarly have to decrease.

Integration into the EU capital markets may provide local investors with access to diversified financial products, along with alternative forms of capital accumulation such as access to venture capital funds. However, in addition to these positive effects, the new regulatory requirements of the EU capital markets may introduce additional administrative and operational burdens on market participants. These requirements include additional prepared statements and higher levels of public accountability, both of which seek to preserve financial stability and mitigate systemic risks.

The actions of the EU, the Bulgarian government and national and international market actors may serve to redress the structural shortfalls and market deficiencies of the Bulgarian capital markets. Continued progress toward market development and integration, along with the materialization of the EU Capital Market Union by 2019, will require sustained, multidimensional and collaborative efforts. Bulgaria's capital market need not remain in the "periphery," despite the current gaps in its developmental indicators. Indeed, recent structural reforms and regulatory changes have already helped to precipitate such a shift in parts of the market. The next five years will be critical in determining whether these incipient changes are the beginning of a broader shift or discrete areas of development.

References

1. Bulgarian Stock Exchange Sofia AD (2015). Annual report for the activities of the Bulgarian Stock Exchange Sofia AD.
2. Bulgarian Stock Exchange Sofia AD. (2012). National code of corporate governance.
3. Demirgue-Kunt, A. Levine, R. (1996a), Stock market corporate finance and economic growth: an overview, The World Bank Review, 10 (2), 120–140.
4. European Central Bank. (2016). Convergence report, June, https://www.ecb.europa.eu/pub/pdf/conrep/cr201606.en.pdf.
5. European Commission (2016) Country report Bulgaria 2016 including an in-depth review on the prevention and correction of macroeconomic imbalances.
6. European Commission (2016) Alert mechanism report.
7. Economic Research Institute at the Bulgarian Academy of Sciences (2012). Annual report economic development and policy of Bulgaria: evaluations and expectations.

8. IMF Working Paper (WP 12/131). Productivity growth and structural reform in Bulgaria: restarting the convergence engine, Washington.
9. Kostenarov, K. (2012). Modifications of the capital asset pricing model applicable to emerging markets. New Bulgarian University. Sofia.
10. Komijani A., Ahmadi H. (2012). Analysis of the role of protecting shareholders' rights in expanding stock market in selected developing countries. International Journal of Business and Social Science, Vol. 3 (17), 45–59.
11. Popescu, Gh.H. (2016). The Role of Multinational Corporations in Global Environmental Politics, Economics, Management, and Financial Markets 11(3):72–78.
12. Nica, E., Ioan H. (2016). The State-led System of Global Environmental Governance, Economics, Management, and Financial Markets 11(3):79–85.
13. Zaga, S.D. (2016). The Impact of Nutritional Programs in Mexico, American Journal of Medical Research 3(1):7–38.
14. Nica, E. (2016). Employee Voluntary Turnover as a Negative Indicator of Organizational Effectiveness, Psychosociological Issues in Human Resource Management 4(2):220–226.
15. Machan, T.R. (2016). Commerce and Its Normative Dimensions, Psychosociological Issues in Human Resource Management 4(1):7–40.
16. Laporta, R., Lopes-de-Silanes, F., Shleifer, A., Vishny, R., (1999). Investor protection: origins, consequences, Reform NBER Working paper 7428.
17. Levine, R., Sarah, Z. (1998). Stock markets, banks, and economic growth, American Economic Review, (88), 537–558.
18. Marinov, E. (2015). Competitiveness of the Bulgarian regions – Bulgaria's place in the EU. In Conference Proceedings: Management, Effectiveness, Integration: In Search of Present-Day Solutions. Foundation Academic Evgeni Mateev. Sofia. ISBN 978-954-392-323-6.
19. Singh, A. (1997). Financial liberalization, stock markets, and economic Development, The Economic Journal 107 (May), 771–82.
20. Stefanova, J. (2014). Integration of the capital markets of the EU applicant countries from Southern and Eastern Europe – problems and challenges. In Conference proceedings from international conference "EU at the crossroads". Sofia. Minerva. ISBN 978-954-8702-30-0. pp. 181–190.
21. Stefanova J. (2013). Strategic priorities of the Bulgarian capital market for deepening of its integration to EU. Economic Studies Journal. (2), 23–40.
22. Stefanova, J. (2015) "Problems and Challenges facing the capital markets of Bulgaria and Macedonia", https://ideas.repec.org/a/vls/rojfme/v2y2015i1p152-161.html.
23. Strategic Framework of The National Programme for the Development of the Republic of Bulgaria: Bulgaria 2020, (2012), [pdf], Sofia, Council for Development at the Council of Ministers, accessible at: http://www.strategy.bg/PublicConsultations/View.aspx?lang=bg-BG&Id=537.
24. Syllignakis, M., Kouretas, G. (2006). Long and short-run linkages in CEE stock markets: implications for portfolio diversification and stock market integration.

25. Stoyanov B. (2011). Integration of the Bulgarian equity market in the equity markets of the European Economic and Monetary Union. University of National and World Economy, abstract.
26. Transparency International (2015) Corruption perception index report.
27. Visa Europe (2013). The shadow economy in Europe 2013.
28. World Bank (2011). Integration of the capital market and application of the markets in financial instruments Directive, The Bulgarian Experience. Report no. 65823.
29. World Bank (2015). Doing business report. Going Beyond Efficiency, http://www.doingbusiness.org/reports/global-reports/doing-business-2015.
30. World Economic Forum (2015). Global competitiveness report 2015–2016, http://reports.weforum.org/global-competitiveness-report-2015-2016/.

Alexandru SANDULESCU

European Union High Level Adviser on Energy Policy in the Republic of Moldova, email: alexandru.sandulescu@eu-advisers.md

Filip CARLEA

Centre for Renewable Energy Sources Promotion and Energy Efficiency - "Costin C. Kirițescu" National Institute for Economic Research, Romanian Academy, email: filip_carlea@yahoo.com

Marta RUDI

European Union High Level Advisers' Mission in the Republic of Moldova, email: marta.rudi@eu-advisers.md

Increasing the Republic of Moldova's Security of Energy Supply through Integration with the Romanian Energy Market

Abstract: The Republic of Moldova (RM) is highly dependent on imports of natural gas, electricity and oil products. The regional context is changing both politically and economically, and consequently energy flows in the region will change in the next decades. This will further increase the energy supply risks of the Republic of Moldova. RM signed an Association Agreement with the European Union in 2014, committing itself to fully transpose EU legislation in key areas, including energy. This will allow it to gradually integrate RM's energy sector into the EU-wide internal energy market, but keeping as competitors RM's traditional eastern suppliers of gas and electricity. To achieve this goal, new gas and electricity interconnections should be built and flows on some of the existing gas interconnections with Romania and Ukraine should be reversed. Despite their role in increasing the level of security of energy supply, commercial viability of some new interconnections is low and regulated mechanisms should be implemented in order to secure the investment recovery. The authors researched and proposed such a mechanism for the new gas interconnection with Romania, fully compatible with EU legislation, and based on a unified gas transmission tariff.

Keywords: security of energy supply, Republic of Moldova, interconnections, energy policy, energy strategy, energy market

Introduction

The Republic of Moldova is highly dependent on energy imports. Domestic consumption of natural gas is covered almost 100% by imports and 75–80% of gross electricity consumption is covered by a power plant, located in Cuciurgan-Transnistria, a geographical area which is not under the control of the Moldavian State. Domestic electricity production is based mainly on imported gas. The high dependence on imports, both on gas and electricity, has as a consequence a low level of security of supply, which ranks Moldova on position 116 out of 125 in the World Energy Council's Energy Trilemma Index 2016, in what concerns security of energy supply indicator.

Besides its great dependency on imports, an even higher vulnerability of the Republic of Moldova comes from the limited number of possible external suppliers of gas and electricity. Except for possible but very unreliable electricity from Ukraine, imports are only from two Russian companies, Gazprom for gas and InterRAO, owner of Cuciurgan Power Plant, for electricity.

Vulnerability also came from the use of a single supply route for gas, through Ukraine. Even if this route is currently also used by Gazprom to supply gas to Romania, Bulgaria, Greece and partially to Turkey, there is a clear intention expressed by the Russian Federation's officials to abandon this route in the future and replace it with other gas pipelines, such as Turk Stream. This is part of the Russian Federation's intent to change the supply routes towards Europe, avoiding crossing Ukraine. The new projects do not provide Moldova's gas supply, and 2020 is expected to be the year in which the gas route will be changed.

The Republic of Moldova has been a contracting party to the Energy Community Treaty since 2010 and as a consequence, it has clear commitments to transpose EU energy acquis, to create competitive electricity and gas markets and to integrate its national energy markets into the internal EU market. These commitments were further developed in the Association Agreement between the European Union and the European Atomic Energy Community and their member states, on the one hand, and the Republic of Moldova, on the other, signed in 2014.

According to these commitments, the Republic of Moldova transposed the Second Energy Package (Directives 2003/54/EC and 2003/55/EC) and more recently, in 2016, the Third Energy Package (Directives 2009/72/EU, 2009/73/EU and two Regulations, 714/2009 and 715/2009). This creates the legal and regulatory environment for the development of competitive electricity and gas markets, but competition remains only in theory due to the lack of competitors on the wholesale segments of the market.

On the institutional level, there is a functional energy regulatory authority, ANRE. Its powers and independence needs further enhancement. In this respect, a new Energy Law is under discussion and should be issued in 2017. In 2015, the legal separation of distribution and supply activities in gas and electricity was done, and the ANRE issued distinct distribution tariffs. Regulated transmission tariffs are also applied.

Correlated with the development of the wholesale market, a Market Operator and balancing mechanisms are envisaged by the new Electricity Law. Balancing mechanisms for gas should also be issued through secondary legislation, according to the Gas Law.

So, the basic conditions to have competitive wholesale markets in gas and electricity are met, except for the first condition regarding competition, which requires more players at unregulated prices to compete with the *de facto* monopolistic external suppliers.

New interconnections are envisaged both for gas and electricity, in order to properly link Moldavian transmission networks to Romanian ones. By this, three goals will be achieved:

- an increase in the level of security of energy supply by increasing the number and diversity of suppliers and supply routes;
- a level of competition in the wholesale gas and electricity markets able to establish prices at the lowest values possible;
- a possibility to couple and further integrate Moldova's gas and electricity markets into the EU internal energy market.

The new interconnections should be regarded not only as interconnections with Romania but also with the continental EU-wide gas and electricity transmission networks, in which gas and electricity are freely traded across Europe.

1. Literature review

There are several documents addressing the increasing of the Republic of Moldova's security of energy supply, starting with the national Energy Strategy 2030[1]. The Strategy envisages the building of new interconnections for gas and electricity and the development of competitive energy markets until 2020. Feasibility studies were also elaborated by foreign consultants for gas in 2015[2] and electricity interconnection in 2016[3]. On electricity, there are also a Synchronous Interconnection Feasibility Study (2016)[4] and two World Bank studies (2015 and 2016). All these documents analyze the need for new interconnections from the perspective of their need and benefits but do not provide any viable solutions for financial recovery of investments in a market environment in which the use of the new infrastructure will be low.

2. New interconnection for gas

A 43km, 500mm diameter pipeline was built between Iasi (RO) and Ungheni (RM) and was commissioned in 2014. With a capacity of 1.5 billion cu.m/yr, it was supposed to entirely cover Moldova's gas consumption of roughly 1 bln. cu.m/yr. This theoretical capacity of 1.5 billion cu.m/yr is calculated at a flat rate of 175,000 cm/h, which represents the maximum capacity of the pipeline. The pipeline's cost of

26.5 million euro was mostly covered by grants from the EU and Romania. This is a first phase of a larger interconnection infrastructure; to make it fully functional there is a need to expand the interconnector with high capacity gas pipelines both on Romanian and Moldavian territories: on the Moldavian side, the Ungheni–Chisinau pipeline of 117km, 600mm diameter, is an investment estimated at 93 million euro[2], out of which ten million euro will be covered by an EU grant, while on the Romanian side there is the Onesti–Gheraiesti–Iasi pipeline and two compression stations in Onesti and Gheraiesti. Investment is estimated at 110 million euro, of which 55 million euro is expected to be covered by EU structural funds.

Works on both sides of the border were expected to end in December 2017[1], but a more realistic completion term will be at the end of 2019.

The Republic of Moldova has two gas transmission operators, Vestmoldtransgaz, a state-owned company operating the new interconnector including the foreseen extension to Chisinau and Moldovagaz, a company controlled by Gazprom owning and operating the rest of the transmission network.

Gas sources

For the Iasi–Ungheni interconnector, gas sources could be Romanian on-shore deposits (existing ones will be depleted in roughly 15 years), central EU sources through the Arad-Szeged interconnection, LNG terminals in Greece and Turkey through the Giurgiu–Ruse interconnector, or Romanian off-shore deposits by the Southern Corridor.

3. New interconnection for electricity

In 2004, Romania technically joined the ENTSO-E[2], but its electricity grids are completely separated from the Republic of Moldova's ones. Moldova is interconnected with the IPS–UPS network, which includes the Russian Federation, Ukraine, Belarus and some Asian countries. The Baltic States, even if they are members of ENTSO-E, are synchronously connected with the IPS–UPS grid (Integrated Power System-Unified power system), a wide area synchronous transmission grid of some CIS countries (*Commonwealth of Independent States*) with a common mode of operation and centralized supervisory control. One 400kV line and three 110kV lines cross the border between Romania and Moldova, and the 110kV lines were used in the past for small cross border trade in "island mode" (capacity up to 150MW). Balancing services are provided by Ukraine to the Republic of Moldova.

---

1 Indicative deadline in the Intergovernmental Agreement between RO and RM on gas and electricity interconnections, 2015.

2 ENTSO-E –European Network of Transmission System Operators for Electricity; UCTE – Union for the Coordination of Transmission of Electricity, the name of the ENTSO-E association at that time.

Synchronous interconnection: a study of the technical feasibility of the synchronous interconnection of the electricity grids of Ukraine and Moldova with the ENTSO-E continental grid was financed by the EU and carried out by the ENTSO-E. It ended in 2016, with the conclusion that interconnection is technically feasible, but the power plants and electricity networks of both candidate countries should meet ENTSO-E Operation Handbook[3] requirements. The author estimates are that meeting these requirements will take 12–15 years and 1.5 to 2.0 billion euro for investments.

Asynchronous interconnection: an interconnection that can be achieved more rapidly, in only 2–3 years, is the asynchronous interconnection. It implies the use of Back to Back (BtB) substations, able to interconnect power systems at different frequencies. There are three such possible interconnections between the Republic of Moldova and Romania:

a) The South interconnection, Isaccea–Vulcanesti–Chisinau, with BtB in Vulcanesti;
b) The North interconnection, Suceava–Balti, with BtB in Bălţi;
c) The central interconnection, RO–Ungheni–Straseni, with BtB in Ungheni or Straseni.

The South interconnection was established to be the most feasible one by the studies mentioned in section 2 for several reasons: the Isaccea–Vulcanesti cross-border power line exists, there are 600MW in interconnection capacity on the Romanian side and this interconnection needs the lowest total costs (Romania and Moldova), currently estimated at 194 million euro. With an envisaged capacity of 2x300MW, and used in base load, this interconnection will be able to cover 70–80% of Moldova's electricity consumption of about 4TWh/yr. As mentioned, a feasibility study was prepared by a consortium led by the ISPE Romania and financed by the EBRD.

In recent years, the asynchronous solution seems to be the preferred way to connect ENTSO-E and IPS–UPS grids. In this respect, we could consider:

- The "Black Sea Transmission Network" between Georgia and Turkey, 2x350MW BtB and 283km of power lines, construction started in 2010 and ended in 2014;
- The "Litpol Interconnection" between Poland and Lithuania, 2x500MW BtB and 341km of power lines, construction started in 2014 and the first 500MW module is ready[4];
- The "NordBalt" submarine cable between Sweden and Lithuania, 700MW, 450km, construction started in 2015;
- The "Estlink 1" and "Estlink 2" submarine cables between Finland and Estonia, the first one of 350MW, 150km, commissioned in 2006 and the second one of 650MW, 151km, commissioned in 2015.

3 "Continental Europe Operation Handbook", European Network of Transmission System Operators for Electricity https://www.entsoe.eu/publications/system-operations-reports/operation-handbook/Pages/default.aspx.

4 "LitPol Link capacity tests successful", November 26, 2015, LiTpol Link project, http://www.litpol-link.com/news/litpol-link-capacity-tests-successful-sM721T.

There is no mutual exclusion between synchronous and asynchronous electricity interconnection solutions, the asynchronous solution being regarded as a transitory solution to the final synchronous solution. In this respect, the BtB substations could be relocated on the next asynchronous border, even if, after ten years of operation they might be fully depreciated.

4. Financing the interconnection infrastructure

The new gas and electricity interconnections between the Republic of Moldova and the EU networks (Romania) could be approached in two ways, in what concerns investment recovery:

a) as pure security of supply infrastructure, which lowers the price of gas or electricity provided from Eastern partners to Moldova, even if the new interconnection is not used;
b) as commercial investments that should be recovered in a reasonable time through effective use of the new infrastructure.

Gas infrastructure

As commercial investment, the Ungheni–Chisinau gas pipeline is currently not feasible. The price of gas supplied by Gazprom to the Republic of Moldova dropped gradually to 146 USD/1000 cu.m in Q_1-2017, much lower than the price of gas bought from Europe. In this case, the gas interconnection will not actually be used and the investment could not be recovered through transmission tariffs. But this situation might change suddenly due to political realities, including the possible recovery of the historical debt of Moldovagaz of about 6 bln. USD (most of it being the debt of Transnistria, a region that is not controlled by the central government of Moldova).

The solution to recover the investment outside the transmission tariff and irrespective of the actual use of the pipeline, compatible with EU acquis in energy, is to impose a public service obligation, such as:

- to establish a "Security of Supply Fund", with incomes from a levy on all imported energy products—electricity, gas and fuels. From this fund, operational costs and investment recovery of the unused interconnection infrastructure will be covered;
- to establish a unified gas transmission tariff and a compensation mechanism between the two transmission operators, Vestmoldtransgaz and Moldovagaz–authors' proposal;
- to impose a mandatory acquisition of gas for state-owned tertiary consumers (hospitals, schools, public buildings) from EU markets;
- to impose a mandatory use of the new pipeline, at a certain rate, to the main gas importers;
- a combination of the above.

Electricity infrastructure

The price of electricity supplied by the Cuciurgan Power Plant in 2015 was 67.95 USD/MWh (59.5 euro/MWh). In 2016, it dropped to 48.995 USD/MWh (42.9 euro/MWh). If we compare these prices with the average electricity spot price in RO of 34.66 euro/MWh in 2014 and 36.42 euro/MWh in 2015, and between 27 and 42 euro/MWh in 2016 (monthly values), the difference is still 6–12 euro/MWh. Considering these differences in prices, the investments in asynchronous interconnections between Romania and Moldova are commercially viable.

It is also to be mentioned that starting in November 2014, RO–HU–CZ–SK wholesale spot markets are included in a single market. Also, there are electricity export and import contracts among the whole region, starting with countries in the Balkans and ending with Central European countries. This has as a consequence the fact that the relevant market is huge, providing a good long-term stability of the prices, and liquidity in the market is high.

Private investments in interconnections

The EU Third Energy Package provides for the possibility of private investments in interconnections, in certain conditions[5][5][6]. This possibility was transposed in Moldavian legislation in 2016, through the new Electricity Law and the new Natural Gas Law. In this respect, the new laws allow more TSOs (Transmission System Operators) for gas and for electricity to co-exist in the Republic of Moldova, but only two of them being allowed to be "system operators", one for gas and one for electricity. So, it is possible to have a private investment in an interconnection, made by a distinct registered TSO. The law goes further, providing the possibility to exempt these investments in interconnections from the normal third-party access rules. By exception, there will be a regulated tariff applied for a limited period of time to a certain part of the new interconnection capacity, all these elements being established such that the investment be recovered, including a profit. The three elements: regulated tariff, application term and capacity are approved by the ANRE, the energy regulatory agency under the supervision of the Energy Community Secretariat. These provisions are aimed to attract private investments in new interconnections, creating a virtual risk-free environment.

5. Unified gas transmission tariff and a compensation mechanism

The authors proposed a very viable solution for the investment recovery of the new gas transmission infrastructure, based on a unified gas transmission tariff and

5 Art. 36 – New infrastructure of Directive 2009/73/EC (gas) and Art. 22 – Network development and powers to make investment decisions of Directive 2009/72/EC.

a compensation mechanism between the two gas transmission operators. The recovery is not affected by the actual use of the new interconnector and provides stable transmission tariffs and equal treatment of end-users in what concerns the gas transmission network.

Instead of calculating two distinct gas transmission tariffs for the existing transmission operators, the ANRE, as a regulatory authority, will establish only one nation-wide transmission tariff, based on the cumulated costs of the operators (CAPEX - capital expenditure, OPEX - operating expense) and the use of the whole national network. This transmission tariff will be applied to all gas transmission pipelines, regardless of ownership.

Considering the very likely situation that the new interconnection is not used, remaining as a security of supply reserve, then the investment is recovered as follows:

- Moldovagaz will apply the unified gas transmission tariff, calculated as to cover all network costs, including those of the new interconnection (both CAPEX and OPEX);
- ANRE will calculate quarterly the value of the difference between the revenue obtained by Moldovagaz applying the unified gas transmission tariff and the revenues needed by Moldovagaz to cover its CAPEX and OPEX costs;
- The calculated difference is transferred by the Moldovagaz to the Vestmoldtransgaz or to the State Budget in order to pay back the loans for financing the interconnection.

Authors' calculations show that according to the current gas transmission tariff of Moldovagaz of 1.53 euro/1000 cm (32.76 lei/1000 cm) and the low-pressure end-user price of 287 euro/1000 cm (6138 lei/1000 cm):

- the increase in the transmission tariff will be 246% and will rise to 5.3 euro/1000 cm;
- the increase in the end-user tariff will be 1.3% and will rise to 290.77 euro/1000 cm.

In these calculations the authors assumed that:

- the total investment is 103 million euro (value from the feasibility study plus extra works envisaged by Moldavian authorities);
- 10 million euro will be received as a grant from the EU;
- the recovery period of the loans will be 25 years;
- the interest rate will be 1.5%.

Sensitivity calculations were also made, considering the use of the new interconnection in covering 0%, 10%, 20%, 50% and 75% of Moldova's current gas consumption. The solution proved to be robust and functional for different gas import patterns.

The solution was proposed by the European Commission DG Energy and Energy Community Secretariat and was considered viable and fully compatible with EU legislation.

Advantages of the proposed solution:

- stability and predictability of the unified gas transmission tariff;
- fairness and transparency for network users and finally for consumers, having to pay the same transmission tariff regardless of the origin of imports;
- full investment cost recovery regardless of the actual use of the newly built infrastructure;
- the solution is more robust and adaptive than the solution involving a security of supply fund and a levy;
- it is fully compatible with the acquis communitaire.

6. Conclusions and Relevant Implications

One of the major vulnerabilities of the Republic of Moldova is its dependence on electricity and gas imports (considering electricity provided by Cuciurgan power plant also an "import").

Moldova's legislation was recently aligned to the provisions of the EU Third Energy Package, creating the legal and regulatory environment needed for the establishment of electricity and gas wholesale and retail markets based on competition. Based on the legislation, these markets will be fully compatible with the acquis communitaire and could be integrated into the EU energy internal market.

The gas and electricity transmission networks have currently weak interconnections with EU networks. New interconnections are envisaged both for gas and for electricity, in order to properly link Moldavian transmission networks to Romanian ones, the only way to interconnect them with EU networks. By this, three goals will be achieved:

- an increase in the level of security of energy supply by diversifying the suppliers and supply routes;
- a level of competition in the wholesale gas and electricity markets able to establish prices at the lowest possible values;
- the possibility to couple and further integrate Moldova's gas and electricity markets into the EU internal energy market.

The new interconnection infrastructure will allow a direct competition in the Republic of Moldova between East and West providers of electricity and gas.

The new interconnections and associated infrastructure are significant investments, which can be built in two to three years after the investment decision is made. Financing could be through loans from the EBRD, EIB, World Bank or through private investments.

A solution to ensure viable investments in commercially non-viable new interconnections for gas was proposed and analyzed by the authors. The solution is based on a unified gas transmission tariff and is fully compatible with the community acquis.

References

1. "Continental Europe Operation Handbook", European Network of Transmission System Operators for Electricity, https://www.entsoe.eu/publications/system-operations-reports/operation-handbook/Pages/default.aspx.
2. "LitPol Link capacity tests successful", November 26, 2015, LiTpol Link project, http://www.litpol-link.com/news/litpol-link-capacity-tests-successful-sM721T.
3. Government Decision No. 102/05.02.2013 on approving the Energy Strategy till 2030.
4. Feasibility Study of the Ungheni–Chisinau gas pipeline elaborated by Fichtner GmbH in 2015.
5. Feasibility Study of the Isaccea–Vulcanesti–Chisinau asynchronous electricity interconnection, elaborated by ISPE 2016.
6. Feasibility Study on Synchronous Interconnection of Ukrainian and Moldovan Power Systems to ENTSO-E Continental Europe Power System.
7. Directive 2009/73/EC of the European Parliament and of the Council of 13 July 2009 concerning common rules for the internal market in natural gas and repealing Directive 2003/55/EC.
8. Directive 2009/72/EC of the European Parliament and of the Council of 13 July 2009 concerning common rules for the internal market in electricity and repealing Directive 2003/54/EC.

Mirjana RADOVIĆ

Institute of Economic Sciences, Belgarde, Serbia,
e-mial: mirjana.radovic@ien.bg.ac.rs

Zvonko BRNJAS

Institute of Economic Sciences, Belgrade, Serbia

Vukica VULIĆEVIĆ

Belgrade Banking Academy, Belgrade, Serbia

Elaboration of the Importance of Fast-Growing Companies Gazelles – New Evidence from Serbia

Abstract: In this paper, attention is focused on the specific segment of small and medium-sized firms, characterized by rapid and stable growth, their ability to quickly adapt to changing market conditions and in the long term to operate at the high-performance level. These companies are today known as "Gazelles", a term that was coined by an American author, David Birch (Birch D. L., The Job Generation Process, M.I.T. Program on Neighborhood and Regional Change, 1979). The paper deals with issues such as definitions and basic characteristics of these companies, the key factors of their business, as well as their level of development in the European Union and the Republic of Serbia. The variety of research methods has been used in accordance with the specifics and the complexity of the case analysis, relying on the relevant domestic and international literature and internet sources. The results of the research clearly show that, with consistent support from economic policy, Gazelles can make an important contribution to solving the comprehensive socio-economic crisis we are facing in today's modern societies.

Keywords: Growth, Small and Medium Enterprises (SMEs), Gazelles, Business Performance, Innovations

1. Introduction

Due to numerous economic and social advantages, such as economic and technological flexibility, job creation and employment, the SME sector is an important support for development in every national economy. They are the dominant form of business organization, accounting for 95% to 99% of total businesses in national economies, employing between 60% and 70% of the total working population in some countries. The main topic of this paper is a special group of SMEs, i.e. a group of fast-growing companies called gazelles. These enterprises attract a lot of attention owing to their above-average growth rate, which makes them important providers of jobes. They have attracted so much attention because they contribute to social well-being by creating new businesses and jobs. They are said to provide a high return on investment, promote regional development, and contribute to the managers' and employees' satisfaction. For these reasons, in the recent years, many governments have aimed to increase the number of gazelles.

2. Definition of Fast-Growing Companies: Gazelles

By studying the prosperity of Silicon Valley in 1980s, David Birch concluded that only three percent of companies would survive and continue to grow and he named them dynamic companies, gazelles. The term gazelle is used to describe companies that show high rates over a specific time course. Studies show that the share of these companies, compared with other companies or businesses that have been created in the current year is very small in any economy, the figures varying between 2% and 15% depending on the study.

David Birch also set the principal elements to be used in applying the gazelle definition, these are: selected growth indicators, measurement method, time period of measurement, as well as other additional criteria. Growth is conditioned by relative or absolute growth as well as a mix of the two. The default time for the company analysis is usually three years.

The most commonly used definition of a gazelle in the world literature is that these enterprises are those whose sales increase by at least 20% per year over the course of three consecutive years.

The most important indicators of a company's growth are:

- Type 1: Absolute growth AR_{t1t2}=aps(x_{t1}-x_{t2}) that measures sales growth and employment growth as a difference between the first year of proportion/size, and last year the share/size
- Type 2: Relative growth $RR_{t1t2}=(x_{t2}/x_{t1})-1$, which measures turnover growth or employment growth as a division between first-year share/size, and last year the share/size
- Type 3: Birch Index $BI_{t1t2}=|AR_{t1t2}|*RR_{t1t2,}$ which calculates the turnover growth and employment growth as a combination and multiplication of the absolute and relative growth.

The OECD (2007) definition is that the fast-growing enterprises are those that generate the average annual growth rate of over 20% per year over a period of three years with at least ten employees in the initial year of the period, whereas gazelles are a group of fast-growing companies with up to five years of existence.

Between 1994 and 2011, three meta-studies and 22 empirical studies were implemented as regards to this topic. The aforementioned empirical studies were based on individual company data collected in the late 1990s and mid 2000s in the USA,

Canada, Germany, Finland, Spain, Great Britain and the Netherlands. Those studies indicated that gazelle companies are not numerous, but with a share of 2% to 5% of the total number of companies, their contribution to the creation of new jobs is proportionally bigger.

Analyzing a few empirical studies on the fast-growing SMEs, members of the PRO INNO team came up with several common characteristics, such as: gazelles have decentralized, participatory organizations and organizations that are willing to adapt to change. Their growth is closely linked to the company's innovation including continuous changes in every aspect of the business. They are distinctively market-oriented firms, connecting technology and markets and adapting their products to respond to customer needs. Subject firms stimulate team work among all employees through daily communications, introducing modern decision-making techniques, developing skills and so on.

3. Characteristics of Gazelles as Economic Development Drivers

There are key strategies that seem to help businesses to become gazelles and as such survive in the market. Successful gazelles are characterized as enterprises with a clear strategy of differentiation, fostering their customers and cleverly using the resources available in their environment, especially those that allow them to reduce the risk and uncertainty, as well as boost knowledge creation and innovation.

3.1. Correlation Between Gazelles and Growth

Fast growth is possible in two situations: formation of the new company created to use innovations of a technological-marketing nature in ceasing market opportunities not identified by the competition, and/or an existing company is introducing new strategies, procedures, conduct and similar. Subject changes, if radical, may contribute to strong company growth. An important element of strategy implementation is the ability of the company to learn from the growth in a certain period and then to apply the lessons learned in the next period. On the other hand, the biggest limitation or barrier to growth, in most cases, is the use of inadequate strategy mix.

Growth nature in these companies is not always continuous and these companies may be subject to nonlinear forms of growth, with frequent booms and plunges, and in spite of all of that they continue to grow in the long term. Understanding what the driver of fast SME growth is is crucial both for managers striving to become or remain competitive, and for the governments responsible for national economies and the creation of new jobs.

3.2. Correlation Between Gazelles and Innovation

The dynamic organizational capabilities of an enterprise are based on the ability to connect internal power to external needs. Gazelles are characterized by the fact that innovations are not only introduced in the production domain, but practically in all domains of operations, including managerial, organizational and technical innovations within the company. Fast-growing companies succeeding with the help of innovative approaches in marketing, organization and/or distribution may be found in all spheres of business. Gazelle innovation represents a change of approach to resource management and the introduction of new organizational structures rather than the creation new technologies or products in general.

3.3. Characteristics of Gazelles in Terms of Size and Age

It is estimated that about 70.5% of gazelles are small-sized businesses, while medium-sized enterprises constitute about 27.5% of all gazelles in the EU. The biggest number of gazelles is certainly among small and young firms. The age of gazelles is an interesting issue. The baseline assumption of David Birch is that fast growing firms are by default young companies. Research conducted in the USA in 2008 found that, however, the average age of fast growing companies is as old as 25 years (Acs Z. J. et al., 2008). On average, the largest number of gazelle founders have significant experience of many years in their profession, in a particular area and branch. One of the most important growth patterns of a company is just the professional experience of the founders and employees.

3.4. Strategic Aspects of Gazelle Operations

Successful gazelles are characterized by the application of clear differentiation strategies, customer care and smart use of available resources in the environment. Subject companies are successful due to their close contact with the customers, listening to identify customer needs and requirements, constant product improvement and, thus, ensuring their superior position compared to their relevant competition. Focus on quality, clients and distribution are by far the most important growth drivers and in that context of marketing it plays key role. The dynamic organizational capacities of the company are based on its ability to connect internal forces with external needs. A crucial factor safeguarding survival of SMEs, and especially gazelles, on the highly competitive market is human resources management, including style, personnel, skills and common values. Style is related to grouping staff by similarities in thinking and conduct, strengthening organizational culture and involving employees in decision-making processes; staff is related to special individuals, engaged. Skills are related to the fact that employees possess special skills required for company strategy implementation.

4. Gazelle Firms in the European Union

Research proved that most important trends of the European economy are connected with fast-growing companies, particularly gazelles. For example, compared to the average, gazelles provide more significant contributions to sales growth than to the employment growth in the total economy; then, young production firms generate more contributions to sales growth and less to employment growth, while service companies generate more significant contributions in both domains, sales growth and employment growth.

4.1. Overall Importance of SMEs and Gazelles for the Economies of EU Countries

Chart 1 shows EU Countries with both the three highest and three lowest numbers of gazelles and fast-growing companies in 2010, according to Eurostat.eu official statistics. Gazelles were characterized as companies of no more than five years of existence with an average annual growth rate above 20% in the last three years. Fast-growing companies are companies with an average annual growth rate of 20% in a three year period.

Fig. 1: The Number of Gazelles in selected EU countries

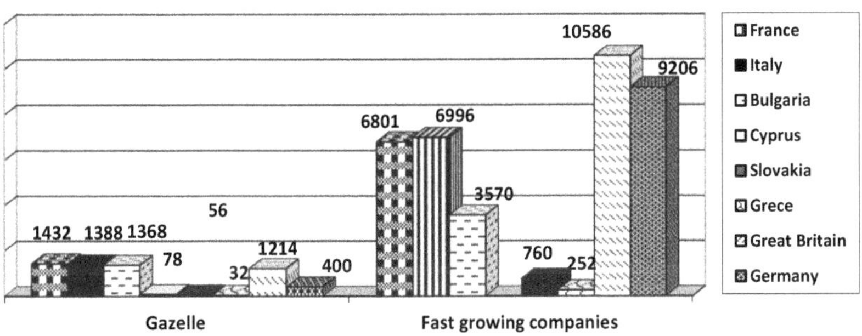

Source: *Eurostat.eu*

4.2. Contribution of Gazelles and Fast-Growing Companies to the EU economies

The share of gazelle firms by country is shown in the study conducted by the European consortium *INNOVA Sectorial Innovation Watch* in January 2011 (Mitusch & Schimke 2011). Research included analysis of gazelle firms share by country within two specific samples: share of 10% and 5% of fast-growing companies. Research was based on the database of *CIS IV*[1]. Chart 2 shows five of the highest and two of the lowest shares of gazelles with both 10% and 5%.

1 *CIS (Community Innovation Surveys)* are statistical researches of innovations in companies in the science and technology segment of the EU. Producing CIS data is on a voluntary basis for all member countries. *CIS IV* was implemented on the basis of 2002–2004 reference period in the following countries: Belgium, Bulgaria, the Czech

Fig. 2: The Share of Gazelles in selected EU Iceland

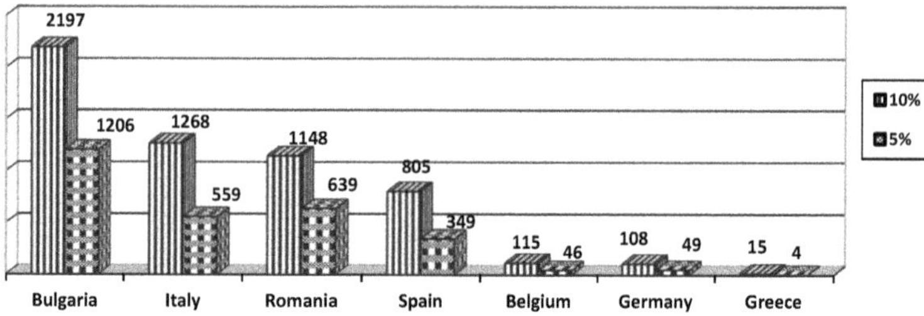

4.3. The share of Gazelles in Individual Sectors of EU Countries

The aforementioned study (Mitusch & Schimke 2011) showed representation of gazelles by industries and sectors in the EU. Research identified gazelle shares by sectors and industries within 5% and 10% groups of all growing companies in the EU within NACE[2]. Chart 3 shows the highest and lowest gazelle shares by sector.

Fig. 3: The Share of Gazelles in selected EU countries by Sector

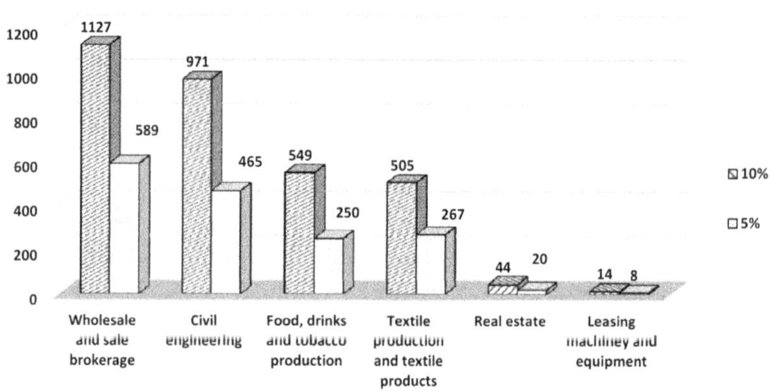

Republic, Denmark, Germany, Estonia, Greece, Spain, Finland, France, Hungary, Italy, Lithuania, Latvia, Portugal, Romania, Slovenia, Sweden, Slovakia, Norway and Island.

2 NACE (European Classification of Economic Activities) is a statistical classification of economic activities in the European Community and a subject of EU legislation.

5. Evidence of Gazelle Performance in the Republic of Serbia

In the most recent period for which data is readily available (2013) and, by analogy in the subsequent period, the SME sector has remained an increasingly important sector of the Serbian economy, with an increasing share of the economic structure and contribution to GDP.

However, the Republic of Serbia's ranking is relatively low compared to EU countries in terms of potential entrepreneurship and innovations. Measured by the global entrepreneurship development index or GEDI[3], which is used as an indicator of the quality of entrepreneurship and innovations that have been influenced by individual and institutional factors, in 2014 Serbia ranked 68 out of 130 countries, which is below most of the countries in the region.

It is argued that Serbian gazelles recorded a dynamic growth of employment and total revenues, primarily thanks to their investments in technical and technological resources and application of the cutting-edge methods and standards taken from successful countries; but also thanks to continuous professional education of employees, continuing improvements of customer relations, product and/or service quality and aspiration towards winning over new positions in the market.

The advantage of these enterprises is primarily in what is considered a fast revenue growth and market share usually accompanied by an increase in company value. Their greatest weaknesses, on the other hand, are mainly associated with the fact that they have not achieved the necessary economies of scale and therefore occasionally enter the zone where they generate losses. In addition, they are usually faced with constraints related to financing their business activities, and have difficulty reconciling growth and profitability. The biggest obstacle in obtaining funds for these enterprises is a brief period of existence, which is why they do not have sufficient credibility among investors, and often record a high level of indebtedness, which prevents further borrowing.

Although, judging strictly from the standpoint of European standards of innovations, economic power and competitiveness, it is still early to talk about dynamic entrepreneurship in Serbia—in its last official research the Republic Institute for Development for the period 2003–2007 identified 532 dynamic enterprises out of which 53 firms can be classified as the most dynamic ones, as gazelles (The Ministry of Economy and Regional Development; the Republic Institute for Development; the National Agency for Regional Development, 2008). In this research, gazelles were identified as small and medium-sized enterprises who in 2003 were employing up to 20 people and no more than 250; whose number of employees and total revenues in 2007 increased by 30% compared to 2003; whose business was continuously solid and who were not part of a larger holding companies.

3 Global Entrepreneurship Development Index (http://thegedi.org/research/gedi-index/).

In 2007, which is the last official research, gazelles in Serbia made up 0.1% of the total number of enterprises and 1.0% of the total number of employees; they managed 0.3% of the equity, generated 1.0% in total revenues and 1.3% in total gain. In the years that followed through 2013, the significance and growth of these companies was doubled or tripled in all major indicators, which will be presented herein after.

Comparative key findings in our study reflecting the period 2007–2013 are the following:

- In 2007 in Serbia there were 532 dynamic enterprises, with 43,311 employees, out of which 53 were gazelles, while in 2013 1,103 dynamic enterprises included 156 gazelles, which means that their significance has doubled.
- Dynamic enterprises accounted for only 0.6% of the total number of enterprises in 2007, and 1.2% in 2013 and they actually created 10,000 new jobs from 2009 to 2013.
- These companies have generated 110.5% of the growth of business revenues of the economy as a whole from 2009 to 2013, and actually covered 10.5% of the losses of the rest of the economy. These companies accounted for one third of all gross profit growth.
- In the rated period of 2009–2013, the net profit of these companies tripled.
- These companies actually created 10,000 new jobs from 2009 to 2013, which is 2% of the total labor force while at the same time employment in the rest of the economy dropped by 78,000.

In the rated period of 2009–2013, the sectoral structure shows that the dynamic enterprise concentrated in the trade sectors (336 companies or 30%) and then in the manufacturing sector (201 companies, i.e. 18.2%). Negative trends in the manufacturing sector are observed through all main indicators: reduced participation in number of employees, operating revenues and in the newly created value.

In the observation period (2009–2013), gazelles, dynamic small and medium-sized companies demonstrated resilience to crisis blows and managed to overcome the crisis fast to achieve outstanding performance.

Obviously, some of the conditions for the operation, strengthening and growth of SMEs in Serbia have been improved in recent years, which is partly attributable to the policies adopted by the government and the improved framework of support provided through business support organizations, including the network of Regional Development Agencies. The 2013 SME Report for Serbia clearly states that what is required is establishing a rounded incentive system and solving key problems of enterprises coupled with specific measures as part of the process of building a system to encourage the development of dynamic enterprises and gazelles. However, since 2013, most of the support organizations and the government unfortunately have not been directly targeting the development and growth of gazelles in the Republic of Serbia.

Considering the aforementioned, one may conclude that gazelle firms in Serbia have very much the same general characteristics as the one identified in other world economies, including the most developed. There are few of them (no more than small percentages of the total number of companies), but they generate outstanding contributions in terms of employment, growth and total business results of the national economies and should therefore receive much more attention from SME policy institutions.

Conclusions and Recommendations

Within the total SME corpus, so-called gazelles, dynamic small and medium-sized companies, play a special role, and many authors believe that they are the biggest development potential of national economies. The present paper elaborated the issue of the definition of this specific group of companies; the gazelle phenomenon was explained, as well as their specific features and characteristics that make them so unique. The most important results of gazelle-related researches conducted in the USA, European Union and, in the final part, in Serbia, were presented.

The principal characteristics of gazelles are innovativeness, both in production and process domains, as well as management practices. Their management and organizational flexibility facilitates faster and streamlined adaptation to changes, providing strong market orientation, focus on quality, clients and distribution. Strong links with consumers and maximum utilization of employees indicate that successful strategic management of the company leads to constant and stable growth, both in large, small and medium enterprises, including gazelles.

Because of this the set of incentive measures for supporting gazelles need to be established, ranging from a friendly environment in general to those specifically supporting the establishment and sustainable development of dynamic and gazelle firms. Formulating and consistently implementing the aforementioned measures of development and support to dynamic and especially gazelle companies would generate significant contributions to a more dynamic national economy as a whole and better performance, thus, creating the conditions required to find solutions for numerous social problems.

References

1. Acs, Z. J., Parsons W., Tracy S. (2008). High-Impact Firms: Gazelles Revisited, Corporate Research Board, LLC, Washington.
2. Ahmad, N. & Petersen D. R. (2007). High-Growth Enterprises and Gazelles – Preliminary and Summary Sensitivity Analysis, OECD-FORA, Paris.
3. David, L. Birch, The Job Generation Process, M.I.T. Program on Neighborhood and Regional Change (1979).
4. Birch, D. (1981). Who creates Jobs?, Public Interest 65.
5. Birch, D. L., Haggerty, Parsons, A. W. (1998). Who's creating jobs?, Cambridge, MA: Cognetics.
6. Birch, D. L., Medoff, J. (1994). Gazelles In L. C. Solmon & A. R. Levenson (Eds.), Labor markets, employment policy and job creation, Boulder, CO: Westview.

7. Boljević, A. (2007). Strategijsko planiranje kao odlučivanje o pravcima razvoja preduzeća, Univerzitet u Novom Sadu, Ekonomski fakultet, Subotica.
8. Brinkley I. (2007), Knowledge economy and enterprise – A knowledge economy working paper, The Work Foundation, 1 November, www.theworkfoundation.com.
9. Brnjas, Z. (2000). Strategijski menadžment, Privredni pregled, Beograd.
10. Draker, F. P. (2006). Moj pogled na menadžment, Adižes, Novi Sad.
11. Dess, G. G., Lumpkin, G. T., Eisner, A. B. (2007). Strategijski menadžment, teorija i slučajevi, treće izdanje, Data Status, Beograd.
12. Dautzenberg K., Ehrlinspiel M., Gude H., Käser J., Schultz P. T., Tenorth J. at al., (2012). Study on Fast Growing Young Companies (Gazelles), Bundesministerium für Wirtschaft und Technologie.
13. Draker, F. P. (2006). Draker iz dana u dan, Adižes, Novi Sad.
14. Đorđević, D., Anđić, Ž., Mala i srednja preduzeća i proces upravljanja, www.indmanager.edu.rs.
15. OECD (2014). Entrepreneurship at a Glance 2014, OECD Publishing, Paris.
16. Europe's 500 je Evropska organizacija i mrežna platforma za rastuće kompanije i njihove preduzetnike (pogledati: http://www.europes500.eu/).
17. Gazelle companies – characteristics and development patterns Appendix 2 – Entrepreneurship and Innovations, www.tillvaxtanalysis.se.
18. Henrekson, M., Johansson, D., Gazelles as Job Creators – A survey and interpretation of the evidence, Research Institute of Industrial Economics, www.ifn.se.
19. High-growth enterprises, What governments can do to make a difference, (2010), OECD studies on SMEs an entrepreneurship, www.oecd.org.
20. Inić, P. B. (2006). Strategic management, Branimir Inić, Beograd.
21. Jakopin, E. (2013). Dynamic Entrepreneurship – the engine of economic growth and development in Serbia, www.scindeks-clanci.ceon.rs.
22. Jancyak, S., Bares, F., High growth SMEs: The evolution of the Gazelles and samo evidence from the field, www.expertise.hec.ca.
23. Kontić, J. (2010). Strategije rasta preduzeća, Zadužbina Andrejević, Beograd.
24. López-Garcia, P., Puente S. (2009). What makes a high-growth firm? A profit analysis using Spanish firm-level data, Doocumentos de Trabajo N.°0920, Banco De España.
25. Nacionalna agencija za regionalni razvoj u 2013. godini, www.narr.gov.rs.
26. Ministarstvo ekomomije i regionalnog razvoja, Republički zavod za razvoj, Nacionalna agencija za regionalni razvoj, Izveštaj o malim i srednjim preduzećima i preduzetništvu za 2009. godinu, www.narr.gov.rs.
27. Ministarstvo ekomomije i regionalnog razvoja, Republički zavod za razvoj, Nacionalna agencija za regionalni razvoj, Izveštaj o malim i srednjim preduzećima i preduzetništvu za 2013. godinu, www.narr.gov.rs.
28. Mitusch K. & Schimke A. (2011), Gazelles – High-Growth Companies, Consortium Europe INNOVA Sectoral Innovation Watch.
29. Mihailović, B. (2007). Formulisanje strategije preduzeća, monografija, Institut za ekonomiku poljoprivrede, Beograd.

30. Moreno A. M., Casillas J. C. (2000). High-growth enterprises (Gazelles):A conceptual framework, http://www.researchgate.net/publication/.
31. Pavlović, N., Tomić, D. (2007). Upravljanje rastom i razvojem preduzeća, Alfa-Graf NS, Novi Sad.
32. Penezić, Ć. N. (2010). Preduzetništvo, savremeni pristup, Akademska knjiga, Novi Sad.
33. http://www.policycafe.rs/Anketa2015/BEP%20Survey%202015%20Executive%20Summary%20-serbian.pdf.
34. Preduzeća sa tendencijom brzog rasta traže informacione sisteme, www.vibilia.rs.
35. Strategija razvoja konkurentnih i inovativnih MSP 2008–2013, www.klasterpolux.rs.
36. Study of Fast Growing Young Companies (Gazelles) – Summary, www.bmwi.de.
37. Vaidyanathan, N., How to spot a Gazelle (with binoculars)!, www.smbconnect.in.
38. Vemić, M. (2013), Evaluation of knowledge-based high-growth enterprises in Serbia's economic development, Online Journal of Applied Knowledge Management, Volume 1, Issue 2, 2013, www.iiakim.org.
39. Vujadinović, M. (2011). Država pomaže "gazelama", Ekonometar, 01.07.2011., str. 26.
40. Popescu, Gh.H. (2016). The Role of Multinational Corporations in Global Environmental Politics, Economics, Management, and Financial Markets 11(3):72–78.
41. Nica, E., Ioan, H. (2016). The State-led System of Global Environmental Governance, Economics, Management, and Financial Markets 11(3):79–85.
42. Shaefer, H.L., Pinghui, W., Kathryn, E. (2017). Can Poverty in America Be Compared to Conditions in the World's Poorest Countries? American Journal of Medical Research 4(1):84–92.
43. Popescu, Gh. H., Florin, C.C., Teodora, I.B. (2016). Environmental Consequences of Liberalized and Expanding Global Trade, Journal of Self-Governance and Management Economics 4(3):66–72.
44. Nica, E., Cristina, M., Ana-Madalina, P. (2016). Competition in the Worldwide Workplace: Economic Globalization and Labor Rights, Journal of Self-Governance and Management Economics 4(3):73–79.
45. Nica, E., (2016). The Effect of Perceived Organizational Support on Organizational Commitment and Employee Performance, Journal of Self-Governance and Management Economics 4(4):34–40.
46. Popescu, Gh. H., Mihaela, C., Oana, M.S. (2016). The Role of Human Capital in the Knowledge-networked Economy, Psychosociological Issues in Human Resource Management 4(1):168–174.
47. Nica, E. (2016). Employee Voluntary Turnover as a Negative Indicator of Organizational Effectiveness, Psychosociological Issues in Human Resource Management 4(2):220–226.

48. Machan, T.R. (2016). Commerce and Its Normative Dimensions, Psychosociological Issues in Human Resource Management 4(1):7–40.
49. http://cordis.europa.eu/innovation/en/policy/pro-inno.htm.
50. www.ebart.rs.
51. http://epp. eurostat.ec.europa.eu/.

Irina ANGHEL

Institute of National Economy, Romanian Academy,
irina_c_anghel@yahoo.com

Steliana SANDU

Institute of National Economy, Romanian Academy,
sandu.steliana55@yahoo.com

The Romanian ICT Sector in the European Context

Abstract: The ICTs stand at the centre of the flagship initiative "The Digital Agenda for Europe", while the Digital Single Market Strategy is among the top ten political priorities for the EU. There are, also, other EU initiatives designed to address the challenge of ICT skills shortages on the European labour market, mobilizing all important stakeholders in the education and business sectors to cooperate to ensure the stock of digital talent and the digital skills necessary for the knowledge economy and information society. Romania has assumed targets regarding ICT, in line with the EU agenda, through the National Strategy on Digital Agenda for Romania. Our paper aims to look into the national capacity to develop its ICT potential in order to reach its targets, to become relevant in the highly virtualized global economy, and to provide viable and effective solutions to the current and future societal demands. To this end, based on international reports and Eurostat data analysis, we will assess the national ICT readiness and potential, its relevance and importance, as well as the ICT skills in the workforce and the population. We would also draw main areas of intervention for improving the Romanian landscape, which seems rather bleak against the EU background.

Keywords: ICTs, digital skills, e-business, business digitisation, information society, knowledge based economy

1. Introduction

The technologies for data storing, processing and retrieving (IT) and the technologies relying on electronic systems to facilitate communication (CT) represent the basic infrastructure for the development of the information society and, even more, of the knowledge-based economy. The high and growing rate of employment in ICT (Eurostat, 2017), the increasing contribution of the ICT sector to GDP, the soaring share of e-commerce in total global sales and of the enterprises recruiting and employing ICT personnel are only a few arguments for the fact that the openness and readiness of the private sector as well as public administration to integrate ICT in all their activities are critical to their relevance, efficacy and long-term viability. Moreover, it becomes obvious that, in the medium and long run, the competitiveness of a whole country's economy, as well as its attractiveness for international investors—within the region and on the global market—depends greatly on the availability of well-trained, ICT literate, human capital. Besides the economic perspective, the advancement in research and innovation regarding other pressing societal challenges and demands—in the health sector, energy, environment protection, social inclusion, urban development, agriculture etc.—relies, to a certain extent, on the ICT infrastructure and on the humans able to harness it to its full potential.

Therefore, at regional and national levels, the development of the ICT sector, the stimulation of the private sector to invest in training their employees to utilize ICT and to become visible in the virtual space, together with enlarging the access and use of broadband internet for the benefit of individuals and companies, setting the stage for, and promoting e-government, as well as ensuring a basic ICT literacy for pupils and young people through school curricula have become priorities on the policy makers' agendas.

At the EU level, the Europe 2020 flagship initiative, "The Digital Agenda for Europe" (EC, 2010), as well as the Digital Single Market Strategy (EC, 2015) focus on facilitating the social, economic and industrial full capitalization on the digital economy towards economic growth and social development. In Romania, the National Strategy for the Digital Agenda (MSI, 2014), whose operationalization, involving an over 2.4 bl. euro investment, is expected to generate, by 2020, a 13% growth in GDP, an 11% increase in jobs and a 12% cut in public costs, facilitates the integration of ICT in public administration, in education, culture and health, and in business and commerce. It also targets enlarging coverage and access to broadband and digital infrastructure services, which is key to the successful strategy implementation. Stimulating the private investment in RDI in the ICT sector is, also, a major strategic objective, that would augment the ICT sector's added value. Among the measurable intended outcomes, by 2020, of all citizens, 35% should use e-government, 60% the internet on a regular basis and 30% should buy online. The broadband networks should reach at least 80% coverage.

2. Literature review on ICT and its relevance to economic and social development

Experts and scientists have turned to ICT to evaluate and substantiate its role as an important vector for change, for social development, and economic growth (Baller et al., 2016; Dutta et al., 2015; EC, 2015; Niebel, 2014; Farhadi et al., 2012; WB, 2012 etc.). It has been confirmed that ICTs improve access to goods and services, enhance inclusion and connectivity, help reduce poverty, facilitate entrepreneurship and employment, and improve the interaction and interface between citizens and public institutions. But probably the most significant direct effect of ICT is on productivity and economic growth. Globalization, trade expansion, international capital flows have been enabled by, and, also, have potentiated, the development of ICTs.

At company level, incorporating ICTs into as many dimensions as possible may boost management effectiveness, internal communication, product diversification, promotion and development, closeness to the market and individual clients, market expansion, market targeting, productivity and cost efficiency. Company and sectoral level studies confirmed this relationship (O'Mahony and Vecchi, 2005)

Yet, the magnitude of the positive impact of ICTs on productivity and economic development varies from company to company, from sector to sector and from country to country, depending on the general economic development level which renders a certain absorptive capacity. The significant positive productivity impact of ICT in developed countries has been confirmed in numerous empirical studies (Cardona et al., 2013; Dahl et al., 2011; Dimelis and Papioannou, 2010; O'Mahony and Vechhi, 2005; Inklaar et al., 2005; Stiroh, 2005 etc), while other studies investigated and confirmed the bidirectional causality between economic growth and ICT investment (Seo et al., 2009).

Still, the impact of ICT capital accumulation in developing countries is rather dim (Niebel, 2014; Cardona et al., 2013; Van Reenen et al., 2010; Draca et al., 2007 etc.) There are studies indicating no significant impact of ICT penetration (Jacobsen, 2003) while others insist on conditional positive effect. On one hand, the relationship between ICT investment and economic growth is dependent on the absorptive capacity of the business sector[1], determined itself by the availability of appropriate human capital and a corresponding level of private R&D expenditures. The catalyst function of the absorptive capacity for ICTs explains why, in many developing countries, the impact of ICT investment on productivity is considerably inferior to that of the developed countries (Niebel 2014; Lee et al., 2005).

On the other hand, if optimally absorbed and capitalized on, through potential spill overs and network effects, as well as lower transaction costs and accelerated knowledge creation processes, ICTs allow for "leapfrog" productivity growth[2] (Steinmueller, 2001), and thus, a higher impact than in developed countries (Stiroh 2002, Pilat, 2004, Seo and Lee, 2006). Nevertheless, these gains are again conditioned by the absorptive capacity of the country's industries, as well as by similar levels or similar types of applied ICTs across the industry or sector (Draca et al., 2007).

Other authors argue for statistically non-significant differences in the elasticities of ICT to GDP growth between countries of various economic development levels (Niebel, 2014), questioning the leapfrog effect. Yet, the positive significant effect is still confirmed in the above-mentioned study, for all three sub-groups of countries

---

1 The absorptive capacity for ICTs has been defined as the effort and ability of employees—management and workers—to appropriate and apply new technology (Kneller, 2005).

2 Companies and countries investing in ICT may by-pass long-term processes of human capital accumulation and fixed investment to narrow the gaps with competitors of the more developed economies (Steinmueller, 2001).

selected for the econometric analysis (developed, emerging and developing, a total of 59 countries).

There are also studies that assess the impact of ICTs' use on economic growth and find a positive correlation, whose intensity depends on the income level (Farhadi et al., 2012, Gruber et al., 2010; Lam and Shiu, 2010)

The Romanian industrial and business sectors seem to be disposing of well-trained human resources, and applying relatively homogenous ICTs within sectors. While breeding one of the largest and fastest expanding IT markets among the newest EU member states, the Romanian economy had a strong and developing ICT industry as well as a dynamic e-business sector, even before becoming an EU member state (Mazurencu et al., 2006) Yet, the degree of exploiting the advantages of available ICTs to the benefit of productivity growth and competitiveness is still unclear.

3. Methodology

Our analysis of the integration of ICTs in the Romanian economic and social landscape relied upon the latest available Eurostat data, the Global Competitiveness Report (WEF, 2015), the DESI (Digital Economy and Society Index) (EC, 2017) and Network Readiness Index (Dutta et al., 2015). The systemic picture presented below is the result of a qualitative analysis that synthesizes our research results.

The Global Competitiveness Report, published yearly by the World Economic Forum, designed a synthetic indicator for the *Technological Readiness* dimension, which assesses the ability of an economy to adopt technologies for high productivity growth, to capitalize upon the ICTs in the current activities and production processes of companies and sectors, thus contributing to higher efficiency and innovation performance.

The World Economic Forum also calculates and provides the Network Readiness Index in their Global IT Report (Baller et al. eds, 2016), designed to measure the capacity of countries to leverage ICTs for higher economic competitiveness and general well-being. It is made up of a total of 53 indicators, grouped into ten pillars and four main categories regarding (a) Environment, (b) Readiness, (c) Usage and (d) Impact. The Environment subindex assesses the quality of the political, legislative, business and innovation context from an ICT development point of view, while the infrastructure for, affordability of, and skills for ICTs are captured in the Readiness dimension. The extent to which people, businesses and public institutions use ICTs is measured by the Usage subindex which, together with the two previously mentioned categories represent the Drivers for ICT development. The Impact subindex determines the social and economic effects associated with ICTs: such as access to education, financial services and healthcare, government efficiency etc, and the propensity to innovation mediated by the ICTs as a social impact and the shift towards knowledge-intensive activities as an economic impact.

In order to monitor the EU member states' progress towards the Digital Agenda strategic targets, the European Community experts calculate and release the Digital

Economy and Society Index (DESI). This composite indicator focuses on five dimensions:

(1) *Connectivity*, expressed in the rate of fixed, mobile broadband take-up, the broadband internet speed and prices;
(2) *Human Capital*, which refers to both basic skills and internet use, and to more advanced skills and the availability of specialists for development;
(3) *Use of Internet*, for communication, getting information and for transactions among the citizens;
(4) *Integration of Digital Economy* in business and commerce
(5) *Digital Public Services*; measuring the amplitude of e-government

The Eurostat database provided the newest data regarding the share of the ICT sector in GDP, the availability of basic and advanced skills in ICT within the workforce and the general population, the intensity of ICT employment and the availability of qualified human capital for ICT.

Based on the various indicators and reports mentioned above, and especially their content relevance from an economic perspective, we will focus on the Human Capital and Integration of Digital Economy dimensions in Romania in comparison with other EU countries.

4. The ICTs in Romania

The last available Global Competitiveness Report (2016–2017) released by the World Economic Forum presents Romania as ranking nine positions below the previous year's report (from 53 to 62), while other new EU member states, such as Bulgaria, advanced along the 138 positions. Yet, together with the Macroeconomic Context and Labor Market Efficiency pillars, the Technological Readiness stands out as a dimension of competitiveness that compensated again for other low and very low positioned pillars and ensured Romania the 62nd rank. Its level of Technological Readiness would rank Romania 38th among the 138 countries included in the survey. This may be an argument that Romania performs fairly well in the ICT field and its potential for ICT-driven growth is promising.

Even though considerably below the 2001–2006 levels (4% and 3.5% respectively), the contribution of the ICT sector to the GDP has increased, as compared to 2008 (3.27%), reaching, in 2014, 3.31%, which placed Romania as sixth to last in the EU 28 ranking, before countries like Austria, Italy and Spain. Ninety 94% of the ICT share in GDP comes from the service sector and only 6% from manufacturing.

Yet, other studies, reports and even indicators may render a different perspective.

The Network Readiness Index calculated for 2016 (Baller et al., 2016) revealed a setback for Romania's position in the 139 analyzed countries. After an important leapfrog of twelve positions (from 65 to 73) from the 2014 to the 2015 reports, it slipped down three positions, with a score of 4.1 (out of seven, the best). The pillars where Romania performs best are related to the *Skills* (41st position, score 5.5) and

Infrastructure and digital content (55th position, score 4.6), which further rendered the highest score, in all subindexes, for the *Readiness subindex* (53rd, score 5.1). The *Skills* pillar, while presenting an individual indicator with a very low position and score (*Quality of the education system* – 90th position, score 3.3), has been on an important upward trend. Romania also registered a steady rising trend for the *Political and regulatory environment, Individual* and *Business usage.* Significant downward slopes have been reported for *Government usage* and *Affordability.* The worst-ranking pillar scores concern the *Business and innovation environment* (71), *Affordability* (73), *Government usage* (96), *Economic impacts* (72) and *Social impacts* (79).

We may conclude that the driving factors (the *Readiness* and *Usage* subindexes) in the political and economic *environment* for ICT are better and more favorably assessed than the ICT *impact* on product, service and organizational innovation, on the development of knowledge-intensive activites, on access to basic social services, and on government efficiency. Therefore, Romania is not able to effectively leverage the available strengths and opportunities in ICT in order to get the highest social and economic impact possible.

Regarding some of the specific objectives of the National Strategy on Digital Agenda, the current levels are far below the assumed targets for 2020 (Table 1).

Table 1: Current levels and targets for some strategic ICT objectives

Objective	RO Target (2020)	Current level (2016)
Online buyers	30%	18%
SMEs with online sales	20%	7%
Citizens using e-government	35%	6%

Source: The National Strategy on Digital Agenda and the Romanian EDPR country profile

Each of the last four years' of calculating the DESI values, even though on an upward trend, has placed Romania not only in the cluster of the low performing countries, but, also as the last of the EU-28 countries. While the high subscription rate to fast broadband and to mobile and fixed internet raise the Connectivity index value close to the EU average, ranking Romania 22nd in the EU, all the other dimension indicators, though slightly ascending (except for the *Use of Internet*), are way below the average EU performance.

Romania lags behind the EU regarding fixed and mobile 4G broadband coverage. But progress has been consistent in mobile broadband take up, in enhancing competition in infrastructure, higher regulation certainty. Romania also secured ESIF funding for improving fixed broadband coverage and the infrastructure in less populated areas.

Beside societal benefits like higher social inclusion, integration, social innovation and social development, depending on the prevailing activity type, the *use of internet* may stimulate, to a greater or lesser extent, the economic growth.

Indeed, the outstanding rate of social network users (74% of internet users, positioning Romania eighth in the EU-28 where the average was only 63%), together with the important usage of the internet for entertaining may have a direct economic impact through the opportunities created for promotion and marketing in the industries of general consumption goods and services, for small businesses, as well as for larger ones. Besides, the wide and dynamic social networks proved to be an important virtual economic space for the small and very small entrepreneurial initiatives that may remain in the shadow economy until they either pass the time and market test, or they fade away.

Unfortunately, Romania ranks as last in the EU-28 regarding this socio-economic digital dimension, mainly because of the two most economically relevant indicators: banking and shopping. While the EU average value for the share of individuals resorting to e-banking in total individuals using internet (in the three months prior to the survey) was 59%, the figure for Romania was 8%, 2 percentage points lower than the DESI 2016 value. The percentage of internet users who shopped online remained the same as one year before, at 18%, less than a third of the EU average values.

In order to address the blurry legal framework as well as the lack of trust in e-commerce, the e-Commerce Action Plan has been designed and the retailers with a turnover higher than 10,000 euros/year have become legally compelled to install POS terminals.

The Digital Public Services sub-index measuring especially e-government and, generally, the extent of applying ICTs in public services is an important instrument for increasing public spending efficiency, for smoothing the interaction and communication between the public institutions, on one hand, and contributors and beneficiaries on the other. It may also encourage the entrepreneurial initiative and augment business efficiency. Moreover, the digitization of public institutions' activity may facilitate social innovation, by easily bringing together, on virtual platforms, stakeholders, ideas, and solutions. This dimension ranks Romania the last, as well, even if the progress in some supply side indicators is important. While the share of internet users that have also used e-government services dropped 2 p.p to 6% in 2016 (DESI 2017), way below the EU average which is almost six times the Romanian figures, the scores for pre-filled Forms, for Online Services Completion and for Open Data indicators increased considerably.

We will later look into the dimensions with the most direct and important economic impact, as they regard the availability of human capital to integrate ICT in business, and the capacity of the business sector to absorb and capitalize upon ICTs.

4.1. Digital Skills and Human Capital for ICT

The share of internet users (56%), as well as the level of at least basic digital skills (28%) has improved compared to the last DESI score (52% and 26% respectively); still, Romania ranks last with both indicators. They are relevant in the economic perspective, as they represent, on one hand, the pool of workers, and, on the other, the consumers, with internet access and the minimum ICT abilities necessary for the business sector to apply ICT in their daily activities and to reach their online market target.

Indeed, according to Eurostat database[3], in 2014, 58% of the active labor force had never used a computer nor done any of the assessed computer activities, while the EU-28 average is 20% and the Finland figures are as low as 5%. About the same percentage of all active labor force—a little above a quarter—reported that they consider their computer or internet skills sufficient and insufficient if they were to apply for a job in 2011. More alarming is that the figures for the student segment are even worse, as 13% of the respondent students had never used a computer (3% for the EU average) and 49% of them considered their computer and internet skills not to be sufficient if applying for a job, compared to the 16% registered for the EU-28 average.

These figures confirm that the process of ensuring basic ICT skills throughout the workforce and consumers, necessary for economic digitization in Romania, is difficult and the gap to the more economically developed EU countries is considerable. The risks to the economic competitiveness and growth prospects are obvious.

Regarding the more advanced ICT users, even if the percentage of specialists has increased along the years (reaching 1.9% in 2014 and 2% in 2016), Romania remained on the 27th position; moreover, despite occupying a favorable rank regarding the pool of STEM graduates (the 17th position, with 16 per 1000 individuals 20–29 years old), the indicator value has dropped by one point and Romania slipped down one position. These indicators stand for the core ICT human capital—employable and potential—that allows the companies to apply available technologies for higher productivity, driving economic growth.

According to Eurostat, in 2014 ICT personnel represented only 1.95% of total employment, with Romania ranking third to last in the EU-28 hierarchy, while the highest figures—above 4%—were reported for Sweden and Denmark. Bulgaria and the other ex-communist countries registered levels above 2%, as well.

The Eurostat file reported low figures for the share of individuals in the population as well as of respondent students that were able to use common software for basic computer use tasks (table 2)

Yet, the human capital potential for ICT development and ICT-driven economic growth is still high. Even if among the EU countries with the least ICT employment intensity, the tendency over the last years has been on an upward slope. The 2014 value (1.95% of total employment) is 0.74 p.p higher than in 2004, and 0.5 p.p. higher than in 2010.

The share of youth in employed ICT specialists is among the highest in the EU (48.4% ICT specialists aged 15–34, with Romania being the sixth country in the EU with the highest share of young specialists), way above the EU average (36.2%) and increasing (46% in 2005).

3 http://appsso.eurostat.ec.europa.eu/nui/show.do?dataset=isoc_sk_cskl_i&lang=en, file name [isoc_sk_cskl_i].

Table 2: Individuals' level of computer skills (percentage of all individuals)

Individuals who have...	**Romania**		**EU-28 av.**		**Max. (FI)**
	% of all pop.	**% of Students**	**% of all pop.**	**% of Students**	**(of all pop.)**
... used basic arithmetic formulae in a spreadsheet	16	47	44	70	63
...written a computer program using a specialized programming language	4	-	11	-	28
... created electronic presentations with presentation software	5	17	38	72	46

Source: Eurostat database, accessed on 20.05.2017 http://appsso.eurostat.ec.europa.eu/nui/show.do?dataset=isoc_sk_cskl_i&lang=en

Also, the share of tertiary educated individuals in total employed ICT specialists has been consistently and steadily increasing. While the total number of specialists increased by 60% from 2005 to 2016, the share of tertiary educated specialists increased from 49% in 2005 to 70% in 2016. The education degree of ICT specialists is another criterion that ranks Romania favourably in the EU (the eighth position).

4.2. ICT in the business sector

The dimension of DESI, which is the most representative for the ability of the national economy to absorb and capitalize on the available ICTs, is *the Integration of Digital Technology by businesses.* It assesses, on the one hand, the level of digitization of the companies' businesses, the degree to which the companies in the private economic sector integrate IT in their operational activities, external relationships and inside dynamics and communication routine. On the other hand, the chosen indicators measure how much the business sector widens its market shares with internet sales.

While the European businesses increasingly adopt digital technologies, the Romanian companies report the same or less propensity towards ICT in sales or in designing the organization as an open system connected to the business environment. The percentage of enterprises with a high or very high Digital Intensity Index in Romania in 2015 was slightly over 10%, while the EU average reached over 20% and the best performing country (Denmark) reported over 45%.

Thus, the same percentage of companies (22%) as in 2016 reported electronic information sharing (24th rank, 13 p.p lower than the EU average) through IT tools such as "Enterprise Resource Planning Software Package" that mediate the information flows between the various functional organizational areas. An even better position—but stagnant over the last two years—is conferred by the RFID indicator, which measures the share of enterprises attaching "smart tags" to their products for after-sales product identification, or for smoothing the production and service delivery processes (4%, 0.1 p.p more than the EU average, which renders Romania in 14th position in the EU-28 hierarchy). Nine percent of enterprises, which is only half of the EU average figures, use e-invoices in standard, automatically processible formats. The other five indicators composing the *Integration of Digital Technology* summary indicator rank Romania in one of the last three positions among the EU-28 countries.

Even if it is two p.p. higher than the previous year's survey, the percentage of the Romanian businesses which, in 2016, were existent and active on social networks, blogs, multimedia content sharing websites etc. was only 8%, which puts Romania in the last place, 12 p.p behind the EU average. A decreasing share of enterprises' purchasing cloud computing services (5%, one p.p. less than the previous year and less than half the EU average percentage) ranks Romania in 26th place. Thus, Romania remained the last in the EU-28 regarding business digitization.

The investment in R&D in the ICT sector in Romania is low. The number of ICT patent applications to the EPO (per million of active population) was, in 2013, only 2.118, while other economically more EU countries registered 100.213 (Finland) or 72.052 (Sweden) and the EU-28 average was 32.315.

Also, the business R&D expenditure in the ICT sector is not steadily and consistently directed towards a particular sector, except for *computer programming, consultancy and related activities.* The digitization process of the business operational activities of the public services and population's social and economic life has increasingly been considered vital to the social development and economic competitiveness and growth. The ICTs are a catalyst for the competitiveness and presence of the Romanian economy on the international market, which will depend more and more on e-commerce and e-business. The development of the ICT sector will also be a key area for future labor market equilibrium, as studies have reported that by 2020 it might absorb up to 600,000 ICT specialists.

Moreover, the ICTs would mediate and facilitate social innovation as the infrastructure of the smart society. Yet, their effectiveness is potentiated or limited by the individual skills and institutional absorptive capacity of ICT, and by the population's and businesses' access to IT and the internet.

5. Conclusions and recommendations

The Romanian progress in social and economic digitization has been steady but slow, and the gaps to the other EU countries and the electronic reality of the global economy are wide. Many of the targets set in the National Digital Agenda Strategy seem unrealistic at present and urgent action is needed to improve the prospects of reaching them.

The key strategic intervention areas concern the development of digital skills among the workforce and consumers, and the incentivization of business digitization (e-commerce and e-business) in the private sector.

The potential for ICT skills is high, but progress is rather slow. The introduction of ICT and programming classes into the general curricula of middle school as of 2017 is a significant step forward, but more systematic and integrated action is needed for encouraging the private sector to improve the digital skills within companies and to attract ICT specialists. Moreover, available Eurostat data make it obvious that the acquirement of digital skills is highly correlated with disposable household income and the population density of the residential area. The share of individuals able to perform medium ICT tasks is about four times higher in urban areas than in sparsely populated areas, and the basic skills and minimum internet and computer usage rate in rural areas is half of the figures in densely populated areas. The ratios are similar when comparing the individuals living in households with income in the first quartile with those living in households with income in the fourth quartile. This requires social and economic public policy instruments to ensure equal opportunities and exposure to ICT, independent of income or residency.

The fiscal advantages offered to ICT personnel have proved effective in attracting and retaining specialists for the Romanian economy. Yet, most of the public action has been focused on the citizens and less on supporting the companies to apply ICTs in their current activities. They are still perceived as an optional expenditure rather than a vital strategic investment for long-term business success.

The ICT sector itself, even if it has registered a significantly higher growth rate than the rest of the economy, needs to develop the hardware sector with niche technologies for both the domestic and foreign markets. While the national performance in software development has been important, and the Romanian IT specialists in software are in the global top-ten ranking, the share of ICT personnel in the labor force needs to increase and the enrolment of students in ST needs to be encouraged.

Regarding the main limitations of our research, we consider that relying on a variety of reports and data sources may have resulted in a somewhat inconsistent and contradictory overall picture for the ICT sector in Romania. This limitation of the paper will further be addressed by integrating the overlapping reference frameworks into a unitary, consolidated set of individual indicators that may also provide a reliable perspective over the evolution of the ICT sector in Romania over the last decade.

References

1. Baller, S., Dutta S., Lanvin B., eds. (2016). The Global Information Technology Report 2016. Innovating in the Digital Economy, WEF, 2016, http://www3.weforum.org/docs/GITR2016/WEF_GITR_Full_Report.pdf.
2. Cardona, M. M., Kretschmer, T., Strobel, T. (2013). ICT and Productivity: Conclusions from the Empirical Literature. Information Economics and Policy 25(3):109–125.

3. Dahl, C. M., Kongsted, H. C., Sorensen, A. (2011). "ICT and Productivity growth in the 1990s: Panel data evidence on Europe". Empirical Economics, 40(1):141–164.
4. Dimelis, S., Papioannou, S. (2010). "FDI and ICT Effects on Productivity Growth: A Comparative Analysis of Developing and Developed Countries". European Journal of Development Research 22(1):79–96.
5. Draca, M., Sadun, R., Van Reenen, J. (2007). Productivity and ICT: A Review of the Evidence, CEP Discussion Paper No. 749, 2007.
6. Dutta, S., Geiger, T., Lanvin, B. (2015). The Global Information Technology Report 2015. ICTs for Inclusive Growth. The World Economic Forum / INSEAD, 2015.
7. European Comission (EC) (2010): A Digital Agenda for Europe. European Commission Communication 245 final /2.
8. European Comission (EC) (2015): The digital single market strategy. European Commission Communication 192 final.
9. European Comission (EC) (2017a): Europe's Digital Progress Report 2017, Country Profile Romania.
10. European Comission (EC) (2017b): Romanian Digital Economy and Society Index, Country Profile.
11. Eurostat: ICT specialists in employment (2017) http://ec.europa.eu/eurostat/statistics-explained/index.php/ICT_specialists_in_employment.
12. Farhadi, M., Ismail, R., Fooladi, M. (2012). Information and Communication Technology Use and Economic Growth. PLoS One 7(11):e48903.
13. Gruber, H., Koutroumpis, P. (2010). Mobile telecommunications and the impact on economic development. Paper presented at the 52nd Economic Policy Panel Meeting, Einaudi Institute for Economics and Finance (EIEF), October 22–23, Rome, Italy.
14. Inklaar, R., O'Mahony, R., Timmer, M. P. (2005). ICT and Europe's Productivity Performance; Industry-level Growth Account Comparisons with the United States. Review of Income and Wealth, 51(4):506–536.
15. Kneller, R. (2005). Frontier Technology, Absorptive Capacity and Distance. Oxford Bulletin of Economics and Statistics 67(1):1–23.
16. Lam, P. L., Shiu, A. (2010). Economic growth, telecommunications development and productivity growth of the telecommunications sector: evidence around the world. Telecommunications Policy, 34:185–199.
17. Lee, S.T., Gholami, R., Tong, T.Y. (2005). Time series analysis in the assessment of ICT impact at the aggregate level—Lessons and implications for the new economy. Information and Management 42:1009–1022.
18. Mazurencu, M., Niculescu-Aron, I., Mihăescu, C. (2006). An overview of the Romanian ICT Sector in the Context of European Emerging Markets, Economy-Informatics, 1–4.
19. Ministerul pentru Societatea Informationala (MSI): National Strategy on Digital Agenda for Romania (2014), Bucharest.

20. Niebel, T. (2014). ICT and Economic Growth – comparing developing, emerging and developed countries., ZEW Discussion Paper no. 14–117, 2014, http://ftp.zew.de/pub/zew-docs/dp/dp14117.pdf.
21. O'Mahony, M., Vecchi, M. (2005). "Quantifying the Impact of ICT Capital on Output Growth: A Heterogeneous Dynamic Panel Approach". Economica 72 (288):615–633.
22. Pilat, D. (2004). The ICT Productivity Paradox: Insights from Micro Data. OECD Economic Studies, pp. 37–65.
23. Seo, H., Lee, Y. (2006). Contribution of information and communication technology to total factor productivity and externalities effects. Information Technology for Development 12 (2):159–173.
24. Seo, H. J., Lee, Y. S., Oh J. H. (2009). "Does ICT investment widen the growth gap?" Telecommunications Policy 33:422–431.
25. Steinmueller, E. W. (2001). ICTs and the possibilities for leapfrogging by developing countries. International Labour Review 140 (2):193–210.
26. Stiroh, K. J. (2002). Are ICT Spillovers Driving the New Economy? Review of Income and Wealth 48(1):33–57.
27. Stiroh, K.J. (2005). Reassessing the Impact of IT in the Production Function: A Meta-Analysis and Sensitivity Tests. Annales d'Economie et de Statistique no. 79/80, 2005, pp. 529–561.
28. Van Reenen, J., Bloom, N., Draca, M., Kretschmer, T., Sadun, R. (2010). The Economic Impact of ICT. Centre for Economic Performance, London School of Economics.
29. World Economic Forum (WEF) (2016): The Global Competitiveness Report 2015–2016, 2015 http://www3.weforum.org/docs/gcr/2015-2016/Global_Competitiveness_Report_2015-2016.pdf.
30. World Bank (2012). ICT for Greater Development Impact. World Bank Group Strategy for Information and Communication Technology.

Andreea-Emanuela DRĂGOI

Institute for World Economy, andreeadragoi@iem.ro

Ana-Cristina BÂLGĂR

Institute for World Economy, anacristinabalgar@gmail.com

Financing the EU Agricultural Sector through Direct Payments: Implications of the CAP Reform

Abstract: The latest reform of the Common Agricultural Policy (CAP) has had a substantial impact on the financing tools of the agricultural sector in the EU Member States. Currently, the most used mechanism for financing agriculture in the European area is represented by the direct payments that constitute an instrument for supporting the European farmers and sustainable rural development in the EU. In this context, our paper aims to assess through a quantitative analysis the financial allocations for direct payments in the member states, and also to underline existing opportunities for Romania using a qualitative analysis as revealed by the current financial framework (2014–2020). For this purpose, we use DG Agriculture & Rural development statistics, and country sheets available in the European Commission database. Our analysis will be supported by the most relevant theoretical approaches in the literature in the field, but also by the latest European Commission reports on CAP reforms. In the final part of our research we will highlight through a quantitative analysis the CAP reform impact on direct payments but also on the sustainability of agricultural practices in the member states.

Keywords: Common Agricultural Policy, Direct Payments, EU Agricultural Sector

1. Introduction – The CAP reform implications for the Direct Payments (DP)

Since 1950 and until now, the CAP has evolved from a policy focused on the subsidisation of production towards a policy that is somewhat aimed at income support, fostering at the same time rural development and environmental protection. A number of analysts (Ghinea, 2009) show that although "agricultural policies represent the most integrated European economic sector," in its 50 years of reforms the CAP has faced the so-called "prisoner's dilemma": although the major objectives have been agreed upon by all member states, in the inter-governmental negotiation process, each country attempts a more moderate or a fiercer support to its own interests. Certain analyses (EC, 2014) show that the Common Agricultural Policy has considerably evolved since its inception to enable European farmers to meet the needs of over 500 million citizens. The specialised literature

(Bleahu, 2005) shows that the main objectives of the CAP are to ensure decent living conditions for farmers, to guarantee a stable, safe and affordable supply of food for the consumers and to foster the balanced development of all the rural territories in the European Union.

In order to harmonise these interests with the EU's major objectives, the CAP has undergone a series of reforms, among which we only remember the most recent ones: the *MacShary Reform* (of 1999, which concerned granting the European farmers compensating payments established per hectare of arable cultures and per capita for cattle), the *Reform for the implementation of Pillar II related to rural development* (finalised in 2001 and characterised by the adoption of measures related to the quality of products and of the production process, the preoccupation for the environment) and the most recent, the *Reform finalized in 2013*, which targeted three major strategic objectives: the preservation of the sustainable food production potential in the entire EU, the support for agricultural communities that offer European citizens valuable and diverse quality food and the preservation of viable rural communities.

The CAP Reform of 2013 entered into force on 1 January 2014. Most of the reform elements have been applicable since 1 January 2014, with the exception of the new direct payment structure, for which the annual direct payment cycle has to be taken into account: the annual statements submitted by the farmers under the CAP will be received during the spring. Based on these statements, the payments corresponding to the new direct payment structure will be made in 2015 together, for example, with the environmental payments and the additional aid for young farmers.

2. Literature review

The direct payment financing instrument was conceived in order to support and stabilise the income of farms in the European area that are facing systemic risks induced by the volatility of the prices of agricultural products, as well as the unpredictability of weather phenomena, which may have severe negative consequences for the quality and quantity of the agricultural production. Direct payments are allocated in the form of an annual direct financial support that the beneficiary farmer receives upon the condition of observing a set of agricultural rules and practices that require compliance with the standards on environmental protection, animal welfare, food safety and product traceability.[1]

However, certain analyses (Dewbre et al., 2001) show that besides the stimulating potential of direct payments for the development of the EU agricultural sector, they also have a negative effect on trade, as European farmers are sometimes disadvantaged if compared to international competitors, because the compliance

1 The term "traceability" refers to the possibility to identify the route of a product along the entire production chain and the compliance with the standards imposed by the EU requirements in the field.

with "green" standards implies higher production costs. We should also note that in the new financing context, attempts have been made to find a solution through the "direct green payments" mechanism, which has to be applied mandatorily in member states and which predominantly finances agricultural activities that observe environmental standards. In order to avoid the distortion of free competition on the internal market, these direct payments are not based on the level of production, but on the area of land used and on the type of agricultural practice. In this context, it must be specified that the increased environmental performance of the CAP financing by means of the mandatory "environmental" element of the direct "green" payment calls for a reconsideration of the priority actions that simultaneously target the compliance with climate objectives and with the targets of the environmental policy. These may take the form of simple, generalised, non-contractual and annual environmental actions that exceed the cross-compliance requirements and that are related to agriculture (for example, permanent pastures, green cover, crop rotation and ecological set-aside). Moreover, the rural development programmes of the member states should analyse the possibility of including the requirements related to the current Natura 2000 areas and improving certain elements of the standards on the good agricultural and environmental conditions (GAEC). Although green payments become a priority in the financing programmes of member states, the experience of the previous financing context (2007–2013) shows that the other objectives of the direct payments are also important. For example, in the 2014–2020 period, in order to take into account the specific problems of certain regions where certain types of agriculture are considered particularly important for economic or social reasons, further facultative coupled aids may need to be granted, provided that certain clearly defined limits are observed (support based on established elements: areas, productivities or number of animals). According to certain authors (Pedersen, 2014), in order to increase competitiveness and the contribution to the viability of rural areas, as well as to reduce bureaucracy, the current system could be replaced by a simple support scheme specifically designed for small farmers. The same analysis underlines the fact that the current system is also simplifying the cross-compliance rules by drawing up, for the use of farmers and of the administrations, a more simple and comprehensive set of rules, without restricting the very scope of the concept of cross-compliance.

According to the provisions imposed by the last CAP reform through the Flexibility Mechanism in the 2014–2020 period, it will be possible to transfer up to 15% of the funds between the two pillars (agriculture and markets – Pillar I; rural development – Pillar II), which will enable the member states to achieve their specific rural development objectives more easily. Concretely, it is a new architecture of direct payments, which become better targeted and fairer, preserving at the same time the "environmental component" and aiming at the strengthening of the safety networks in the field of rural development.

Against this background, we should note that the mechanism of the compliance with the criteria related to direct payments, the so-called "cross-compliance" which represents the general legal framework guiding member states in obtaining financing under the Common Agricultural Policy, has become, since 1 January 2015, better targeted with respect to the environmental component through the introduction of a new instrument: the direct "green" payments. This type of financial support will amount to up to 30% of the total of funds allocated to direct payments and will be accessible for farmers who observe three mandatory agricultural practices: the maintenance of permanent pastures, culture areas based on ecological production and crop diversification. It is worth mentioning that direct "green" payments must be included in the rural development programmes of the member states because they have the advantage of stimulating agricultural practices that respect the environment and ecosystems. Certain analyses (Was et al., 2014) indicate the immense potential existing in the context of the Common Agricultural Policy financing in the 2014–2020 period, in terms of sustainability and the "greening" of agricultural practices employed by EU farmers. The financing framework comprises certain mandatory regulations for the member states (such as "green payments per hectare"), but it also leaves room for the national authorities to achieve certain rural development priority objectives, among which is the construction of an economically sustainable rural area by complying with environmental objectives and the fight against climate change.

As a result of the changes determined by all the reform processes that modelled it over half of a century of existence, the Common Agricultural Policy has now become more adaptable to external changes and challenges (for example, the Russian embargo that affected the agricultural markets and for which funds were deployed in support of the farmers on an exceptional basis under the Flexibility Mechanism), but also more capable of stimulating a competitive development of the rural area.

3. Key changes caused by the new regulations in the DP in the Member States

For the 2015–2020 period, the direct payment schemes represent the main mechanism of support for the European farmers. Through these payments, financial support will be granted only to farmers, legal persons or groups of natural or legal persons who can prove their legal right to use farms and who perform such an agricultural activity within their farms—they cultivate the land and breed animals, they employ usual technologies to maintain the agricultural area in an adequate condition to be used as pasture or for cultivation. The current CAP framework makes a distinction between a series of types of direct payments, among which the most important is the Single Area Payment Scheme (SAPS), and the element of novelty is the Simplified Small Farmers Scheme (see Figure 1).

Fig. 1: Direct payments – an instrument to support the European farmers

The SINGLE AREA PAYMENT SCHEME	AGRI-ENVIRONMENT AND CLIMATE MEASURES	The YOUNG FARMER PAYMENT	
TRANSITIONAL NATIONAL AID	The REDISTRIBUTIVE PAYMENT	The COUPLED SUPPORT SCHEME[2]	The SIMPLIFIED SMALL FARMERS SCHEME

Source: The authors' synthesis is based on the information provided by DG Agriculture & Rural Development

The Single Area Payment Scheme, according to Regulation (EU) No. 1307/2013, Article 36, consists of granting a single payment per eligible hectare declared by the farmer on an annual basis and separated from production. In order to receive this payment, the farmers must observe eligibility conditions, among which we note: to submit the payment application with accurate and complete data, together with all the documents requested by the Agency for Payments and Interventions in Agriculture, and to observe the cross-compliance rules.[3]

As regards the SAP, although considerable progress has been made through the CAP reform, a series of problems persist regarding its implementation, as we will explain below. According to EU Report no. 5/2013 on the SAP—*Single Area Payment*

---

2 *The Coupled Support Scheme* is granted, in accordance with Regulation (EU) No. 1307/2013, Articles 52–55, only in those sectors or regions where certain types of agriculture or certain agricultural sectors that are particularly important for economic, social and environmental reasons are affected by certain difficulties. Sectors and productions concerned: protein crops, grain legumes, hemp, rice, seeds, hops, sugar beet, fruits and vegetables, milk, sheep meat and goat meat, beef and veal, silkworms. For this scheme, Romania allocates 13.7% in 2015 and 14.9% in 2020 from the annual EAGF national ceiling.

3 In Romania, farmers who in the year prior to the application submission received direct payment of over EUR 5,000 must prove at least their capacity as authorised natural persons, individual enterprises or family enterprises in accordance with the Emergency Government Ordinance no. 44/2008 on the conduct of economic activities by authorised natural persons, individual enterprises and family enterprises, as amended and supplemented. In this context, it must be noted that in March 2015, the Government of Romania approved an Emergency Ordinance concerning SAP for the 2015–2020 period, according to which farmers who own between five and 30 hectares receive a redistributive payment and those who benefit from support of over EUR 5,000 must prove that they are active farmers.

Scheme: aspects that must be approached in order to consolidate the proper financial management of this mechanism, given that the SAPS beneficiaries are imprecisely defined—"farmers" who perform an "agricultural activity" and who have "eligible land", situations have emerged at the level of the EU-28 in which persons or entities without any agricultural activity or with negligible agricultural activities received this type of payment. Moreover, given that member states have been provided with several models for SAPS implementation, which has had a major impact on the distribution of support among farmers in each of the member states, the SAPS does not represent at present a very precise mechanism in terms of directing income support. As regards the "internal convergence" of the SAPS, the member states that maintain allocations based on historical references[4] must evolve towards more similar levels of payment per hectare. In this regard, the New Regulatory Framework offers member states a range of various options.

Therefore, they may adopt a national or regional approach (based on administrative or agronomic criteria), reaching a national/regional flat rate by 2019, or they may guarantee that the farms receiving support below 90% of the average national/regional rate benefit from a gradual increase in support, with an additional condition that each farmer should receive a minimum payment of 60% of the national/regional rate by 2019. The amounts allocated to the farmers who receive more than the regional/national average will be adjusted pro rata, the member states being allowed to limit the possible support "losses" to 30%. However, it must also be noted that the new direct payment system also offers, within the Reformed Agricultural Policy, a series of opportunities. Therefore, according to the regulations in force, the member states are also entitled to make redistributive payments for the first hectares, whereby they may use up to 30% of the national package, either for the first 30 hectares, or up to the average area of the farms if this is larger than 30 hectares. Another option refers to the application of the maximum payment per hectare. Member states that use redistributive payment may be exempted from the mandatory degressivity of the basic payments starting with the amount of EUR 150,000. In the new financing framework, it has been decided at the EU level to reduce the payment for large farms: an agreement has been reached to mandatorily reduce payments exceeding EUR 150,000 granted to individual farms ("degressivity"). In practice, this means that the amount of support that any individual farm may receive within the basic payment scheme (BPS) will be cut by at least 5% for amounts exceeding EUR 150,000. In order to take employment into account, wage costs may be deducted before the calculation is made. This reduction must not apply to the

4 Most member states that have so far implemented the Single Area Payment opted for the historical model. In this model, the amount of support granted is essentially based on a series of parameters established in the 2000–2002 period, which are no longer consistent with the current agricultural activity. If the authorities of member states do not implement adequate restrictions, this model may generate transfers and the speculative accumulation of payment entitlements by the beneficiaries.

member states that use "redistributive payment" within which at least 5% of the national financial package is retained for redistribution for the first hectares of all farms. The funds that are "saved" by this mechanism remain in the member state/region concerned and are transferred to the rural development package in question, and may be used without co-financing applications. Also, member states have the option to impose a ceiling of EUR 300,000 on the amounts that each farmer may receive, taking into account wage costs as well.

4. DP in the Member States – Challenges and achievements

According to DG Agriculture & Rural Development data, in the 2015–2020 period, EUR 252.2 billion have been allocated at the EU-28 level for direct payments; the states that granted the largest funds were France (over EUR 45 billion), Germany (over EUR 30 billion) and Spain (over EUR 29 billion). As far as Romania is concerned, it ranks in the middle of the EU classification, with an allocation of over EUR 10 billion (see Table 1.).

Table 1: The distribution of financial allocations in member states by means of direct payments in the period 2015–2020 (EUR billion)

Member State	2015	2016	2017	2018	2019	2020
Belgium	0.544	0.536	0.528	0.520	0.515	0.505
Bulgaria	0.642	0.721	0.792	0.793	0.794	0.796
Czech Rep.	0.875	0.874	0.873	0.872	0.872	0.872
Denmark	0.926	0.916	0.907	0.897	0.889	0.880
Germany	5.148	5.144	5.110	5.076	5.047	5.018
Estonia	0.110	0.121	0.133	0.145	0.157	0.169
Ireland	1.216	1.215	1.213	1.211	1.211	1.211
Greece	2.047	2.039	2.015	1.991	1.969	1.947
Spain	4.833	4.824	4.815	4.886	4.880	4.893
France	7.586	7.553	7.521	7.488	7.462	7.437
Croatia	0.113	0.130	0.149	0.186	0.223	0.261
Italy	3.953	3.902	3.850	3.799	3.751	3.704
Cyprus	0.051	0.050	0.050	0.049	0.049	0.048
Latvia	0.168	0.195	0.222	0.249	0.275	0.302
Lithuania	0.393	0.417	0.442	0.467	0.492	0.517
Luxembourg	0.033	0.033	0.033	0.033	0.033	0.033

Member State	2015	2016	2017	2018	2019	2020
Hungary	1.272	1.271	1.270	1.269	1.269	1.269
Malta	0.005	0.005	0.005	0.004	0.004	0.004
Holland	0.793	0.780	0.768	0.755	0.744	0.732
Austria	0.693	0.693	0.692	0.691	0.691	0.691
Poland	2.970	2.987	3.004	3.021	3.041	3.061
Portugal	0.557	0.565	0.573	0.572	0.590	0.599
Romania	1.428	1.629	1.813	1.842	1.872	1.903
Slovenia	0.138	0.137	0.136	0.136	0.135	0.134
Slovakia	0.377	0.380	0.383	0.387	0.390	0.394
Finland	0.523	0.523	0.523	0.523	0.524	0.524
Sweden	0.696	0.696	0.697	0.697	0.698	0.699
United Kingdom	3.548	3.555	3.563	3.570	3.581	3.591

Source: DG Agriculture & Rural Development (2015) – *Regulation Direct payments – ceilings by Member State.*

As shown in the European Commission Communication on the role of the Common Agricultural Policy in addressing the challenges to be faced by the rural environment on the horizon 2020 (EC, 2011), the component related to the financing of sustainable agriculture through the direct "green" payment mechanism must represent a priority for member states.

So far, most member states have complied with the new financing directions by prioritising this type of direct "green" payments, although the Single Area Payment remains the most commonly used in the total of direct payments at the level of member states (see figure 1).

Fig. 1: The situation of financial allocations by "direct green payments" in the member states in 2015 (% of total direct payments)

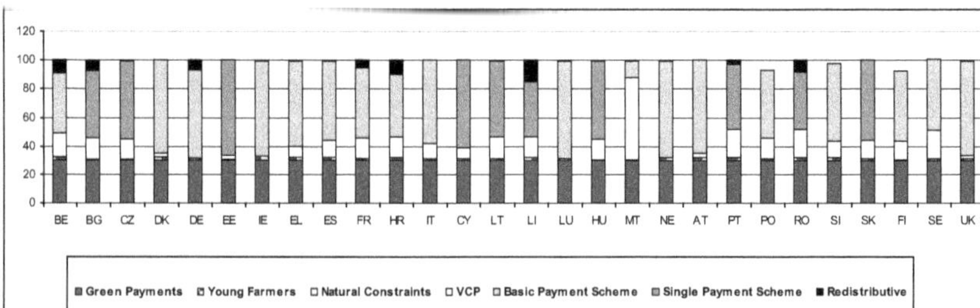

Source: The authors, based on the DG Competition data.

According to the most recent EU statistics (Direct Payments 2015–2020, Decisions taken by member states), by 31 January 2016, most member states had notified about the decisions regarding payment schemes for young farmers, the use of national reserves for supplementing the funds for the single area payment, as well as those regarding the transfer mechanism within the "greening" process. Within the transfer mechanism for "greening", five member states (France, Austria, the Netherlands, Poland and Ireland) notified about the transfers of funds, and the European Commission has three months, beginning on the notification date, to send its comments or possible objections, and seven months to reject such transfers (in accordance with Article 10(4) of Commission Regulation 614/2016). According to the possibility conferred by the EU provisions concerning the CAP flexibility mechanism, certain member states decided to transfer funds from Pillar I (Direct Payments – DP) to Pillar II (Rural Development – RD) (see Table 2).

Table 2: The distribution of financial allocations per member states within the CAP flexibility mechanism (in % of the national ceilings)

FROM DP to RD (PERCENTAGE OF NATIONAL CEILINGS, MAX. 15%)						
Financial year	**2015**	**2016**	**2017**	**2018**	**2019**	**2020**
Claim year	**2014**	**2015**	**2016**	**2017**	**2018**	**2019**
France	3.0%	3.3%	3.3%	3.3%	3.3%	3.3%
Latvia	7.5%	7.5%	7.5%	7.5%	7.5%	7.5%
UK	10.8%	10.8%	10.8%	10.8%	10.8%	10.8%
Belgium	-	2.3%	3.5%	3.5%	4.6%	4.6%
Czech Rep.	-	3.4%	3.4%	3.4%	1.3%	1.3%
Denmark	-	5.0%	6.0%	7.0%	7.0%	7.0%
Germany	-	4.5%	4.5%	4.5%	4.5%	4.5%
Estonia	-	6.1%	14.3%	15.0%	14.9%	15%
Greece	-	5.0%	5.0%	5.0%	5.0%	5.0%
Holland	-	4.0%	4.1%	4.2%	4.2%	4.3%
Romania	-	1.8%	2.3%	2.2%	0.0%	0.0%

FROM RD TO DP PERCENTAGE OF NATIONAL CEILINGS, MAX. 25%)						
Financial year	**2015**	**2016**	**2017**	**2018**	**2019**	**2020**
Claim year	**2014**	**2015**	**2016**	**2017**	**2018**	**2019**
Croatia	15.0%	15.0%	15.0%	15.0%	15.0%	15.0%
Malta	0.0%	0.8%	1.6%	2.4%	3.1%	3.8%
Poland	25.0%	25.0%	25.0%	25.0%	25.0%	25.0%
Slovakia	21.3%	21.3%	21.3%	21.3%	21.3%	21.3%
Hungary	-	15.0%	15.0%	15.0%	15.0%	15.0%

Source: The authors' processing based on the DG Agriculture & Rural Development statistics.

According to Table 2, Romania is among the countries with the lowest transfer rate under the CAP flexibility mechanism, as it did not transfer any payments to the Pillar II direct payments, and transferred the smallest funds from direct payments to rural development. Although recently integrated into the EU (in 2013), Croatia is among the countries that used the flexibility mechanism very well in order to increase its funds for direct payments, but the member state with the highest transfers is Poland (25%). As regards the areas of interest for granting direct payments, most member states opted for the voluntary coupled support (VCS) and for the small farmers scheme (SFS), see Table 3.

Table 3: Areas of interest for granting direct payments in member states

MEMBER STATE	SAPS	REGIONALIZED BPS	REDISTRIBUTIVE PAYMENT	NATURAL CONSTRAINTS	VCS	SFS
Belgium			x		x	
Bulgaria	x		x		x	x
Czech Rep.	x				x	
Denmark				x	x	
Germany		x	x			
Estonia	x					x
Ireland					x	x
Greece		x			x	
Spain					x	x
France		x	x		x	
Croatia			x		x	x

MEMBER STATE	SAPS	REGIONALIZED BPS	REDISTRIBU-TIVE PAYMENT	NATURAL CONSTRAINTS	VCS	SFS
Italy					x	x
Cyprus	x				x	
Latvia	x				x	x
Lithuania	x		x		x	
Luxembourg					x	
Hungary	x				x	x
Malta					x	x
Holland					x	x
Austria					x	x
Poland	x		x		x	x
Romania	x		x		x	x
Slovenia					x	x
Slovakia	x				x	
Finland		x			x	
Sweden					x	
UK		x	x		x	
Total	**10**	**6**	**9**	**1**	**27**	**15**

Source: Authors' processing based on the DG Agriculture & Rural Development statistics.

As shown in Table 3, the type of direct payments less used by member states refers to areas with natural constraints; among the states with the most types of direct payments we find France, Romania, Germany and the United Kingdom. According to the data provided by DG Agriculture & Rural Development, the ten new member states (who joined the EU in 2004) decided to maintain the basic direct payment until 2020, and not to opt for the differential single area payment scheme, as they could have done in 2018. Among the member states, only six opted for regionalising of the basic payment scheme and only nine member states opted for the redistributive payment, while almost all (27 states) opted for voluntary coupled support, and 15 states opted for the small farmer schemes. As regards financial allocations per type of direct payment, most of the member states decided to allocate funds for the basic payment scheme, for the single area payment, for coupled support and for young farmers (YFP), a reduced support being granted to the areas with natural constraints (ANC) (see Table 4).

Table 4: Financial allocations per types of direct payment in 2016 (% of the total)

MEMBER STATE	BPS	SAPS	REDISTRIBUTIVE PAYMENT	YFP	ANC	VCS
Belgium	42.2		9.5	1.7		16.7
Bulgaria		47.8	7.1	0.1		15.0
Czech Rep.		54.8		0.2		15.0
Denmark	66.2			0.6	0.3	2.8
Germany	62.0		7.0	1.0		
Estonia		66.0		0.3		3.7
Ireland	67.8			2.0		0.2
Greece	60.2			2.0		7.8
Spain	55.9			2.0		12.1
France	44.0		10.0	1.0		15.0
Croatia	43.5		10.0	1.5		15.0
Italy	58.0			1.0		11.0
Cyprus		61.3		0.7		8.0
Latvia		53.4		1.6		15.0
Lithuania		38.8	15.0	1.3		15.0
Luxembourg	68.0			1.5		0.5
Hungary		54.6		0.4		15.0
Malta	12.4			0.4		57.2
Holland	67.5			2.0		0.5
Austria	65.9			2.0		2.1
Poland		45.7	8.3	1.0		15.0
Romania	47.5			2.0		20.5
Slovenia		50.7	5.3	0.8		13.1
Slovakia	53.5			1.5		15.0
Finland		56.7		0.3		13.0
Sweden	49.4			1.0		19.6
UK	55.5			1.5		13.0
Belgium	65.8		1.0	1.6		1.7

Source: Author's processing based on the DG Agriculture & Rural Development statistics.

In 2016, the basic payment scheme prevails in the EU-28, followed by the single area payment scheme, this situation being similar in many member states, with some exceptions (for example, in Malta, most direct payments, 57% of the total, have been allocated for voluntary coupled support, much more than the EU average). In Romania, SAPS is dominant in all direct payment allocations, while the support for young farmers was below the EU average. It must also be noted that Romania is among the few member states without financial allocations for basic payments and is not among the states who grant considerable support for redistributive payment.

5. Conclusions

One of the fundamental changes determined by the most recent CAP reform is the increase in transparency regarding the financing of the rural environment in the Member States (DG Agriculture & Rural Development, 2014). The new regulations regarding the increased transparency of the financing of the rural environment have been introduced by Regulation 1306/2013, and according to these provisions the beneficiaries who receive funds under the CAP mechanisms will be offered an advantage as a result of the improvement of the management procedures regarding the financial support granted, doubled however by a more rigorous control procedure for the financed projects.

Certain analyses (Hogan, 2015) show that the role of the new transparency requirements is decisive for the real support of European farmers under the CAP (in the context in which they are often forced to abide by stricter rules regarding ecological agriculture, environmental and animal welfare requirements compared to their competitors at the international level), whether by the direct payment financing mechanism, or by personal investment projects. By improving transparency with regard to the financing of rural projects in the member states, the reformed Agricultural Policy imposes the annual publication by the member states of the beneficiaries of direct payments, together with details regarding the exact amounts and their intended uses, including the type of measures for which financing will be granted and the specific objectives targeted by that financing.

As regards the new DP regulations, it has been stated in the literature (Gray, 2012) that they discharge the EU authority of part of the administrative burden related to the funds for projects in the rural environment, and at the same time transfer a more significant part of the responsibility to the national and local actors (the national and regional paying agencies). These regulations on shared management stipulated that before requesting financing from the EU budget, they national rural development agencies must be accredited based on criteria clearly set out by the European Commission and, after the accreditation, they must meet certain eligibility conditions in order to be authorised to manage the granting of financial support. The payments made by these agencies are reimbursed afterwards by the European Commission (on an annual basis for EAGGF[5] financing and on a quarterly basis for EAFRD[6]).

Concerning the impact of CAP reforms on direct payments, Zahrnt (2015) considers that, in over fifty years of existence, this common policy has uncontestably improved its performance, but there still are aspects of its regulations that may cause distortions of free competition on the EU internal market, sometimes disadvantaging low-income farmers. Some CAP critics (Brunner and Huyton, 2008) pointed out that this policy was insufficiently oriented towards providing an efficient response to the unprecedented challenges that may be faced by the EU agricultural sector in the event of major natural disasters. For example, a study by the European Court of Auditors (ECA, 2008) identified a series of structural "weaknesses" of the CAP, from the insufficient targeting of the sustainable economic development to the fact that, from an economic point of view, the only net beneficiaries of the CAP continue to be farmers, landowners who pay less in terms of contributions to the EU budget, meaning less than what they receive through this policy. The ECA showed in its analyses that the new CAP financing context is characterised by the payment to each beneficiary of a single payment, regardless of production (a process known as "decoupling"). An essential element of the new common agricultural policy implies, however, that the payments due may be reduced if the beneficiaries have not complied with certain existent rules in terms of environment, food and plant safety, animal welfare or if they did not meet the newly-established requirement regarding the maintenance of the entire agricultural land in good agricultural and environmental conditions.

Regarding the difficulties of the control of cross-compliance, Brunner and Huyton (2008) point out that more strictness is necessary when there are fears that direct green payments may be used as a disguise for subsidies for certain farms, rather than as incentives for sustainable agricultural practices. In relation to such fears, it must be noted that there have been examples in certain member states where direct payments classified as "green" financed activities actually caused damages to the environment.

However, in our opinion, the future of CAP financing must be governed by the "green" component of this policy, because the relation between agriculture and biodiversity in the European environment is a symbiotic one. Moreover, the current common policy regarding the use of the agricultural land represents, as shown by the experience of recent years, an adequate instrument for correcting the so-called "market failures", while at the same time stopping the decline of biodiversity (as demonstrated by the success of the Natura 2000 direct payments).

---

5 EAGGF – The European Agricultural Guidance and Guarantee Fund primarily finances direct payments to European farmers and the support measures for agricultural markets.

6 EAFRD – The European Agricultural Fund for Rural Development finances the rural development programmes of member states.

The agri-environment schemes for European farmers enabled them to continue the agricultural activities and to adopt at the same time certain more "environmentally friendly" techniques and practices. Leitao (2006) and Vickery (2004) consider that these types of financing measures proved to be both an economic success and an aid for the preservation of the bio-habitat, while other analysts (Donald and Evans, 2006) underline that this financing may determine long-term benefits for environmental protection and the preservation of the natural landscapes on the EU territory.

While the climate change continues to have a strong impact on economic development in the European environment, the "green" component of the financing of the European rural environment must act as a catalyst in member states' rural development strategies, because the quality of agricultural habitats will determine the EU's ability to ensure the future sustainability of quality food supply and to be competitive on the international stage of agricultural product trade. Through the direct "green" payments, member states may ensure a viable food production in order to improve the competitiveness of the agricultural sector and to increase its share in the food chain, because the agricultural sector is very fragmented compared to other sectors of the food chain, which are better organised and therefore have greater negotiation power. Moreover, European farmers face competition on the world market, having to comply at the same time with the high standards related to environmental, food safety, food quality and animal welfare objectives required by the European citizens, and "green" payments may represent a compensating incentive for them. For the horizon 2020, the new financing framework enables member states to encourage ecological growth through innovation, which may incentivise the adoption of new technologies, the development of new products, the change of production processes and the support for new application templates, in particular in the context of the emerging bio-economy.

References

1. Bleahu, A. (2005). Dezvoltarea Rurală în Uniunea Europeană, in "Calitatea Vieţii" Journal, XVI, nr.3–4, pp. 289–300.
2. Brunner, A., Huyton, H. (2008). The Environmental Impact of European Union Green Box Subsidies, ICTSD Working Papers.
3. Dewbre, J., Antón, J., Thompson, W. (2001). The Transfer Efficiency and Trade Effects of Direct Payments, in Journal of Agricultural Economics, vol. 83, no. 5, pp. 1204–1214.
4. Drăgoi, A. E, Bâlgăr, A.C. (2016), "Financing the European Agriculture: A Comparative Approach across the Member States", Global Economic Observer, Vol. 4, http://nos.iem.ro/bitstream/handle/123456789/992/geo_2016_vol4_no1_art_002.pdf?isAllowed=y&sequence=1.
5. Ghinea, C. (2009). O ţară şi două agriculturi. România şi reforma Politicii Agricole a UE, CRPE Study, No. 4.
6. Donald, P., Evans, A. (2006). Habitat Connectivity and Matrix Restoration, in "Journal of Applied Ecology" vol. 43, no. 2, pp. 209–218.

7. European Commission (2011). Impact Assessment – Common Agricultural Policy towards 2020, Brussels, SEC (2011) 1153 final.
8. European Court of Auditors (2008). Information note of the European Court of Auditors concerning Special Report No 8/2008 "Is cross-compliance an effective policy?", ECA/08/30.
9. Gray, J. (2012). The Common Agricultural Policy and the Re-Invention of the Rural in the European Community, in Sociologia Ruralis Jounrnal, Vol. 40, pp. 30–52.
10. Hogan, P. (2015). New CAP transparency rules take effect, in World Grain, 6/1/2015.
11. Leitao, D., Jolivet C., Rodriguez M. & Tavares J. P. (2006). Bustard Conservation in Europe in the last 15 Years: Trends, Best Practice and Future Priorities, RSPB/BirdLife, Sandy, Bedfordshire, UK.
12. Pedersen, J., H. (2014). The Common Agricultural Policy made simple – cutting out red tape, DG Agricultural &Rural Development Working Paper, No. 143.
13. Vickery, J.A., Bradbury R., Henderson I.G., Eaton M.A. (2004). The role of agri-environment schemes and farm management practices in reversing the decline of farmland birds in England, Biological Conservation vol. 119, nr. 1, pp. 19–39.
14. Was, A., Zawalińska, K., Britz, W. (2014). Impact of "Greening" the Common Agricultural Policy on Sustainability of European Agriculture: from the Perspective of the Baltic Sea Countries in "Journal of Agribusiness and Rural Development", 4(34), p. 191–212.
15. Zahrnt, V. (2015). Public Money for Public Goods: Winners and Losers from CAP Reform, ECIPE Working Papers no. 8.

Rodrigo CASTAÑEDA

FAO, Roma, email: rodrigo.castaneda@fao.org

Ignacio DE LOS RÍOS

Universidad Politécnica de Madrid, GESPLAN,
email: ignacio.delosrios@upm.es

Larissa DOMÍNGUEZ

FAO, Roma, email: Larissa.DominguezFuentes@fao.org

Responsible Governance of Tenure of Land: Towards Voluntary Guidelines in the Context of Food Security

Abstract: Previous approaches of land governance led to large-scale investments that responded to economic models based on intensive extraction and exploitation of natural resources. As available resources decrease, tension is building up increasingly. For this reason, the international community is very interested in finding a new approach for land governance. The governance of land has become crucial for political and scientific research on rural development and environmental conservation. Especially within the framework of food security, it became increasingly important as land became the target of large-scale investments. This research revises the previous approaches that the international community has used for land governance and how their consequences led to the wide negotiation process that concluded with the creation of the Voluntary Guidelines on Responsible Governance of Tenure of Land, Fisheries and Forests in the Context of National Food Security is analyzed.

The results show two fundamental facts suggesting that these guidelines represent a valuable tool to solve natural resources conflicts and strengthen peace processes, especially in the post-conflict countries. Firstly, they emphasize a multi-sectoral approach and permanent dialogue between the various actors involved, which favors reconciliation and enhancement of solidarity linkages among them. Secondly, it emphasizes a new model of action for FAO, which embraces this strong openness to include different stakeholders in its processes.

Keywords: Land governance, food security; poverty eradication; rural development, social conflicts

Introduction

In the light of an international context where conflicts arise due to the high demand for land and natural resources, the Food and Agriculture Organization of the United Nations (FAO) has taken a step forward by developing a mechanism to achieve global consensus regarding land tenure: The Voluntary Guidelines on the Responsible Governance of Tenure of Land, Fisheries and Forests in the Context of National Food Security (VGGT). With this, solutions to land and resource conflicts are facilitated through open dialogue processes where the different actors are encouraged to express their concerns, opinions and priorities on land governance. Even though the VGGT can be used by anyone, its implementation mostly focuses on supporting civil society and grassroots organizations, the private sector and governments on legal, technical and political aspects of land tenure in order to create a legitimate path for dialogue and conflict solution.

The enhancement of a responsible governance of land is crucial for the creation of a model that will accelerate peace-building processes in conflict or post-conflict countries. The VGGT are an innovative tool that not only create a legitimate path for the concerns of the different actors, but also provide guidance and recommendations for achieving consent. The following article analyzes how international processes led to the favorable environment for the creation of a mechanism such as the VGGT. It analyzes the negotiation process, and the pilot implementation phase. The information contained herein further analyzes and emphasizes the need to exploit the potential of the VGGT for the resolution of land conflicts. The objective of the paper is to create a conceptual review of land governance and its relation with peace and food security in post-conflict countries.

The concept of "governance" has been widely used in social sciences since its creation at the end of the last century. However, its meaning has changed over time according to the context and priorities of each period. The concept of governance has acquired great political importance, its meaning now covers all political interventions, especially in the context of social development (Moyano, 2010). The Institute on Governance defines it as "the interaction among structures, processes and traditions that determine how power and responsibilities are used, how decisions are made and how citizens and other stakeholders express their opinion" (2017). The White Paper on European Governance from the European Commission includes the rules, procedures and conducts that affect the way in which power is implemented, their definition emphasizes the importance of participation, responsibility, effectivity and coherence (European Commission, 2001).

In its current interpretation, governance refers to the whole governing process, including how society is managed and how the different priorities and interests reconcile. It not only refers to the governing bodies, but to all stakeholders that contribute to and are affected by such processes. The "governance of tenure" refers to the way in which the access to land is managed and regulated (UNITERM, 2012). The sensitivity of the governance of tenure, lies in its relation with livelihoods. When it comes to land, the governance of tenure is strictly connected to human rights, such as the right to a standard of living adequate for the health and well-being of each person and their family, including food, clothing, housing and medical care. It particularly affects the right to adequate food (UDHR, 1948; ICESCR, 1966).

Today, when approximately 795 million people suffer from hunger around the world, good governance of natural resources is a crucial matter for the population. In spite of the decreasing trend in hunger figures, by which the number of people suffering from hunger is 216 million less than in 1990, hunger still remains a big challenge for countries (FAO, 2015). Efforts to achieve food security are weakened due to political instability, reduction of and access to natural resources, economic crisis, or lack of participatory and inclusive social policies, thus leaving out the most vulnerable sectors of the population from the economic opportunities and income distribution. Considering that global food demand in 2050 is projected to increase by at least 60 percent above 2006 levels (FAO, 2016), and it is expected that the major contribution in the fight against hunger will come from the increase in food production, the distribution of land will become crucial. There are approximately 4400 million hectares of arable land in the world (FAO, 2011); this land must be fairly distributed to allow every country to respond to its demand for food production and land. The pressure for the access to land is expected to increase, especially in developing countries, and there is an urgent need to adopt good governance practices (FAO, 2013). Access to land inherently supports people's means of livelihood, which allows the possibility of achieving food and nutrition security for their families.

Land governance is a critical issue for the 46% of the world's population that live in rural areas (World Bank, 2016), which makes them more vulnerable to climate change and food crisis. Other crucial factors that jeopardize food security are civil wars and political instability in general. These also represent the two main factors for migration of rural populations, both to the cities and to other countries. Each year, 65 million people leave their farms due to extreme poverty. From those, 45 million move to the cities, which increases urban population, food demand and in many cases, political tension (FMAT, 2016). Today's hunger crisis is fed by the lack of policies regulating access to land, which leads to the rural population's loss of food security. During the food crisis in 2008, the food insecurity created by the crisis and the food riots that came as a consequence exposed how dispossession of assets and reductions in food subsidies can create or aggravate conflict (FAO, 2016).

Literature review

The results of this research are based on a methodology that incorporates different information sources, the first being the collection and review of numerous secondary sources on the above concepts and documental revision of the main events that led to the negotiation of the VGGT from the international organizations' official documents (IFAD et al., 2015). Moreover, the research methodology incorporates empirical information obtained from fieldwork on the implementation of the Guidelines, interviews with the main actors, CSO's reports on the pilot phase implementation of the VGGT, CFS reporters, and FAO's fieldwork on the implementation of the VGGT.

For the collection of experience knowledge about the VGGT, different focus groups and workshops were applied (Madriz, 2003) as part of the activities of the implementation of the Guidelines, including the stakeholders and applying the same methodological framework. This common methodological framework, for the gathering and systematization of the expert and experimented knowledge, integrates social learning processes from the conceptual elements of the Working with People model (WWP) (Cazorla et al., 2013, 2017; De los Ríos et al., 2013).

For the analysis and systematization of experience knowledge about the processes that led to the negotiation of the VGGT and their importance for the international community, four periods are determined, from 1970 to 2015. The criteria for determining the periods were the following: historical landmarks, the actors involved in the process and the change of priorities and paradigms in relation to land governance. These periods constitute a revision of the different approaches that have been used for achieving the responsible governance of tenure and how its consequences led to the creation of the VGGT. They focus on the results each period had depending on the context and highlight that the problem of land governance is still present. The first period revises the first steps towards the responsible governance of natural resources. It starts with the agrarian reforms that took place around the world and the first land governance conference in the 1970s. Then it focuses on the how the market model was introduced and took over the land governance systems. The second period comes as a natural consequence of the two phenomena mentioned before. It is marked by the food crisis that exploded in 2008 and was catalyzed by the economic and energetic crises of the same year. The third period focused on how this crisis led to a change of paradigm, which allowed for the reform of the Committee on World Food Security (CFS) and the negotiation of the VGGT in 2009. The fourth and last period focuses on the implementation and potential of the Guidelines: I) Main approaches for the governance of land: Agrarian reform and the market model; II) Food crisis; III) Elaboration of the VGGT: Multistakeholder's dialogue; IV) The Voluntary Guidelines: Implementation and current situation.

Results and discussion

The international community has followed different approaches for the distribution and access to land. Such approaches go from the agrarian reform to the adoption of a market model. Even though none had solved the issue of land governance, the social, economic and cultural lessons that came out of them led to the creation of an innovative mechanism based on dialogue and consensus, the VGGT.

The first steps towards the governance of land: Agrarian reform and the market model

Up to the 1960s, many countries implemented different models of agrarian reforms with the objective of reducing the concentration of land to allow for the modernization of agriculture. The reforms aimed at attaining a more equal distribution of income, through the agrarian reform, they intended to increase the size of the internal market and open the doors for industrialized products. Agricultural production was supposed to boost the industrialization process (Gomez, 2013). Under this assumption, the industrialization of agriculture would facilitate the social integration of farmers. However, it didn't have the same results in every country.

It is important to consider that some models of agrarian reform were *imported* from other countries, and therefore they did not respond to the specific context and needs of the countries, especially in Latin America (FAO, 2012). In cases such as Chile, Romania and Peru, land reform failed and rapidly backlashed and aggravated land concentration. This was largely due to the lack of social and productivity programs to support farmers. On the other hand, in cases such as Vietnam, and later Brazil, it had a positive impact and is still considered as a good example of agrarian reform (FMAT, 2016).

At the end of the 20th century, several governments decided to implement the market assisted land reform led by the World Bank based on the creation of a land market (Aiyar et al., 1995). According to this strategy the market allocates the resources instead of the state. The new role of the state was to create the enabling conditions for the land market to develop; if there is no longer direct intervention from the state, at the most, it could facilitate the access to financing (Machado, 2009). However, due to the lack of regulation in the financing systems in some countries, this was not always a successful strategy. Separately, this model highlighted the negotiation disadvantages smallholders had in front of big international enterprises (Reydon y Plata, 1996). Much discussion has taken place on the results of this reform. Many argue that it led to the current dynamics of the land market, which are defined regional and global value chains and do not take into consideration the social function of land, its association to cultural heritage, the environment and livelihoods of the rural poor. (Losano, 2006)

The land market followed the economic principle of intensive extraction and exploitation of natural resources allowing both privatization and concentration of natural resources (Bryceson et al., 1999). Early in the 20th century, the world was facing the challenge of responding to an increasing demand for food in developing countries, and an increasing demand for natural resources for new kinds of energy, both framed by the need to adapt to climate change and to the rapid decrease of available non-renewable resources (Fernandes et al., 2010, Franco et al., 2010, Nalepa and Bauer, 2012; Nalepa and Bauer, 2012; Wilkinson and Herrera, 2010). In order to satisfy the demand, more land was needed and the opportunity for making economic profit increased. These changes made investments shift from traditional commodities to food and natural resources, and land became one of the main sources of large-scale investment (Amanor, 2012; Cotula, 2012; Deininger, 2012). These changes led to the accumulation of tension regarding access to land, which increased the possibility of resulting in conflict, particularly when climate change became part of the equation.

The increase in investment in land, in some cases, represented a risk for traditional rights. Due to the lack of registration systems for traditional lands, local and foreign agents took extensions of land that already belonged to rural communities, whose traditional rights were not taken into consideration and lacked resistance vis-à-vis freehold titles. The lack of regulations on this process, turned land grabbing into a common phenomenon (FAO, 2012). These changes led to the accumulation of tension regarding access to land, which increase the possibility to trigger conflicts, particularly in the new context of climate change.

This scenario left smallholders behind and focused on mass production. Family farmers, indigenous peoples, small scale fisher folk and other vulnerable sectors of the population—some of the most affected—were overlooked. The lack of land regulation allowed for this exclusion, causing significant hazards in the fight against hunger and malnutrition. Recognizing that five hundred million smallholder farms worldwide support around one third of humanity's food supply means that they are a crucial element in the fight against hunger. Family farms are the predominant form of production in both developed and developing countries (FAO, 2016), but smallholders possess a small proportion of land, with 72% of the smallholders owning a piece of land less than one ha, and 85% less than two ha. As such, the exclusion of smallholders in land regulation has a direct and severe impact on food security.

Fig. 1: Amount of land possessed by smallholders

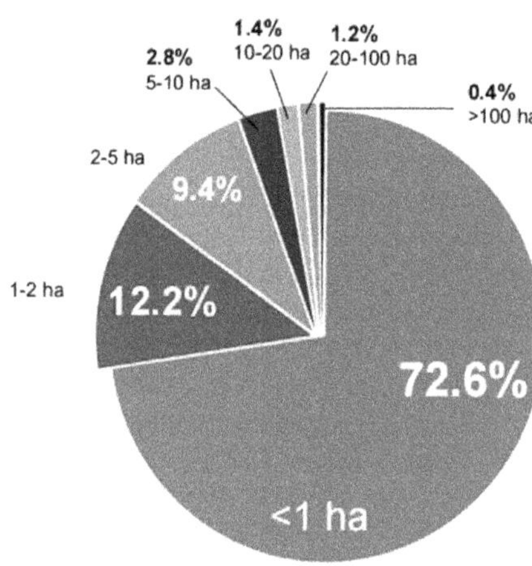

Source: Prepared by FAO for the Family Farming team

The pressure for land and lack of proper regulation of the land market—which is the most common scenario in the developing countries—has led to speculation (Borras and Franco, 2010) and in some cases land grabbing (McMichael, 2012). The globalization of trade has opened the door for large enterprises that increasingly compete with smallholders. Due to the size and economic power of these enterprises, smallholders usually end up forsaking their rights, which allows enterprises to benefit from low land values and labor costs. Further, in some cases local governments support these enterprises, thus becoming a critical issue if there is no registration system for the smallholder lands. With no land registries, lands that are managed under traditional systems can be re-allocated (FMAT, 2016). The demand for land increases the risk of conflicts and emphasizes the need for responsible governance of land tenure, in particular to protect smallholders and rural communities.

Further, leasing, seed pools and state concessions can also result in land concentration. The concept includes dispossession of rural communities through appropriation by external players for farming activities, infrastructure, urban expansion, etc., and the concentration of user rights to land and natural resources. Over the last 30 years the discussion regarding responsible governance of land tenure has somehow been abandoned by the governments. The discussions have focused on increasing production and economic profits, allowing natural resources to become a commodity. This approach undermines not only the environment but also human rights to food and traditions (FMAT, 2016).

The food crisis

The 2007–2008 food crisis represented the breaking point of the situation. The crisis reaffirmed that the problem did not reside in the lack of food, but in the access to food, which links back to land governance. The food crisis was a result of the previous approaches, and brought to light that previously smallholders had not been integrated in the agriculture value chain, which demonstrated how important it was to include smallholders in policy dialogue. Land was turned into a commodity that was handed out to the best bidder. The problem was that for the rural population, land not only provides food, but it is where tradition, identity and history are embedded (FAO, 2012). The food crisis was accompanied by economic and energy crises. Together these three crises triggered a rampant land-grabbing process of unexpected dimensions. This breaking point highlighted the need to establish codes of conduct and good practices that would reduce its negative effects, both on people and natural resources (FAO, 2012). This scenario called for the establishment of a new mechanism for the governance of natural resources; this mechanism would be the VGGT.

The food crisis in 2008 emphasized the relation between conflict and hunger. The proportion of people that suffer from hunger is three times higher in countries in conflict than in other developing countries (FAO, 2016). Approximately one-fifth of undernourished[1] people live in countries in conflict, nearly 167 million people. Food riots that were occasioned by food insecurity reflected how dispossession of assets and reductions in food subsidies create or increase the risk of conflict in a country (FAO, 2016). Secure and sustainable access to land and other natural resources is crucial in the fight against hunger and poverty, they contribute directly to sustainable development and peace building. Addressing issues of land tenure is necessary for post-conflict recovery to be effective.

1 Undernourishment is defined as a person who is not able to acquire enough food to meet the daily minimum dietary energy requirements over a one-year period. The FAO defines hunger as being synonymous with chronic undernourishment (FAO, 2015).

Since 2000, 48% of civil conflicts have occurred in Africa. Access to rural land underpins the livelihoods of many and in 27 out of 30 conflicts, land access has played a significant role (FAO, 2016). Land is not only an important economic asset and source of livelihoods, it is the foundation for community identity, traditions and culture, making it a sensitive issue for displaced communities. However, such sensitivities are often ignored due to political priorities or economic interests (UNEP, 2012). While it is crucial to address land conflicts and to understand the underlying land rights to achieve sustainable peace, land is often considered too politically sensitive or too technically complicated to help achieve any solution. In fact, recent studies have shown that conflicts associated with natural resources are twice as likely to relapse into conflict within the first five years after the end of hostilities (UNEP, 2012). Further, in solving land conflicts, one key weakness is the lack of institutionality. In most countries, there is no specific institutional body responsible for land issues. Given the lack of institutional responsibility, the implementation of land policies is usually placed in the hands of various ministers, leading to a lack of continuity and harmony within the policies. This can create legitimacy problems resulting in a lack of responsible administration for land issues.

Fig. 2: Relation between hunger and conflict

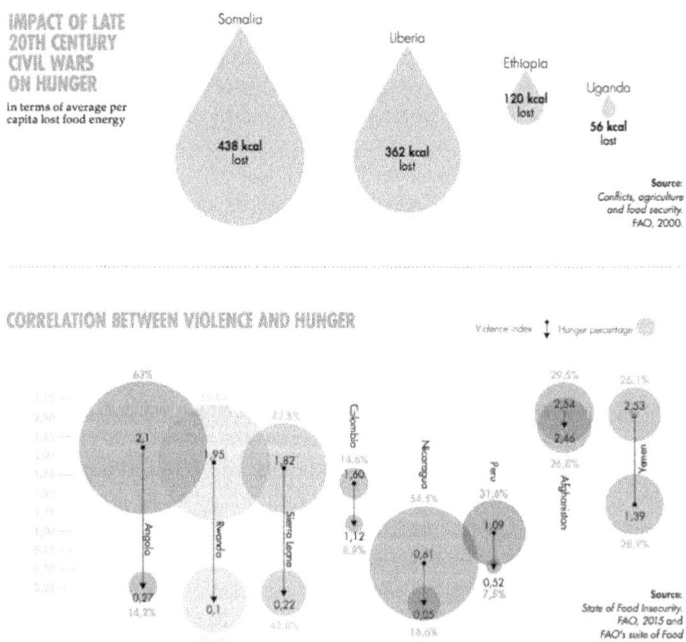

Source: State of food insecurity. FAO, 2015 and FAO's suite of Food Security Indicators

The relation between violence, natural resources and hunger is not new; it has existed for years. The FAO mandate originates in the need for an international organization to coordinate policies and global interventions in the interests of the most vulnerable sectors of the population. When created in 1945, FAO's objective was to support governments in increasing agricultural production to solve the hunger problem resulting from the Second World War (FAO, 2011; FAO, 1985). Through the creation of FAO, the international community recognized not only the crucial role of agriculture in human development and peace, but also the need to give a voice to the millions of men, women and children who were unheard. The previous experiences brought to light the need to encourage an open dialogue among the different stakeholders and paved the way for the creation of an alternative and inclusive mechanism that would leave no voices unheard, the VGGT.

Elaboration of the VGGT: multistakeholder's dialogue

After the experiences with the agrarian reforms and the introduction of the market system, the international community had exhausted its options for dealing with land conflicts. It could not continue ignoring the problem and eternalizing land conflict. They needed a new approach that would cover the empty spaces that were not included in the previous strategies. The pressure that came out of the large-scale land acquisitions forced them to bring the issue of land governance to the table. The failure of agrarian reforms and the market model crisis underlined the need to include the different stakeholders in the negotiations and policy making. Only then, with the tension that kept building up, did land governance become a priority for policy makers. It was in this scenario that the VGGT came up as a possible solution; they represent an innovative holistic instrument for solving land conflicts through dialogue and consent.

Main conferences and meetings that led to the VGGT

In 1970 the issue of responsible governance of land tenure was brought to the table for the first time in the World Conference on Agrarian Reform and Rural Development. After the conference, the governments requested that FAO create the Committee on World Food Security (CFS), recognizing the importance of land tenure in international discussions. This is considered the first time that an international organization raised the subject and prepared a path for the international community to discuss the responsible governance of tenure. The World Forum on Agrarian Reform followed the conversations in 2004, but it was not until after the 2008 food crisis that the international community felt the pressure to make responsible governance of tenure a priority in their agenda. The International Conference on Agrarian Reform and Rural Development that took place in 2006 recognized the agrarian reform as a central issue for the eradication of hunger and poverty.

A first important step was the formal reform of the CFS in 2009. The Committee opened its doors to the different stakeholders to create a neutral forum for policy dialogue. After its reform, the CFS provided a neutral forum for discussions among the civil society, private sector, academia and the member states. In 2009, stakeholders started the negotiations for the Voluntary Guidelines on the Responsible Governance of Tenure. The different stakeholders knew that in order to avoid and solve land conflicts, they needed a mechanism that would give them the tools for achieving an open and transparent dialogue.

None of the stakeholders were benefiting from the land conflicts. The alternative was to open the neutral forum where they could participate and express their concerns in order to reach a win-win situation. Each stakeholder would benefit from the discussions:

- Governments needed to solve conflicts and create standard settings
- Civil society and indigenous peoples needed to create paths to solve their conflicts and a legitimate channel to express their concerns
- The private sector needed to achieve sustainability and ensure transparency in the investment processes in order to avoid conflict

Fig. 3: Timeline: Main political milestones towards VGGT

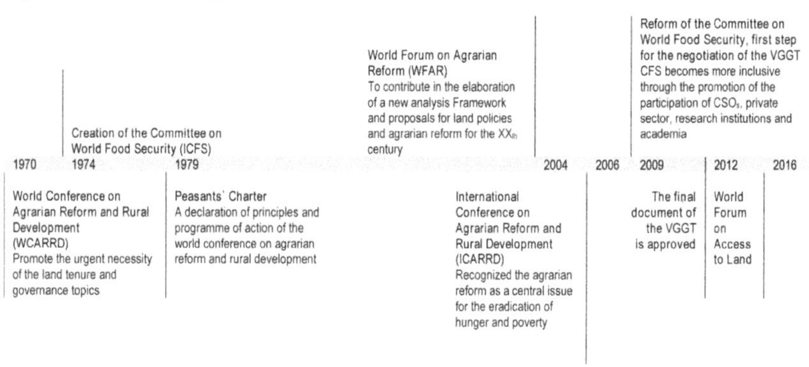

Source: Author based on a chronological revision

The actors and the negotiations

The aim of the negotiations was to achieve a document that encompassed the priorities and concerns of the different stakeholders, especially civil society, the private sector and governments. However, given the political sensitivity of the subject, tensions were raised during the negotiations. The differences among the positions of the stakeholders divided the participants and in many cases blocked the negotiations. The civil society, being the most vulnerable and affected by the lack of responsible public institutions, focused their interventions on demonstrations of how the governance of land and other natural resources is crucial to achieve food sovereignty. For the first time, groups that are often marginalized and overlooked were able to convey points of view, experiences, voices and proposals and to actually be heard. Even though civil society managed to include most of their demands regarding subjects such as eviction, restitution, access to law, traditional land rights and women's rights, the other stakeholders remained reluctant to include details on the access to water.

As for the private sector, their concerns focused on the need to obtain complete and transparent information, especially when it came to the status of the land they wanted to invest in. The document however emphasized that the governments are not the only actor to be accountable for responsible investments, it specifically mentions that the private sector needs to step in and accept its responsibilities. Another issue the private sector raised was the need to fight against corruption and the need to strengthen governments and accountability systems. During the negotiations, the governments agreed to the commitment of improving land governance. Nevertheless, they demanded that the VGGT be as flexible as possible so that they could be adapted to the different national contexts, legal systems, and local institutions. They emphasized that the VGGT should respect and not interfere with each country's legal system. Other concerns for the governments included the restitution mechanisms, regulation of investments and the definition of legitimate land rights.

The Voluntary Guidelines: Implementation and current situation

The VGGT define five general principles and ten principles for implementation. These principles emphasize the need to protect the basic tenure rights of people, and include key subjects that are not always covered by the legal system. One such subject is the need to recognize and respect alternative tenancy registries, which means traditional rights should become legitimate. They further call on the need to have one single legal system to avoid overlapping laws that could lead to conflict and misunderstandings among the different stakeholders. The principles further highlight the need to guarantee free prior and informed consent whenever investments are undertaken, and when such consent is violated, the access to justice should be guaranteed by the government. Stakeholders are urged to accept the VGGT, even if, as their name states, they are voluntary, and thus no stakeholder is forced to apply them.

As for the implementation, the VGGTs identify ten principles. The principles are based on the Universal Declaration of Human Rights and they focus on: human dignity, no discrimination, equity and justice, gender equality, a holistic and sustainable focus, consultation and participation, the rule of law, accountability and monitoring, and documenting. The document attempts to encompass the different priorities of the stakeholders and their suggestions.

After the negotiation and creation of the VGGTs, governments and stakeholders identified the need for and importance of responsible investment guidelines. The result was the development of an annex document to VGGT, Responsible Agriculture Investment (RAI). Recognizing that the majority of people that suffer from hunger live in rural areas of developing countries, investment in rural development and agriculture is key to achieving a world free of hunger. RAI proposes a series of principles and guidance for achieving responsible investments in agriculture. This complementary document highlights the need for responsible investments that create an enabling environment and better capacities for investing responsibly, and improve the existing monitoring systems and assessment tools for the impact of rural investment (FAO, 2016).

FAO and several civil society organizations are having a positive impact with the implementation of the Guidelines. They have developed information and capacity developed materials, often with the support of rural communities in order for the material to respond to their real needs. They have also focused on awareness raising and on capacity development for the constructive and proactive engagement of CSOs in processes of political dialogue on the subject. The map below summarizes the implementation of the VGGT to date, identifying the 18 countries where FAO has implemented the VGGT. It is important to take into consideration that this map is based on FAO reports; if other countries have used the Guidelines without FAO support they might not be included in the map.

Fig. 4: Ongoing implementation of VGGT

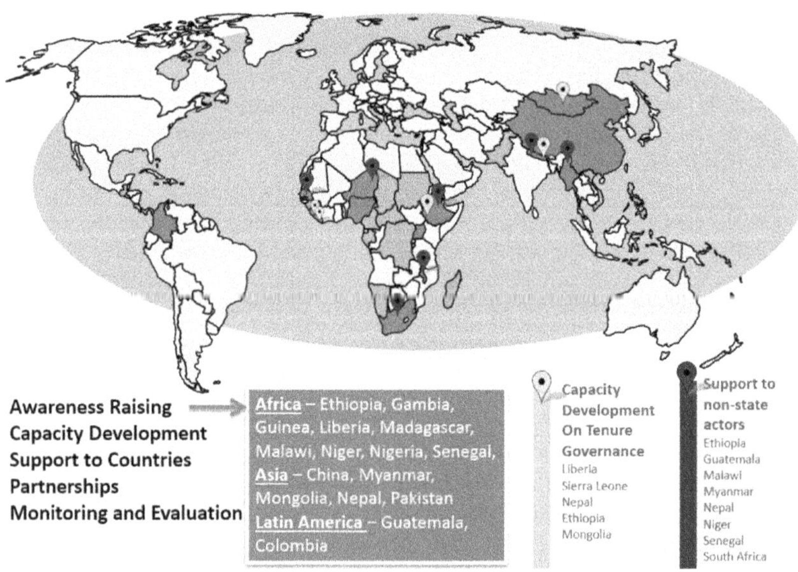

Source: FAO for the implementation of the Belgium Project

Conclusions

The five-year anniversary of the VGGT, in May 2017, will celebrate the success of the negotiations and highlight their achievements. However, the VGGT still face many challenges for achieving their full potential. One key challenge they are facing is that they are not a legally binding document. After four years of negotiation, stakeholders finally agreed on the VGGT, but only with the condition that they would be voluntary. The term "voluntary" tends to create some controversy, especially among civil society organizations. The term implies that the implementation of the Guidelines relies on the will of the governments, as they are not required to sign or ratify them. Further, there is no coercive mechanism to ensure that policymaking is in accordance with the VGGT or guarantee that investments are aligned with RAI.

In spite of this, the VGGT have a high level of legitimacy. This is due to the way they were created and the subjects they cover, especially as land governance has become a central issue in today's conflict solving and policy making. Up to a certain point, this legitimacy relativizes the non-binding controversy. The VGGT are an orientation document that can be used for analyzing or elaborating specific policies for each country. They are written to be flexible and to adapt to different country contexts. The VGGT can be helpful for identifying and facing challenges when tenure governance is causing conflicts in the countries. The document is flexible enough to respond to the different needs and the difficulties encountered in reaching a consensus among the stakeholders.

Civil society organizations have continually expressed their concerns with the voluntary nature of the VGGT (FMAT 2016). Given that civil society organizations constitute one of the most vulnerable stakeholders, often without a voice in policy dialogue, it can be difficult to convey their demands without such a mechanism. For them, the VGGT represent a legitimate way to start dialogue with the governments and other stakeholders. However, the voluntary aspect should not be considered the only factor for the implementation problems, just because a document is legally binding it does not mean it will be successfully implemented (Mereminskaya, 2011).

Due to the difficulty of the negotiations, the final text of the VGGT is not easy to read or assimilate. This represents a great challenge for the implementation of the VGGT among civil society, especially grassroots organizations. Mainly because the document remains abstract and rough, a deep analysis should be undertaken to connect and associate the VGGT to the local contexts. FAO attempted to fill this void in the first phase of the implementation, and even though the results have been positive, there is still much work to be done. Such work includes awareness raising, capacity building, and support in the adoption process.

Another key challenge is the implementation strategy of the VGGT. To date, a mechanism for implementation has not been defined. It is important to consider that the VGGT and RAI are not property of FAO, they are public tools that should be recognized and implemented by all the stakeholders.

The universal character of the VGGT makes monitoring difficult. There is an urgent need to strengthen the monitoring processes. It becomes difficult to monitor how and by whom the VGGT are being used around the world. This lack of monitoring mechanisms makes it even harder for FAO to identify weaknesses and areas of opportunity for the VGGT. Together, they can turn land policy, land administration, dispute resolution, land reform, capacity development, mediation, peace agreements, peace building and stabilization plans as entry points for the implementation of the VGGT (GLTN, 2014).

Perhaps the main problem with the *voluntary* aspect and the lack of the implementation strategy, is that so far, in order to implement the VGGT, FAO requires the permission of the government, this is considered one of the main criteria. The uptake and implementation of the VGGT lie with the governments, and where there is political instability, or where conflict is taking place, governments might refuse international support, especially in policy dialogue. This weakens the VGGT's potential because there is still no path for entering into such countries, mainly because instability is rising because of land issues. As such, these countries would benefit the most from the VGGT, which is why it is crucial to define a strategy for creating an entry point in these situations. The post-conflict countries need early response, and they need more than diplomatic action; they need support in solving the pressure for natural resources. The coordination among the different UN agencies, regional and sub-regional platforms needs to be strengthened in order to increase the reach of the monitoring and implementation of the VGGT.

The VGGT are also facing the challenge of defining one specific approach and strategy. The text identifies the Guidelines as a reference document for the responsible governance of tenure, and that they aim at the achievement of food security, social stability and improvement of livelihoods. However, stakeholders struggle with defining how and why they would use the VGGT in their own countries and contexts. This was observed in most of the capacity development activities that FAO undertook with civil society; the flexibility and difficulty of the text makes it hard for the stakeholders to truly understand how the Guidelines will contribute to their efforts. The VGGT are so broad and can be used in so many contexts and environments that defining one strategy and/or approach could affect their dynamic nature. There is a need for a constant review and a case-by-case analysis for the VGGT to be effective and to adapt the strategy to the needs of each of the countries and its national processes.

The implementation and use of the VGGT varies and depends entirely on the perception that stakeholders have of the document. Therefore, it is necessary to insist on the win-win aspect of the VGGT and on its capacity to adapt to the local contexts in order to create a more homogenous perception. Only through this approach will stakeholders realize that the main objective of the VGGT is to solve land governance issues through the creation of a participatory and inclusive dialogue process where all actors can participate.

The VGGT have great potential and there is an urgent need to implement them to face today's land governance situation. It is a unique tool that includes the most important ethical and normative principles for the use and governance of land and supports governments through the design and implementation of public policies for the governance of natural resources. It is a mechanism that facilitates the identification of information through dialogue and allows different stakeholders to convey their concerns. Moreover, if multistakeholder mechanisms are created at the local level, the VGGT can also become an instrument for monitoring and accountability of the implementation of land policies.

The first phase of VGGT implementation has been positive but it has also brought to light the weaknesses and challenges that must be faced. The question is how to address these challenges so as not to waste a crucial instrument that is key to solving one of the greatest problems of our generation. It is necessary that the stakeholders work together to meet these challenges and to use the VGGT's potential of becoming a mechanism for strengthening peace-building processes through the promotion of an open dialogue on land governance. Five years from their adoption in the CFS, the VGGT are an outstanding example of a new approach to governance and they need to be in the core of the world's effort to eradicate hunger. Their inclusive and participatory nature is the key to the success of their implementation. If the international community keeps its focus on their participatory and inclusive nature on land governance dialogue, the VGGT can represent the next milestone for strengthening peace-building processes.

Acknowledgments

The authors are grateful for the participation of FAO colleagues Marcela Villarreal, Sergio Gomez and Francesco Pierri for providing information that has contributed to the research. The authors also want to acknowledge Vanessa Passafaro's contribution to the final editing of this paper.

References

1. Aiyar, S., Parker, A., Van Zyl, J. (1995). Market-assisted land reform: a new solution to old problems. World Bank. 1995. Retrieved from http://documents.worldbank.org/curated/en/708351468740977892/Market-assisted-land-reform-a-new-solution-to-old-problems.
2. Amanor, K.S. (2012). "Global resource grabs agribusiness concentration and the smallholder: two West African case studies". Journal of Peasant Studies, 39(3–4), 2012, pp. 731–49.
3. Borras, S. Jr., Franco, J. C. (2010). "From Threat to Opportunity? Problems with the Idea of a 'Code of Conduct' for Land-Grabbing". Yale Human Rights and Development Law Journal, vol. 13, no. 2, 2010, pp. 507–23.
4. Bryceson, D. F., Kay, D. F., Mooij J. (eds.) (2000). Disappearing Peasantries? Rural Labor in Africa, Asia and Latin America. London: Intermediate Technology Publications, 2000.

5. Cazorla, A., De los Rios, I., Salvo, M. (2013). "Working With People (WWP) in Rural Development Projects: a proposal from Social Learning". Cuadernos de Desarrollo Rural 10: 131–157.
6. Cazorla, A., De los Ríos, I. (2017). Rural Community Management in the Global Economy: a planning model based on innovation and Entrepreneurial Activity. In: I. Nicolae, I. De los Ríos and AJ. Vasile (eds.). Rural Communities in the Global Economy: Beyond The Classical Rural Economy Paradigms. Nova Science Publishers: New York. 2017, pp. 1–22.
7. Popescu, Gh. H. (2016). The Role of Multinational Corporations in Global Environmental Politics, Economics, Management, and Financial Markets 11(3):72–78.
8. Nica, E., Ioan, H. (2016). The State-led System of Global Environmental Governance, Economics, Management, and Financial Markets 11(3):79–85.
9. Zaga, S.D. (2016). The Impact of Nutritional Programs in Mexico, American Journal of Medical Research 3(1):7–38.
10. Popescu, Gh. H., Florin, Cristian, C., Teodora I.B. (2016). Environmental Consequences of Liberalized and Expanding Global Trade, Journal of Self-Governance and Management Economics 4(3):66–72.
11. Nica, E. (2016). Employee Voluntary Turnover as a Negative Indicator of Organizational Effectiveness, Psychosociological Issues in Human Resource Management 4(2):220–226.
12. Machan, T.R. (2016). Commerce and Its Normative Dimensions, Psychosociological Issues in Human Resource Management 4(1):7–40.
13. Commission of the European Communities: European Governance. A White Paper. July 2001. Retrieved from http://europa.eu/rapid/press-release_DOC-01-10_en.htm.
14. De los Rios-Carmenado, I., Turek, A., Afonso, A. (2013). Project management competencies for regional development in Romania: analysis from Working with People Model. Procedia Economics and Finance, 8, 2013, pp. 614–621.
15. Fernandes, B. M., Clifford A.W., Goncalves E. C. (2010). Agrofuel policies in Brazil: paradigmatic and territorial disputes. Journal of Peasant Studies, 37(4):793–819.
16. Food and Agriculture Organization of the United Nations (FAO). Achieving Zero Hunger: the critical role of investments in social protection and agriculture. Rome: FAO, 2015. Retrieved from http://www.fao.org/fileadmin/user_upload/newsroom/docs/Report-Achieving-Zero-Hunger.pdf.
17. Food and Agriculture Organization of the United Nations (FAO). Conflict and hunger. Le Monde Diplomatique, Peace and Security Supplement by FAO, 2016. Retrieved from http://www.fao.org/3/a-i5638e.pdf.
18. Food and Agriculture Organization of the United Nations (FAO). Fast facts: The State of the World's Water and Land Resources. 2011. Retrieved from http://www.fao.org/fileadmin/user_upload/newsroom/docs/en-solaw-facts_1.pdf.

19. Food and Agriculture Organization of the United Nations (FAO): FAO's work on the ground. Le Monde Diplomatique, Peace and Security Supplement by FAO. May 2016. Retrieved from http://www.fao.org/3/a-i5638e.pdf.
20. Food and Agriculture Organization of the United Nations (FAO). FAO, the first 40 years. Rome: FAO, 2015.
21. Food and Agriculture Organization of the United Nations (FAO). FAO in Italy: history in the making. Rome: FAO, 2011.
22. Food and Agriculture Organization of the United Nations (FAO). Overview of the FAO Umbrella Programme Supporting Responsible Investments in Agriculture and Food Systems. Rome: FAO 2016.
23. Food and Agriculture Organization of the United Nations (FAO). State of Food Insecurity in the World. 2015. Retrieved from http://www.fao.org/fileadmin/user_upload/newsroom/docs/en-solaw-facts_1.pdf.
24. Food and Agriculture Organization of the United Nations (FAO). World Food Programme Glossary. 2012. Retrieved from http://www.fao.org/faoterm/en/.
25. Foro Mundial sobre el Acceso a la Tierra (FMAT). AGTER 2016. Retrieved from http://www.agter.asso.fr/rubrique170_en.html.
26. Global Land Network Tool (GLNT): Support peacemaking and peace-building efforts in fragile states. 2014. Retreived from http://www.gltn.net/index.php/work-stream/land-and-conflict.
27. Gómez, Sergio; Soto Baquero, F. (2013). Reflexiones sobre la concentración y extranjerización de la tierra en América Latina y el Caribe. Rome: FAO, 2013.
28. Graham, J., Amos, B., Plumtree, T. (2003). Principles for Good Governance in the 21st Century, Policy brief no. 15. Ottawa: Institute on Governance.
29. International Fund for Agricultural Development (IFAD) et al: Objetivo Hambre Cero: el papel decisivo de las inversiones en protección social y agricultura. 2015. Retrieved from: http://www.fao.org/3/a-i4951s.pdf.
30. International Fund for Agricultural Development (IFAD). Smallholders, food security and the environment. 2013. Retrieved from http://www.unep.org/pdf/SmallholderReport_WEB.pdf.
31. Institute on Governance: Defining Governance. 2017. Retrieved from http://iog.ca/defining-governance/.
32. McMichael, P. (2012). The land grab and corporate food regime restructuring". Journal of Peasant Studies, 39(3–4):681–701.
33. Mereminskaya, Elina: El Convenio 169 de la OIT sobre Pueblos Indígenas y Tribales: Derecho Internacional y Experiencias Comparadas, Estudios Públicos n° 121, 2011, p. 215.
34. Moyano, E. E. (2009). Capital Social Gobernanza y Desarrollo en Áreas Rurales. Ambienta, 2009. Retrieved from http://www.mapama.gob.es/ministerio/pags/Biblioteca/Revistas/pdf_AM%2FAmbienta_2009_88_112_126.pdf.
35. Millennium project: The 0.7% target: An in-depth look. 2006. Retrieved from http://www.unmillenniumproject.org/press/07.htm.
36. Losano, M.G. (2006). Función social de la propiedad y latifundios ocupados: los "Sin Tierra" de Brasil. Dykinson: 2006.

37. Organization for Economic Cooperation and Development (OECD). Adoption of technologies for sustainable farming systems. Wageningen Workshop proceedings. 2001. Retrieved from http://www.oecd.org/greengrowth/sustainable-agriculture/2739771.pdf.
38. UN General Assembly, International Covenant on Economic, Social and Cultural Rights, 16 December 1966, United Nations, Treaty Series, vol. 993, p. 3. Retrieved from: http://www.refworld.org/docid/3ae6b36c0.html.
39. UN General Assembly, Universal Declaration of Human Rights, 10 December 1948, 217 A (III). Retrieved from: http://www.refworld.org/docid/3ae6b3712c.html.
40. United Nations Conference on Trade and Development (UNCTAD): Achieving the SDGs requires rich countries to meet their 0.7% aid target. May 2016. Retrieved from (http://unctad.org/en/pages/newsdetails.aspx?OriginalVersionID=1283.
41. United Nations Interagency framework for preventive action (UNEP). The United Nations Interagency Toolkit and guidance for preventing and managing land and natural resources conflict, Land and Conflict. 2012. Retrieved from http://www.un.org/en/land-natural-resources conflict/pdfs/GN_Land%20and%20Conflict.pdf.
42. World Bank. World Bank Statistics. Retrieved from http://data.worldbank.org/indicator/SP.RUR.TOTL.ZS.

Jovan ZUBOVIĆ

Institute of Economic Sciences, Belgrade, Serbia.
e-mail: jovan.zubovic@ien.bg.ac.rs

Marko JELOČNIK

Institute of Agricultural Economics, Belgrade, Serbia

Jonel SUBIĆ

Institute of Agricultural Economics, Belgrade, Serbia

Farmland Affordability in Serbia

Abstract: By signing the SAA agreement Serbia is committed by 01/09/2017 to change regulations related to sale of agricultural land, which is to grant EU citizens the same rights as the local population have in buying land in Serbia. The aim of this paper is to assess availability of farmland by applying the affordability index, as well as to compare the farmland affordability for EU citizens in their respective countries and in Serbia. Comparative analysis has been conducted with all EU countries, with a special emphasis on Romania, Poland and Slovenia, countries that have a similar environment to Serbia in the field of agriculture. The results show that when comparing the price of agricultural land in Serbia in 2014 and 2015, it is less affordable for Poles and Romanians. On the other hand, it is more affordable for Slovenians, and significantly affordable for Germans, French, Italians, Belgians, Danes and the Dutch. In other words, for farmers from those countries buying agricultural land in Serbia land is five to eleven times more affordable compared with the purchasing power of the local population. Further research in this field is required, especially given the fact that there is a methodological mismatch in recording and calculating average prices of farmland in the EU.

Keywords: Farmland affordability; Republic of Serbia; Farmland price

Introduction

The transition processes in Serbia started at the beginning of the 21st century, when basic conditions for its implementation appeared. In the following years, trade relations and capital accounts have been gradually liberalized, which has enabled the integration of the economic system of Serbia into the international financial and commodity flows (Cvijanović et al., 2009). With its market open, Serbia is becoming more and more interesting to foreign investors, whereby certain industries have started with the process of adapting the existing regulations and business policies, institution building and market autonomy expansion, which altogether leads to a correction of general image and investment attractiveness of the economy (Sredojević et al., 2011).

The transition in agriculture represents the transfer from the former, primarily public and centralized model of agricultural production to a new, market economy concept that characterizes developed EU countries. It implies changes in all levels and in all areas (sectors) of human activities, i.e. both changes in the organization and functioning of the material sphere and changes in the attitude and behavior of market actors. Therefore, the focus is on the change of the paradigm of economy, as well as on changes of a strategic approach of individual actors (Pejanović et al., 2006).

The Republic of Serbia is at its transitional peak, which is the stage representing a radical change of the future development of the national economy. Further acceleration in the development of a market economy would be certainly initiated by investment in new companies (job creation), capital increase of the existing ones, as well as the consolidation of the financial system. It should be noted that the adoption of a large number of public policies and regulations during the last decade has led to a significant improvement of the business environment in Serbia, whereby the primary goal of legal reforms, harmonized with EU regulations, is recognized in the administrative simplification of business activities and strengthening of investment security (Subić et al., 2011).

Along with the transition, in late 2005 Serbia began with negotiations with the EU in defining the Stabilization and Association Agreement (SAA), which once ratified by all EU Member States was concluded in 2008, and according to the decision of the European Council entered into force at the beginning of September 2013. This agreement establishes all the rules of a comprehensive partnership between Serbia and the EU, which will later initiate the accession and full membership of Serbia to the EU. As the primary aspect of the SAA is the gradual establishment of a free trade zone, it should be noted that Serbia and the EU already established a high level of trade integrations through the implementation of the Interim Agreement in early 2010 (DEURS, 2016).

According to the *Law on Agricultural Land,* agricultural land is defined as goods of general interest, and their owner cannot be a foreign natural nor a legal person. Unfortunately, the signing of the SAA activated the clause with changes to the existing regulation that would allow the purchase and disposal of agricultural land by nationals of the EU starting from September 2017, under the same conditions that exist for the local population. The subject of the paper is related to the affordability of agricultural land. The goal of the paper is to assess farmland accessibility in terms of the economic strength of the domestic and EU population interested in agriculture, i.e. marking potential primary buyers (EU member states) of agricultural land in Serbia at the moment when it becomes legally possible. In addition, a comparative analysis is conducted with special emphasis on Romania, Poland and Slovenia, given that these countries share relatively similar natural and economic environment with Serbia in the field of agricultural production.

The conducted research is accompanied by the following methodological framework: desktop research, in-depth interview and the methods of comparative analysis and synthesis. Preparation of the paper is primarily based on secondary (statistical) data obtained at personal request, whereby the sources of information were most often national or multinational (Eurostat) statistical organizations and public institutions (the line ministry, administrations, agencies and scientific institutions in the sphere of agriculture). Primary data was primarily the result of completed in-depth interviews with policy makers. All resulting conclusions were agreed with the statements from the available national and international scientific and professional literature focused on the researched topic.

1. Literature review

The index of farmland affordability (FLA) is a new indicator developed for assessing the degree of accessibility of land to the local population in accordance with their economic strength relative to the strength of foreign investors. In methodological terms, it evolved from the affordability index of real estate sale and rent (Rodda, 2005). The use of FLA in the Western Balkans was first initiated during the pre-accession negotiations between the EU and the Republic of Croatia at the end of the first decade of this century. The index simulates the level of income that local population of average economic strength must spend in order to purchase one hectare of agricultural land. In methodological terms, the index best reflects the relation between the unit price of farmland and the average income in the agricultural sector of a specific territorial unit.

In practice, the above-mentioned is contradicted by several crucial constraints arising from agricultural statistics, such as the low level of comparability of the estimated price of agricultural land in selected countries, as a result of its methodological inconsistency, as well as incomparability of income generated in the agricultural sector. Therefore, income is usually replaced by gross value added (GVA) per person employed in agriculture, forestry and fisheries, based on its comparability and satisfactory approximation of the value of agricultural income. It is pointed out that the number of employees in agriculture, forestry and fisheries resulted from methodologically harmonized Labour Force Survey for all EU member states, and not based on administrative records of the number of employees. Similarly, GVA achieved for overall economic activity, or a sector of the economy, is methodologically uniform in the statistics of national calculations of each EU member state. Finally, Serbia is methodologically adapted to EU statistics.

GA index is presented in the paper as the ratio of the price of agricultural land and GVA per employee in the agricultural sector in the observed territorial unit in a given period intersection. Higher index values imply lower levels of affordability of agricultural land to the local population and vice versa (GRC, 2008; Lovrinčević, Vizek, 2009).

2. The available fund and structure of agricultural land and holdings in the Republic of Serbia

Review of available resources, i.e. the capacity of agricultural land and its structure, as well as the review of the total number and structure of agricultural holdings in Serbia is based on data from the last census of agriculture in 2012.

The largest part of the agricultural land (over 70%) is privately owned, while the remaining part is owned by the state or other forms of ownership. The total available land owned by agricultural holdings (AH), over 5.3 million hectares, is dominated by utilized agricultural land (UAA) accounting for almost 65% (Table 1). It is noted that the sum of agricultural holdings (AH) includes family agricultural holdings (FAH) and legal entities and entrepreneurs (LEE).

Table 1: Available land of agricultural holdings in Serbia in 2012

Element	Available land of agricultural holdings					
	Total	Agricultural land			Forest land	Other
		Total	UAA	Unused		
Area (in ha)	5,346,596.5	3,861,477.4	3,437,423.5	424,053.9	1,023,035.5	462,083.6
Structure (%)	100.0	72.2	64.3	7.9	19.1	8.7

Source: SORS, 2013.

According to their organizational and legal form (Table 2), the structure of agricultural holdings is dominated by family agricultural holdings with more than 99%. Furthermore, almost 80% of the available land of FAH is UAA (Table 3), whereas LEE own approximately an identical proportion of UAA and forest land (over 30%).

Table 2: Agricultural holdings according to their organizational and legal form in 2012

Element	AH			Structure (%)		
	AH, total	FAH	LEE	AH, total	FAH	LEE
Republic of Serbia	631,552	628,552	3,000	100.0	99.5	0.5

Source: SORS, 2013.

Table 3: Available land by legal and organizational form of AH in 2012

Element Total		Available land				
		UAA	Unused AL	Forest land	Other	
FAH						
Area	in ha	3,538,376	2,825,068	158,196	468,018	87,095
	%	100.0	79.8	4.5	13.2	2.5
LEE						
Area	in ha	1,808,221	612,355	265,858	555,018	374,989
	%	100.0	33.9	14.7	30.7	20.7

Source: Ševarlić, 2015.

The average size of agricultural holding viewed through UAA is about 5.4 ha (Table 4), which is considerably higher in the segment of LEE than in FAH. Expressed atomization of land owned by agricultural holdings (average of six plots) is a limiting factor of technological development and strengthening of competitiveness of domestic agriculture.

On the other hand, increase in the average size of UAA is obvious with the growth of economic size (strength) of AH, as well as the expressed differentiation of holdings in the segment of FAH and LEE in the classes of high economic value. Economic size of AH is represented by the value of the total standard output realized during normal operating conditions of agricultural holding (average monetary value of agricultural production calculated at manufacturer's price without direct payments and accrued taxes).

Table 4: Average size of AH according to available UAA and average UAA by AH economic size classes in 2012 (in ha)

Element	Average UAA per AH	AH economic size (in EUR)							
		0-1,999	2,000-3,999	4,000-7,999	8,000-14,999	15,000-24,999	25,000-49,999	50,000-99,999	100,000 and higher
AH	5.4	1.2	2.8	5.0	8.8	15.5	30.2	71.1	375.2
FAH	4.5	1.2	2.8	5.0	8.7	15.3	29.4	64.8	140.7
LEE	204.1	1.5	4.1	12.5	20.3	31.8	63.5	193.4	840.8

Source: SORS, 2013.

Average AH in Serbia has the economic strength of about EUR 6,000, i.e. about EUR 5,000 in the segment of FAH, and nearly EUR 205,000 in the segment of LEE. Since the

FAH segment accounts for about 99.5% of the total number of AH, and given that the group of AH in economic classes from 0–1,999 EUR and 2,000–3,999 EUR accounts for 68% of the total number of AH, with an average size of almost three ha of available UAA, it can be concluded that the national agriculture is dominated by small agricultural holdings, given their property size, with low economic strength (Paraušić, Cvijanović, 2015).

3. The price of agricultural land in Serbia and selected countries

Although the principle of civilizational and religious ethics presupposes equal rights for all people to use and dispose of land as one of the basic existential resources, in reality it is not available to everyone (George, 2005). Physical and financial affordability of agricultural land is one of the primary factors of investment in agricultural production and the consolidation of AH. The determination of the price of agricultural land (intended for sale or lease) is globally a very sensitive issue. Eurostat only kept track of the prices of agricultural land as of 2009. Available data are characterized by frequent interruptions in the offered data series, without the inclusion of all EU member states and methodological inconsistency of displayed parameter values.

On the other hand, Serbia lacks a systematic tracking of rental prices and the value of agricultural land in private ownership. Concluded contracts include the total value of the transaction and the number of cadastral plot, but they often fail to include the area that was traded, which is a major constraint to sales transactions of agricultural land.

Table 5: Average purchase prices of agricultural land (EUR/ha)

Year/Country	Serbia	Poland	Romania	Slovenia
2015	3,500	8,115	4,000	14,000
2014	3,500	7,550	-	15,000
2013	-	6,154	-	14,000
2012		5,944	1,021	14,000
2011	-	4,673	904	15,000
2010	-	4,214	872	15,800
2009	-	3,981	932	17,500
2008	-	3,595	1,303	18,100
2007	-	2,835	1,020	18,450

Source: IAE, 2016; FADNPL, 2016; GIS, 2016; Luca, 2014; FADNRO, 2016.

Consequently, prices of agricultural land in Serbia are generated based on data collected through field research, while prices for Poland are taken from the national FADN database. In the case of Slovenia, data are used from the National Institute of Geodesy, while data for Romania are based on a national expert's estimate. Average purchase prices of agricultural land in Serbia and selected EU countries (Poland, Romania, Slovenia) are provided in the following table (Table 5).

The presented data imply a trend of falling sales prices of agricultural land in Slovenia, their stagnation in Serbia and a trend of growth in Poland and Romania. Compared to the initial year of the observed period, the price of agricultural land in the final year was about three times greater in Poland, about four times higher in Romania, while in the same period in Slovenia it was lower by almost 32%. In the last reporting year, Romania and Serbia have the lowest prices of agricultural land, whereas in Serbia it was as much as four times lower than the current prices in Slovenia, i.e. over two times lower than prices in Poland. In Serbia, higher land prices are found in the region of Vojvodina, while lower prices are estimated for Southern and Eastern Serbia.

4. Affordability of agricultural land

An introduction to the analysis of the affordability of agricultural land in Serbia is used to primarily highlight the importance of agriculture to the national economy. This was achieved by presenting and comparing the share of GVA in the sector of agriculture, forestry and fishery in total GVA realized in the entire economy, and by comparing GVA per employee in the sector of agriculture, forestry and fishery in the Republic of Serbia with the actual values of these indicators in selected EU countries, i.e. Romania, Slovenia and Poland.

Thus, the share of GVA of agriculture, forestry and fishery in total GVA realized in the territory of Serbia implies how important agriculture is to the national economy. The value of this indicator varied over the 2007–2015 period in the range from 6.7–8.4% (Table 6), whereby in 2014 and 2015 it amounted to 7.9% and 6.7%, respectively. This is significantly higher than the value of the same indicator for the EU-28 (1.3% and 1.2%), or the analyzed member states, Romania (5.3% and 4.6%), Poland (2.3% and 2.2%) or Slovenia (1.5% and 1.6%). It can be concluded that with the liberalization of the market of agricultural land in Serbia, foreign investors would initiate a more pronounced technical and technological transfer in agriculture and stricter adherence to the principles of good agricultural practice, which would ultimately lead to increased yields and total value of the agricultural production, i.e. further growth of the agricultural sector's share in total GVA.

Table 6: Share of GVA from the sector of agriculture, forestry and fishery in total GVA realized in Serbia (period 2007–2015)

Element/year	2007	2008	2009	2010	2011	2012	2013	2014	2015[2]
GVA of agriculture, forestry and fishery[1] (in millions of EUR, current prices)	1,860.0	2,394.0	1,934.0	1,975.0	2,371.4	2,027.8	2,212.3	2,191.6	2,199.1
Share of GVA of agriculture, forestry and fishery in total GVA (in %)	7.6	8.4	7.5	8.0	8.4	7.6	7.7	7.9	6.7

Source: SORS, 2016 and authors' calculations based on SORS, 2016.

Note: [1]GVA for the sector of agriculture, forestry and fishery without data for perennial plants; [2]GVA for the sector of agriculture, forestry and fishery and total GVA represent an estimate of the sum for the four quarters, according to calculations of quarterly national calculations.

The contribution of the agriculture sector to the strength of the national economy is visible through the share of employees (aged 15–64) in the sector of agriculture, forestry and fisheries in the total number of employees (Table 7). During the 2007–2015 period, the indicator for the territory of Serbia had a value in the range of 17.1–20.6%, while in 2014 and 2015 it amounted to 18.0%. Its value is significantly higher than the recorded value for the EU-28 over the last two years of the observed period (4.3% and 4.2%). The comparison of the values for Serbia with the values for the analyzed EU member states reveals that greater participation of employees in agriculture, forestry and fisheries is found only for Romania (25.4% and 23.1%), while it is significantly lower in Poland (11.2% and 11.3%) and Slovenia (7.7% and 5.8%).

It can be concluded that the liberalization of agricultural land and the inevitable land consolidation in Serbia would lead to the transfer of a proportionally large part of currently employed people in the agriculture sector to the category of the unemployed or the employed in other industries, which already occurred in the observed EU countries. The average GVA per employee in the sector of agriculture, forestry and fisheries in Serbia varied from EUR 3,976–5,916 (Table 7). Significant increase in the value of the indicator since 2011 was primarily a result of downsizing employees in the agricultural sector. Direct comparison of the value of this indicator achieved in 2014 and 2015 in Serbia (EUR 5,315 and EUR 5,284) with the value achieved in the EU-28 (EUR 17,897 and EUR 18,134), reveals that in both years it was almost three and a half times lower than the EU average. However, the value of the indicator is higher than the value in Poland (EUR 4,827 in 2014, and EUR 4,637 in 2015) and Romania (EUR 3,386 and EUR 3,391), but also significantly lower than the value in Slovenia (EUR 7,232 in 2014, and EUR 10,016 in 2015).

Table 7: GVA per person employed in the sector of agriculture, forestry and fisheries in Serbia (2007–2015)

Element/ year	2007	2008	2009	2010	2011	2012	2013	2014	2015
Number of employees in agriculture, forestry and fisheries[1]	433,025	545,938	486,392	420,731	400,898	391,690	396,961	412,343	416,200
Share of the employed in agriculture, forestry and fisheries in the total number of employees (in %)	17.1	20.6	19.8	18.5	18.5	18.3	18.1	18.0	18.0
GVA per person employed in agriculture, forestry and fisheries (in EUR)	4,295	4,385	3,976	4,694	5,916	5,177	5,573	5,315	5,284

Source: SORS, 2016 and authors' calculations based on SORS, 2016.

Note: [1]Number of employees is generated based on the Labour Force Survey. Since methodological differences occurred in 2008 and 2014, the values of data for 2014 and 2015 are adjusted to previous years, enabling their comparability in the entire period.

The prevailing conclusion is that Serbia has a great potential for technological progress of agriculture. As the previous indicator embodies the current competitiveness and efficiency of national agriculture, it is expected that countries that achieve high values of this indicator are technologically better equipped and have greater economic strength, which provides them with a better position in the purchasing of agricultural land.

Mutual comparison of FLA indexes for Serbia and selected EU member states is primarily limited by methodologically non-conforming record keeping and price determination of agricultural land by Eurostat, national statistical offices and other authorized institutions.

Upon the completion of the analysis (Table 8), it can be concluded that agricultural land, relative to its price and the income-generating strength of the people engaged in agriculture, forestry and fisheries, is utterly unaffordable to the local population in Slovenia, Poland, Romania, Denmark or the Netherlands, while on the other hand, it is very affordable to the local population in France, Bulgaria, Sweden, Slovakia and Spain.

The results of the comparative analysis reveal that during 2014 and 2015, agricultural land in Serbia was a lot more affordable for the local population in relation to the situation in Romania (FLA value of 1.18 in 2015), Slovenia (2.07 in 2015, 1.40 in 2014) or Poland (1.56, 1.75). In addition, the decrease in the value of the FLA index in Poland after joining the EU was the result of the rapid rise in prices of agricultural land, while increase of the FLA index in Slovenia resulted primarily from the growth of GVA and reduction of the number of employees in the agricultural sector.

Comparing the value of FLA index between groups of countries that are old and new EU member states (like Bulgaria and Croatia, including Serbia, as a candidate country for EU accession), it can be seen that affordability of agricultural land to local people is higher in the second group of countries. It is assumed that the perceived gap for the value of FLA will be mitigated in the future as a result of the expected decrease in the number of employees in the agricultural sector, and faster growth of GVA per employee in relation to the rise in prices of agricultural land.

Table 8: FLA index for Serbia and selected EU countries (2009–2015 period)

Year/country	2009	2010	2011	2012	2013	2014	2015
Serbia	-	-	-	-	-	0.67	0.67
Poland	0.27	1.04	1.00	1.23	1.16	1.56	1.75
Romania	0.33	0.30	0.24	0.36	-	-	1.18
Slovenia	3.00	2.53	1.96	2.31	2.16	2.07	1.40
Belgium	0.85[1]	-	-	-	-	-	-
Bulgaria	0.26	-	-	-	-	-	-
Czech Republic	0.47	-	-	-	-	-	-
Denmark	0.97	-	-	-	-	-	-
Finland	0.54	-	-	-	-	-	-
France	0.17	-	-	-	-	-	-
The Netherlands	1.18	-	-	-	-	-	-

Year/country	2009	2010	2011	2012	2013	2014	2015
Croatia	0.29[1]	-	-	-	-	-	-
Luxembourg	0.67	-	-	-	-	-	-
Germany	0.54[1]	-	-	-	-	-	-
Slovakia	0.37	-	-	-	-	-	-
Spain	0.38	-	-	-	-	-	-
Sweden	0.30	-	-	-	-	-	-
UK	0.59[1]	-	-	-	-	-	-

Source: Authors' calculations based on Eurostat data, 2016; SORS, 2016; IAE, 2016; FADNPL, 2016; GIS, 2016; Luca, 2014; FADNRO, 2016.

Note: [1]The data for Germany, Belgium and Croatia are for 2006, while data for the UK are for 2008.

Differences in the income-generating strength of employees in agriculture lead to the assumption that investment in the purchase of agricultural land in Serbia would be most interesting to the populations of the EU member states from the immediate (Slovenia) or wider surroundings (Germany, the Netherlands, France, Belgium and others), that have an agricultural tradition and in which agricultural land is less affordable to the local population.

Table 9: Affordability of agricultural land in Serbia to farmers in selected EU member states

Year/country	2014	2015
Serbia	0.67	0.67
Poland	0.72	0.75
Romania	1.03	1.03
Slovenia	0.48	0.35
Belgium	0.08	0.08
Denmark	0.07	0.08
France	0.09	0.08
The Netherlands	0.06	0.06
Italy	0.09	0.08
Germany	0.10	0.13

Source: Author's calculations based on data from Table 8.

The previous table (Table 9) reveals that compared to the current prices of agricultural land in Serbia (in 2014 and 2015) and the income-generating strength of farmers in certain EU countries, agricultural land in Serbia is unaffordable to Poles (FLA index 0.72, or 0.75) and Romanians (1.03 in both years), while it is more affordable to Slovenians (0.48 or 0.35) and significantly more affordable to Germans, French, Italians, Belgians, Danes or the Dutch (for these countries the values of FLA index range from 0.06–0.13). Therefore, agricultural land in Serbia is five to almost twelve times more affordable to German, French, Belgian, Italian, Danish or Dutch farmers than to Serbian farmers.

Conclusion

During the process of EU accession negotiations, following the provisions set by the Stabilization and Association Agreement, Serbia was obliged to adjust the legislation related to farmland acquisition so that by 1st September 2017 EU citizens could purchase and dispose land under the same conditions as Serbian entities do. Taking into account current prices of agricultural land in Serbia and countries in the region, it is to be expected that after fiberizing farmland trade domestic farmers could economically compete with EU citizens. According to projections, initial buyers of Serbian farmland are expected to originate from Western EU member states, such as Germany, France, Belgium, Italy, Denmark or the Netherlands. After liberalization, growth of households' farmland size is expected, as well as improvement of current technical–technological bases and agricultural production competitiveness. On the other hand, it can also be expected to increase unemployment at the national level.

Some administrative and methodological limitations in our research resulted in setting some recommendations in order to facilitate monitoring and forecasting of capital flow in the EU farmland market; a) methodological convergence of farmland price assessment processes (administrative recording); and b) making obligatory reporting on farmland prices in the FADN survey.

Acknowledgement

This paper is a part of projects III–46006 and 179015, funded by the Ministry of Education, Science and Technical Development of the Republic of Serbia, for the project period 2011–2017.

References

1. Cvijanović, D., Mihajlović, B., Simonović, Z. (2009). Tranzicija u Srbiji: Efekti i ograničenja. Tranzicija, 10 (21–22):87–100.
2. DEURS (2016). Stabilization and accession agreement. Portal of the Delegation of the European Union in the Republic of Serbia, Belgrade, Serbia, 2016,

accessed at: April 2017, available at: http://europa.rs/srbija-i-evropska-unija/kljucni-dokumenti/sporazum-o-stabilizaciji-i-pridruzivanju/.
3. EUROSTAT. (2016). Data available in the database active at the portal of EUROSTAT, Luxembourg, accessed: July 2016, available at: http://ec.europa.eu/eurostat/data/database.
4. FADNPL. (2016). Price of agricultural land in Poland. on demand received data, FADN Poland: Warsaw, Poland, received July 2016.
5. FADNRO. (2016). Price of agricultural land in Romania. on demand received data, FADN Romania: Bucharest, Romania, received July 2016.
6. George, H. (2005). Progress and Poverty. Cosimo Inc.: NY, USA, 2005, p. 420.
7. GIS: Price of agricultural land in Slovenia. Portal of GIS, Geodetski Institut Slovenije: Ljubljana, Slovenia, accessed July 2016, available at: http://www.trgnepremicnin.si/sl/vsebine-portala/periodicna-porocila.
8. GRC: Pregovaračko stajalište Republike Hrvatske: Poglavlje 4. - Sloboda kretanja kapitala. report, Government of the Republic of Croatia, Zagreb, Croatia, June 2008, p. 25, available at: http://eupregovori.bos.rs/progovori-o-pregovorima/uploaded/04.pdf.
9. IAE: Price of agricultural land in Serbia. Internal documentation, Institute of Agricultural Economics: Belgrade, Serbia, 2016.
10. Law on agricultural land. Official gazette of the Republic of Serbia, no. 62/06, 65/08 – other laws, 41/09 and 112/15.
11. Lovrinčević, Ž., Vizek, M. (2009). Poljoprivredno zemljište u novim zemljama članicama EU i u Hrvatskoj: Cijene, priuštivost i konvergencijski potencijal. Ekonomski pregled, 60(1–2). 28–49.
12. Luca, L. (2014). Romanian land market regulatory framework: The legislative corrections in 2014. Agricultural Economics and Rural Development - New Series, 11(2), 2014, pp. 203–212.
13. Popescu, Gh.H. (2016). The Role of Multinational Corporations in Global Environmental Politics, Economics, Management, and Financial Markets 11(3):72–78.
14. Nica, E., Ioan H. (2016). The State-led System of Global Environmental Governance, Economics, Management, and Financial Markets 11(3):79–85.
15. Zaga, S. D. (2016). The Impact of Nutritional Programs in Mexico, American Journal of Medical Research 3(1):7–38.
16. Popescu, Gh. H., Florin, C. C., Teodora I. B. (2016). Environmental Consequences of Liberalized and Expanding Global Trade, Journal of Self-Governance and Management Economics 4(3):66–72.
17. Nica, E., Cristina, M., Ana-Madalina, P. (2016). "Competition in the Worldwide Workplace: Economic Globalization and Labor Rights," Journal of Self-Governance and Management Economics 4(3):73–79.
18. Nica, E. (2016). The Effect of Perceived Organizational Support on Organizational Commitment and Employee Performance, Journal of Self-Governance and Management Economics 4(4):34–40.

19. Nica, E. (2016). Employee Voluntary Turnover as a Negative Indicator of Organizational Effectiveness, Psychosociological Issues in Human Resource Management 4(2):220–226.
20. Machan, T.R. (2016). Commerce and Its Normative Dimensions, Psychosociological Issues in Human Resource Management 4(1):7–40.
21. Paraušić, V., Cvijanović, D. (2014). Ekonomska veličina poljoprivrednih gazdinstva u Srbiji i preporuka mera za njihovo osnaživanje, proceedings, Konferencija – Primena podataka Popisa poljoprivrede 2012. u analizi stanja poljoprivrede i u planiranju agrarne politike u Republici Srbiji, Subotica, Maj 2014, RZS: Beograd, Srbija, 2014, pp. 25–61.
22. Pejanović, R., Milanović, M., Cvijanović, D. (2006). Tranzicija (poljo)privrede Republike Srbije: Dometi, efekti i ograničenja. Ekonomika poljoprivrede, 53(4):937–946.
23. Rodda, D. T. (2005). Recent house price trends and homeownership affordability. U.S. Department of Housing and Urban Development: Washington DC, USA, 2005, p. 77.
24. SORS: Agricultural census in the Republic of Serbia – 2012, Agriculture in Serbia. book I and II, Statistical office of the Republic of Serbia: Belgrade, Serbia, 2013.
25. SORS: Data available in the database active at the portal of the Statistical Office of the Republic of Serbia, SORS, Belgrade, Serbia, accessed: July 2016, available at: http://www.stat.gov.rs/WebSite/public/ReportView.aspx.
26. Sredojević, Z., Jeločnik, M., Subić, J. (2011). Economic indicators of condition and tendencies of Serbian economy. Economia. Seria Management, 14(2):348–358.
27. Subić, J., Ivanović, L., Bekić, B. (2011). Characteristics of investment process in Republic of Serbia: Overview on municipalities Apatin, Inđija and Zrenjanin. Scientific Papers. Management, Economic Engineering in Agriculture and Rural Development, 11(2):220–226.
28. Ševarlić, M. (2015). Poljoprivredno zemljište. study within the edition of Agriculture in the Republic of Serbia: Agricultural census - 2012, SORS: Belgrade, Serbia, 2015, p. 260, available at: https://issuu.com/zavodstatistika/docs/poljo privredno_zemljiste_-_web.

Constantin POPESCU

The Bucharest University of Economic Studies, Piața Romană nr. 6, sector 1, Bucharest, Romania, email: pop.costica@gmail.com

Vasile Miltiade STANCIU

Spiru Haret University, str. Ion Ghica nr. 13., sector 3, Bucharest, Romania, email: miltiade_stanciu@yahoo.com

Respiritualization of Basic Education – A Great Urgency in Romania

Abstract: The purpose of this paper is to promote re-thinking (respiritualization) of education in Romania, starting from the basic one. Our research highlights that at present there are opposite directions of basic education, as education for a start in life has negative consequences that jeopardise "the health of the entire living system". The "illiteracy of people who have not studied" and the "illiteracy of people who have studied" are the greatest dangers to the future of human life. We argue that the family, the community, the business environment, the society, the church, and the state bear the entire responsibility for the opposite directions of the basic education. By respiritualization of basic education in Romania, we understand integral reconsideration of this process from the inside to the outside of the people in the spirit of the following principles: gratuity out of love, liberty in responsibility and faith in meaning values.

Keywords: systemic wisdom (ecological conscience), basic education, respiritualization, fruitage, loving gratuity, illiteracy of people who have studied

Introduction

The research in the latest decades, especially that of a transdisciplinary character, highlights that the serious problems we face in life as "existence in relation" have generated the current global systemic crisis affecting "the health of the entire living system" (Popescu, 2012).

The global poverty, systemic pollution, cosmo-technical arming, wars, terrorism, etc. that humanity faces did not fall from the sky; they are not the result of God's will or hostile nature, but originate in human and institutional behaviours in the opposite direction. According to "systemic wisdom" (Bateson, 1987), Mother Nature keeping us in her lap invented sexuality for life diversity as "integrated live wholes" and death for its individuality under uncertain conditions.

Human society, hosted by planet Earth, as "a live and conscious organism" (Capra, 2004), invented education as an internal transformation process of man, in order to adapt to life conditions under unavoidable circumstances of incertitude, limitation, and certitude of death.

When man's education and the fruitage of the behaviours resulting from it are in harmony with the exigencies of "the health of the entire living system", with people aspiring towards life in decency and flourishing, we say they are in the "torrent of evolution" (Adler, 1995, p. 194). By "the health of the entire living system" we understand the assembly of the processes making up the homeostasis of the "integrated live wholes" ensuring their dynamic structural balance and the flexibility of the status parameters.

The human and institutional behaviours that jeopardise "the health of the entire living system" alienate people's expectations of a life in decency and happiness, and are in the opposite direction of our common evolution. As man during the adaptation and transformation process is both nature and society all the time, "education in and for life" (Pope Francis, 2014) must turn the available natural endowment into maximum profit, enriching it with life experience, results of scientific knowledge and faith in meaning values, as natural-spiritual capital specific to each human being that is used day by day and hour by hour.

As a continuous and conscious process, the education of the human being seems to start long before birth (Szent-Györgyi, 1981); it takes place in the natural time before birth, becomes "home" education in the first seven years, develops through institutional education in school, grows up during the working process as education for productive active life and ends when preparing the life decline and understanding of death's certitude.

Within this process integrating "memory of the past", life in harmony with the bearing mother and the present lived in the family, community, school, and social-spiritual environment, pre-existing natural values harmonise with traditional scientific, religious, cultural and spiritual values representing the foundation of the way we think, choose and build, the way we live and love.

Therefore, each human behaviour in the direction or in the opposite direction of the evolution torrent originates both in the nature in man and in the society in man, from the way the natural-spiritual makes or does not make the consciousness of meaning and of the understanding of life as "existence in relation". It is difficult, if not impossible to establish how much of the human behaviours in the direction or in the opposite direction are due to nature in man and to society in man.

Although such a distinction is difficult to be made, it is good to remember that education must shape the nature inside man, in order to transform its creative potential into values, the eternity becoming the debt of the ancestors for the life lived by each generation coexisting and following (Adler, *ibid.*, p. 198).

1. From Scientific Knowledge Wisdom

Education as a continuous and conscious process, under the direct responsibility of human individuals and all interest bearers: family, community, working organizations, church, state, society, and the environment was, is and will be studied by enlightened spirits in understanding this social phenomenon. From them we inherit reflection models, psychologies, methods, faiths, wisdom, traditions, etc., which we have to learn to adapt in order to live in harmony, all the time getting us out of the habit of doing all those useless things that are not in the life direction nor in its service, and do not help us to relieve pain and achieve happiness.

The integrating learning process is researched from various points of view, depending on *the imperatives of the life lived* (Adler, *ibid.*, p. 34) and from the knowledge perspective as well, and there results the main idea that it includes, at the same time, both understanding the need to learn the useful and to create new things, and the need to give up the habit of doing useless and harmful things. Such a process implies, at the same time, learning how to learn and learning how to unlearn.

In this respect, Lev Tolstoi (2009) in his reflections at the end of his life reached the wisdom that: "The actual knowledge is only one: to know how to live. People know many things, but this is something they do not know and they even think that they do not have to know and do not need to know how to live. Useless knowledge occupies their mind and prevents them from knowing what they must know". Love for All and for Everything represents the universal law of understanding that education needs to help human beings to form and to grow up with freedom in love, in social responsibility and community, in compassion and human solidarity.

The winner of the Nobel Prize for medicine Albert Szent-Györgyi (1981, p. 215), having studied human life and having interpreted human behaviors in terms of meaning values, evaluated that: "... people cannot have another higher purpose than ennobling their lives, creating a world without hunger, fear and diseases, a peaceful world where decency, equity, good will, harmony and fairness prevail and which is led by wisdom and competence". In this respect, the humanist scientist Albert Szent-Györgyi builds the model of institutional education from the same perspective as Tolstoi and as many other researchers in the field, formulating the functions of school education as a conscious and live process. School, the scientist says, "must mainly teach us how to learn, waken our desire for knowledge, teach us the joy of having done something well and the creation emotion, teach us how to love what we do and help us discover what we would like to do" (*Ibid.*, pp. 130–131).

From the perspective of understanding life as "love in action" as lived and interpreted by Mother Teresa and by other people as well, the entire educational process must also be finalized by the capacity of getting closer to understanding Truth, Beauty and Goodness, are fundamental values, a "human trinity" that orients our choices, even under the most difficult conditions. Human beings getting closer to these fundamental values is a permanent process, started by "home education" and continued by all steps of formation and growing up and feeling like a human being, where we learn how to learn and to unlearn as well, as Alexandr Solzhenitsyn also said (1978) in his speech at Harvard University in 1978. The courage of saying the truth in your conscience and of getting the truth in your soul, no matter whether it is convenient for you or not, is the key to human beings growing up with freedom in responsibility, love and faith. Without this courage by which we live the truth in our conscience within acts and facts of human and institutional behavior, the education of human beings remains a "dead storage", that transforms from the inside neither the man nor the society where the man lives. Lack of courage to say or receive the truth is evaluated by Solzhenitsyn as the start of the decline in life as "existence in relation".

In Einstein and Krishnamurti we meet close wisdoms as regards the fundamental problems of education in the life direction and at its service when they evaluate that "only a life lived at the service of others is worth living" and that "no human problem can be solved without love". These two enlightened spirits in knowing wisdom allow us to evaluate that the actual education is that made for life fulfilment (Rosemberg, 2005). Such a universal educational model is one that cultivates pupils' authentic feelings, promotes sincerity in manifesting young people's behavior, and strengthens pupils' trust in the following values: truth, beauty and the good of humanity. It teaches the pupil to search for the future in the "memory of 'systemic wisdom' and in the 'dream in hope'" (Popescu, 2015).

Having his vision in the same universal educational model, Pope Francis (2014) develops this systemic vision of education as "education for difficult times", when a human being is asked for solidarity and social communion, compassion and commitment, love in action in acts and facts of human and institutional behavior.

Thinking about a *perfect society*, John Kenneth Galbraith (1997) thinks that education is the most important function of the society and that the basic education is needed mostly by the poor, in order to learn how to fight poverty, take responsibility for their own lives and refuse a servant behavior, which not only makes performance of appropriate direction, but also produces serious dependences in opposite directions and human inequalities.

In "...an ABC of human wisdom", Stephan R. Covey (1996) highlighted that the actual transformation only takes place inside human beings, where lenses are created through which we see and interpret the world, paradigms through which we relate to life as "existence in relation". The actual change for good, Covey said, is produced from inside the human being to its outside, by tenacious work at the roots.

When transformation is borrowed from outside, the power of change, Covey said, "generates weakness in the borrower, as it strengthens his/her dependency on external factors in solving his/her problems. It generates weakness in the person seeing himself/herself obliged to 'make himself/herself acceptable to someone', preventing him/her from thinking independently, preventing his/her evolution and his/her deliberate obedience to inside discipline. And, in the last resort, it lowers the quality of the relation. Fear replaces cooperation and the parties involved occupy defensive and arbitrary positions" (Covey, *ibid.*).

Understanding the organic union between learning and unlearning, John Maynard Keynes (2009), at the end of the preface written to *General theory of using labour force, interest and money*, said that the difficulty for the human being is not represented by assimilating to the new, but by getting rid of old and useless things that have nestled in all corners of our minds, hearts and souls, by virtue of the education we received.

From the wisdoms presented and from other interpretations conceiving the actual education from the perspective of human life fulfillment, it results that Einstein is right when he states that the evil in the current educational school model, both in basic education and in higher education, originates mainly from: "applying fear-based methods", "pursuing the aim by using force" and "using artificial authority in the education process" (Einstein, 2008).

While Amartya Sen demonstrates in *Development as freedom* (2004) that "there is no substitute for individual responsibility", Pope Francis updates this interpretation in the context of the current global crisis, underlying that "no one is liable for anything; either for what was bad in the past or for what should be done".

We also believe that a deficit in freedom in love and in responsibility in displaying human and institutional behaviors is the deepest cause originating, in fact, in the current educational model based on self-centred egoism, individualism without limits, generator of excesses and deficits in growing that disturb the homeostasis of individual and social life, unbalancing the flexibility of social life and its relation with ecological flexibility and promoting an "economy that kills the life of the integrated life wholes" (Wijckman, Rockstrom, 2012).

In the spirit of what was said before, the winner of the Nobel Prize for economics, Joseph Stiglitz (2015), demonstrates that the huge inhumane and social inequalities in the most developed country in the world (1% of the population ownes as much wealth as the rest of 99%), USA did not fall from the sky, they are not the result of market mechanisms, but they are the direct result of wrong public policies, of certain institutional behaviors in the opposite direction.

In the recent report to the Rome Club, referred to as *Reinventing prosperity* issued in November 2016, Maxton and Randers, starting from the systemic analysis of the urgent problems of globalization of the business world, underlie the need to rethink the current model of producing and distributing wealth, orienting the economic growth processes towards increasing occupation and reducing social inequalities, but keeping climate change consequences under control.

2. Systemic Crisis of Basic Education

The research in the education field and our analyses taking Romania as an example (Popescu, Stanciu, 2015) highlight that the current global systemic crisis originates mainly from the current model of basic education, where the deficits and excesses of human and institutional behaviors emerge.

Considering that life is an "existence in relation", it is normal to interpret these deficits and excesses in a systemic, integrating vision, choosing both the cause-consequence relation and the system of the mechanism for manifesting the simple and multiple propagated effect in social life (Capra, 2004).

Within the deficit system causing the crisis in the basic education, we can integrate the following: *home deficit* (Popescu, Taşnadi, 2009), the increasing number of children left by their parents who left to work abroad, children under irresponsible care of authorities; the *increasing deficit in vocational teachers* in most schools and especially in the rural environment; *deficit in school subjects related to life in community, work for life fulfilment, love of truth, beauty and goodness; deficit in individual, familial, communitarian, institutional responsibility and in faith in appropriate development of school activity; deficit in love of promoting social education (Adler, 1995, p. 203)* that promotes collaboration and cooperation, human solidarity and social communion; *deficit in full understanding of life* (Krishnamurti, 2012) as "existence in relation".

In their unity and interdependency, these deficits of the base education are the expression and condition of certain human and institutional behaviors that prevent wise self-government of their own lives and the responsible government of social life as a whole, in the name of the common good and based on the values of direction durability.

As a result of these deficits in the educational process, we have a complex system of excesses of human and institutional behaviours that are in the opposite direction of evolution. In fact, wherever there are "gaps" in human beings' education, they automatically fill with useless and harmful things, generating behaviors governed by greed, hatred, intolerance, lies, etc. (Osho, 2006).

All these excesses of education and behavior did not fall from the sky, but are the result of the current education model, and we can highlight the following aspects: *excess of school subjects*, so-called modern and useless ones that prevent appropriate organization of pupils' learning time; *excess of meaningless examinations and evaluations*, from the perspective of education in the service of life; *excess of artificial authority*, of methods based on fear and force; *excess of freedom outside love*, without responsibility, authentic knowledge and faith in the hope certitude; *increasing number of illiterates "who have not studied"*, especially in areas dominated by poverty and corruption; *excesses in the number of people "who have not studied"* in almost all urban and rural regions and centres where inhuman inequalities are registered between citizens' duties and rights.

Watched in their dynamic union and interdependency in their actual movement in the time of our common space, these excesses and deficits in education reflect in what we call the "behaviour of second hand minds" (Albert Szent-Györgyi, 1981).

Essentially, these integrating behaviors generating opposite directions in our common evolution are, according to doctor Viktor Frankl, "in the majority position" in any larger or smaller social group. What is even worse, according to Frankl, is that this majority group was, is and will be dominant related to the minority group of "common sense" people, educated in love and in full understanding of life (Frankl, 2009).

In our opinion as well, "man's failure", dealt with a long time ago by Heraclit, can be explained today by the existence of opposite directions related to: a decrease in individual responsibility for the wise self-government of one's own life; emphasis of "live pigs" behavior, thick-skinned people who are dominant in all social groups; extension of human behaviors of "live dead bodies" at the level of all public and private authorities, where a lot of money is earned for little or no work (watch and win!); promotion of the principles "right person in the place right for another person" and "right person in the wrong place"; emphasis on inhumane inequalities in life as "existence in relation" with significant consequences upon "the health of the entire living system"; increase of the impact of "second hand minds" on administrating the general business of the human community; decrease of people's competition against themselves in a social environment that does not favor collaboration and cooperation for the sustainable good of human communities.

Accepting Einstein's thesis that we cannot get out of a crisis using the thinking that led us to that crisis, we believe that the solution to the crisis of the basic education is another "borrowed mind", a different way of looking at education's role and functions, another paradigm used to destroy in a creative way, by learning and unlearning the current educational model, laying the bases of education in the life direction and at its service.

We are experiencing a progress originating from scientific knowledge and from the usefulness of people's hands, which does not seem to be human when these wonderful achievements are transformed into instruments for destroying life as "integrated live wholes" (Pope John Paul II, 2008).

Interpreting this crisis from the perspective of the dangers and opportunities that it contains, it is appropriate to learn how to unlearn the opposite directions generating dangers and, at the same time, to learn the need to respiritualize basic education, transforming it into acts and facts of human individual, social and institutional behavior in harmony with the exigencies of "the health of the entire living system".

3. For the Respiritualization of Basic Education in Romania

The worrying phenomena that develop continuously in our basic education, considered to be in an "actual reform" such as: the increase in school drop-outs and the number of illiterates among the young population, the increase in the number of pupils who studied but do not have appropriate knowledge, having only one diploma without any scientific or educational coverage in many cases, as well as the occurrence of basic education graduates, of people in high school without any practical job to offer them a productive occupation or a vocational continuation of their training, etc. are all persuasive evidence that this educational system must be reinvented, rethought and respiritualized.

Such a process is part of the large scope of "consciousness revolution", as imagined by Laszlo, Grof și Russell (2009) where a new paradigm needs to be present and allow young human beings to be formed and to grow up in liberty and responsibility, in love and solidarity.

It is essential in the beginning that this unique institutional process underlies a system of principles originating from knowledge of the legities of "the health of the entire living system", becoming in actual terms individual and institutional values governing choices and behaviors in life as "existence in relation".

We do not claim that we are able to present these principles exhaustively, but we do believe that none of the principles below should be absent: Man is the organic part of "the entire living system" (Capra, 2004); People have the sacred duty to collaborate and cooperate to solve the big problems defining their lives (Gavriliu, 1995); The whole prevails upon the part in life homeostasis (Pope Francis); Harmony is superior to freedom in the evolution torrent, where there is no rest (Semaschko); Time is governed by the eternity of fruitage of people's work (Pope Francis); "Everything can be different as well" if it does not jeopardize "the health of the entire living system" (Adler, 1995); Let us become the change we want to take place for humanity's sake (Ghandi); "Only a life lived in the cause of others is worth living" (Einstein); A meaningful life needs a noble and inspiring aim and creative effort (Tolstoi); A common part of human life from anywhere and from any time is subordinated to "relieving pain and getting happiness" (Dalai Lama); Only what is healthy for the entire living system is healthy for Man and for all people (Popescu); Let us love the people close to us like ourselves, justly gaining the love of the people close to us (Selye); Let us promote long-term efforts whose results do not face death, bringing pure joy, as perpetuation forever (Brâncuși); Let us harmonize excellence in skills with excellence in wisdom (Pope Francis); Let us harmonize our body, soul and social functions in order to tie individuals to society (Adler); Let us form an independent, inventive, innovative and creative thinking (Frankl); Let us promote liberty in love, responsibility and faith in hope certitude (Pope Francis); There is no substitute for individual responsibility (Sen); Health cannot be substituted (Popescu); Basic education must be free out of love, in responsibility and efficiency, out of the faith in hope certitude (Pope Francis); Let us promote the culture of dialogue for collaboration and cooperation for the common good and for solving major existential problems (Pope Francis).

Conclusions and proposals

Pursuant to these principles, the model of basic education that we propose for Romania can be built in the following key directions of action and collaboration of all bearers of interests. These concrete actions form in union and interdependency the system of responsibilities for the building and good operation of basic education.

Essentially, our proposals imply that: Basic education is compulsory for each human individual until finishing high school; The responsibility belongs to the individual, family, community, school, church and state; In each urban and rural community there must be a Committee for Responsibility in Basic Education (CREB) made up of the representatives of: families, community, church, business environment, etc., democratically elected and taking into account mental health (CSM1), material (CSM2) and moral (CSM3) criteria; Punishment threat is established by law for all bearers of interests and responsibilities in the basic education field, for school drop-out or inadequate training cases; Each general school or school of "educational maturity" (high school) is lead by a Council of Representatives (CR) comprised of pupils, teachers, families, church, community, business environment, etc. The CR annually presents public reports of community importance on the status of basic education in school; The responsibility of financing schools belongs to the state, regions, counties and local communities, as percentages established by law, depending on the number of pupils taken care of by one teacher; Funds can also be attracted from other sources following the improvement in education quality and solving of special social problems; Responsibility for the school curriculum is ensured by harmonizing an obligatory part, common to all schools (a percentage of the school time) with a concrete part, specific to the community; The CR is responsible for applying the school curriculum, directly or indirectly improving it after each education cycle, graduated by a generation (after four grades, after eight grades, after twelve grades); The CR is lead by a president on behalf of teachers and by a vice-president for pupils' happiness on behalf of families, both elected democratically.

The organization and operation system for basic education that we design could be oriented towards the following: Organization in cycles: primary cycle, for initiation (I) first four grades (6–10 years); secondary cycle II, for training (10–14 years) and cycle III, for growing up (14–18 years); Each cycle is concluded with a final evaluation, diploma for primary education, diploma for secondary education and diploma for educational maturity; The pupils pass from one cycle to another based on graduation average marks, ranking the pupils for training groups: excellent, very good, good and satisfactory; Depending on the average marks obtained after each year of study, pupils pass from one category to another; Depending on the coefficient for ranking study groups, one for the first (satisfactory) and 1.5 for good, two for very good and three for excellent, a scholarship to encourage creativity is awarded; Depending on the scores received by the teachers, it is established which class of pupils each teacher is to work with and teachers' salaries are also established, including bonuses for excellence.

For the last four-year cycle of basic education, which falls into various categories: professional schools, job schools, vocational schools, high schools, etc. we propose the following institutional exigencies: The last cycle of basic education is chosen based on a vocational test, practical skills, etc. that is definitive for pupils' distribution; The last cycle of basic education is performed in: philology, philosophy, nature sciences, agricultural sciences, human sciences, administrative sciences, social sciences, political sciences, art, etc. Graduation from the last cycle of basic education is finalized by a maturity diploma in various fields and is based on two types of assessments: An assessment of general culture, valid for all graduates, with an integrating character and a vocational assessment, based on a project presented before a specialized commission. It is compulsory to obtain the minimum score of five for each of the two assessments; One or two assessments can be repeated only once in the same school year; if a student fails to pass in the respective year they can repeat in the next year; If in the next school year no pass is obtained, the last school year in the maturity cycle is repeated, but paying for the schooling, until the minimum graduation score is obtained.

Without developing the structure of training within basic education, at various stages, considering the lack of space, we think that subject matters related to life lived in the community, work based on social division, knowing and understanding natural and social phenomena and trust in the laws of love, solidarity, social communion and compassion, structured from simple to complex and related to the specifics of the region, of humane, urban and rural communities, on normal interactions generated by international phenomena must be wisely included in the school curriculum in order to be embedded as seeds in the fertile soil of the lives of young people called to form and grow up in freedom and responsibility.

As the young human being is being formed and growing up it is essential to harmonize pupils' loading level with the time for study and recreation, so that the time spent at school does not exceed two to three hours for cycle I, three to four hours for cycle II and four to five hours for cycle III. We also recommend choosing teachers for subjects and performing the assessment in an integrating form, by combining two or three related subjects and having no more than two or three assessments a year.

The difficulties in implementing the model we have proposed relate to: learning the unlearning process both at the institutional behavior level and at the human, individual and social behavior level; understanding human freedom as the responsibility of undertaking self-government of one's own life in freedom and harmony; real appraising of the teacher by all bearers of interest in the education field; rethinking public educational policies in terms of the exigencies of "the health of the entire living system" and not of right or left party ideologies that do not ensure continuity as essential feature of these policies; institutional and human understanding of gratuity of basic education in tight connection with love, with responsibility of all bearers of interest based on economic, social-human, spiritual and ecological efficiency implying that faith without education gives us nothing but ignorance, and difficult and boring labor, poverty and appeal to crime and violence.

Our conclusion is that such a project for Romania, as a country of education in love and full understanding of life must be debated with all bearers of interest and based on the principles of life as "exigency in harmony", in an institutional form that should live, as Spiru Haret said (*apud.* Maliţa, 2012): "somebody who will not have love for family and for country, honesty, civic and military courage, abnegation, justice feeling, activity, energy is unlikely to be a good citizen; on the contrary, he/she will be more than an ignorant, an obstacle, if not a danger for his/her country and family".

References

1. Adler, A. (1995). Sensul vieţii. IRI: Bucharest.
2. Bateson, G. (1987). Steps to an Ecology of Mind. Jason Aronson Inc: Nortvale.
3. Capra, F. (2004). Momentul adevărului. Ştiinţă, societate şi cultură. O viziune fascinantă asupra unei noi realităţi înconjurătoare. O reconciliere a ştiinţei cu spiritul uman, pentru un viitor durabil. Tehnică: Bucharest.
4. Covey, S. (1996). Eficienţa în 7 trepte. Un Abecedar al înţelepciunii umane. All: Bucharest.
5. Dalai L. (2010). Despre fericire, viaţă şi multe altele. Conversaţii cu Rajiv Mehrotra. Curtea Veche: Bucharest.

6. Einstein, A. (2008). Cuvinte memorabile, culese şi adnotate de Alice Calaprice. Humanitas: Bucharest.
7. Frankl, V. (2009). Omul în căutarea sensului vieţii. Meteor Press: Bucharest.
8. Galbraith, J. (1997). Societatea perfectă. La ordinea zilei: binele omului. Eurosong&Book: Bucharest.
9. Gavriliu, L. (1995). Prefaţă la Adler, Alfred: 1995, Sensul vieţii. IRI: Bucharest.
10. Keynes, John, Maynard: 2009, Teoria generală a ocupării forţei de muncă, a dobânzii şi a banilor. Publica: Bucharest.
11. Krishnamurti: (2012). Despre educaţie. Arta învăţării şi valoarea vieţii. Herald: Bucharest.
12. Laszlo, E., Grof, S., Russell, P. (2009). Revoluţia conştiinţei. Noua spiritualitate şi transformare planetară. Elena Francisc: Bucharest.
13. Maliţa, M. (2012). Strategii de supravieţuire in istoria poporului român, Ed a II-a revăzută şi adăugită. Compania: Bucharest.
14. Osho. (2006). Cartea înţelegerii. Crearea propriei tale căi spre libertate. Mar: Constanţa.
15. Pope, F. (2014). Educaţia în slujba vieţii. Propuneri pentru vremuri grele. ARCB: Bucharest.
16. Pope John Paul II: 2008, Enciclice. ARCB: Bucharest.
17. Popescu, C. (2015). Visul din speranţă. Eco Print: Satu Mare.
18. Popescu, C., Stanciu, V.M. (2015). A Holistic Vision of an Ecolonomic Society Model. National Strategies Observer, no.1/vol 1, pp. 65–74.
19. Popescu, C. (2012). Despre viaţă şi economie. ASE: Bucharest, p. 450.
20. Popescu, C., Taşnadi, A. (2009). Respiritualizarea. Învaţă să fii OM. ASE: Bucharest.
21. Rosemberg, M.B. (2005). Adevărata educaţie pentru o viaţă împlinită. Elena Francisc: Bucharest.
22. Maxton, G., Randers, J. (2016). Reinventing prosperity. Managing Economic Growth to Reduce Unemployment, Inequality and Climate Change. Greystone Books: Vancouver/Berkeley.
23. Semaschko, L.S.(coord) (2008). Academia Armoniei / Păcii Mondiale şi a Educaţiei Armonioase Generale într-o societate a informaţiei. Asociaţia Armoniei Globale (GHA): Sankt Petersburg.
24. Sen, A. (2004). Dezvoltarea ca libertate. Economica: Bucharest.
25. Soljeniţin, A. (1978). The exhausted West, Harvard Magazine, http://harvardmagazine.com/sites/default/files/1978_Alexander_Solzhenitsyn.pdf, accesed in 10 January 2017.
26. Stiglitz, J. (2015). Marea divizare. Societăţile inegale şi ce putem face în privinţa lor. Publica: Bucharest.
27. Szent-Györgyi, A. (1981). Pledoarie pentru viaţă. Politică: Bucharest.
28. Tolstoi, L. (2009). Despre Dumnezeu şi om, din jurnalul ultimilor ani (1907–1910). Humanitas: Bucharest.
29. Wijkman, A., Rockstrom, J. (2012). Bankrupting Nature. Denying our planetary boundaries Routledge: New York.

Florin-Marius PAVELESCU

Institute of National Economy, pavelescu.florin@yahoo.com

Disembodied Technical Progress and Structural Change in Romania's Interwar Economy

Abstract: The paper is especially dedicated to the identification of the form of the trajectory of economic growth and of the sense and intensity of sectoral structural changes in the case of Romania's economy during the interwar period. The estimations regarding the average yearly rate of the gross value-added and the rate of disembodied technical change proper reveal a relatively fast economic growth on a concave trajectory. Also, we are able to show that the main direction of sectoral structural changes in terms of gross added value was industrialization, while the secondary one was de-agrarianization. In the conclusions chapter, the average yearly rate and the form of the trajectory of the gross value-added growth related to the 1921–1939 period are compared with those registered during the 1888–1913 period. This way, we are able to highlight that during the interwar period the economic growth was faster in comparison to the 1888–1913 period, even on a concave trajectory instead of a convex one.

Keywords: Juglar Cycle, Kuznets cycle, Kondratieff cycle, economic sectors, senses of structural change, average yearly rate, representative rate, trajectory of economic growth

Introduction

During the interwar period, Romania experienced an important economic growth. The accomplishment of the process of the re-unification of Romanian territories in a national-unitary state and also the end of the first transition to a market economy, as an outcome of the implementation of extensive agrarian reform, created conditions for the increase of the rate of economic and social development.

But the respective favorable premises were different at the level of economic sectors, depending on their development degree and on the policy promoted by the governmental authorities and also on the external shocks, which were manifest during the analyzed period. Therefore, the economic activity registered important fluctuations both at the macroeconomic and sectoral levels.

Consequently, an analysis of the features of the economic growth trajectory registered at the macroeconomic and sectoral levels, on the one hand, and of sectoral structural changes on the other can reveal interesting aspects of one of the most important stages of Romania's economic and social evolution.

1. Literature review related to the periodization of Romania's interwar economy

The fluctuations of economic activity in Romania during the interwar period were determinated by both internal and external factors. Among the internal factors, the most important were: a) the reconstruction of the economy after the huge damages registered during World War One; b) the important stimulus for economy activity generated by the implementation of the agrarian reform voted by the Parliament in 1921 and by the extension of the internal market; c) the protectionist policy adopted by governmental authorities in order to support the development of the manufacturing industry and the entrepreneurs, which invested in the respective economic branch. The main external factors that modelled Romania's economic development during the analyzed period were: a) re-orientation of foreign trade as an outcome of the new economic and political order established after the end of World War One; b) the agrarian crisis, which was manifest in the late 1920s; c) the great economic crisis during the 1929–1933 period; d) the intensification of political and economic tensions in Europe during the second half of 1930s, which generated an arms race.

In this context, Romania's economy experienced an important growth during the 1919–1928 period. V. Axenciuc (2008) shows that economic historians agree that the 1919–1924 period may be considered as one of the reconstructions of the economic potential after the huge damages caused by World War One. Hence, the 1925–1928 period may be characterized as a period when the economy growth took place in the context of re-evaluation of the extension of the internal market, which resulted from the re-unification of Romanian territories. Also, the economic dynamics during the 1919–1928 period may also be viewed as a Juglar-type cycle,[1] which had two phases, the 1919–1924 period and 1925–1928 period.

The time interval between 1929 and 1939 was marked by the great economic crisis during the 1929–1933 period and by a notable economic recovery during the 1934–1939 period. The respective time interval has been thoroughly analyzed by Romanian historians from various points of view. Because we deal with an alternation of an economic crisis period with a period of economic recovery, we may consider the 1929–1939 time interval as the second Juglar-type cycle of Romania's economy during the interwar period.

---

1 Business cycles of Juglar-type have a length of time which is comprised between 7 and 12 years and are essentially generated by the renewal of fixed capital. F.M. Pavelescu (2016 a) claims that we may admit the Juglar-type cycles are practically decennial economic cycles. In case of interwar Romania's economy, another argument in favour of considering the 1919–1928 period as a Juglar-type cycle is the contraction of gross domestic product in 1928 due to agrarian crisis and the sensible change of macroeconomic policy operated in 1929.

2. The dynamics of gross value added at macroeconomic and sectoral levels

If we use the data presented in V. Axenciuc (2012), we note that at the macroeconomic level, the average yearly rate of the gross value-added was 8.08% during the 1921–1924 period and 3.49% during the 1925–1928 period (Table 1). The sensible differentiation of the average yearly rate of economic growth during the abovementioned periods can be explained by particular conditions of the first interwar decade. In the first part of the 1920s, the economic reconstruction after World War One was the dominant process and favored the achievement of high rates of economic growth. During the 1925–1928 period, the rates of economic growth tended to moderate. Also, the agrarian crisis had a negative impact on the dynamics of gross value-added.

Table 1: Average yearly rate of gross value-added at whole economy and sectoral levels during the economic cycles of the 1921–1939 period (%)

Period	Whole economy	Primary sector	Secondary sector	Tertiary sector
1921–1924	8.08	3.67	12.99	9.84
1925–1928	3.49	1.19	6.49	3.46
1929–1933	0.62	2.53	-0.04	-0.65
1934–1939	3.55	2.97	4.63	3.25
1921–1928	4.51	2.42	7.88	4.16
1929–1939	2.21	2.77	2.48	1.46
1921–1939	3.69	2.62	5.46	3.60

Source: Author based on V. Axenciuc (2012)

If we adopt the vision of an economy with three sectors, initially defined by C. Clark (1960)[2], we can reveal that the average yearly rate of growth of the gross value-added of the primary sector was slower than that registered at the level of the whole economy, during both the 1921–1924 and 1925–1928 periods. On the contrary, the secondary sector experienced a higher average yearly rate of growth of the gross value-added in comparison with the dynamics of the respective indicator registered at the level of the whole economy during each of the two phases of the 1920–1928 Juglar-type cycle.

2 The three sectors of the economy are: a) primary sector, which includes agriculture, forestry, hunting and fishing; b) secondary sector, which includes mining and quarrying, manufacturing and energy, gas and water and c) tertiary sector, which includes services.

The gross value-added created in the tertiary sector grew sensibly slowly in comparison with the dynamics registered by the secondary sector. But we may note that, during the 1921–1928 period, in comparison with the dynamics registered by the whole economy, the gross value-added created in the tertiary sector grew more rapidly. During the 1925–1928 period, the average yearly rate of growth of the value-added created in the tertiary sector was practically equal to that registered at the whole economy level.

During the 1929–1933 period, due to economic crisis, we can detect a trend of decrease of the gross value-added created in both the secondary and tertiary sectors, the average yearly rate being equal to -0.04% and -0.65% respectively. The gross value-added created by the primary sector grew moderately, the average yearly rate being equal to 2.53%. This way, at the level of the whole economy, the gross value-added registered a small positive growth, the average yearly rate being equal to 0.62%.

In the context of economic recovery of the 1934–1939 period, the average yearly rate of value-added created at the level of the whole economy (3.55%) was very near to that obtained during the 1925–1928 period, 3.49%. But the above-mentioned dynamics were the result of different sectoral dynamics. In comparison with the 1925–1928 period, during the 1934–1939 period we may observe a higher average yearly rate of gross value-added in the case of the primary sector. On the contrary, the gross value-added grew slowly both in the secondary and tertiary sectors.

Because the 1929–1933 crisis had a major negative impact on the economic activity, the gross value-added growth during the 1929–1939 Juglar-type cycle was slower in comparison with that registered during the 1921–1928 period. The average yearly rate of the above-mentioned indicator was 4.51% during the 1921–1928 period and 2.21% during the 1929–1939 period. The slower economic growth observed during the 1929–1939 period in comparison with that registered during the 1921–1928 period was caused by the lower average yearly rates of growth of the gross value-added in the secondary and tertiary sectors. During the 1929–1939 period, the average yearly rate of growth of the gross value-added created in the primary sector (2.77%) was higher in comparison with that registered during the first interwar Juglar-type cycle (2.42%). The above-mentioned average yearly rate of growth was also higher in comparison with those registered both in the secondary and tertiary sectors (2.48% and 1.46% respectively).

If we consider the length of the Interwar period, we may appreciate the respective time interval as one of the Kuznets-type cycles of Romania's economy.[3] In this

3 Kuznets cycle was firstly defined in Kuznets (1973) and its length was estimated at 15–25 years. Initially, the main cause of the manifestation of this cycle was considered the demographic phenomena, such as migration, which generates cycles of constructions. Later on, the Kuznets cycles were explained by the extension and re-novelling of the infrastructure. In the case of Romania's interwar economy, the length of the respective time interval is 21 years. During this period, the economic and social development took place in the context of the consolidation of market mechanisms. Also, on the one hand, we may detect some important changes in demographic behavior,

context, we note that the average yearly rate of the gross value-added was 3.69% during the 1921–1939 period, which reveals a certain trend of economic growth. This way, in 1939, in real terms, the gross value-added created at the macroeconomic level was practically double in comparison with that registered in 1920.

The main contribution to the above-mentioned rate of economic growth was brought by the secondary sector, where the average yearly rate of the gross value-added was 5.46%. The average yearly rates of gross value-added related to primary and secondary sectors (2.62% and 3.60% respectively) were lower in comparison not only with the average yearly rate registered at the level of the secondary sector, but also at the level of the whole economy. The sectoral dynamics of the gross value-added, during the analyzed period highlight that the incentives granted by public authorities in the context of a protectionist policy determined a fast expansion of industrial activities.

3. Estimation of the rate proper of the disembodied technical progress during 1921–1939 period

The average yearly rate of growth of the gross value-added (RMY) is not the only indicator that can be used in order to reveal trends of economic activity. If the dynamics of economic activities are not stable, due to their cyclical nature, external shocks or other internal changes, the respective average yearly rate loses some of its relevance.

In this context, it is recommendable to use another indicator, such as representative rate (RRY)[4] or rate proper of disembodied technical progress (g_1)[5], which permit the identification of the form of the trajectory[6]. The estimation of the simple linear

---

especially related to demographic transition and internal migration. On the other hand, we may remark the efforts made by official authorities to harmonize and modernize the institutional framework and to develop the different components of the infrastructure.

4 The representative rate of the considered variable (RRX) is defined in F. M. Pavelescu (1986) with the help of the formula: $(n+1)*\ln(1+RRX) = 2*\ln IRX$, where: n = number of the years of the analyzed period, IRX = representative index of the considered dependent variable, which is defined as the geometrical mean of the fixed-base indices.

5 The rate proper of the disembodied technical progress (g_1), is the estimated parameter of the linear regression $\ln IX= a_1+g_1*t$, where ln IX = natural logarithm of the fixed-base indices of the considered variable, t= time factor.

6 We distinguish between two major forms of trajectory of the considered variable dynamics, namely: concave and convex. A concave trajectory is an outcome of a deceleration of the yearly rate of growth of the analyzed variable. A convex trajectory reveals an acceleration of the yearly rate of growth of the analyzed variable.
F. M. Pavelescu (2016, b) has in view the algebraical properties of the estimated parameters of the simple linear regression $\ln GVA= c_1+g_{1*}t$ and the relationship between the average yearly rate and the representative rate. This way, it is possible to demonstrate that we deal with a strong concave trajectory if we have: $\ln(1+RRX)>\ln(1+RMX)>g_1$ and a moderate concave trajectory if we have: $\ln(1+RRX)> g_1> \ln(1+RMX)$, where

regression lnGVA= c_1+g_{1*}t related to the 1921–1939 period shows that the rate proper of the disembodied technical progress was 0.018 in the case of the primary sector, 0.024 in the case of the tertiary sector and 0.042 in the case of the secondary sector. In the case of the whole economy, the above-mentioned estimated parameter was equal to 0.027 (Table 2). This way, we may reveal once again the faster dynamics of the gross value-added created of the secondary sector in comparison with those of the primary and secondary sectors and also with the dynamics registered at the level of the whole economy. Also, the rate proper of the disembodied technical progress related to the tertiary sector appears to be near that registered at the level of the whole economy.

All the estimated parameters are significant from statistical point of view, i.e. student test statistics are higher than three. The highest coefficient of correlation of the natural logarithms of the fixed base indices of the gross value-added and the time factor (R(lnIGVAT; t)) is obtained in the case of the secondary sector (0.9467), while the respective indicator related to the whole economy is equal to 0.9304. In other words, the dynamics of the value-added created in the secondary sector were not only the fastest but also the most stable in time. A high stability of the dynamics of the gross value-added can be also observed at the level of the whole economy.

Table 2: Indicators of the dynamics of the gross value at the whole economy and sectoral level during the 1921–1939 period (%)

Indicators	Whole economy	Primary sector	Secondary sector	Tertiary sector
c_1	0.203 (7.038)	0.114 (3.194)	0.276 (7.025)	0.262 (7.548)
g_1	0.027 (10.464)	0.018 (5.670)	0.042 (12.119)	0.024 (7.858)
ln(1+RRY)	0.050	0.029	0.069	0.050
ln(1+RMY)	0.036	0.026	0.053	0.035
R(ln IGVA;t)	0.930	0.809	0.947	0.886
R^2	0.866	0.654	0.896	0.784
F	109.510	32.151	14.877	61.748

Source: Author based on V. Axenciuc (2012)

N.B. c_1 and g_1 are the estimated parameters of the simple linear regression lnIGVA = c_1 +g_1*t, where: lnIGVA= natural logarithm of the fixed-based indices of the gross value-added, t= time factor. R (lnIGVA; t) = coefficient of correlation of the natural logarithm of fixed base indices of gross value-added and time factor. The student test statistics are presented in the brackets. R^2 = coefficient of determination, F= Fisher test statistics, RRY= representative rate of the gross value-added, RMY= average yearly rate of the gross value-added.

RMX= average yearly rate of the considered dependent variable. Analogously, we may consider that we face a strong convex trajectory if we have: g_1> ln (1+RMX)>ln (1+RRX) and a moderate convex trajectory if we have: ln (1+RMX)> g_1> ln (1+RRX).

The form of the trajectory of the dynamics of the gross value-added is a strong concave one both in the case of the whole economy and each of the three sectors, because in all four simple linear regressions we face the relationship: ln (1+RRY)>ln (1+RMY)>g_1. The concave form of the trajectory of Romania's economic growth during the interwar period can be explained mainly by the reconstruction phase after the damages of World War One, when the rate of economic growth was very fast, and by the impact of the 1929–1933 crisis, when the dynamics of gross value-added slowed down at the macroeconomic level and were negative in the secondary and tertiary sectors.

4. Features of the changes of the gross value-added sectoral structure

During the interwar period, the differentiation of the sectoral rates of growth determinated notable changes in the sectoral structure of the gross value-added. Therefore, in 1920, the primary sector contribution to gross value-added created at the level of the whole economy was 42.9%, while the tertiary sector contributed with 35.3%, and secondary sector with 21.8% (Table 3).

Table 3: Sectoral structure of gross value-added during the 1920–1939 period (%)

Year	Primary sector	Secondary sector	Tertiary sector
1920	42.9	21.8	35.3
1924	36.4	26.0	37.6
1928	33.2	29.2	37.6
1933	36.5	28.2	35.3
1939	35.3	30.0	34.7

Source: Author based on V. Axenciuc (2012)

The above-mentioned sectorial structure of the gross value-added was essentially influenced by the considerable damages caused by World War One and by the re-unification of Romanian territories. In this context, in comparison with 1913, the best year of the Romanian economy before World War One, in the year 1920, the weight of the primary sector in the gross value-added created at the level of the whole economy increased from 36.7% to 42.9%, while the weight of the secondary sector decreased from 27.8% to 21.8% and the weight of the tertiary sector decreased from 35.6% to 35.3%.

During the 1920–1928 period, due to the fast development of industrial and construction activities, the weight of the secondary sector in the total gross value-added increased from 21.8% to 29.2%. The weight of the tertiary sector increased slowly, from 35.3% to 37.6%. In the same time, the weight of the primary sector decreased from 42.9% to 33.2%.

During the 1929–1933 economic crisis, the gross value-added created by the secondary and tertiary sectors diminished. Consequently, the weights of the respective sectors decreased to 28.2% and to 35.3% respectively. In this context, in 1933, the last year of the crisis, the sectoral structure of the gross value-added was very near to that registered in the year 1913.

As an outcome of the boom of the 1934–1939 period, in 1939, the weight of the secondary sector increased to 30.0%. Due to slower dynamics, the weights of the primary and tertiary sector decreased to 35.3% and 34.7% respectively.

The sense of the structural change was dependent not only on development of the industrial and construction activities, but also on the expansion of the services sector. Therefore, during the 1921–1928 period, the Coefficient of Intensity of Structural Change (CISC) was equal to 12.42%, while the weights transfer was equal to 9.72% (Table 4). The main sense of structural change was the de-agrarianization, while the secondary sense was the industrialization.[7] The international experience showed that the respective type of structural change was a typical one during the periods when the base industrial structures were built.

7 F. M. Pavelescu (2014) demonstrates that in the case of an economy with three sectors we are able to identify six types of structural changes during the analyzed period, i.e.: a) re-agrarianization if the weight of the primary sector increased, b) de-agrarianization if the weight of the primary sector decreased, c) industrialization if the weight of the secondary sector increased, d) de-industrialization if the weight of the secondary sector decreased, e) tertialization if the weight of the tertiary sector increasesd, f) de-tertialization if the weight of the tertiary sector decreased. The coefficient of intensity of structural changes (CISC) is a product of the weights transfer (WT) and a structural index (SI). In the case of an economy with three sectors, structural index (SI) takes values between 122.47% and 141.42%. The weights transfer reveals the main sense of the structural change. The secondary sense of structural change is given by the modification of the weight, which is the second from the absolute value point of view. Hence, we can identify twelve situations of main and secondary sense of structural change.

Table 4: Features of the structural change of the sectoral gross value-added during the period 1920–1939

%

Period	Coefficient of Intensity of Structural Change (CISC)	Weights Transfer (WT)	Structural Index (SI)	Main Sense of Structural Change	Secondary Sense of Structural Change
1921–1924	8.19	6.60	124.08	de-agrarianization	industrialization
1925–1928	4.43	3.13	141.87	industrialization	de-agragrianization
1929–1933	4.12	3.28	125.59	re-agrarianization	de-tertialization
1934–1939	2.27	1.81	125.10	industrialization	de-agrarianization
1921–1928	12.42	9.72	127.76	de-agrarianization	industrialization
1929–1939	3.67	2.91	126.05	de-tertialization	re-agrarianization
1921–1939	11.27	8.25	136.70	industrialization	de-agrarianization

Source: Author based on V. Axenciuc (2012)

During the 1929–1939 period, as an outcome of a slower development of the services activities, the main sense of structural changes was de-tertialization, while the secondary one was de-agrarization. CISC is equal to 3.67%, in the context of a weights transfer of 2.91%. In other words, the intensity of change of the sectoral structure of the gross value-added during the second Juglar-type cycle of Romania's interwar economy was lower in comparison with that registered during the first one. Also, we may remark that the 1929–1933 economic crisis generated important blockages of the services activities, which were not entirely surpassed during the 1934–1939 boom.

If we consider the 1921–1939 period as a Kuznets-type cycle, we find that CISC= 11.27% and WT= 8.25%. The main sense of the structural change was industrialization, while the secondary sense was de-agrarianization. If we have in view the length of the respective period we may appreciate that the intensity of structural change related to sectoral gross value-added was a moderate one.

Conclusions

The analysis of the dynamics of the gross value-added at macroeconomic and sectoral levels, during the 1921–1939 period allows us to reveal the important role played by the extension of industrial activities in supporting the economic growth. Therefore, the secondary sector sensibly increased its weight in the gross value-added generated at the whole economy level. Also, the estimated rate proper of the disembodied technical progress for the secondary sector is higher than the estimation related to the whole economy level. The gross value-added created in the primary sector grew at a moderate rate, but was slower than the dynamics of the services sector. It is notable that the development of the services may be considered as a moderated one, too, especially if we consider the 1929–1939 period.

Comparison of the indicators related to the rate proper of the disembodied technical progress estimated for the 1929–1939 period with those estimated for the 1888–1913 period[8], presented in F. M. Pavelescu (2016, b) highlights that during the interwar period Romania's economy experienced a faster growth and a change of the development pattern. Therefore, the average rate of growth at the maroeconomic level was 3.69% instead of 2.73%. This performance was obtained due to higher rates of growth registered in all three economic sectors. Thus, in the case of the primary sector, the average yearly rate was 2.62% instead of 1.78%, in the case of the secondary sector 5.46% instead of 3.50%, while in the case of the tertiary sector the above-mentioned indicator was 3.60% instead of 3.32%.

On this basis, we can conclude that the higher rate of economic growth was a result of the implementation of the agrarian reform adopted in 1921 and of the protectionist measures designed to support mainly the expansion of the industry and the activities of indigenous investors. The average yearly rate of gross value-added created in the tertiary sector was very near to that estimated for the 1888–1913 period.

The higher rate of economic growth during the 1921–1939 period was obtained in the context of a strong concave trajectory both at macroeconomic and sectoral levels instead of a moderate convex trajectory as it happened during the 1888–1913 period at the macroeconomic level and in the case of the secondary and tertiary sectors. The strong concave trajectory of the dynamics of gross value-added during

8 F. M. Pavelescu (2016, a) considers 1888–1914 as the first (upward) phase of the second Kondratieff-type cycle of modern Romania's economy evolution. The second (downward) phase of the above-mentioned long cycle lasted between 1919 and 1947. Also, the fact has been revealed that, in the case of Romania, the 1888–1914 period is a part of the first transition to market economy, which took place during the 1860–1921 period. There is the assumption that the first transition to market economy ended in Romania in the context of the legiferation of the Agrarian Reform. Thus, the 1919–1939 period was in fact a time interval when the market mechanisms acted on a consolidated basis and the economy and other social activities continued their modernization processes.

the 1921–1939 period is essentially the outcome of a re-construction process after World War One, and of the 1929–1933 economic crisis. But the respective form of trajectory suggests that the interwar period was a part of the downward phase of a Kondratieff-type cycle. We may also note that the moderate convex trajectory of value-added growth during the 1888–1913 period acts in favour of the idea that the respective time interval was the upward phase of a Kondratieff-type cycle.

References

1. Axenciuc, V. (2012). Produsul intern brut al României 1862–2000. Serii statistice seculare şi argumente metodologice, Volumul II Produsul intern brut 1862–1947. Calcule detaliate şi metode de constituire a seriilor de indicatori pe activităţi-resurse. Editura Economică, Bucureşti, 2012.
2. Axenciuc, V. (2008). La formation et le development du marche interieur moderne en Roumanie. Etude et séries statistiques à long terme (1860–1947), Academie Roumaine, Institute National de Recherches Economique, 2008.
3. Clark, C. (1960). Les conditions du progrès économique, PUF, Paris, 1960.
4. Juglar, C. (1862). Des crises économiques et leurs retours en France, en Angleterre et aux Etats Unies, Guillaumin, Paris, 1862.
5. Kondratieff, N.D. (1935). The long waves in economic life. The Review of Economic Statistics, vol. XVII, no. 6/1935.
6. Kuznets, S. "Modern economic growth. Main findings and reflections." American Economic Review, Vol. 60, No. 3.
7. Pavelescu, F. M. (1986). Some considerations regarding the estimated parameters of the Cobb-Douglas production function. A new approach. Revue Roumaine des Sciences Sociales no.1–2/1986.
8. Pavelescu, F. M. (2013). Some considerations regarding the economic cycles in Romania during the period 1859–2010, Romanian Journal of Economics, 2013(XXIII), Volume 36, Issue 1(45).
9. Pavelescu, F. M. (2014). Methodological considerations on the size of coefficient of intensity of structural changes (CISC), Romanian Statistical Review no.2/2014.
10. Pavelescu, F. M. (2016a). Features of long cycles of Romania's economy evolution in Chivu Luminita, Ciutacu Constantin, Ioan Franc Valeriu, Andrei Jean-Vasile (ed.) – Economic Dynamics and Sustainable Development. Ressources. Factors. Structures. Proceedings of ESPERA 2015, Part 1, Peter Lang, 2016.
11. Pavelescu, F.M. (2016b). "Economic cycles and disembodied technical change of Romania's economy during the period 1863–1913" Romanian Journal of Economics, (XXIII), Volume 36, Issue 1(45).
12. Schumpeter, J. (1939). Business Cycles. Mc. Graw-Hill, New York, 1939, vol. 1.

George GEORGESCU

National Institute of Economic Research "Costin C. Kiritescu", Romanian Academy, 13 Calea 13 Septembrie, Academy House, postcode 050711, Bucharest, Romania, georgescu@ince.ro

Bank De-Risking Impacts on Finance and Development. The Case of Romania

Abstract: The study aims to investigate the causes, external manifestations and impacts of the phenomenon of de-risking, increasingly rendered visible in the last years on international financial markets, under the circumstances of the post-crisis global economic developments. The paper reveals that this phenomenon is still little discussed and understood by academics and institutional organizations, consequently being ignored by any theoretical foundation or arguments for the possible guidance, between one direction or the other, of policies, norms and regulatory practices in order to monitor and address the slippages with adverse effects. In the paper, the stage of actual knowledge of this phenomenon, as concerns the different forms of manifestation, the main causes and factors of influence, the adverse impact observed and possible counteracting measures are presented. The paper presents some reference points for decoding this phenomenon, proposing new directions for more in-depth scientific researches, focusing on the identification of specific solutions based on customized analysis, including for Romania's case, considering the trade-off options, such as stability versus prudentiality in risk taking and risk management, profitability versus social responsibility under uncertainty conditions, banking system interests versus interests of regulatory and supervisory institutions, and monetary policies versus government policy and strategies.

Keywords: de-risking; banking system; corresponding banks; AML/CFT; financial stability; non-performing loans; financial inclusion

Introduction

The phenomenon called de-risking, which has recently emerged—at least as a visible manifestation—entered almost by force just two to three years ago into the attention of researchers, academics, banking authorities and international and global institutions, who have not reached a consensus on its definition. It seems that economics and, particularly, its financial branch, is yet again facing a deadlock, being constrained to react *post-factum* and trying to explain the fundamentals of an event that was not included in its object of study and research, imposed by the new realities of globalization and international practices, situated outside its theoretical and methodological precepts.

In our opinion, on the one hand, in terms of a strict conceptual delimitation, the phenomenon could not be defined unambiguously in the absence of clear terms of reference: essence, features, external forms of manifestation, development, effects, benchmarks for evaluation. On the other hand, being expressed by an antinomian grammatical composition, e.g. associating the prefix *de* to the gerund *risking*, in economic terminology it may be included in the broader concept of risk management, meaning, *per se*, an exclusion of risks as sources of uncertainty.

In other words, under the circumstances of compliance with the new financial standards of the post-crisis period, especially by the banking entities that operate globally and intermediate international financial transactions, this new approach implies, in practice, the formal improvement of risk management through avoidance or elimination from the risk assessment system of potential threats that are considered too likely to occur and bearing excessive adverse effects, and/or whose prevention would be inefficient in terms of cost-benefit.

Thus, according to the new pseudo-paradigm, lacking any theoretical support and macroeconomic or social reliability, we are witnessing a reality of some financial services decommittment, chaotic and totally opaque, contrary to the role and functions assumed by the banking system as the claimed principles of sustainable development, inclusive growth and the broad access of the population to these financial services. The phenomenon, which has become of global magnitude, hides, in fact, the conflict of interests between the finance industry and the society as a whole, both at intra and inter-country levels, indirectly feeding the anti-globalization movement.

Looked at from a different angle, the meaning of the term de-risking can be associated to the one of deleveraging, which has had a wide circulation in the post-crisis period, with much clearer connotations, essentially meaning the reducing of risk exposure by withdrawing the credit lines from the geographic areas considered to be of high risk, as did the parent banks with their subsidiaries in Central and Eastern Europe, it is true, in a controlled manner, as agreed according to the Vienna Initiative in 2009 (Gattini, 2016, p. 92).

Considering that it only concerns the banking sector, the current range of de-risking meaning covers a very broad area, from avoiding market/business risk and reputational risk, to defining any kind of financial services withdrawal. Erbenova et al. (2016, p. 3) argue, rightly, that the indiscriminational use of the term has led to misunderstandings and created confusion in the dialogue on determinants and trends of the phenomenon.

In this article, having the objective of a better understanding of the essence of de-risking, we intend to point out the main external manifestations of this phenomenon, several causes and influencing factors, a number of adverse effects and possible measures mitigating them, and how they particularly affected Romania.

Our research tries, based on the current state of knowledge and an analytical approach, as much as it was possible, to investigate this phenomenon, looking for an answer, even incomplete, to the dilemma "how risky is de-risking?".

1. A worldwide phenomenon: external manifestations, causes and determinants

In the banking system, in practice, the phenomenon of de-risking manifests as financial transactions contraction, including restricting access to finance, reducing or eliminating exposures to a range of clients, individuals or legal entities and/ or geographical areas, jurisdictions, sectors, and services considered to be high potential risks.

In fact, the emergence of this phenomenon signifies a market failure, the banking sector trying to eliminate its own weaknesses without taking into account the outside effects, mainly on economic and social development, which, for restoring the market mechanisms' functionality and safeguarding the financial stability, requires an intervention by the national public authorities and international institutions.

Among the external manifestations of de-risking revealed by the literature and international institutions' reports (Alier, 2016; Canuto & Ramcharan, 2016; Corazza, 2016; Erbenova et al., 2016; IMF, 2016; World Bank, 2015) are the reduction of corresponding banking relationships (CBRs), the restricting access to certain services related to financial transfers (Money Service Businesses or MSBs), the non-banking market operators (Money Transfer Operators or MTOs), which mainly affect the remittances. Also, according to a report by Goldman Sachs (2016), due to the introduction of a stricter risk management, the de-risking phenomenon can occur in the form of reducing credit exposures by lowering, through externalization, non-performing loans (NPL).

Recent studies issued by the World Bank (World Bank, 2015) revealed that, out of the 170 regional banks and small local banks included in the survey, about half reported a moderate or significant decline in CBRs,[1] and in the case of the 20 large international banks, the share was about 75%. The main categories of causes raised by banks consisted, on the one hand, of business reasons (costs versus profitability) and, on the other, the regulations and risks (systemic, operational, legal, reputational).

As concerns the correspondent banks, de-risking has also reached those headquartered in Europe, some of which have subsidiaries in Eastern Europe, including Romania. As found by a study by the European Central Bank (2015, p. 5), under the circumstances of post-crisis decreasing of transactions with correspondent banks, several large EU banks discarded some of these transactions, namely those recording low volume/significant value, due to the introduction of the Single Euro Payments Area (SEPA) in 2014.

The Panama Papers scandal, which severely hit the global finance, showed how difficult it is for large banks to know exactly the origin of funds handled through correspondent banks and how they are used (Mendoza, 2016). It should be noted that the incidence of de-risking and the name of the banks involved are difficult

1 Correspondent banking relationships are established on the basis of bilateral agreements according to which, typically, a large international bank and a small regional/ local bank are authorizing each other to provide financial services, generally payments to third parties, consisting particularly of crossborder trade-related transactions, money transfers, short-term loans and investments and others; the local correspondent banks act as intermediaries, therefore substituting the setting up of subsidiaries/branches by the international banks in the countries (jurisdictions) concerned (Bank for International Settlements, 2016, p. 9).

to detect, due to concerns over reputational risk. The global banks do not officially notify such operations, but neither are the affected correspondent banks rushing to make them public, fearing the creation of a negative perception from customers.

Also, as another influencing factor, the adoption of new rules during the post-crisis period (under Basel III Accords), focusing, *inter alia*, on the minimum capital requirements and increasing the provisions for assets held by international banks in correspondent banks, has reduced their lending capacity, also impacting profitability indicators.

In this context, it should be noted that financial services run by major banks through correspondent banks, are characterized, in general, by minor profit margins and low volumes of transactions. All in all, it has become so that the costs of compliance with the AML/CFT rules on combating money laundering and financing terrorism introduced by the intergovernmental body FATF (Financial Action Task Force), including those related to conducting due diligences, increased by over 50% (International Finance Corporation, 2016, p. 2). These costs, in many cases, exceeded the related benefits, which have led international banks to reduce or eliminate relations with those correspondent banks considered as bearing too high risks to reward their managing (Artingstall et al., 2016, p. 14).

As concerns other reasons for international banks' decisions towards de-risking, the fear of penalties and international/regional sanctions for potential infringement of those rules, which count more than they explicitly appear, are added.

2. Adverse effects and possible countermeasures

As long as the de-risking phenomenon is manifested essentially by reducing access to financial services, it becomes clear that the very foundations of development are undermined, the investment loans, private and/or public, the international trade in goods and services and related transactions, including the value-added global chains, the flows of foreign direct investments, and the private and institutional international transfers are all affected (Erbenova et al., 2016).

Direct and indirect effects on international trade can be significant. A study by BIS (Bank for International Settlements, 2014, p. 45) revealed that about one third of the world trade, which reached 19 trillion dollars in 2014, is supported by trade finance instruments, intermediated, for the most part, by the international banks through a network of correspondent banks. They are asked, for example, to confirm payments to exporters (by documentary credit or letter of credit), based on documentation for the shipment of goods, supplying the lack of direct banking link between buyers and sellers.

The de-risking phenomenon in the CBR area deepens the deficit in trade financing, mainly affecting the underdeveloped or developing countries (Auboin & DiCaprio, 2017, p. 7), which may explain the weak recent developments in the world trade, which entered decline in 2015 (down about 10% compared to 2014). The de-risking implications for the world trade has been also pointed out by the IMF Managing Director (2016, p. 8).

Beside macroeconomic effects at the national and global level, there are adverse social costs, among other things. By restricting the consumer loans and remittances of expatriates, disadvantaged groups of the population are financially excluded. Most affected by this phenomenon, paradoxically, are those most in need, whether countries or companies, especially SMEs or individuals from both developing and advanced countries, and, as it has been revealed, even humanitarian organizations are hindered in carrying out their missions.

Another paradox is that the de-risking phenomenon in the banking system—its main motivation being the improvement of risk management through the elimination of risk sources—may at the macroeconomic level lead to the increase in financial and monetary instability, turning by feedback loop on the banking system itself while its spillover effects on different transmission channels culminate in a global financial crisis. This risk of de-risking is also highlighted by diverting the financing means of those excluded to alternative credit providers as shadow banking, whose oversized expansion, out of any control, was at the origin of the financial crisis in 2008, with dramatic long-term global effects.

The adverse effects of de-risking are asymmetric, by decoupling whole regions from the global growth. The literature refers, as an example of regional imbalances, to the Caribbean as the most affected region by de-risking. Particular to this area, located in the Caribbean Sea, is the small size of the states (islands) and the almost total dependence of foreign exchange receipts on tourism, exports and remittances, with the related financial operations conducted through correspondent accounts.

The annual meeting of central bank governors in the region under the CDB (Caribbean Development Bank) discussed the severity of the problems facing these countries, over which hangs the threat of a balance of payments crisis, the increase in external debt, weakening of the financing of development projects, many of them requiring external payments for imported equipment, worsening the business environment (Canuto & Ramcharan, 2016). In fact, the CDB itself, whose activities are constrained by closing the correspondent accounts with most transactions running into dollars, noting also that banks in the region are dependent on the US financial system, is affected by de-risking.

As mentioned above, the adverse effects of de-risking that have emerged recently have only shown its main source, i.e. the banking system or more precisely the international banks, but have so far not succeeded in drawing a full picture of these effects at the global level. Many studies or investigations by international organizations (in particular the IMF and World Bank) focusing on this research objective have only provided partial results or have not been finalized yet.

Other analyses, including pilot studies, aimed at the assessment of de-risking side effects, on macroeconomic and/or social areas, are only at the stage of data collection, at least at the World Bank, the proposed measures to counter adverse effects have rather the attributes of recommendations (Corazza, 2016).

Thus, these general recommendations refer to the prevention and mitigation of adverse effects by "freezing" de-risking actions pending the clarification of the essential aspects of the phenomenon and the completion of various studies in progress at the global level, taking into account the possibility of introducing global financial regulation standards, that allow, based on a case-by-case risk-based approach, the improvement of risk management, a faster intervention of central banks and regulatory authorities, as well as better regional coordination of their actions (Canuto & Ramcharan, 2016).

Other specific recommendations focus on providing assistance to facilitate compliance with AML/CFT regulations and reduce its costs, including through the SWIFT network, improving transparency regarding information on the origin/real beneficiary of cross-border financial transfers, setting a minimum limit for remittances under the AML/CFT regulations and setting daily ceilings for the volume of transactions.

Countries severely affected by de-risking through limiting their access to the global financial system, especially in the CBR area, are advised that banking sector initiatives are to be accompanied by the introduction of temporary mechanisms and alternative payment channels for international transactions, supported by state authorities, with the possible technical assistance from the IMF, if available (Erbenova et al., 2016, p. 5; IMF, 2016, p. 5).

Further on, we shall attempt to identify several defining aspects of the de-risking presence in the banking system in Romania, as well as some adverse effects that can be assigned to it, at least to some extent.

3. How is Romania affected by de-risking

Under the circumstances of structural weaknesses inherent in the transition to a market economy and the accumulation of significant twin deficits (budgetary and BoP current account) during the pre-accession period, Romania experienced the severe global crisis triggered in 2008, managing to maintain its financial stability only by receiving a financial support package from the IMF and the EU, through a sovereign loan amounting to 20 billion euros.

Although de-risking phenomenon has not been perceived, as such, at the global scale, it was present in Romania in multifaceted forms during the post-crisis period.

In the context of a banking sector dominated by foreign capital in a proportion of about 90%, the deleveraging, albeit controlled, resulted in the withdrawal of credit lines by the parent banks from their subsidiaries in Romania amounting to 13 billion euros over the 2009–2015 period, which contributed, among other factors, to the contraction, in real terms, of bank lending in the post-crisis years.

The reduction of the total number of retail clients represents, although partially, another expression of the same de-risking phenomenon. In the case of Commercial Romanian Bank-Erste Group, the largest bank in the system, it lost more than one million clients in the post-crisis period, but, with its remaining 2.8 million clients in 2016, is still ranked as the first among banks in this regard.

The number of banking transactions with payment instructions has decreased (to below 210 million annually during the 2009–2016 period, by 20 % less compared to 2007) and the remittances have also tended to decrease (less than four billion euros annually in the 2009–2016 period, compared to amounts between five and seven billion euros in 2007 and 2008).

All this can be considered defining aspects of the evolution of the banking system in Romania, partly attributable to the more or less significant impact of de-risking. Further, the impact of de-risking on reducing bad loans and the low level of financial inclusion in Romania will be examined in a more analytical manner.

3.1 De-risking and bad loans

The non-performing loans (NPL) in the banking system in Romania followed an evolution in two phases: first, under the post-crisis impact, the NPL ratio recorded an increase to over 20% of the total assets in the latter part of 2013 and early 2014, after which, being also subject to de-risking, the ratio declined, falling below 10% at the end of 2016 (NBR, 2016, p. 58), taking into account the methodological changes introduced in 2014 (Table 1).

It should be noted that these ratios, especially at peak levels, were significantly above the alert thresholds recommended by the international financial institutions throughout the reference period, remaining currently slightly above them. It is worth mentioning that these NPL ratio thresholds range from two to four percent considered by the IMF to eight percent as envisaged by the European Banking Association (EBA), compared with an EU average of about 5.5% recorded in 2016.

Table 1: The NPL ratio of Romania's banking system between 2010 and 2016

-%-

Year	NPL ratio according to NBR definition	NPL ratio according to EBA definition**
2016	-	9.46
2015	-	13.51
2014*	13.94	20.71
2013	21.87	-
2012	18.24	-
2011	14.33	-
2010	11.85	-

*Calculations based on reporting by all banks: both those using the standardized approach to assessing credit risk and those that use the internal ratings-based approach.

**According to the EBA definition, the non-perfoming exposures are those that meet any of the following criteria: i) significant exposure overdue more than 90 days; ii) it considers that, in the absence of the collateral execution, the borrower is unlikely to pay its credit obligations in full, regardless of the existence of any outstanding amounts or number of late payment days. Starting from June 2015, the non-performing exposures of cash balances in the central bank and other deposits held at credit institutions were included.

Source: Monthly Bulletin, NBR, November 2016, p. 58.

The halving of the NPL ratio in just three years in the case of Romania is considered a good performance, appreciated, among others under the Vienna Initiative, by EBRD experts (Montes-Negret & Cloutier, 2016), who showed that from this experience six lessons can be learned: data and information system is accessible and reliable; positive role of the regulatory authority; insolvency framework consistent with the practices of restructuring; incentivizing tax structure for NPL trading; development of a debt market allowing banks to partially deleverage the NPL portfolio.

A report of the European Investment Bank concerning the supervision of banking systems in Central and Eastern Europe also noted that, following the implementation of an action plan of the central bank in this regard,[2] the asset quality improved significantly in Romania, both in the corporate and the retail sectors (Gattini, 2016, pp. 91–98).

According to a recent study by Deloitte (2017, pp. 7, 16, 31), Romania has proven to be the most active among the countries of Central and Eastern Europe in terms of the liquidation of bad loans portfolios, with a total value of transactions of about five billion euro (representing almost 50% of the total NPL) between 2014 and 2016, compared with Hungary (3.2 billion euros) and Poland (1.4 billion euros). However, the average sale prices of bad loans portfolios in Romania stood at a very low level (about 11%), half of that achieved by the Czech Republic or Slovakia.

If it is true that reducing the share of NPL helps the improvement of assets quality and, thereby, the recovery of the banking system, in Romania's case the fundamental question is how it was possible that alert thresholds were exceeded by so much and for so long, without banking supervisory authority and with the European institutions empowered to act only late, albeit in a radical manner. In our opinion, the reduction in the NPL ratio by writing off the portfolio of bad loans at derisory prices does not reflect a real recovery of the banking system in Romania, as it materialized in the financial losses suffered by banks in the years 2009 to 2014 as a result of hazardous credit policies from 2004 to 2008.

This reduction, by the manner in which it occurred, is merely a form of de-risking, with adverse effects outside the banking system, mainly by the decrease in lending, affecting the resources to finance the economy and reducing the number of customers, thus limiting companies' and the population's access to financing.

3.2 De-risking and financial inclusion

By restricting certain categories of customers' access to to financial services, including individuals, it is estimated that one of the biggest threats of de-risking is

2 The NBR bad loans restructuring plan, implemented since 2014, has provided measures aimed to help banks balance sheets cleaning up through writing off provisioned NPL that were deemed unrecoverable, selling the uncovered NPL portfolios that were overdue by more than one year (except in bankruptcy or insolvency), removing off balance NPL and revaluation of collaterals at market value by external auditors.

to financial inclusion (Artingstall et al., 2016, p. 15; Durner & Shetret, 2015, p. 21; Erbenova et al., 2016, p. 5).

Under the circumstances of increasing concerns for reducing inequality and poverty in the world, financial inclusion has become a global objective, and is a subject of the UN *2030 Agenda for Sustainable Development*, the World Bank's initiative on universal access to financial services (WB - *Universal Financial Access 2020*), and the G20 *Global Partnership for Financial Inclusion* (GPFI). Also, more than 50 countries have launched national strategies for financial inclusion, with a roadmap stipulating concrete measures, supported by the allocation of necessary resources to implement them.

The World Bank monitors the degree of financial inclusion globally by creating a database (*Global Findex*) that includes over 140 countries and more than 100 indicators (Asli et al., 2015). As can be seen from the data presented in Table 2, in 2014 financial inclusion in Romania was at a low level, the majority of the selected indicators standing below the average of the country group to which it belongs (upper-middle income) according to the World Bank classification, and well below the average of OECD advanced countries.

Table 2: Indicators of financial inclusion

-% of population aged 15+ -

Indicators	**Romania**	**Average of countries *upper-middle income***	**Average of countries OECD *high-income***
Account held in a financial institution	60.8	70.4	94.0
Debit card	45.8	45.9	61.9
Savings in the past year	13.3	32.2	51.6
Credit in the past year	11.8	10.4	18.4
Bills paid by internet	11.5	15.3	54.1

Source: Data book on Financial Inclusion, Global Findex, World Bank, 2015, pp. 122–125.

At EU level, the measurement of financial inclusion is done using a composite indicator, on a scale from zero to one, a FIS (Financial Inclusion Score) estimated based on the weighted average of a series of indicators relating to the infrastructure of financial services, including their quality, as well as their use, the share of the adult population holding current and savings accounts, the share that takes consumer credits, or has life insurance. In the ranking of the degree of financial inclusion according to FIS, compared to countries rated 1.00 (Sweden, Denmark, Finland, Ireland) and to an average score of 0.91 at EU level, Romania is ranked last with a score of 0.554 (European Commission, 2015, p. 5).

In Romania, the low level of financial inclusion is explained. In addition to the large share of people at risk of poverty or social exclusion (37.3% according to

Eurostat) that do not qualify for bank loans, during the 2009–2015 period a total of about 700,000 people (60% more than in 2008) were recorded as having late payments more than 30 days overdue to the Central Credit Risk, appearing on the black list of banks and thus being excluded from aplying for another credit.

4. Concluding remarks

The de-risking phenomenon has recently come to the attention of international financial institutions and researchers, particularly due to events that have emerged in the area of banking that have had adverse macroeconomic and social effects and are increasingly perceived as a global threat, constituting, by itself, a major risk factor.

The main difficulty encountered by the attempts to prevent and counteract these adverse effects is caused by the lack of proper assessment of the de-risking impact, given insufficient data and inability of separating the cause-effect relation on the alignment of various forms and complex event phenomena, the multitude of involved actors and the conflict, most often hidden, between the interests of the banking system, dominated by global banks, and those of national and international institutions and society as a whole. The banking system, which gathers most causes of de-risking, is faced with extremely difficult trade-off options, each of which are associated with a particular set of costs and benefits, variable in time and space, under the pressure of fitting the stability/prudential standards versus risk taking, under a complex of interdependent conditions and high uncertainty, and the achievement of the bank's top management performance indicators.

Given the early stage of researches on de-risking phenomenon, while following the global studies, especially by the IMF and World Bank, this paper aimed at clarifying the key issues and assessing the implications of this phenomenon to their real dimension, specifically for Romania. As revealed in this paper, Romania is also affected, more severely in terms of financial inclusion, therefore it is important that regulatory and supervision authorities of financial markets (mainly NBR and FSA), which have basic information and specific data, start a customized analysis in order to identify particular solutions to mitigate the adverse effects of de-risking for our country.

References

1. Alier, M. (2016). The withdrawal of correspondent banking relationships, IMF, July 8, 2016.
2. Artingstall, D. (2016). Drivers and impacts of Derisking, John Howell ed., February 2016.
3. Asli, D.K., Klapper, L., Singer, D., Van Oudheusden, P. (2015). The Global Findex Database 2014: Measuring Financial Inclusion around the World, Policy Research Working Paper 7255, World Bank, Washington, 2015.
4. Auboin, M., DiCaprio, A. (2017). Why do trade finance gaps persists: and does it matter for trade and development?, WTO Working Paper, ERSD, 23 March, 2017.

5. Association of Supervisors of Banks of the Americas. (2016). Impact of Compliance/Regulatory Risk in Financial Activity ('De-Risking') in the Americas, ASBA, Mexico City, 2016.
6. Bank for International Settlements (2016). Corresponding Banking, BIS, Committee on Payments and Market Infrastructure, Basel, July 2016.
7. Bank for International Settlements (2014). Trade finance: developments and issues, BIS, CGFS Papers, No. 50, January 2014.
8. Canuto, O., Ramcharan, V. (2016). De-Risking Is De-linking Small States from Global Finance, World Post, 22 October 2016.
9. Corazza, C. (2016). The World Bank's Data Gathering Efforts: De-risking? Key Findings and Recommendations, World Bank Group, January 2016.
10. Deloitte Auditing and Consulting (2017). CEE NPL markets in full swing. A record year 2016, Budapest, January 2017.
11. Durner, T., Shetret, L. (2015). Understanding Bank De-risking and its Effects on Financial Inclusion. An Exploratory Study, Global Center of Cooperative Security, November 2015.
12. Erbenova, M. (2016). The Withdrawal of Correspondent Banking Relationships: A Case for Policy Action, IMF Staff Discussion Note, June 2016.
13. European Central Bank (2016). Ninth Survey on Correspondent Banking in Euro, Frankfurt, 2016.
14. European Commission (2015). Measuring financial inclusion in the EU: the new Financial Inclusion Score, Policy Paper, Brussels, 2015.
15. Financial Action Task Force (2016). Guidance on correspondent banking services, FATF, Paris, October 2016.
16. Financial Action Task Force (2015). "Statement on de-risking", FATF, Paris, 23 October 2015.
17. Gattini, L. (2016). CESEE Bank Lending Survey, European Investment Bank, June 2016.
18. Goldman Sachs Global Investment Research (2016). In line with expectation: De-risking continues, NPL formation stabilized, Goldman Sachs Equity Research, 26 August 2016.
19. International Finance Corporation (2016). De-risking by banks in emerging markets – effects and responses for trade, IFC, WB Group, EM Compass, Note 24, November 2016.
20. International Monetary Fund (2016). The Managing Director's Spring Global Policy Agenda Decisive Action, Durable Growth, IMF, Washington, April 2016.
21. KPMG (2016). European Debt Sales – Romania, KPMG Insights, 21 February 2016.
22. Mendoza, N. (2016). How banks de-risking can undermine development, DevexImpact, 2016.
23. Montes-Negret F., Cloutier, E. (2016). What lessons from Romania's early success in NPL reduction?, EBRD's Note, NPL Initiative, Vienna, March 2016.
24. National Bank of Romania (2015). NPL resolution in the case of Romania, Financial Stability Department, NBR, Bucharest, June 2015.

25. National Bank of Romania (2016). Financial Stability Report, NBR, Bucharest, December 2016.
26. Raiffeisen Research (2016). CEE Banking Sector Report 2016, Raiffeisen Bank, Vienna, June 2016.
27. Staci, W. (2015). Global Correspondent Banking: De-Risking and Its Consequences for Global Commerce and the Financial System, Center for Financial Markets, Milken Institute, July 2015.
28. World Bank (2015). "Withdrawal from correspondent banking: where, why, and what to do about it", Working Paper No. 101098, Washington, 2015.
29. World Bank (2015). Report on the G20 Survey on De-risking activities in the remittance market, Working Paper No. 101071, Washington, 2015.

Elena PELINESCU

Institute for Economic Forecasting of the Romanian Academy, 13, Calea 13 Septembrie, Bucharest, email: elena_pelinescu@yahoo.com

Mihaela SIMIONESCU

Institute for Economic Forecasting of the Romanian Academy, 13, Calea 13 Septembrie, Bucharest, email: mihaela_mb1@yahoo.com

Crisis and Monetary Policy – the Romanian Experience

Abstract: The international financial crisis that started in 2007 changed the monetary policy. Old instruments became ineffective and new instruments were applied. The Romanian economy followed the experience of other countries and also applied new instruments in order to reach the monetary objective to keep inflation under control and sustain the economic development. This paper tries to highlight the impact of monetary policy during the crises on development and ISD flow in Romania using the VAR and VEC models on the quarterly data. The results show that before the crisis there was no long-term relation between money demand and GDP as a theory, but, after the crisis, there was a negative long-term relation, probably as a result of the financial instability and the great injection of money in order to cover the bad loans and to prevent a banking system crisis. Hagmayr and Haiss (2007) and Haiss and Kichler (2009) also highlight a negative relation between the domestic bad credit and GDP.

Keywords: Macroeconomic forecast, economic crisis, monetary policy, central banks, financial markets

1. Introduction

The economic-financial crisis that started in 2007 compelled the banking system to closely watch their way of conducting operations and to review the system of regulations and risks, particularly those of the system itself. The real experience showed that the monetary policy alone could not provide the stabilization of the economies, seriously damaged by the effects of the financial crisis, and this required the application of a mixture of economic policies that combined the restructure policies with those concerning the fiscal consolidation and a cautious monetary policy.

The economic-financial crisis also had a major impact upon the monetary policy regarding the highlighting of the weakness and insufficiency of the classical instruments used by the central banks and the need for development of new instruments in order to provide the stability of prices, but also to protect and monitor the stability of the financial system in its entirety. Such a point of view was also supported by Cecchetti (2008), Bernanke (2009), Bernanke and Reinhart (2004) Bernanke, Reinhart, Sack (2004), J. C. Trichet (2009) and others who wrote about inventory strategies and possible measures in the case that the interest rate is zero.

The purpose of this paper is the analysis of the influences of the economic-fiananical crisis on the instruments of monetary policy and the assesment of the change impact for the monetary variables and ISD for the Romanian economy.

The methodology used in order to reach the objectives includes the usage of comparative analyses, the documentary syntheses, the statistical and mathemathical analyses, but also the application of some complex econometric techniques such as the autoregression vectors (VAR) and the vectors of errors correction (VEC). The models such as VAR are the most often used in the literature dedicated to the analysis of the influence of the economic-financial crisis on the monetary policies (Bernanke, Reinhart, Sack, 2004; Eggertsson and Woodford, 2003 and others). In order to achieve this objective, this paper is structured in three parts.

2. The evolution of the instruments used by BNR in order to reduce the crisis impact over the economy

For Romania, the period of time between 2000 and 2006 signified a focus of efforts on monetary policy, but not only that; in order to meet the criteria from Maastricht regarding nominal convergence, the inflation decrease had to go from two figures to one figure. In this respect, a new strategy of monetary policy was developed, meaning "a direct targeting of inflation", aiming at maintenance, in a relative steady interval with a variation of ±15%, of the exchange movements, whose influences over the inflationary expectations are determined in Romania. Romania's economic climate from 2007 to 2015 was characterized, first of all, by Romania joining the EU member countries on January 1st 2007, which signified a new stage in the economic-social evolution of the country. Besides, efforts have been made for the harmonization of the monetary policy and, especially, of the instruments of the monetary policy used at national level, with those of the European Central Bank, and counteraction of the effects of the global economic-financial crisis of summer 2007, through the credit crisis with high risk in USA. In Figure 1, during the 2000–2008 period, you can notice the real increase of gross domestic product (GDP) together, during the same time, with the decrease of the interest of the monetary policy that led to the increase of the domestic credit, which also influenced the level of gross domestic product.

The interest rates also had an essential contribution in Romania, both before the crisis and during the crisis, and after that too. The understanding of the mechanism of changing these interest rates on the monetary market and of conveyance towards the interests used for the clients by the banks, shows an image of the way the monetary policy affects the economy (R. Radu, 2010).

Fig. 1: The evolution of GDP real increase, of the intern credit change and of the monetary policy interest during 2000–2016

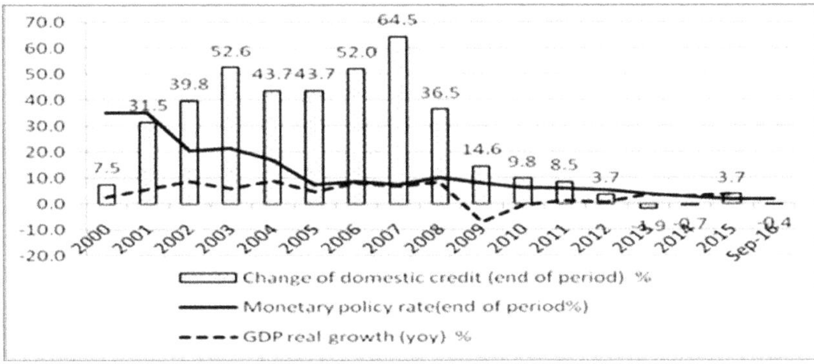

Source: BNR Annual reports during 2000–2015, BNR Monthly newsletters

Yet, the deepening of the conveyance mechanism analysis of the interest rates during the 2008–2010 period revealed, both in Romania and other countries (Poland, Hungary, the Czech Republic), the appearance of some disorders (Enache Raluca, R. Radu, 2015). Analyzing the evolution of the daily interest rates on the monetary market in Romania and the Euro Zone, of the interest of the monetary policy established by BNR between January 2007 and September 2016 and of the inflation evolution in the two zones, it is noticed that at the beginning of the crisis (2007–2008) interest rates were increased, with wider fluctuations for Romania compared to the Euro Zone. The Romanian evolution could be a result of the external shocks of the price increases for oil and food (reflected in an inflation increase), but also of the capital account liberalization, through which it was allowed for non-residents in Romania to make lei deposits, which led to the national currency depreciation with 25 percentage between the middle of 2007 and the end of March 2009, despite the increase of the interest rate of monetary policy, from 7% in August 2007 to 10.25% in August 2008 (see Figure 2).

Fig. 2a: The evolution of the interest rates *Fig. 2b: Annual changes of the inflation rate*

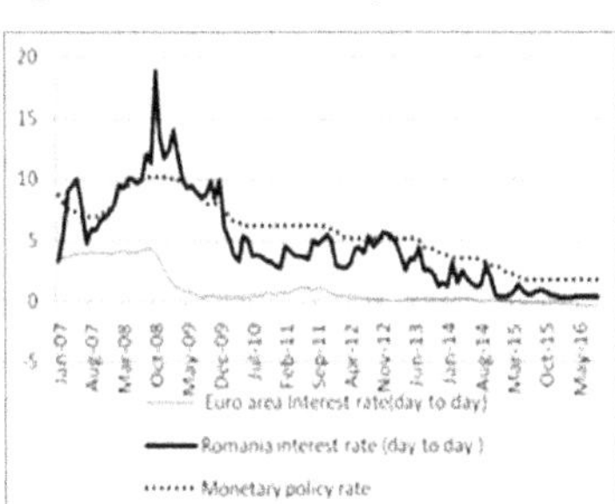

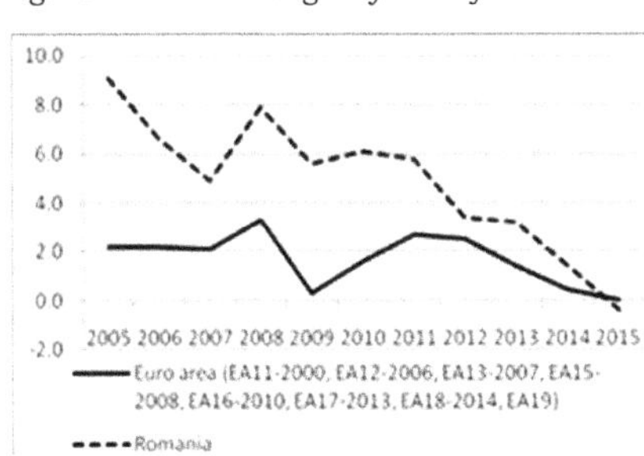

Source: Eurostat data and BNR data, accessed 26.10.2016

The inflation increase was a signal for BNR in the decision to change the interest rate of monetary policy. In Borio's opinion (2016, p. 2016), this approach, in Wicksellian spirit, to the natural rate is quite narrow, the present economic situation demanding an expansion of the context to include other indicators in the analysis, indicators that have a signalizing role, such as the credit evolution, the assets price and the risk. This assertion is important if we take into consideration the fact that in Romania, the pressure increase over the interest rate was due, on one hand, to the segmentation of the interbank market because of the lack of trust in the banks, and on the other, the change of banks' attitude towards BNR, meaning that they had a very clear negative attitude. The general increase of liquidity demand can be added to this, taking into consideration the uncertainties as far as the economic evolution is concerned (IMF Country Report No. 10/47, February 2010, p. 8).

Besides this, the daily interbank interest rates and the three months interest rate are inside this corridor and it oscillates around the interest of monetary policy, with bigger variations for the daily interbank interest rate (fig.3).

Fig. 3: The evolution of the interest rate for the monetary policy for the interest on the daily interbank market, the three months interest rate, and the credit and deposit in Romania from January 2005 to September 2016

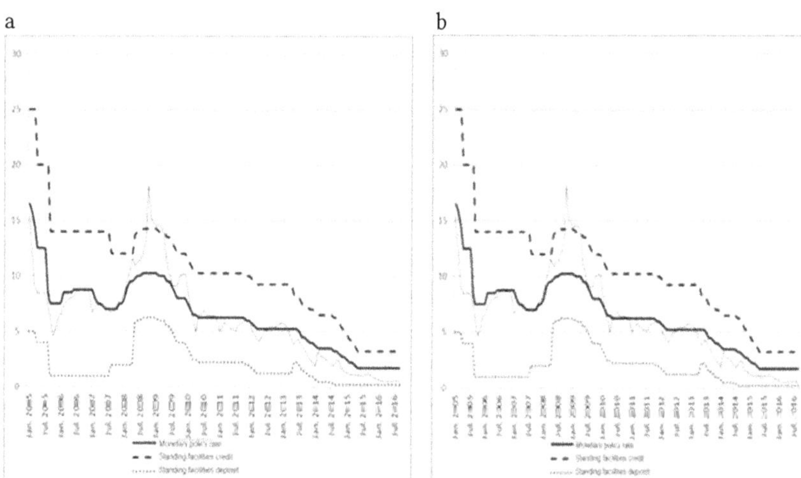

Source: Eurostat data and BNR data, accessed 26.10.2016

There is a big difference between the credit and deposit interest rate, which, although it experienced a deeper decrease tendency starting in April 2005 when it reached 16 percentage points (compared with 25 percentage points in December 2004 and 20 percentage points in January 2005), it maintained itself at a high level, the difference being halved starting in May 2008 and maintaining itself at

8 percentage points (p.p) until April 2013. After this date, it experienced a deeper decrease process, reaching only three p.p. in September 2016. The impact of the variations for the mandatory minimum deposits rate can be noticed in the structure of BNR's sheet balance during the 2007–2014 period where the level of the mandatory deposits has values between 61–23%, the way it is presented in table 1.

Table 1: The restricted structure of the BNR balance sheet during 2007–2014 (%)

Indicators	**2007**	**2008**	**2009**	**2010**	**2011**	**2012**	**2013**	**2014**
Total assets	100	100	100	100	100	100	100	100
External assets	98	97	92.0	96.6	95.0	91.0	97.5	98.5
Credits granted to the credit institutions	0	1.0	6.5	2.0	4.0	7.0	0.6	0.0
Other assets	2.0	2	1.6	1.4	1.0	2.0	1.9	1.5
Total obligations	100	100	100	100	100	100	100	100
Minimum mandatory savings in lei	22	18	16.0	15.0	16.0	12.0	16.9	13.2
Minimum mandatory savings in foreign currency	36	43	22.7	17.7	15.0	15.0	14.4	10.6
Deposits received from the credit institutions	4	0.4	0.0	0.2	0.0	0.0	0.0	3.7
Cash in circulation	25	24	19.0	18.2	20.0	20.0	24.0	27.7
External obligations	5	5	23.0[1]	30.0[2]	30.0[3]	28.0[4]	18.6[5]	10.3[6]
Treasury availabilities	8	1.2	9.0	7.8	8.0	14.0	18.6	24.9
Others (share capitol, savings, etc)	0.3	8.4	10.0	10.8	11.0	11.0	7.5	4.2

Source: Data from the Annual Reports of BNR during 2007–2014

Note: 1. Out of which 20% represents the sums obtained from the FMI loan.
2. Out of which 27% represents the sums obtained in 2009–2010 from the FMI loan.
3. Out of which 28% represents the sums obtained in 2009–2011 from the FMI loan.
4. Out of which 25% represents the sums obtained in 2009–2012 from the FMI loan.
5. Out of which 15.6% represents the sums remained to be paid from the FMI loan.
6. Out of which 7.1% represents the sums remained to be paid from the FMI loan.

The permanent facilities used by BNR as deposits received and the credits granted to the credit institutions represent another instrument used by BNR in order to implement the monetary policy. Figure 3 presents the evolution of the monetary indicators that show the usage of this instrument by BNR. There can be noticed the fact that between December 2006 and September 2016, the instrument *deposits received* was more frequently used in the implementation of the BNR's monetary policy, while in comparison the credit granting acted more for draining the liquidity excess. The credit instrument was used more between March to June 2007, August 2008 to December 2009 and December 2012 to February 2013, with a credit top in October 2009 (48993,9 million lei) followed by a lower injection of 38625,2 million lei in February 2009, and another one of 24014,2 million lei in December 2009, taking into consideration the delay as the economic-financial crisis was felt in Europe, but also in Romania (see figure 4).

Fig. 4: Permanent facilities used by BNR between December 2006 and September 2016

a b

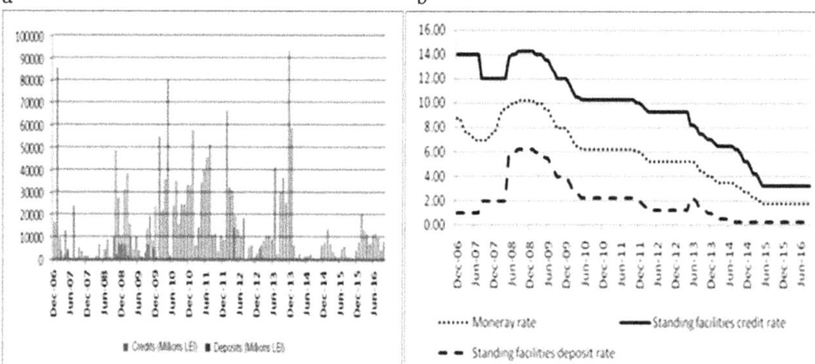

Source: Data from the BNR Monthly Newsletters no. 12 during 2007–2015 and no.9/2016, table no. 3.2 Permanent facilities granted to the eligible participants by BNR

The literature revision

The VAR models were used by Benanke and Blinder (1992), but also by Sims (1992) in order to identify the direction and the amplitude of the monetary shocks over the different variables of the economy.

Hoke and Tuzcuoglu (2016) used a FAVAR model, based on Bayesiene techniques, with a big data number from the real, monetary, financial sector in order to highlight the reaction of some variables to different shocks. Using the answering function to an impulse, they proved that the industrial production is reduced to a contraction of the monetary policy, that an unemployment increase causes a decrease of the inflation and of the financial factors, that the money factor is affected in a negative way by a shock to the interest rate, that the expectations factor, after a slight increase in the first phase of the shock, changes its trajectory and becomes negative in accordance with the expectations theory that follows a contraction period of the monetary policy.

Frank and Hesse (2009) used a VAR model with two variables in order to estimate the response to the liquidity stress of the interest used in the USA and the Euro

Zone, using the spread between LIBOR and OIS, instead of using the liquidity and the credit components. The model was estimated for the crisis period, meaning from 1st July 2007 until 3rd April 2008. Thus, they could quantify the cumulative effect of the central bank interventions over the interbank monetary market, showing that the announcement of LTRO facility interventions reduced the stress on the monetary market by around ten percentage points; the spread average between LIBOR and OIS was 55 important percentage points during the crisis, and would have been significantly smaller if the interventions would not have taken place.

Čihák, Harjes, Stavrev (2009) used a bi variant VAR model, estimated both in levels through Bayesiene methods and first order differences for monthly data during January 1999 to April 2009 for the interbank interests and the corporate bonds and January 2003 to April 2009 for the loans of the non-financial corporations and the households. The models' results showed that the changes of the interests of the monetary policy were transmitted in the interests rates on the monetary market with amplitudes and different speeds. More than that, the data proved that transmitting to the interest rates on the market was poor during the crisis, indicating their inefficiency during the crisis and that is why there was a need for new instruments.

Analyses through VAR techniques regarding this mechanism of the transmission of the impulses of monetary policy through the channel of the interest rates were also accomplished for Romania by Radu (2010) and Enache Raluca, R. Radu, (2015), the results being similar to those from the study by Čihák, Harjes and Stavrev (2009).

For four states from south-east Europe, Hagmayr and Haiss (2007) indentified a negative correlation between GDP and domestic credit, and Haiss and Kichler (2009) also identified an inverse relation between the underperforming credits and GDP.

The models and results presentation

The analysis method used is represented by: the models with the error correction (VEC-error correction vector) and autoregression-vector models (VAR).

The VAR model has the following form:

$$y_i = A(L)y_{i-1} + Cy*_i + e_i, e_i \rightarrow (0, \Sigma_e)$$

Regressors number: k= mq+m*
Coefficients number: c=mk

Initially, it can be considered that the vector y_i has "m" variables. Each of these variables has "p" lags. The rest of the variables (the determinist variables and the free term) can be found in the vector written with y_{*_i} with m* elements.

The VAR model is written in two equivalent forms (X- a matrix of size Tk, Y and E- matrices of size Tm, Im- the matrix size unit m, α- vector with mk elements, y and e- vector with some mT components):

$$Y = XA + E$$
$$y = (Im * X)\, a + e, e \rightarrow (0, \Sigma_e * I_T)$$

In the literature, two structural VAR approaches are mentioned. The first one is used by Canova (1995) and then by Gordon and Leeper (1994) and it implies the usage of the normal distribution: Wishart for the size with reduced parameters. Extractions for structural parameters are achieved in a conditional form, using the identification restrictions. If Aj are the coefficients of the model and $\sum_e = A_0^{-1} A_0^{-1'}$, then Aj=$A_0^{-1} Aj$. This method neglects the restrictions if A_0 is overidentified.

Sims and Zha (1999) considered a different structural form, where A0 is non-singular and $\overline{y}$ contains determinist variables.

$$A_0 y_t - A(l) y_{t-1} + C\overline{y}_t = e_t, e_t - > (0, I)$$

The VEC models are restricted VAR models, meaning that they use series of unsteady data which are cointegrated. The VEC model has cointegration relations even in its specification, the long-term behavior of the endogenous variables being restricted in order to converge towards the cointegration relations, also allowing for the short-term adjustment of the dynamics.

The cointegration term is named error correction term, because the deviation from the short-term equilibrium is adjusted through the short-term partial corrections.

For two variables y1 and y2, the cointegration equation is:

$$y_{2t} = \beta y_{1t}$$

The right VEC model is:

$$\Delta y_{1t} = \alpha_1 (y_{2t-1} - \beta y_{1t-1}) + \varepsilon_{1t}$$

$$\Delta y_{2t} = \alpha_2 (y_{2t-1} - \beta y_{1t-1}) + \varepsilon_{2t}$$

The variable that is only on the right side is the term of error correction. For the long-term equilibrium, this term is null. If the two variables divert from the equilibrium, the term of error correction will not be null and each variable is adjusted in order to partially re-establish the equilibrium relation. The coefficients α_1 şi α_2 measure the adjustment speed of the variable y_{1t}, respectively y_{2t} towards equilibrium.

The relation between the monetary policy is analyzed empirically through variables like the real currency demand (M2), the intern credit, the direct foreign investment inflows (ISD) and the economic growth analyzed through the dynamics of industrial production. The data series have monthly frequency and they can be considered as the models on two different periods of time: January 1994 to March 2016 and the period of time after the start of the recent economic crisis in Romania: January 2009 to March 2016.

According to the correlation matrix, the production varietion correlates poorly with the variation of the real currency demand and very poorly with the variation of the intern credit and with the ISD inflows in the country. A stronger correlation (coefficient of linear correlation of almost 0.27) could be noticed between the variation of the real currency demand and ISD.

The data having monthly frequency was deseasoned for the series where the presence of seasonal factors was detected. For the intern credit and ISD the data deseasonalization was not necessary. The data series for the index of the industrial production (2000=100) and the real demand currency were seasonally adjusted based on the Tramo-Seats method. The unit root tests were also applied on the series without seasonal factors and a series of stationary data was obtained in the ISD case. For the other variables the series in first difference is stationary at a significance level of 5%, according to the ADF test (the results can be offered on request).

On the stationary series, a vector-autoregression model (VAR) was built. According to the Schwartz criteria, the right lag is two, but other criteria indicate a lag equal with four. Taking into consideration the data of economic theory, it is preferred to choose a lag as small as possible.

A VAR(2) model is estimated for the variables: the change of the industrial production index (D_PRODUCTIE), the change of the real monetary mass (D_M2), the change of the intern credit (D_CREDIT) and ISD.

The impact of the currency demand, the intern credit and ISD over the dynamics of the industrial production is almost null. There can be noticed a slightly positive impact of the intern credit variation from the two previous periods of time over the change of Romania's industrial production index from January 1994 to March 2016, which is in accordance with the expectations, because in Romania, the economic growth was mostly achieved based on consumption. There could be noticed a significant positive impact of ISD over the variation of the currency demand during this period of time. On the other hand, the variation of the currency request and the variation of the intern credit had a positive impact on ISD.

D_PRODUCTION = - 0.3071308322*D_PRODUCTION(-1) - 0.1225587257*D_PRODUCTION(-2) + 0.0001503554058*D_M2(-1) - 0.0001597578556*D_M2(-2) + 5.935107815e-06*D_CREDIT(-1) + 7.407113982e-06*D_CREDIT(-2) - 0.0005825516507*ISD(-1) - 0.0005353879583*ISD(-2) + 0.4626300683

D_M2 = - 4.013160928*D_PRODUCTION(-1) - 42.03044882*D_PRODUCTION(-2) + 0.1218220964*D_M2(-1) + 0.115440863*D_M2(-2) - 0.004558333734*D_CREDIT(-1) + 0.0005475286599*D_CREDIT(-2) + 0.7697452156*ISD(-1) + 0.5472892686*ISD(-2) + 464.952733

D_CREDIT = - 741.3906404*D_PRODUCTION(-1) - 318.2057244*D_PRODUCTION(-2) + 0.7024684912*D_M2(-1) + 1.222278848*D_M2(-2) - 0.1377199972*D_CREDIT(-1) + 0.287627237*D_CREDIT(-2) + 24.17490116*ISD(-1) - 35.56608587*ISD(-2) + 1810.495603

ISD = - 6.097916433*D_PRODUCTION(-1) + 3.333799041*D_PRODUCTION(-2) + 0.01830485687*D_M2(-1) + 0.03371145022*D_M2(-2) + 5.444142645e-05*D_CREDIT(-1) + 0.0007314482964*D_CREDIT(-2) + 0.176816751*ISD(-1) + 0.2140761936*ISD(-2) + 106.5193359

Yet, the suggested VAR(2) model represents a strong autocorrelation of errors and heteroscedasticity.

A VAR(2) model is reestimated only for the variation of the production dynamics and the change of the intern credit. There can be noticed a positive impact of the change of the intern credit on the change of the industrial production, meaning that besides the increase of the intern credit from one period of time to another in the two previous months, the industrial production also grew at present. The results are in accordance with the economic theory, because there is a posivite relation between the intern credit and the production increase.

D_PRODUCTION=-0.2976739365*D_PRODUCTION(-1) - 0.123231363*D_PRODUCTION(-2) + 5.129260404e-06*D_CREDIT(-1) + 6.204645536e-06*D_CREDIT(-2) + 0.1603178181

D_CREDIT= - 559.0656489*D_PRODUCTION(-1) - 486.47959*D_PRODUCTION(-2) - 0.1985063841*D_CREDIT(-1) + 0.2673777706*D_CREDIT(-2) + 949.5687734

The errors are independent until the twelve lag. The estimation results can be offered on request. At a shock in the production change, this variable responds quickly and positively after a month. At a shock in the variation of the intern credit, the industrial production does not respond immediately. There is an adjustment positive response after only two months. At a shock in the variation of the dynamics of the industrial production, the credit responds negatively in the first three months after the shock, while at a credit shock, the credit variation responds positively after a month and negatively after two months, the signs alternating during the ten months after the shock.

According to the decomposition by each variable, in a month after a shock in the change of the dynamics of the industrial production, the changes in this variable are exclusively due to this shock. After two months, 13.85% from the change of the credit variation is due to the variations in the dynamics of the industrial production in order for the influence of this shock over the intern credit to increase suddenly in the second period of time and to be stabilized starting the fifth lag around the value 22%.

In a month after a shock in the variation of the intern credit, 99.99% of the change of this variable is due to this shock. After two to ten months, around 99.4% of the variation of the intern credit is due to the changes of this variable and only 0.5% of the change of industrial production is due to a shock in the intern credit. Therefore, these results are in accordance with the expectations. The changes in the intern credit affected the industrial production quite little, while the variations of the industrial production had even less impact on the intern credit. An explanation could be the fact that the intern credit was more targeted towards consumption and less towards the stimulation of the industrial production.

In order to analyze the short and long-term relations, an error correction model will be created (VEC) with the intern credit variables and the index of the industrial production, which are cointegrated by the I order (the results can be offered on request). There is only one cointegration relation between the two variables.

D(CREDIT) = C(1)*(CREDIT(-1) - 3759.066092*PRODUCTION_SA(-1) + 332160.0799) + C(2)*D(CREDIT(-1)) + C(3)*D(CREDIT(-2)) + C(4)*D(PRODUCTION_SA(-1)) + C(5)*D(PRODUCTION_SA(-2)) + C(6)

D(PRODUCTION_SA) = C(7)*(CREDIT(-1) - 3759.066092*PRODUCTION_SA(-1) + 332160.0799) + C(8)*D(CREDIT(-1)) + C(9)*D(CREDIT(-2)) + C(10)*D(PRODUCTION_SA(-1)) + C(11)*D(PRODUCTION_SA(-2)) + C(12)

D(CREDIT) = - 0.06978189595*(CREDIT(-1) - 3759.066092*PRODUCTION_SA(-1) + 332160.0799) - 0.15341211*D(CREDIT(-1)) + 0.2975039214*D(CREDIT(-2)) - 669.7345866*D(PRODUCTION_SA(-1)) - 544.8582492*D(PRODUCTION_SA(-2)) + 911.0930431

D(PRODUCTION_SA)=4.192920239e-06*(CREDIT(-1) - 3759.066092*PRODUCTION_SA(-1) + 332160.0799) + 2.419722466e-06*D(CREDIT(-1)) + 4.394483375e-06*D(CREDIT(-2)) - 0.2910242744*D(PRODUCTION_SA(-1)) - 0.1197236185*D(PRODUCTION_SA(-2)) + 0.1626296737

The coefficient C(1) represents the error correction term or the adjustment speed towards the equilibrium. There are two types of causality: the long-term causality and the short-term causality. In the long term, if the coefficient C(1) is negative, then there is a long-term causality from the intern credit to the index of the industrial production. In this case, C(1) has the value -0.069, less than zero. So, there was a long-term causality between the index of the industrial production and the intern credit in Romania from January 1994 to March 2016. In other words, the need to support the investments in the industrial production caused an increase in the intern credit.

In order to verify the existence of a short-term causality, it is tested if C(4)=0 and C(5)=0. In this purpose, the Wald test is applied. The probabilities associated to the Wald statistics test are higher than 0.05 (results in the Table). So, the coefficients are null from the statistics point of view, which implies the fact that there is no short-term causality relation from the industrial production to the intern credit.

The coefficient C(7) is positive, which indicates the fact there is no long term causality relation for the index of the industrial production. The short-term causality is verified through the testing of the coefficients C(8) and C(9), which is not different from zero in a significant way from a statistics point of view. Therefore, there is no short-term causality between the two variables.

Table 8: The results of the Wald test for the coefficients

Null hypothesis	**Test statistics**	**Prob.**
C(4)=0	2.046678	0.152539
C(5)=0	1.358071	0.243872
C(8)=0	0.088993	0.765461
C(9)=0	0.303613	0.581626

Source: Own calculations

So, we can conclude that there is only one long-term causality relation from the change of the industrial production to the intern credit in Romania, from January 1994 to March 2016. In the long term, in order to cover the extension needs of the industrial production, the intern credit was also brought into discussion.

The model is resumed for the period after the start of the economic crisis: January 2009 until March 2016. This time, there is a long-term causality relation between the variables in both ways: from the index for the industrial production to the intern credit and from the intern credit to the change of the industrial production. In the long term, in order to support the increase of the industrial production, credit is needed, and the production is financed based on credit.

D(CREDIT) = - 0.006342304422*(CREDIT(-1) + 4478.554676*PRODUCTION_SA(-1) - 876328.2709) + 0.004434989409*D(CREDIT(-1)) - 25.28014764*D(PRODUCTION_SA(-1)) + 255.2456857

D(PRODUCTION_SA) = - 1.89993284e-05*(CREDIT(-1) + 4478.554676*PRODUCTION_SA(-1) - 876328.2709) + 0.0001063158355*D(CREDIT(-1)) - 0.2003541068*D(PRODUCTION_SA(-1)) + 0.0696005924

Still, in the short term, the causality relations between the variables do not exist. Therefore, the intern credit supported the industrial production, and, implicitly, the economic growth during the economic crisis only in the long term. In order to fight against the negative effects of the crisis, the economy made slow adjustments.

Conclusions

In conclusion, a few common elements can be highlighted in the implementation of the monetary policy taken from the central banks for the purpose of avoiding the negative effects of the financial crisis, meaning:

- the reduction of the interest rate in many cases up to zero, this leading to analyses and debates regarding the efficiency of the monetary policy in such conditions;
- a liquidity management, including through extension measures of the maturity for the loans and the deposits at the central bank for the current terms;
- the extension of the titles and duties range that can represnt collateral guarantees in the interbank loans;
- currency swaps between the central banks, FED and BCE in order to provide the necessary currency; changes in the structure of the balances of the central banks.

Also, the analyses highlighted that BNR used a mixture of conventional and non-convetional instruments in order to insure the implementation of the monetary policy. The international and economic crisis also affected the Romanian industry, which entered into a very fast and sharp decline from November 2008. The most industrial sectors affected by the crisis had the export as their destination of production. There are more explanations of the effects of the economic-financial crisis over these activity sectors:

- the restriction of the foreign markets based on the economic crisis in the member states for Romania (Germany, Italy, France, etc.);
- the restriction of the credit offered to the economic agents by the commercial banks, in accordance with the prudence norms of BNR;
- the decrease of the activity in the construction sector, which affected the production in the connected industrial activities in a negative way;
- the propagation of the effects horizontally in the sectors joined in the activity.

Therefore, the empiric analysis on monthly data revealed that the relations between the intern credit and the industrial production were more powerful during the economic crisis. The economic crisis affected both the monetary policy and the economic growth, reordering the dependences between the variables.

References

1. Bernanke B. S., Reinhart V, Sack B. P. (2004). Monetary Policy Alternatives at Zero Bound: An Empirical Assesment, în Brooking Papers on Economic Activity, No. 2, https://www.brookings.edu/wp-content/uploads/2004/06/2004b_bpea_bernanke.pdf, accesat în 6 12.2016.
2. Bernanke B. S., (2009). The crisis and the policy response, in Speech at the Stamp Lecture, London School of Economics, London, 13 January, https://www.federalreserve.gov/ newsevents/speech/bernanke20090113a.htm.
3. Bernanke B, Reinhart V, (2004). Conducting Monetary Policy at very low short term interest rate, in Policy to deal with deflation, vol. 94, (2), pp. 85–90, AEA Papers and Proceedings, May, http://public.econ.duke.edu/~staff/wrkshop_papers/20082009%20Papers/Bernanke_Reinhart_AER_2004.pdf, accesat în 6 12.2016.
4. Borio C. (2016). Revisiting the three intelectual pillars of monetary policy, in Cato Journal, Vol. 36, No. 2 (Spring/Summer 2016), pp. 213–238, https://object.cato.org/sites/cato.org/files/serials/files/cato-journal/2016/5/cj-v36n2-1.pdf, accesat în 8.12.2016.
5. Canova, F. (1995). VAR Models: Specification, Estimation, Inference and Forecasting, in H. Pesaran and M. Wickens, Handbook of Applied Econometrics, Ch.2, Blackwell, Oxford, UK.
6. Cecchetti S. G. (2008). Monetary Policy and the Financial Crisis of 2007–2008, in http://citeseerx.ist.psu.edu/viewdoc/download?doi=10.1.1.464.161&rep=rep1&type=pdf, accesat în 22.06.2016.
7. Čihák, M., Harjes, T., Stavre, E. (2009). Euro Area Monetary Policy in Uncharted Waters, IMF Working Paper WP/09/185, International Monetary Fund.
8. Eggertsson, G., Woodford, M. (2003). The zero bound on interest rates and optimal monetary policy, în Booking Papers of Economic Activity nr.1, pp. 139–233 https://www.brookings.edu/wp-content/uploads/2003/01/2003a_bpea_eggertsson.pdf, accesat în 6.12.2016.

9. Enache, R. Radu, R. (2015). Transmisia ratelor dobânzilor în România. Estimări recente şi comparaţii regionale, în Caiete de Studii No. 37/2015, Banca Naţională a României.
10. Frank, N., Hesse, H. (2009). The Effectiveness of Central Bank Interventions during the First Phase of the Subprime Crisis. IMF Working Paper 09/206.
11. Gordon, D.B., Leeper, E. M. (1994). The Dynamic Impacts of Monetary Policy: An Exercise in Tentative Identification, Journal of Political Economy, University of Chicago Press, vol. 102(6), pp. 1228–47, December.
12. Hagmayr, B., Haiss, P. R., Sümegi, K. (2007). Financial sector development and economic growth-evidence for southeastern Europe. Available at SSRN 968253.
13. Haiss, P. R., Kichler, E. (2009). Leasing, credit and economic growth: Evidence for Central and South-Eastern Europe. Hoke S. H, K. Tuzcuoglu, (2016), Interpreting the latent dynamic factors by threshold FAVAR model, Staff Working Paper No. 622, Bank of England.
14. Hoke S. H., Tuzcuoglu, K. (2016). Interpreting the latent dynamic factors by the thereshold FAVAR model, Staff Working Paaper No. 622, Bank of England.
15. International Monetay Fund, (2010). Romania. Financial System Stability Assessment, in IMF Country Report No. 10/47, February 2010, cr.1047.
16. Radu, R. (2010). Mecanismul de transmisie a ratelor dobânzilor, în Caiete de Studii no.28/2010, Banca Naţională a României.
17. Sims, C. A. (1992). Interpreting the macroeconomic time series facts: The effects of monetary policy, European Economic Review, no36, 5 (June), pp. 975–1000.
18. Sims, C., Zha, T. (1999). Error Bands for Impulse Responses Econometrica, 67:1113–1155.
19. Trichet, J. C. (2009). The ECB's enhanced credit support, in Keynote address by Jean-Claude Trichet, President of the ECB at the University of Munich Munich, 13 July 2009 https://www.ecb.europa.eu/press/key/date/2009/html/sp090713.en.html.

Iulia LUPU

Victor Slăvescu Centre for Financial and Monetary Research,
email: iulia_lupu@icfm.ro

Adina CRISTE

Victor Slăvescu Centre for Financial and Monetary Research,
email: criste.adina@gmail.com

Central Banks' Forecasts – An Orientation Tool for the Public and the Financial Markets

Abstract: In the area of macroeconomic forecasts, central banks have at all times been in the forefront, but the manner in which they develop and dispose the forecasts has changed a lot over the last decades. Changes emerged that reflect evolutions in economic theory, as well in the monetary policy strategies adopted over time. Publishing their own forecasts may take the form of a self-discipline imposed by central banks, coming (or not) to support the credibility of central banks in meeting their objectives. According to recent studies, forecasts made by central banks influence the forecasts of the private sector and monetary policy means more than private expectations management, which is a subtle channel of monetary policy transmission. The issue regarding the central bank forecasting can be seen from two perspectives: development of forecasts, on the one hand, and their communication (public broadcasting), on the other. In relation to the financial markets, the second perspective is dominant–how to communicate forecasts and their impact on financial markets, based on the influence of financial variables.

Keywords: Macroeconomic forecast, central banks, financial markets

Introduction

The international context is now characterized by geopolitical uncertainties that are present everywhere, and even protectionist tendencies in some cases, and political uncertainties bearing economic risks. Furthermore, the effects of the referendum in the United Kingdom to leave the European Union are still unknown and prospects for growth in the euro area and the OECD countries remain limited.

The central banks' forecasts affect economic stability and sustainability. Therefore, it is necessary to understand the relation between the performance of macroeconomic forecasts and the reaction of the public and financial markets in order to identify ways to prevent excessive volatility in economic indicators and to ensure a stable economic framework.

The financial crisis provided evidence of the problems faced by those that perform economic forecasts. These new challenges refer to both the instruments for forecasting and macroeconomic policies, especially monetary policy, which has undergone a great pressure in the post-crisis time.

The macroeconomic forecasts process has a fundamental contribution for economic policymaking. This contribution is considerably higher than the simple forecasts of GDP and inflation, which taken separately are not sufficient for decision making. The forecasting regarding the macroeconomic variables represents a useful instrument in making decisions about monetary policy, whereas the central bank increasingly takes into account the prospect and the foresight.

The motivation of looking forward is embedded in monetary policy and also drives at the evolution of macroeconomic variables in the medium-term, it is given by the lags occurrences in the transmission of monetary signals in the real economy. The central bank cannot influence the current inflation and production, but identify the paths of macroeconomic variables in the future, thus guiding the public expectations towards certain targets.

In this article, we intend to identify the necessary elements to generate effective macroeconomic forecasts and also to outline the influence of central banks' forecasts on the public and financial markets. In order to attain the paper objective, it is important to point out both the main characteristics of central bank forecasting and the role of these forecasts in influencing the public expectations.

1. Central bank's forecasting – main characteristics

In general, for a forecasting process to be effective, it should meet three general functions that support each other. First of all, the forecasting process should contribute to the promotion of understanding the evolution of the economy, the likely perspectives for the economy and the risks around that forecast. In the same time, the forecasting process should consider the various advantages and disadvantages offered by alternative strategies. Not the least, the forecast is a good means of communication, which is essential in formulating the public expectations.

Regarding the central banks' forecasting, in addition to results from models, the published forecasts often include subjective adjustments, arising from the need to take into account information that is not included in the models. Most often, the results based only on forecasts models are not publicly available. Such judgments are necessary to adjust the projected track of monetary policy instruments in order to achieve a balanced policy, ensuring an appropriate pace. Even in developed countries, the monetary policy actions are seen later in the economy, requiring up to six to eight quarters. A longer horizon targeting may allow monetary policy to promote better adjustment for prolonged weakness in the economy or financial imbalances. Moreover, it is recognized that optimal horizon targeting may vary over time, depending on the shocks that hit the economy.

An observation that should be taken into account is one concerning those who produce macroeconomic forecasts; they cannot learn quickly from their mistakes, a result that can lead to related forecasting errors.

The actual way in which projections from central banks are produced and used has changed substantially over the last decades. The changes reflected both developments in economic theory (and econometric) and monetary policy regimes.

In general, central banks rely on an inflation target in the short and medium term to help anchor expectations and eliminate or at least mitigate uncertainties regarding their primary objective (the price stability).

The widespread use of the conditioning assumptions, involving a variety of models, a common assessment for reasonableness and consistency of results and an important role given to expert judgments, are some common characteristics of the forecasting process in the modern central banks.

The problem of central bank forecasting can be seen from two perspectives: the development of forecasts, on the one hand, and their communication (public broadcasting), on the other hand.

In relation with the financial markets, the second perspective is dominant–how to communicate forecasts and the impact of these forecasts on the financial markets, based on the influence of financial variables.

2. The role of central banks' forecasts

By issuing macroeconomic forecasts, the public expectations may change depending on the messages formulated, but the central bank continuously strives that its behavior is adjusted to the assumed objectives.

For the central bank policy, a clear and transparent communication is seen as essential, including risks that could affect the published forecasts of the economic indicators. In the case of inflation targeting strategy, the forecasts of macroeconomic variables (especially inflation and GDP) are the basic ingredients for monetary policy implementation.

The central banks' disclosure has been a longer process, based on development of publications issued by central banks. Thus, in 1993, the Bank of England began publishing a quarterly Inflation Report, in which were presented a detailed analysis of the economy and forecasts of inflation, used by the Monetary Policy Committee to take decisions on monetary policy rate.

Today, many central banks regularly publish forecasts for a large number of variables to support and motivate their monetary policy decisions. Overall, the forecast horizon is between two and three years, but there are central banks that publish a long-term prediction (for example the Federal Reserve offers the estimates projected by the individual members of the Federal Open Market Committee). Recently, the European Central Bank increased the forecast horizon and widened the scope of its forecasts. Based on the number of variables predicted, a hierarchy of central banks is presented in the following figure (Fig.1).

Fig. 1: A hierarchy of central banks based on the number of macroeconomic variables

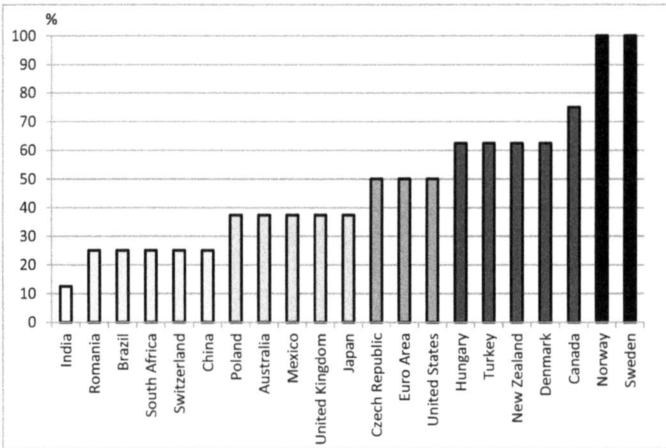

Source: *Authors' representation, according to information provided by central banks' websites.*

Note: The ranking is calculated as a ratio between the number of variables forecasted by the central bank and all identified (eight macroeconomic variables: CPI inflation, core inflation, interest rates, GDP growth, components of GDP growth, output gap or potential GDP; salaries or labor costs; unemployment)

According to Figure 1, the most advanced central banks concerning the number of forecasted macroeconomic variables are the central banks of Norway and Sweden. However, there is no correlation between the level of economic development and the number of macroeconomic variables forecasted by central banks. In this regard, the Swiss National Bank, the Bank of England, and the Federal Reserve Bank of Australia limit the forecasting to one or two macroeconomic variables (CPI inflation, GDP growth).

The next table (Table 1) presents the main communication features of macroeconomic forecasts applied by important central banks of some developed countries. Most central banks provide a point estimate for their projections, sometimes adding a confidence interval around this value. There are also central banks that use alternative scenarios as forecast profiles.

One of the advanced tools of communication for some central banks is the publishing the endogenous interest rate, a measure adopted by Fed, the Bank of Japan, the Bank of Canada, the Czech National Bank etc. Besides, the forward guidance policy becomes increasingly important as communication policy of central banks during crisis (see Table 1).

Table 1: Main communication features of macroeconomic forecasts for central banks of some developed countries

	ECB	BoE	Fed	BoJ	SNB	BoC	SRB	NB	RBA	RBNZ
Forecast Horizon *(years, aprox.)*	2.25 –2.75	3	2–3; long-term	2	3	2	3	3	2	2–3
Forecast profile										
- Interval	Yes	-	Yes	Yes	-	-	-	-	Yes	-
- Point	Yes	Yes			Yes	Yes	Yes	Yes	Yes	Yes
- Fan chart	-	Yes	Yes	Yes	-	Yes	Yes	Yes	Yes	-
- Alternative scenarios	-	-	-	-	-	-	Yes	Yes	-	-
Number of forecast profiles	2	2	2	2	1	2	3	3	3	1
Number of annual publications	4	4	4	2	4	4	6	3	4	4
Endogenous interest rate	-	-	Yes	Yes	-	Yes	Yes	Yes	-	Yes
Forward guidance during crisis	Yes	Yes	Yes	Yes	-	Yes	Yes	Yes	-	Yes

Source: *Authors' representation, according to information provided by central banks' websites. Stockton (2012); Kedan and Stuart (2014).*

Abbreviations: ECB – European Central Bank; BoE – Bank of England; Fed – Federal Reserve Bank; BoJ – Bank of Japan; SNB – Swiss National Bank; BoC – Bank of Canada; SRB – Sveriges Riksbank (Central Bank of Sweden); NB – Norges Bank (Central Bank of Norway); RBA – Reserve Bank of Australia; RBNZ – Reserve Bank of New Zealand.

In terms of the communication tools, the central banks of Norway and Sweden are advanced. They publish the path of the endogenous interest rate, and they also have an extended forecast profile (point, fan chart, alternative scenarios).

3. The relevance of central banks' communication for the financial markets

The economic literature recognizes the relevance of central banks' communication for the financial markets (Kohn and Sack 2004; Ehrmann and Fratzscher 2007; Lamla and Lein 2011). If before 1990 the main approach was to say as little and as encryptedly as possible about the monetary policy, with the transition to the strategy of inflation targeting the transparency on policy goals of central banks has increased, being known that it improves anticipation regarding the monetary policy decisions.

Influencing the market expectations by creating and publishing their own economic forecasts represents the primary channel through which the monetary policy operates. By the same token, the transparency of central banks' policies may allow a better prediction of their future actions (Woodford, 2005; Bernanke, 2004). On the other hand, although desirable, an excessive transparency could complicate the communication with the public and markets (Mishkin, 2007).

A series of studies have shown that the dissemination of information made by central banks can increase the accuracy of private forecasts' anticipation of interest rate.

Analyzing the situation of Japan regarding the impact of publishing the inflation and GDP forecasts by the Bank of Japan (in October 2000), Fujiwara (2005) showed that this action diminished the spread of forecasts made by the private sector, and this can be considered as a decrease of the economic environment's uncertainty.

On the other hand, there are studies that do not find such a relationship to be explicit. Thus, the results of the study conducted by Hubert (2009) for six developed countries (Sweden, Japan, Canada, Switzerland, the UK and the USA) demonstrated that there is no clear evidence regarding improved forecasting capabilities after the publication of the central bank forecasts. However, for Sweden, the UK and Japan, we can empirically observe a strong influence on private agents through projections on inflation.

Moessner and Nelson (2008) studied how the provision of forecasts related to future interest rates could affect the functioning of financial markets. Based on the communication strategies of central banks, the paper analyzes the behavior of financial markets in the US, Eurozone and New Zealand. The authors conclude that the assumption that the provision of central bank forecasts will affect the financial markets is not confirmed in reality.

The results obtained by Knütter, Mohr and Wagner (2011) indicate a generally pronounced effect of central banks' communication on financial variables, whatever the communication channel is considered. The most effective channels of communication in the sense that they may influence the financial markets are the statements and press conferences, while written reports tend to especially influence the asset prices on different segments of the financial market.

Fracasso, Genberg, and Wyplosz (2003) analyze for 20 countries the influence of the quality of inflation reports on the surprises of interest rates (monetary policy surprises). The authors observed a negative correlation between the two variables, suggesting that a high clarity of the diffused information reduces the uncertainty in the financial markets.

According to Bulíř, Čihák and Jansen (2014), the impact of the global financial crisis nuanced the obtained results. Thus, empirically analyzing at the central bank level (the Czech National Bank, the European Central Bank, the Bank of England and the National Bank of Sweden) the relationship between the clarity of the inflation reports and the volatility of the financial markets, the authors noted that this is negative, especially at the Eurozone level, and also before the global financial crisis outbreak. Instead, after the financial crisis, this relationship is not as strong. The authors conclude that it is possible to reduce the uncertainty in financial markets by increasing the quality of written reports, but this is not without challenges, especially in times of crisis.

Conclusions

Methodological advances will shape the future of the macroeconomic forecasting process. The models will become more complete and complex, real-time forecasts will be possible and more frequent, and the data with different frequencies will be better incorporated in future forecasts.

At present, the financial variables are already used in the forecasting and the tendency for future forecasts is to use specialists from financial systems to identify the development of financial markets and the macro-financial linkages.

The lack of data in due time for many important economic and financial indicators and the limited understanding of macro-financial linkages have been the main vulnerabilities of the forecasting system, complemented by normal difficulties encountered in the delicate moments of economic history.

The idea of separating the base model (the econometric one) results from the forecasts published by central banks (containing additional reasoning) would help in a better understanding of the conditioning assumptions and would allow the users of the macroeconomic forecasts to identify the degree of added value applied to the basic model.

A clearer appreciation regarding the way and the distance whereby the forecasts based on the model deviate from the forecasts completed by additional judgments may be useful, especially when forecasting is done in times of change, which coincides with periods when the need for forecasts is more imperative.

References

1. Bernanke, B. (2004). Fedspeak, speech at American Economic Association, San Diego, 3 January 2004.
2. Bulíř, A., Čihák, M., Jansen, D. Jan (2014). Does the Clarity of Inflation Reports Affect Volatility in Financial Markets?, International Monetary Fund, WP/14/175, 2014.
3. Ehrmann, M., Fratzscher, M. (2007). Communication by Central Bank Committee Members: Different Strategies, Same Effectiveness?, Journal of Money, Credit and Banking 39(2–3):509–541.
4. Fracasso, A., Genberg, H., Wyplosz, C. (2003). How do Central Banks Write? An Evaluation of Inflation Reports by Inflation Targeting Central Banks, Geneva Reports on the World Economy Special Report 2. Geneva: International Center for Monetary and Banking Studies / London: Centre for Economic Policy Research, 2003.

5. Fujiwara, I. (2005). Is the central bank's publication of economic forecasts influential?, Economics Letters, 89:255–261.
6. Hubert, P. (2009). Informational Advantage and Influence of Communicating Central Banks, Observatoire Français des Conjonctures Economiques, Documents de Travail de l'OFCE, 2009.
7. Kedan, D., Stuart, R. (2014). Central Bank Communications: A Comparative Study. Central bank of Ireland Quarterly Bulletin, 2 (April):89–104.
8. Knütter, R., Mohr, B., Wagner, H. (2011). "The Effects of Central Bank Communication on Financial Stability: A Systematization of the Empirical Evidence", Fern Universität in Hagen, Discussion Paper No. 463, 2011.
9. Kohn, D., Sack, B. S. (2004). Central Bank Talk: Does it Matter and Why?, in: Macroeconomics, Monetary Policy, and Financial Stability. Ottawa: Bank of Canada, 2004, pp. 175–206.
10. Lamla, M.J., Lein, S.M. (2011). What Matters When? The Impact of ECB Communication on Financial Market Expectations. Applied Economics, 43(28):4289–4309.
11. Mishkin, F.S. (2007). Can Central Bank Transparency Go Too Far?, in Mishkin, Frederic S. (ed.), Monetary Policy Strategy. MIT Press: Cambridge, 2007, pp. 89–107.
12. Moessner, R., Nelson, W.R. (2008). Central Bank Policy Rate Guidance and Financial Market Functioning, International Journal of Central Banking, 4(4):193–226.
13. Stockton, D. (2012). Review of the Monetary Policy Committee's Forecasting Capability, Report Presented to the Court of the Bank of England, 2012, available at: www.bankofengland.co.uk/publications/Documents/news/2012/cr3stockton.pdf.
14. Woodford, M. (2005). Central bank communication and policy effectiveness, Proceedings – Economic Policy Symposium – Jackson Hole, Federal Reserve Bank of Kansas City, 2005, pp. 399–474.

Dorina CLICHICI

Institute for World Economy, Romanian Academy, Calea 13 Septembrie 13, Bucharest, Romania, dorina.clichici@iem.ro

The Financial Cycle and the Monetary Policy Conduct

Abstract: The article has the purpose to argue for the necessity of taking into account the financial cycle by central banks and conducting a countercyclical monetary policy in order to provide financial and macroeconomic stability. Disregard of the countercyclical principle in the process of implementation of economic policies over the last decades has triggered and amplified the economic downturn during the recent global financial and economic crisis. Being focused on the monetary stability, central banks have generated a background that stimulated excessive risk-taking by banks and credit booms, and fostered speculative bubbles, making the economic cycle more prominent. These developments in the global financial system have had a major impact in shaping macroeconomic results, leading to serious financial disruptions and economic imbalances. The article highlights the roots of the procyclicality of the financial system and briefly presents the current views and some conclusions regarding the policies of central banks for smoothing out the financial cycle and preventing financial imbalances.

Keywords: central banking, monetary policy, procyclicality of the financial system, credit growth

Introduction

Developments in financial markets have greatly influenced the real economy globally over the past decades. The recent global financial crisis is the latest in a long list of economic events shaped by cycles in financial markets, which has revealed once again the procyclical character of the financial system. Financial variables' fluctuations have led to serious economic imbalances, and in some cases, have generated a complete break in the link between savers and investors. Historically, these fluctuations have been magnified by loosened international capital flows as a result of financial system deregulation, which started in the 1970s, with the end of the Bretton Woods system. In the 1990s the repealing of the Glass-Steagall Act in the United States removed constraints on capital movement, fostering speculative bubbles. As well as the pursued objective of monetary stability by major central banks, by maintaining a low level of inflation of consumer goods and ignoring inflated asset prices (Schoenmaker and Wierts, 2016) has created a favorable background for encouraging excessive risk-taking by banks.

Moreover, macroprudential supervision was a missing link in the broader monetary and financial policy framework. As a consequence, from 2000 to 2008, speculative capital flows between US and European investment banks increased and created a bubble based on inflated prices, which has degenerated into a severe bust. In this regard, the article supports the idea that central bankers should be more focused on "preemptive tightening" to moderate credit bubbles than on "preemptive easing" to deal with the effects of the busts. The research argues for the necessity of taking into account the financial cycle by central banks in conducting the monetary policy, as an additional tool to macroprudential policies in order to provide financial and macroeconomic stability.

1. Literature review

The factors of the financial system's procyclicality are the starting point in determining the opportunity of using the monetary policy in addressing the financial cycle. Referring to the major impact of financial sector developments in shaping macroeconomic results, Borio (2012) emphasizes the role of the *excess elasticity* of the financial sector, i.e. the supply of credit to the real economy is much more elastic than would be justified by macroeconomic fundamentals. He presents an analytical definition linked to the concept of the procyclicality of the financial system, which denotes self-reinforcing interactions between perceptions of value and risk, attitudes towards risk and financing constraints, which translate into booms followed by busts.

These interactions can amplify economic fluctuations and lead to financial and economic imbalances. "Irrational exuberance" is considered another important driver of financial variables fluctuations (Praet, 2016), which leads investors to radically upgrade their future income expectations, and the capacity of financial intermediaries to transfer this expected increase in future income into the present through credit creation. According to Borio et al. (2001), there are two powerful *factors* of the financial sector's procyclicality: the information asymmetry between borrowers and lenders and inappropriate responses of financial market participants to changes in risk over time.

The information asymmetry means that in good times when collateral values rise, firms are able to obtain easier access to external financing, which acts as an economic stimulus, known as the "financial accelerator". And vice versa, when economic conditions worsen, even firms with high creditworthiness have difficulties to make a credit. The second amplifying factor is caused by difficulties in measuring the time dimension of risk and is derived from market participants having incentives to react to risk in ways that are socially suboptimal. The underestimation of risk in booms contributes to excessively rapid credit growth, to inflated collateral values, to artificially low lending spreads, and to financial institutions holding relatively low capital and provisions. This factor is also described by Dell'Ariccia and Marquez (2006) and Saurina and Jimenez (2006), who present empirical evidence of eased credit standards during boom periods, both in terms of screening of borrowers and in collateral.

The authors find empirical support of a positive lagged relationship between rapid credit growth and loan losses. In this regard, Schularick and Taylor (2008) showed that an upward trend of loans is an important predictor of financial crises, suggesting that such crises are "credit booms that went wrong" and are a result of disregarding the credit risk. As credit fuels consumption power during boom periods, the financial cycle is best described in terms of credit and real estate prices, variables which tend to co-vary rather closely, confirming the importance of credit to finance real estate activity. This is one of the main arguments for monitoring the upward trend of credit and asset prices in real time, which helps to detect excessive accumulation of risks and take further steps to mitigate them.

Based on the literature in the field, the article summarizes policy alternatives for addressing financial imbalances, namely smoothing out the financial cycle, in order to provide a picture of the most relevant ones.

2. Addressing financial imbalances by central banks

2.1. From macroprudential tools to monetary policy

Proper functioning of financial markets was distorted in the period that preceded the crisis by excessive volatility in asset prices, which diverged from their equilibrium values. Moreover, the mistakes of financial institutions regarding the credit policy (generalized underestimation of risk exposure) have generated excessive risk-taking, which significantly increased the leverage and the maturity gap in assets and liabilities of financial institutions. In the US, domestic credit provided by the financial sector and its leverage has increased rapidly in the run-up to the global financial crisis (Fig. 1), degenerating into the subprime credit crisis. A similar trend was noted in the EU, but the moment of time when domestic credit was on a downtrend differs from that in the US, being influenced by the sovereign debt crisis.

Fig. 1: Domestic credit provided *by* financial sector *(% of* GDP*) and banking sector leverage (total, % of net value added) in the US and the EU, 2005–2015*

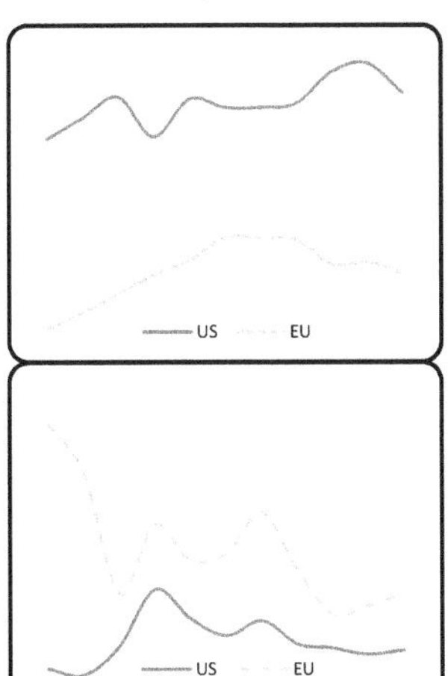

Source: *Author's representation based on the World Bank (2016) and OECD (2016) data.*

Booms and busts in asset prices and rapid credit expansion are symptoms of financial imbalances that may generate future situations of fragility and can amplify financial cycles (Borio and Lowe, 2002). This is an argument for identifying such imbalances in good time and applying the relevant set of tools in order to flatten the financial system's fluctuations.

Research papers addressing financial imbalances are divided regarding the appropriate directions for action to mitigate the negative effects of such imbalances on economic variables. There are authors *focused on macro-prudential policies* as optimal remedies (Bernanke, 2016; Isarescu, 2013; Aikman et al., 2015; Schoenmaker and Wierts, 2016), who argue that promoting monetary policy in order to counteract a speculative bubble, and to avoid overheating the economy, may harm other objectives of the monetary policy. Therefore, it is preferable to act by macroprudential policies, once monetary policy has only the interest rate at its independent disposal, which is not sufficient for this purpose.

It is essential in this regard to adopt appropriate policies in the period of economic expansion in order to mitigate the negative effects of a recession. Recent studies that promote this approach recommend acting through the following macroprudential tools: strengthening the defense capacity through the creation of provisions in times of boom to be used during the period of decline (capital buffers recommended by the global regulatory framework Basel III); discretionary adjustments in capital standards, provisions, collateral valuations and loan-to-value ratios; and greater reliance on stress testing and a heightening of the system-wide focus in assessments of vulnerabilities. Schoenmaker and Wierts (2016) argue that in the run-up of the crisis the monetary policy was not sufficient to prevent the build-up of financial imbalances, central bankers being concerned only with the inflation of consumer goods, ignoring inflated asset prices. Considering this they stress the relevance of macroprudential supervision as a missing link in the broader monetary and financial policy framework.

Another approach takes into consideration a more *active role for monetary policy* in addressing financial imbalances (White, 2009; Taylor, 2010), or point out *the relevance of monetary policy as an additional tool to macroprudential policies* (Yellen, 2009; Borio and Lowe, 2002; Borio, 2003; Trichet, 2005; Praet, 2016). Some authors believe that interest rates were held below what a "policy rules" framework suggests (Taylor, 2010). Empirically it has been shown that monetary policy deviated from the rules-based framework, and that has been a major factor in the crisis. The suggested policy implication for monetary policy in the future is getting back to the rules-based policy framework, the interest rate should rise by a certain amount when inflation increases above its target, and the interest rate falls by a certain amount when the economy goes into a recession (Taylor and Williams, 2010).

Monetary policy should be an additional tool to macroprudential policies that leans against bubble expansion. It may be applied especially when an upward trend of credit is the driving factor of a bubble expansion, and it may enhance financial stability by slowing credit booms and lowering overall leverage (Yellen, 2009). Credit booms are especially prone to generating adverse feedback loops between financial markets and real economic activity. And higher short-term interest rates would have restrained the demand for housing by raising mortgage interest rates, and slowed the pace of house price increases. However, central banks should intervene only if the effects are quite severe and it would be difficult to mitigate them after the fact. Despite the difficulties involved, a monetary policy response to imbalances as they build up is appropriate in some circumstances, and a co-operation between monetary and prudential authorities is essential.

2.1. Monetary stability and financial imbalances

Another factor that created a favorable environment for the development of financial imbalances during the pre-crisis period (Criste and Lupu, 2014) and limited further room for manoeuvre actions of monetary authorities to support growth was an excessive monetary stability focus of central banks (Shirakawa, 2012). Low and stable inflation promotes financial stability, but it also increases the likelihood that excess demand pressures show up first in credit aggregates and asset prices, rather than in goods and services prices (Borio and Lowe, 2002). It could create a too optimistic view on the future development of the economy and a distorted perception about safety, which may increase the value of assets, amplifying the financial fluctuations. In this context, a monetary response to credit and asset markets may be appropriate to assure financial stability and central banks may opt for higher interest rates than justified by the inflation outlook in the short term. According to Borio and Lowe (2002), the opportunity of such a monetary policy regime depends on a number of factors: (a) the ability of authorities to identify financial imbalances; (b) the utility of other instruments, including prudential policy; (c) the effectiveness of interest rate increases as a tool to limit imbalances; (d) the extent to which central bank reactions can create moral hazard.

A relevant approach of a countercyclical monetary policy is the so-called principle *"leaning-against-the-wind"*, where central banks cautiously raise interest rates even beyond the level necessary to maintain price stability over the short to medium term when a potentially detrimental asset price boom is identified (Trichet, 2005). Such a monetary regime could ameliorate the moral hazard problem, discourage excessive risk-taking and reduce over-investment, which in turn would lead to a lower level of indebtedness and less severe consequences of a possible future bust. This approach guided ECB monetary policy already prior to the crisis and backs its prevailing accommodative monetary policy stance today (Praet, 2016). The liquidity and demand support provided by ECB has countered the downturn and reversed the financial cycle, thus preventing it from transforming into a chronic credit crisis. However, the "leaning-against-the-wind" approach was not sufficient to preempt major imbalances. A weak institutional and macroeconomic framework put strains on any type of monetary policy strategy. A more effective first line of defense (Fig. 2) will support a "leaning-against-the-wind" approach, because other policy domains reinforce the thrust of monetary policy. Another key issue to be taken into account by monetary authorities to address them is to identify the unstable *funding patterns* of "irrational exuberance" in the economy (Praet, 2016). That is, to identify if the increase in asset prices is fueled by an excessive level of indebtedness and by the funding of long-term assets with short-term funding in the interbank market by financial intermediaries, which will have systemic consequences when the cycle turns.

However, developments of the post-crisis period have affected the traditional monetary transmission channels, the main refinancing rate was not effective in influencing other interest rates in so far as it was before the crisis (Szczerbowicz, 2012). As a consequence, since 2009 the ECB has completed its countercyclical arms with several unconventional instruments: providing unlimited liquidity provisions in euro and other currencies, extending the maturity of refinancing operations, accepting a wider range of collateral and outright purchases of private and government assets. Its main concern was to maintain the availability of credit for households and companies at accessible rates. Empirical evidence shows that when economic recessions coincide with the financial crisis, monetary policy is less effective and the benefits for subsequent revival of production are illusory. The idea is that excessively indebted economic agents do not want to borrow or spend. In addition, commercial banks' expectations regarding increased capital requirements make them keep additional liquidity at central banks rather than lend. Thus, in most developed economies, there were large increases in the monetary base and moderate increases in broad money without increasing inflation. This liquidity trap that developed economies have faced has revealed that shocks able to push inflation to zero can still take place and has put the optimal level of inflation under discussion. The main argument is that reduced levels of inflation may fall more slightly into negative territory, while central banks in this situation are forced to resort to unconventional measures. In this context, Blanchard et al. (2010) suggest the expediency of amending the current inflation target from 2% to 4%, which would provide a greater possibility of manoeuver for central banks in the event of shocks, and would allow wider variations of nominal interest rates.

Considering the fact that the efficiency of monetary policy is severely constrained in the post-crisis period, is essential in this regard to adopt appropriate policies in the period of economic expansion in order to mitigate the negative effects of recession. Both macroprudential policies and a countercyclical monetary regime should be put in place (Fig. 2).

Central banks should act systematically and may opt for higher interest rates than justified by the inflation outlook in the short term if there are clear signs of financial imbalances, such as rapid credit growth and quick rise of asset prices. The approach of financial stability-oriented monetary policy is the most recommended (Caruana, 2016), which implies that monetary policy acts against the early build-up of financial imbalances, even when the prospect of a crisis is remote. In this respect, central banks should consider two financial cycle indicators that could have a significant influence on private sector expenditure and output, and could result in the model generating recessions—the debt service burden of the private sector and the leverage. It is important that monetary policy should focus on expanding the forecasting horizon (longer than two years usually taken into account by central banks) on risk assessment and should use information contained in asset prices, for early detection of financial imbalances.

Fig. 2: Policies for flattening the financial cycle

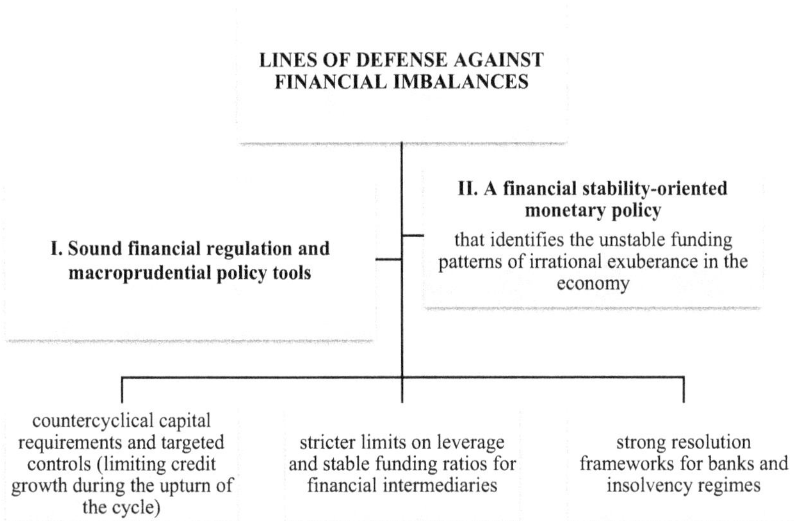

Source: Author's representation based on studied literature.

Conclusions

The credit cycle has been particularly severe and synchronous during the last global financial crisis. The cyclicality in financial variables was determined by various frictions as information asymmetry between borrowers and lenders, and inappropriate responses of financial market participants to changes in risk over time. Irrational exuberance that determines investors to upgrade their future income expectations and the ability of banks to transfer this expected rise in future income into the present through credit granting are also drivers of financial fluctuations.

Taking into consideration these frictions, an exclusive focus on macroprudential policies as optimal remedies for mitigating financial imbalances could not be sufficient to counteract a speculative bubble and to avoid overheating the economy. In this regard, a financial stability-oriented monetary policy is the most recommended, which implies that monetary policy acts against the early build-up of financial imbalances. One important action is to identify the unstable funding patterns by financial intermediaries of the irrational exuberance and to use monetary tools in order to limit this kind of funding. Moreover, the pre-crisis period has revealed that financial imbalances can build up in low inflation environments and that in some cases it is appropriate for policy to respond to these imbalances. This is the argument why central banks should explicitly and systematically incorporate financial stability considerations in their policy. Therefore, central banks may opt for higher interest rates than justified by the inflation outlook in the short term, if there are clear signs of financial imbalances, such as rapid credit growth and rise of asset prices.

References

1. Aikman, D. (2015). Curbing the Credit Cycle. The Economic Journal 125(585):1072–1109.
2. Caruana, J. (2016). Monetary policy for financial stability. Paper presented at 52nd SEACEN Governors' Conference, Naypyidaw, Myanmar, November 2016.
3. Bernanke, B. S. (2010). "Monetary policy and the housing bubble". Paper presented at the 2010 AEA meetings.
4. Blanchard, Olivier et al.: Rethinking Macroeconomic Policy. IMF Staff Position Note SPN/10/03.
5. Borio, C. (2012). The Financial Cycle and Macroeconomics: What Have We Learnt?. BIS Working Papers No. 395, December 2012.
6. Borio, C. (2001). Procyclicality of the Financial System and Financial Stability: Issues and Policy Options. BIS Papers 1 Marrying the macro-and microprudential dimensions of financial stability, March 2001, pp. 1–57.
7. Borio, C., Lowe, P. (2002). Asset prices, financial and monetary stability: exploring the nexus. BIS Working Papers 114, July 2002.
8. Criste, A., Lupu, I. (2015). The Central Bank Policy between the Price Stability Objective and Promoting Financial Stability, Procedia Economics and Finance Vol. 8: 219–225.
9. Dell'Ariccia, G., Marquez, R. "Lending Booms and Lending Standards". Journal of Finance, vol. 61(5):2511–2546.
10. Isărescu, M. (2013). "What can and cannot do a central bank". NBR, The Project "Academica NBR", organized in collaboration with Transilvania University of Brasov, 2013.
11. Praet, P. (2016). Financial cycles and monetary policy. Paper presented in the context of a panel on "International Monetary Policy", Beijing, August 2016.
12. Saurina, J., Jimenez, G. (2006). Credit Cycles, Credit Risk, and Prudential Regulation. International Journal of Central Banking, 2:65–98.
13. Schoenmaker, D., Wierts, P. (2016). Macroprudential supervision: From theory to policy. European Systemic Risk Board Working Paper Series No 2 / February 2016.
14. Schularick, M., Taylor, A. M. (2009). Credit Booms Gone Bust: Monetary Policy, Leverage Cycles and Financial crises, 1870–2008. NBER Working Paper No. 15512, November 2009.

15. Shirakawa, M. (2012). Deleveraging and Growth: Is the Developed World Following Japan's Long and Winding Road?. Paper presented at the London School of Economics and Political Science, January 2012.
16. Szczerbowicz, U. (2012). The ECB Unconventional monetary policies: Have they Lowered Market Borrowing Costs for Banks and Governments?. CEPII, Working Paper No 2012–36.
17. Taylor, J.B. 2010). Commentary: Monetary Policy after the Fall. Presentation at the Symposium "Macroeconomic Challenges: The Decade Ahead", Jackson Hole, Wyoming, August 28, 2010.
18. Taylor, J. B., Williams, J. C. Z. (2010). Simple and Robust Rules for Monetary Policy. Federal Reserve Bank of San Francisco, Working Paper 2010–10.
19. Trichet, J. (2005). Asset price bubbles and monetary policy. Paper presented at Mas lecture, June 2005, Singapore.
20. White, W. (2009). Should Monetary Policy "Lean or Clean"?. Federal Reserve Bank of Dallas, Globalization and Monetary Policy Institute, Working Paper No. 34, August 2009.
21. Yellen, J. (2009). Speech presented at panel discussion for the Federal Reserve Board/Journal of Money, Credit, and Banking conference on "Financial Markets and Monetary Policy" Washington D.C., June 2009.

Corneliu RUSSU

Centre of Industry and Services Economy, Romanian Academy, email: corneliu_russu2007@yahoo.com

Daniel CIUIU

Technical University of Civil Engineering Bucharest, Department of Mathematics and Computer Science; Institute for Economic Forecasting, email: dciuiu@yahoo.com

Influence of Foreign Direct Investment on the Romanian Economy

Abstract: The article deals with the influence of the stock of foreign direct investment (FDI) on the component activities of the Romanian economy, expressed in terms of changes in the turnover of companies, labor utilization, overall productivity, value added and exports. The main conclusion of the analysis is that the beneficial changes that occurred were, however, still far from the ones expected, which means that the model of structuring and development of the Romanian economy specific to the centralized economy period remains broadly the same.

Keywords: FDI; correlation; linear regression; resultant variables

Introduction

The effects of foreign direct investments (FDI) on the economic structure and growth of the host countries are significant and apparent in many fields. FDI inflow effects may be direct or indirect. Direct effects, easier to locate and rate, consist of assimilating new technology brought by foreign investors, in the structural changes in the industries and sectors that have absorbed the FDI inflows, in the productivity growth in these sectors, in the labor market adjustment to the demands for raising the skill levels of the workforce to make it capable to cope with new technologies, and in the substantial growth of the value added achieved by the sectors that represent the main destination of the FDI. Indirect effects, much less clear and, therefore, more difficult to estimate, consist, mainly, of the technological diffusion from MNCs subsidiaries through their connections, upstream to suppliers, downstream to clients, and horizontally to other firms in the same industry; in its turn, the technological diffusion determines additional effects on the other mentioned economic agents in terms of labor skills, number of employees, productivity and achieved value added.

However, the listed effects are potential, their materialization depending on the location advantages presented by the host country's economy, the characteristics of the firms targeted by foreign investors, the investor's characteristics and other favorable or unfavorable circumstances.

For the Romanian economy, which was in a serious decline in the first decade of its transition to a market economy after 1990, the FDI inflows had a salutary role, shown more strongly especially after 2000 and felt on multiple levels. Among the attractiveness determinants for FDI, we can mention the Romanian economy, its specific business environment and the Romanian companies that show positive attraction aspects to foreign capital, but there are also many negative aspects, deterrent to foreign investors seeking new markets to penetrate.

The research results are systematized on sequences devoted to the influence of FDI on GDP, GDP per capita, occupied population, number of employees, labor productivity, tangible and intangible assets, gross value-added (GVA) and total exports.

1. Literature review

The wide range of theories regarding FDI advanced by many researchers can be systematized according to different criteria, most of them subordinating to the essential idea that an investor expands its business abroad in order to efficiently capitalize the benefits resulting from the location advantages, the capabilities of the firm and the internationalization of markets.

a) Theories related to international trade
   From the pioneering attempts of A. Smith and D. Ricardo explaining trade flows between countries, integrative approaches between the theory of international trade and the FDI theory have gradually been reached: E. Hecksher (1919) and B. Ohlin's (1933) approaches, the theory of the product life cycle (Vernon 1966), the combined theory of international trade and investment (Hirsch, 1976), the general equilibrium model of international trade, with MNCs playing the leading role (Helpman, 1984), the theory of the FDI distribution (Nock and Zeaple, 2004);
b) Theories based on the industrial organization approach (Hymer, 1976);
c) Theories based on monopoly power (imperfect markets) (Kindleberger, 1969);
d) Theory of FDI internalization (imperfect markets) (Buckley & Casson, 1976);
e) Oligopolistic theory of FDI (imperfect markets) (Knickerbocker, 1973);
f) Eclectic theory of FDI (OLI paradigm) (Dunning, 1993);
g) Theories based on the national currency strength (Aliber, 1970);
h) Theories explaining FDI made by the companies from developing countries (Mathews, 2002).

The positive impact of FDI on the economic growth of the host countries is convincingly demonstrated by the overwhelming majority of empirical research devoted to this topic and presented in literature. Between the FDI volume and the size of the resulting variables mentioned there are different relationships, which reflect the more or less positive or negative sensitivity of variables to the FDI influence.

The FDI influence on the resulting variables in a certain period can be measured with simple linear regression (Jula and Jula, 2010) as: $Y = \alpha + \beta X + \varepsilon$, where Y is the dependent variable, GDP respectively; α - free period; β - independent variable parameter; X - independent variable; ε - error term of the equation. To determine the model adjustment accuracy, R^2 and adjusted R^2 determinant coefficients have been used. Both values represent the proportion of resulting variable variation estimated in the real values variation of the variable concerned. The difference is that the number of degrees of freedom in the calculation of dispersion for R^2 is not taken into account, while for the adjusted R^2 it is.

To clarify the interpretations, the significance of R and adjusted R, as well as the DW (Durbin-Watson) statistics are presented in the following table.

Table 1: Significances of R, adjusted R and DW (Durbin-Watson) statistics

	Correlations of variables				
R	**>0.9**	**0.75**	**0.5**	**0.25**	**0**
	Strong positive correlation	Mean-high correlation	Mean correlation	Mean-low correlation	Lack of correlation
Durbin Watson statistics					
Number of observations	**Correlation of errors**				
	Strong correlated +	**Correlated +**	**Uncorrelated**	**Correlated -**	**Strong correlated -**
7	< 0.70	0.70–1.36	1.36–2.64	2.64–3.30	> 3.30
8	< 0.76	0.76–1.33	1.33–2.67	2.67–3.24	> 3.24
9	< 0.82	0.82–1.32	1.32–2.68	2.68–3.18	> 3.18
10	< 0.88	0.88–1.32	1.32–2.68	2.68–3.12	> 3.12

2. Influence of FDI on main variables of the Romanian economy

Calculations using EViews 4.0. program led, at national level, to the results in the table below. It should be noted that the reference period was chosen on the basis of the availability of data for the independent variable (FDI) and the independent ones (GDP, GDP/capita, etc.).

Table 2: Correlations of FDI with mentioned resultant variables, 2005–2013

Resultant variable	Equation	R	Student statistics for FDI coefficient	Durbin Watson statistics
GDP	GDP=38256.46+1.754821xFDI+ε	0.932283	6.818882	1.446082
GDP/capita	GDP/cap=1867.741+0.086658xFDI+ε	0.94877	7.94464	1.86162
Occupied population	OP=9875.79524-0.02016xFDI+ε	-0.70711	-2.64582	0.85775
Average number of employees	ANE=4866.78205-0.00538xFDI+ε	-0.26548	-0.72852	0.84110
Labor productivity	PROD=3440.574+0.944482xFDI+ε	0.97263	10.25193	1.51422
Tangible assets	TA=2061.153+0.448742xFDI+ε	0.98028	14.02873	1.53831
GVA	GVA=146587.3+1.502648xFDI+ε	0.97221	10.17256	1.74495
Total export	TE=2231.181+0.709169xFDI+ε	0.89008	5.166492	1.01383

Note: For Labor productivity – 2005–2012 period; for Tangible assets – 2005–2014 period

Source: *Calculations by the authors based on data from Romania's Statistical Yearbook, different issues, Bucharest*

The previous table shows that the FDI influence on most resultant variables was positive, with variations in its intensity: strong positive for tangible assets, productivity, GVA, GDP/capita and GDP; positive medium-high for total export. In contrast, the influence proved to be mean-negative for occupied population and average number of employees.

The strong positive influence of FDI on the most relevant variables of the Romanian economy and its competitiveness on the international arena is particularly encouraging, as it certifies the role of foreign investment as a driver of economic development, structural adjustment and modernization of the economy. Lack of correlation of FDI with employment and the average number of employees is explained by the ambivalent role of the first variable: on the one hand, by the creation of new businesses and developing the existing ones, FDI contributes to job growth and, implicitly, to employment; on the other hand, FDI provides a substantial influx of modern technology with higher yields, which significantly reduces the number of workers needed. By joining these opposing tendencies where the latter is, probably, more consistent, the result is a lack of correlation of the FDI stock with the two resultant variables.

Assessment of FDI contribution to the evolution of mentioned resultant variables can be complemented with other relevant aspects.

Thus, **the contribution of FDI to GDP formation and economic growth** can be completed by taking into account the share in the economy of foreign-owned companies compared to that of the Romanian private and state-owned companies on the basis of the relevant indicator of turnover. In 2014, foreign companies' participation in the social capital had a share of 49% (536 billion lei) of the total turnover of companies in Romania, the Romanian companies with private capital had a share of 47% (509 billion lei) and the Romanian state companies, 4% (Ziarul financiar, 2015). At the end of 2014, 38,260 foreign companies were registered with a turnover greater than zero, most of them operating in the industry, and companies with Romanian private capital numbered 422,384, operating, mainly, in the service sector, particularly trade, restaurants and hotels. The figures presented demonstrate the considerable difference of productive and commercial potential existing between companies with foreign capital and those with Romanian private capital, synthesized in average annual turnover of each of the two categories of companies: the first ones with 14 million lei, the second ones with 1.2 million lei.

The analisys of the share of the total turnover of the two mentioned categories of companies in the total turnover of commercial companies in Romania leads to the conclusion that their contribution to GDP—depending on the value added to the factor cost—is also balanced. In these circumstances, the correlation between the FDI stock increase and the GDP growth should not induce the idea that increasing the level of the second indicator is due to the prevailing FDI, as to this augmentation the Romanian companies also have a substantial contribution.

FDI influence on the use of labor in the whole economy can also be analyzed in terms of the contribution of companies according to the nature of capital. Thus, during the 2008–2014 period, the number of registered companies decreased, with some fluctuations, both for those with foreign participation and those with Romanian private capital; as a result, the number of employees declined during that period, by 1.7% for foreign companies and 22.8% for Romanian companies. The main cause of reducing the number of employees in the two categories of companies was the productive capacity upgrading, the increased uptake of technological progress and the activity restructuring; further reducing the number of employees in companies with Romanian private capital compared to that produced in companies with foreign capital reflects greater intensity of these activities in the first category.

For the productivity indicator, considered the most relevant for economic competitiveness, FDI companies are significantly superior to the domestic capital companies. In the year 2014 the ratio between FDI companies and the state capital companies was 3.06:1, and between FDI companies and Romanian private capital companies 2.17:1 (Ziarul financiar, 2015). The more than double productivity level, measured by the ratio turnover/number of employees, achieved as an average by foreign companies compared to that obtained by Romanian private companies is explained by the superior technical endowment of work, better organization and management of activity in the first category of companies, competitive advantages that allowed them to more easily withstand the pressures of the global financial and economic crisis triggered in 2008, which were particularly severe in the Romanian economy in 2009 and 2010. To this explanation one can add that the FDI companies operate, mostly, in industry, whose specific features allow the achievement of higher productivity, while the companies with Romanian private capital operate, mostly, in the service sector where, at least in the current circumstances of their development in Romania, the achieved productivity is significantly reduced.

The significant difference in productivity between the two categories of companies showed its strong effects on the payroll of employees: although the share of staff costs is at significantly close levels, average monthly net salary in FDI companies was, in 2014, 90.71% higher than that registered in companies with Romanian private capital, representing, thus, a particularly effective factor of productivity growth.

Compared, however, to state-owned companies, the average wages of FDI companies were lower by about 10% in 2013 and by 2% in 2014, the share of staff costs in turnover in the first category of companies was more than three times higher, despite the extremely low level of productivity, which highlights the lack of correlation in the state companies' wages and productivity and explains their poor performance.

According to CAEN (Classification of National Economy Activities) activity Rev. 2, in 67 out of 70 FDI companies the productivity, expressed in turnover/employee, is superior compared with the Romanian private and state companies, except for air transport, IT and manpower services.

An interesting case, to which the industrial policies of the Executive should give special attention, is that of the IT services, in which the productivity of the FDI companies (204,365 lei/employee/year) was considerably lower than that of the companies with Romanian private capital (267,501 lei/employee/year), which means that there are broad prospects for considerable expansion of the latter.

Small differences between the average productivity achieved by the two categories of companies were registered in Agriculture and Apparel, and the biggest differences in favor of foreign companies were in Coke products and refined petroleum products (ratio 8.2:1), wholesale and retail trade (5.8:1), river and sea transport (3.2:1), production and supply of electric and thermal energy, gas, steam and air conditioning (3.2:1), telecommunications (2.6:1), advertising (1.7:1), and hotels (1.6:1).

The shortage of statistical data provided by qualified institutions in Romania on **the contribution of FDI companies and of Romanian private capital to achieve GVA** prevents a thorough and precise analysis in this regard, constraining us in accepting approximations with a reasonable degree of tolerance. The available figures (National Institute of Statistics, 2014) highlight the reality that the FDI company subsidiaries registered a share of GVA at factor cost in the turnover lower than that achieved by Romanian companies—21% and 24% respectively.

The mining and manufacturing industry was the branch that achieved the highest GVA compared to other branches: its share in the total turnover in the economy was 37.4%, in 2013, and 43.4% from the total GVA; for comparison, trade—which had a share of 39.9% of the total turnover—only accounted for 17.4% of the total GVA. Regarding the GVA share in turnover, the performance of foreign company subsidiaries was lower than that of Romanian companies in three sectors: Industry, Construction and Trade; except for the Services, where the massive presence of foreign capital in banks and insurance companies explains this situation.

It should be noted that, by far, the largest share in turnover and, thus, in GVA at factor cost, according to the same source, is held by the subsidiaries of foreign companies originating in the European Union; the share in the indicator referred to above of foreign company subsidiaries from the Community area was 81.4% in 2013, 8.0% for the subsidiaries of European companies outside the EU, and 10.6 % for companies in non-European countries.

The contribution of FDI companies to the increase and beneficial change of the export structure was appreciable, proving their redoubtable competitive strength, exports accounting for a strong primary growth vector of the Romanian economy in the last decade.

To the country's total exports, which reached a record level of 35.585 billion euros in 2014, the FDI companies contributed in a proportion of 70.9%; to imports, which amounted to 36.240 billion euros (the foreign trade deficit of 655 million euros, in considerable diminution compared to previous years); the contribution of the FDI companies was of 64.7% (National Bank of Romania, 2015).

The manufacturing industry is the sector with the largest share of the FDI companies in the total volume of both exports and imports, far away from the other branches. Within the import sector the foreign companies have, also, a high share, lower than that recorded by the mining industry—which counts insignificantly in foreign trade—and at a level close to that of information and communication technologies, which recorded an extremely low volume of foreign trade too.

3. Influence of FDI on the main economic variables of development regions of Romania

By deepening the analysis of the FDI influence on the level of relevant indicators for the economic competitiveness of development regions of Romania one can confirm the considerable disparities between regions and emphasize the reduced chances of regions with lower levels of economic and social development to reduce the gaps that separate them from the advanced regions.

The link between the intensity of the FDI inflows and the FDI stock at regional level and GDP at the same level is evident, which is convincingly demonstrated by the figures in the following table, which refers to two development regions—the most advanced (Bucharest-Ilfov) and the last of the eight regions (North-East)—in 2012, the last year for which the Romanian Statistical Yearbook provides data on regional GDP. The particular FDI attraction force towards the Bucharest-Ilfov region, where the level of the two indicators is almost the same, can easily be observed.

Table 3: Correlations of FDI with resultant GDP variables and employed population at the level of development regions Bucharest-Ilfov and North-East, in 2005–2012 (for GDP) and 2005–2013 (for employed population)

Resultant variable	Development region	Equation	R	Student statistics for FDI coefficient	Durbin Watson statistics
Regional GDP	**Bucharest-Ilfov**	GDP=7560.626+ 0.812751xFDI+ε	0.914729	5.545227	2.5743
	North-East	GDP=10140.11+ 2.577442xFDI+ε	0.707107	2.514421	0.826581
Employed population	**Bucharest-Ilfov**	EP=925.0791+ 0.003605xFDI+ε	0.923141	6.352703	1.924602
	North-East	EP=1674.957+ 0.001977xFDI+ε	0.017029	0.045024	1.849631

Source: *Calculations by the authors based on data from Romanian Statistical Yearbook, different issues, Bucharest*

For these two regions, as for the other six, the link between FDI and regional GDP is one-to-one: the existence of high regional GDP indicates that there are advantages of superior location, which causes a more intense FDI inflow; the latter, in turn, stimulates more intensive development of the region and GDP growth.

The correlation between FDI and the employed population is strongly positive in the Bucharest-Ilfov region (R>0.9), which indicates the significant influence of the first variable on the second, and low in the North East region (R<0.75), representing the low effect of the modest FDI volume on the creation of jobs and population employment.

Conclusions

The main positive effects of FDI on the Romanian economy, some revealed by the correlations shown above, proved to be the following:

- acquisition of new sources of capital;
- increased state budget revenues, affiliates of TNCs and MNCs operating in Romania having a particularly significant contribution that improves the balance of payments;
- transfer of complex and substantial know-how (technological, financial, managerial, organizational, commercial, legal, environmental) from the companies with foreign capital to the domestic ones;

- significant changes in the production nomenclature of the firms, meaning their more pronounced specialization, the addition of new products and services, and their quality improvement;
- pursuit of increased pressure on labor to raise its level of qualification, knowledge and professional skills;
- significant increase in labor productivity, especially in some manufacturing activities; employment of many Romanian private or public businesses, including SMEs, as subcontractors (suppliers of raw materials and intermediate products, as well as specialized services) of companies with foreign capital, forcing Romanian companies to significantly improve quality, organization and market behavior for their products and services;
- integration of the Romanian producers into the international value chains, benefiting from the expertise of FDI companies and their international distribution chains;
- the inflow of FDI and the growth of the stock of developement regions were found to be approximately proportional to the economic potential of the regions and to their social state, i.e. the most developed regions have attracted the most consistent inflows, Bucharest-Ilfov region standing, in this respect, far away from the rest of the regions.

The main negative aspects of FDI's impact on Romanian economic activity were:

- failure of many foreign investors to comply with obligations resulting from privatization contracts, concerning the provisions of post-privatization program commitments related to maintaining the activity profile of the privatized enterprises, the full payment of capital at the level of the subscribed capital, and the improvement of the efficiency of acquired businesses;
- manufacture of industrial products for the domestic market or for exports relying on massive imports of raw materials and intermediate products, most often even from the country of origin of the foreign investors, which means that in such cases the value added performed in Romania is reduced (the case, for example, of some manufacturing activities of high and medium-high technological intensity—manufacture of computers, electronic, optical and electrical devices) which in Romania has registered modest shares (the same situation is encountered in traditional activities, with low value added, where the Lohn system greatly reduces its share in production value);
- orientation of significant shares of FDI inflows towards the services sector, particularly for the financial, insurance and consulting activities, negatively influenced by the global financial crisis, forcing the central authorities to take steps to support them, sometimes by expensive measures;
- widening disparities between development regions, the FDI inflows focusing, naturally, on regions with superior location advantages, i.e. the developed ones, contributing substantially to the development of their economic performance;
- repatriation of profits made by the FDI companies in a higher proportion than those reinvested in the economy of the host country, a practice otherwise existing

worldwide (Durham, 2004), which causes the gains achieved by foreign investors to be often superior to those enjoyed by the domestic firms in the host country. A consistent study referring to this problem points out that, in 2003–2010, the FDI firms in Romania repatriated a total profit (dividends + net interest income) of 14.1 billion euro at a capital stock of 52.0 billion euro, representing a value of about two times higher than the reinvested profit, with variations between CAEN activities (Zaman et al., 2011);

- transfer price practice, whereby MNCs' subsidiaries in Romania export towards the country of origin (in fact, towards the parent companies) products whose processing is deepened or completed with additional operations (superior conditioning, respectively packing and marking with the brand of the parent company), after which they are exported to Romania (for the internal market, being sold at prices higher than those of the initially exported products) or in other countries (that means export of national wealth at prices below the current prices on international markets, disfavoring domestic producers, and reducing foreign currency earnings from exports);
- bringing on the domestic market, by foreign-owned companies, products that are substitutes of the same Romanian product or that have a worse quality than the one offered by the domestic producers, whose access to distribution networks, however, is difficult for various reasons (reduced quantitative offer, insufficient advertising, discriminatory practices of some wholesalers and retailers, etc.).

The final conclusion is that the FDI, which stood for the dynamic component of the total investment in the Romanian economy, had a determining role in stimulating its economic growth, the benefits of their presence by far outrunning the negative sides.

References

1. Aliber, R. Z. (1970). A theory of direct foreign investment, in: Kindleberger, C.P. (ed.). The International Corporation, MIT Press, Cambridge, MA, United States.
2. Buckley, P., Casson, M. (1976). The Future of the Multinational Enterprises, MacMillan, London.
3. Dunning, J.H. (1993). Multinational Enterprises and the Global Economy, Addison Wesley Publication Company, Harlow, Essex.
4. Hecksher, E. (1919). The effects of foreign trade on the distribution of income, Tidskrift, XXI.
5. Helpman, E. (1984). A simple theory of international trade with multinational corporations, The Journal of Political Economy, Vol. 92, No. 3, 1984.
6. Hirsch, S. (1976). An international trade and investment theory, Oxford Economic Papers, New Series, Vol. 28, No. 2.
7. Hymer, S. (1976). The International Operation of National Firms: A Study of Direct Foreign Investment, MIT Press, Cambridge, MA, United States.
8. Jula, D., Jula, N. M. (2010). Econometrie, Editura Mustang, Bucureşti.

9. Kindleberger, C. (1969). American Business Abroad, Yale University Press, New Haven, CT, United States.
10. Knickerbocker, F. T. (1973). Oligopolistic reaction and multinational enterprise, Division of Research, Harvard University, Cambridge, MA, United States.
11. Mathews, J. (2002). Dragon multinational: Towards a new model of global growth, Oxford University Press, New York, 2002.
12. Nocke, V., Yeaple, S. (2004). An Assignment Theory of Foreign Direct Investment, National Bureau of Economic Research Working Paper Series, No. 11003, NBER, Cambridge, MA, United States.
13. Ohlin, B. (1933). Interregional and International Trade, Harvard University Press, Cambridge.
14. Vernon, R. (1966). International Investment and International Trade in the Product Life Cycle, Quarterly Journal of Economics, May 1966, pp. 190–207.
15. Zaman, G. et al. Aspecte ale impactului ISD din România asupra exportului şi dezvoltării durabile, lucrare realizată în cadrul POSDRU 2007–2013, Contractul de finanţare POSDRU/89/1.5/S/62988, variantă completată şi actualizată a articolului "Some challenging (macro)economic aspects of FDI in Romania", Romanian Journal of Economics, Anul XXI, Vol. 33, No. 2 (42)/2011.
16. ***Institutul Naţional de Statistică. Activitatea filialelor străine în România, Bucureşti, 2014.
17. ***Institutul Naţional de Statistică. Anuarul Statistic al României, ediţii anuale, Bucureşti.
18. ***National Bank of Romania. Foreign direct investment in Romania, 2014, Bucharest, 2015.
19. ***Ziarul financiar. Capitalul privat românesc, 2015, Bucureşti.

Maria-Ramona SÂRBU

"Alexandru Ioan Cuza" University of Iaşi, Doctoral School of Economics and Business Administration,
email: sarbumariar@gmail.com

Foreign Direct Investments and their Impact on Wages in the Romanian Economy

Abstract: One of the research topics on the effects of foreign direct investments (FDI) refers to the impact of foreign direct investments on wages. As a result, this paper aims to analyse the link between the FDI stocks and the gross average earning in Romania. The data are recorded per annum over the 2004–2014 period. The statistical methods applied in order to assess the impact of the FDI stocks on the gross average earning are correlation analysis and regression analysis. The results show that FDI stocks affect average wages in the Romanian economy. Therefore, if foreign direct investment stocks increase by one million euros, the variable of the gross average earning will increase, on average, by 0.006 Euros.

Keywords: standard of living, employment, foreign companies, statistical methods

Introduction

The study represents a modest attempt to deal with issues related to the contribution of FDI to the increase in wage income in the Romanian economy. The wage levels are in constant evolution, as they are the basis of the standard of living for the persons employed, and that is why any changes in the amount of the wage may cause significant social problems. Over time, there have been numerous theoretical and empirical studies presented from different points of view taking into account foreign direct investments as one of the explanatory factors of the rise of the wages. Therefore, the purpose of this study is to provide an analysis of the impact of FDI on the gross average earning in Romania.

The established objectives of the research are the following: identifying the studies concerning the correlation between foreign direct investments and wages, analysing the impact of the FDI on wages in Romania. The statistical methods applied in order to assess the impact of FDI on average salaries are correlation analysis and regression analysis. Regarding the structure of this paper, besides this introductory chapter, the study comprises three sections, namely: Section 1 includes literature review; Section 2 includes the research methodology, while Section 3 presents the results of the research. The final part contains the conclusion.

1. Literature review

One of the research topics dealing with the effects of FDI refers to the impact of foreign direct investments on wages. Therefore, in the literature, we can find empirical evidence supporting the idea that employees in industries with a greater presence of foreign direct investments enjoy higher wages and a higher wage increase (Bedi and Cielik, 2002). Taking into consideration the concerns regarding the impact of multinationals on the local employees, some authors, such as Tomohara and Taki (2011), investigated whether foreign direct investments have a positive impact on employees in local companies by generating a rise in wages. The results showed that the activities of foreign companies bring as an advantage for the employees in local companies a growth in their wages, adding thereby to the list of possible benefits of foreign direct investments also the positive effects of the FDI on wages, such as creating jobs, an advantage frequently highlighted by the literature.

In turn, Saglam and Sayec (2011) studied the implications of the activities of multinational enterprises on wages. The results of the study show that an increase in the activities of the multinational enterprises influences the growth of average wages in the local economy, contributing, at the same time, to a higher dispersion of wages between multinational and local enterprises. Noria (2015) evaluates the relative importance of the openness of trade and of foreign direct investments in explaining the interindustrial wage differences in the case of Mexico. The main findings of the study show that trade openness has a statistically significant effect on the interindustrial wage differences, while in the case of FDI, they show that a positive linear relationship exists.

Munoz-Bulloni and Sanchez-Bueno (2013) examine whether the presence of subsidiaries of multinational enterprises in the Spanish processing industry affect domestic firms in the same industry. The study shows that the impact of these foreign firms on local wages is significantly positive in the case of employees in local enterprises with a higher level of competence.

The authors (Munoz-Bulloni and Sanchez-Bueno, 2013) point out a very important aspect: only the employees in local enterprises with a highly qualified workforce benefit from the salary advantages, as a result the foreign industry and the policymakers must take into account that not all the foreign direct investments automatically generate co-benefits for the local businesses. Also, te Velde and Morrissey (2002) argue that foreign-owned enterprises tend to pay higher wages in developing countries, where skilled workers tend to benefit more than the less-skilled workers.

In contrast, there are studies that argue that the takeovers by the foreign investors tend not to have any effect on wages or, on the contrary, have a negative effect (Heyman et al., 2007). Vijaya and Kaltan (2015) present an empirical investigation of the impact of foreign direct investments on wages in the manufacturing sector for the following economies: Australia, Mexico, Austria, the Netherlands, Belgium, Norway, Brazil, the Philippines, Costa Rica, Paraguay, Cyprus, Great Britain, Denmark, Finland, Singapore, Korea (South), France, Sweden, Ireland. The results of the authors indicate that foreign direct investments generally have a negative impact on wages in the manufacturing sector and the impact is stronger on wages received by women. The paper argues that one possible explanation may be the lower bargaining power of labour, thanks to the new arrangements of the labour market in a global economy, where the capital is free to move between countries in search of more favourable conditions.

Another study by Chen et al. (2010) offers evidence at the micro level of a close link between foreign holdings and wage inequality. The results indicate that the presence of foreign investments in Hong Kong, Macao and Taiwan (HMT) has a significant negative impact in terms of salary levels on local firms, and also discourages the growth of salaries in such companies. Overall, the evidence discovered by the authors of the study (Chen et al. (2010)) suggests that the exposure to foreign investments deepens the wage inequalities between domestic enterprises.

2. The research methodology

We used data sources from databases such as Eurostat, the National Bank of Romania (NBR), and the National Institute of Statistics (NIS) for the variables: the stock of FDI and the gross average earning per the economy.

Given that the data concerning the gross average earning are presented by the NIS in the national currency, we used the NBR average exchange rate to convert the gross average earning from lei (RON) into euro.

The data are recorded annually over the 2004–2014 period. We considered this period of analysis due to the availability of statistical information.

The statistical methods applied to assess the impact of FDI on gross average earning are correlation analysis and regression analysis.

Thus, the simple linear regression model is represented by the following equation:

$$GAE = \beta 0 + \beta 1 * FDIs + \varepsilon,$$

where:

- $\beta 0$ – the constant;
- $\beta 1$ – the regression coefficient;
- GAE – gross average earning (dependent variable);
- FDIs – the foreign direct investment stocks (independent variable).

Within the present study the following hypothesis was considered:

Hypothesis 1 - The foreign direct investment stocks in the Romanian economy influences gross average earning.

3. Results and discussion

Results show that the Pearson correlation coefficient between the FDI and the gross average earning is equal to 0.974.

The positive value close to one means that the link between the two variables is direct and very strong.

The significance level of correlation equals Sig = 0.000, a lower value compared to the assumed risk of 1%, so we can consider that the relationship between the two variables is statistically significant.

Table 1: The Pearson correlation coefficient between the FDI indicator and the wages in Romania - Correlations

		Foreign direct investment stocks (Million EUR)	**Gross average earning (EUR/ employee)**
Foreign direct investment stocks (Million EUR)	Pearson Correlation	1	.974**
	Sig. (2-tailed)		.000
	N	11	11
Gross average earning per economy (EUR/ employee)	Pearson Correlation	.974**	1
	Sig. (2-tailed)	.000	
	N	11	11

***Correlation is significant at the 0.01 level (2-tailed).*

Source: *Own computations*

We assume further that the link between the two variables is linear. The correlation curve graph allows the visual approximation of the link between the FDI variables and the average wages in Romania. We see in Figure 1 that the shape of the point cloud shows a direct linear relationship between the FDI variables and wages.

Fig. 1: The relationship between foreign direct investment stocks and the average earning in Romania during the 2004–2014 period

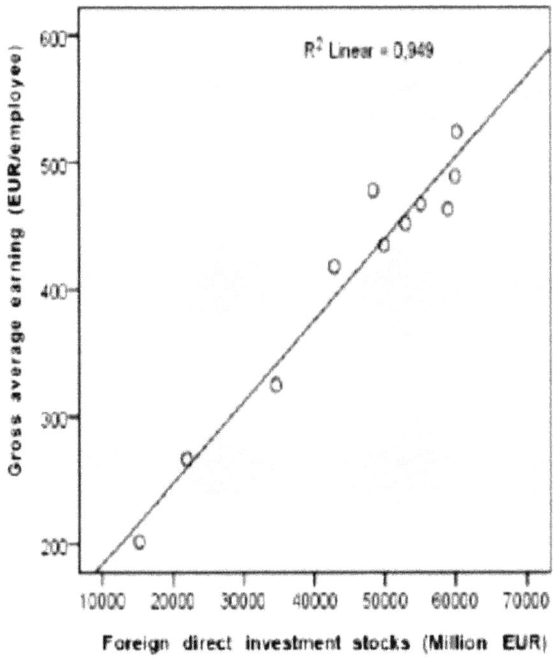

Source: *Own processing.*

The correlation ration (R) of the FDI variables to wages is shown in Table 2. We can also see the value of the determination report (R Square or R^2). The value of the determination ratio R^2 is 0.949, which shows that 94.9% of the variation in wages in Romania is explained by the variation in foreign direct investment stocks.

Table 2: The quality indicators of the linear regression model between the FDI and the average wages

Model Summary

Model	R	R Square	Adjusted R Square	Std. Error of the Estimate
1	.974[a]	.949	.943	24.174

a. Predictors: (Constant), Foreign direct investment stocks (Million EUR)

Source: *Own computations*

The testing results of the simple linear regression model between FDI and the wages are shown in the ANOVA regression Table 3. Analysing the values in Table 3, we see that the Fisher test is statistically significant (because the level of significance of the test Sig. = 0.000, which is lower than the assumed risk of 1%). Therefore, with a probability of 99%, we can admit that the linear relationship between the two variables is statistically significant.

Table 3: The ANOVA results for the regression model between the foreign direct investments variables and wages

ANOVA[a]

Model		Sum of Squares	df	Mean Square	F	Sig.
1	Regression	98041,418	1	98041,418	167,768	.000[b]
	Residual	5259,491	9	584,388		
	Total	103300,909	10			

a. Dependent Variable: Gross average earning per economy (EUR/employee)
b. Predictors: (Constant), Foreign direct investment stocks (Million EUR)

Source: Own computations

The estimates of the regression coefficients are shown in Table 4. The regression equation between FDI stocks and the average wage is:

GAE = 120.303 + 0.006*FDIs + e

If foreign direct investment stocks are increased by one million euro, the variable concerning wages increases on average by 0.006 euro.

Table 4: The regression coefficients for the regression model between foreign direct investments variables and wages

Coefficients[a]

Model		Unstandardised Coefficients		Standardised Coefficients		
		B	Std. Error	Beta	t	Sig.
1	(Constant)	120.303	23.591		5.100	.001
	Foreign direct investment stocks (Million EUR)	.006	.000	.974	12.953	.000

a. Dependent Variable: Gross average earning per economy (EUR/employee)

Source: *Own computations*

The testing of the regression slope involves checking the following statistical hypotheses:

H_0: $\beta_1 = 0$ (the slope is not statistically significant);
H_1: $\beta_1 \neq 0$ (the slope is statistically significant)

The checking of the H_0 hypothesis is performed by using the t test (Student test) for the regression coefficient. The value of the Student test calculated for the observed data is:

$$t = \frac{b_1}{s_{\hat{\beta}_1}} = 12{,}953$$

For the calculated value of the t test, we report a significance level Sig. = 0.000, which is lower than the considered threshold of 1%. So, the H_0 hypothesis is rejected.

With a 99% probability we can affirm that the slope of the regression line is statistically significant, so the stock of FDI has a significant impact on the average wage. Therefore, if foreign direct investment stocks increase by one million euro, the average earning variable increases, on average, by 0.006 euro.

Conclusions

The earnings from the work performed takes various forms, but the wage is the most common form in all the economies around the world. In Romania, the wages offered by the companies with foreign capital depend significantly on the domain of activity, on the professional experience and the level of qualifications.

Also, the employees enjoy other benefits, such as: health insurance, meal vouchers, employers bear the costs related to the training of the employees regarding their career development, free transport where appropriate, or even ensuring the transport.

The purpose of this paper is to provide an analysis of the impact of foreign direct investment stocks on the gross average earning in Romania. Therefore, the statistical methods applied to determine whether there is a link between the FDI and the average wages in the Romanian economy show that foreign direct investments influence the average wages in Romania. For future research, we intend to extend the analysis by including in the model other possible explanatory variables for the wage rise, such as exports, imports and innovation.

References

1. Bedi, A. S., Cielik, A. (2002). Wages and wage growth in Poland: The role of foreign direct investment. Economics of Transition 10(1):1–27.
2. Chen, Z., Ge, Y., Lai, H. (2011). Foreign direct investment and wage inequality: Evidence from China. World Development 39(8), 2011, pp. 1322–1332.

3. Heyman, F., Sjöholm, F., Tingvall, P.G. (2007). Is there really a foreign ownership wage premium? Evidence from matched employer–employee data. Journal of International Economics 73(2):355–376.
4. Muñoz-Bullón, F., Sánchez-Bueno, M. J. (2013). Multinational enterprises and domestic wages: The contingent effect of skill composition. International Business Review 22(6):918–931.
5. Noria, G. L. (2015). The effect of trade and FDI on inter-industry wage differentials: The case of Mexico. The North American Journal of Economics and Finance 34:381–397.
6. Saglam, B.B., Sayek, S. (2011). MNEs and wages: the role of productivity spillovers and imperfect labor markets. Economic Modelling 28(6):2736–2742.
7. Te Velde, D. W., Morrissey, O. (2002). Foreign direct investment: Who gains. ODI Briefing Paper, 2002.
8. Tomohara, A., Takii, S. (2011). "Does globalization benefit developing countries? Effects of FDI on local wages". Journal of Policy Modeling 33(3):511–521.
9. Vijaya, R. M., Linda, K. (2015). Foreign direct investment and wages: a bargaining power approach. Journal of World-Systems Research 13(1):83–95.

Mihai-Sabin MUSCALU

Centre for Industry and Services Economics, Bucharest, Romania

Marius BULEARCĂ

Centre for Industry and Services Economics, Romanian Academy, mariusbulearca@yahoo.com

Cornelia NEAGU

Centre for Industry and Services Economics, Bucharest, Romania

Cristian SIMA

Centre for Industry and Services Economics, Bucharest

Strategic Options to Capitalize the Mineral and Energy Resources of Romania

Abstract: As globalization is increasingly manifest, an urgent mission of great responsibility is more clearly emerging, that is the right mediation between the trend of integration into the global structures, on one hand, and national identity on the other, much in line with current and future objectives of the Romanian economy in general, and the extractive industry in particular. In this context, risks and threats to accessing energy and non-energy strategic resources are increasingly diversified. Therefore, the strategic options were based on the strengths and opportunities identified in the SWOT analysis (presented in our previous works), and intended to offset weaknesses and avoid threats, according to prioritization, the efficient use of mineral and energy resources (crude oil, natural gas, coal, metal ores and uranium) and positive experiences. Based on these assumptions, in this article we have identified several possible strategic options for achieving the objectives for the exploitation of mineral and energy resources in Romania until 2035. The magnitude of benefits resulting from the implementation of these options will depend on the quality of the decisions that society will take as a political and administrative system, and guarantor of security and welfare of the population.

Keywords: oil, natural gas, coal, non-ferrous ores, uranium ores, energy strategy

1. Introduction

As globalization is increasingly manifest, tending to downplay the role of states and national features, an urgent mission of great responsibility is more clearly emerging, that is the right mediation between the trend of integration into the global structures, on one hand, and national identity on the other, much in line with current and future objectives of the Romanian economy in general, and the extractive industry in particular.

If current laws and energy policies remain unchanged until 2035, global energy demand will increase by almost 50% compared to 2007. By 2035, the largest share in the energy consumption growth will occur in countries outside the Organization for Economic Cooperation and Development (non-OECD countries) by 84%, compared to only 14% for OECD countries.

In an increasingly globalized context, the energy policy of Romania is implemented through changes and developments at national and European levels. In this context, Romania's energy policy must be correlated with similar documents at European level to ensure the convergence of our country's policy with the EU's policy in this field [1].

Risks and threats to the access to strategic energy and non-energy resources are increasingly diversified. The sharp growth in global energy and mineral resources consumption has led to gradually "controlled" restriction access to sources of supply and, along with limiting the number of suppliers, to the emergence of monopolies and oligopolies. All these elements have a direct influence on economic security, in which the mining industry development strategy of a country clearly becomes a component of national security [2].

The strategic options have been based on the strengths and opportunities identified in the SWOT analysis (Neagu, Bulearcă et al., 2015), while watching to offset weaknesses and to avoid threats, according to prioritization, efficient use of mineral resources and energy, and positive experience.

Strategic options for hydrocarbon extraction

Based on the analysis of the hydrocarbon extraction sector, aiming to identify the most important problems of the sector and the vision of the functioning of this industry after 2018, the general objective of the hydrocarbon sector is the efficient management and sustainable use of internal oil and gas resources, as well as harmonization of national interests to attract investment capital, in accordance with the requirements of sustainability in oil and gas exploitation.

To achieve this general objective, the measures to be taken must follow some general guidelines:

- Intensifying geological research in order to find new oil and gas deposits.
- Increasing safety in gas supply by diversifying the imported supply sources and developing new interconnections with neighbouring countries' transport systems.
- Increasing the transport capacity of gas extracted from the continental shelf of the Black Sea.
- Promotion of cross-border interconnection projects.

- Increasing natural gas underground storage capacity for the peak demand during the cold season, and for a secure gas supply to customers.
- Development of the gas national transport system and networks, and increasing security of supply and exploitation.
- Ensuring conditions for achieving business portfolio diversification for companies in the oil sector to increase companies' economic performance and competitiveness.

We have identified several possible strategic options for achieving the targeted objectives in oil and gas operations in Romania by the 2035 time horizon:

- Increasing the reserve base by exploiting oil and gas deposits in the Black Sea offshore and unconventional gas.
- Achieving interconnections of national transport systems with those of neighboring countries.
- Resizing underground storage capacity of natural gas.
- Remodelling the gas market.
- Fundraising and investments in exploitation of hydrocarbon resources.

On the 2035 time horizon, in view of discovering new indigenous oil and gas sources, and new regional import sources, as well as an increased interconnection with neighboring markets, Romania can become aregional. regional hub. This would boost industrial competitiveness by optimal energy prices and would generate economic growth and new jobs. The interest of the country and its sustainable development should be promoted while creating an attractive business environment, where the government, regulatory agencies and legislators must be competent partners of investors.

Strategic options for coal extraction

Considering the analysis of the coal extraction sector, mainly the identification of the most important problems of the sector and the vision of the functioning of this industry after 2018, the general objective of the coal sector is the efficient and rational management of coal deposits located on the Romanian territory so that these resources serve the next generations.

To achieve this general objective, the measures to be taken must be subject to the following general guidelines:

- Adapting the coal mining production capacity to market demand.
- Maintaining coal production costs at a level competitive with coal prices, thus maintaining the economic viability of coal mining companies.
- Maintaining a satisfactory level of liquidity and solvency of the coal mining companies.
- Providing economically stable and secure jobs in coal mining companies.
- Tracking the efficiency of unproductive fixed assets and the long-term financial asset policy management by the coal mining companies' boards.

- Implementation of measures to increase revenues from by-products and waste management by coal mining companies.
- Implementation of measures to minimize costs between producers and consumers (that is distribution and transmission costs).
- Identifying new opportunities for coal use, as well as new beneficiaries.

We have identified several possible strategic options for achieving the targeted objectives for coal mining in Romania by the time horizon 2035:

- Making organizational changes in coal resources exploitation.
- Reviewing the legal framework in this field.
- Privatization in the coal mining industry.
- Fundraising and investments in the coal mining industry.
- Human resource development in the coal mining industry.
- Mitigating the impacts of coal mining on the environment.
- Implementing social, education and training programs for former employees.
- Production of liquid and gaseous fuels from coal in the future.

On the 2035 time horizon, the expected results of the implementation of these strategic options in the coal mining industry may lead to: the Romanian coal mining sector functioning in terms of efficiency; environmental protection and sustainable recovery; meeting the necessary quantity of coal for the energy sector (that covers 36% of Romania's energy balance) from domestic production shut-down and closing of unprofitable mines within a coherent process, after informing local communities and involving them in this process; coal resources exploitation in terms of environmental protection in accordance with laws and regulations in this field; social protection of people affected by layoffs from this industry.

Strategic options in non-ferrous ore extraction

Based on the analysis of the non-ferrous ore extraction sector aiming to identify the most important problems of the sector, and the vision of the functioning of this industry after 2018, the general objective of the non-ferrous ore mining sector is the conservation of the existing resources to an optimal exploitation level in the future, the harmonization of national interest with the need for investments in non-ferrous ore exploitation, as well as drawing a larger number and variety of metal resources into the economic cycle.

To achieve this general objective the measures to be taken must comply with the following general guidelines:

- Conservation of closed mines.
- Concession of perimeters to interested companies.
- Capitalization of useful elements from waste dumps and tailings ponds.
- Greening mines affected by extraction.

We have identified several possible strategic options for achieving the objectives of non-ferrous ore mining in Romania by the 2035 time horizon:

- Reviewing regulatory framework in this field.
- Reviewing institutional framework in this field.
- Fundraising and investments in the non-ferrous mining industry.
- Development of education and research in the non-ferrous mining industry.
- Mitigating the impact of the mining industry on the environment.
- Social protection programs for dismissed staff and their families.

The non-ferrous mineral reserves decline and their low useful content caused the shut-down of most mines. The lack of state involvement in major projects, such as gold mining, resulted in the abandonment of the mining activity. At the European level, raw materials extracted inside the Union occupy an important place in the industrial development strategy. In this context, it has made a number of recommendations that our country must take into account, and further develop the mining industry.

Strategic options for uranium ore extraction

Based on the analysis of the uranium ore extraction sector aiming to identify the most important problems of the sector, and the vision of the functioning of this industry after 2018, the general objective of the uranium ore mining sector consists in ensuring nuclear fuel resources from domestic production for the first and the second units of Cernavodă Nuclear Power Plant, and reducing dependence on primary energy resources imports.

To achieve this general objective, the measures to be taken must follow some general guidelines:

- Exploiting the Crucea-Botuşana deposit up to exhaustion under acceptable efficiency conditions.
- Adopting the most appropriate knowledge and technologies, based on the best practice and the most modern management methods in order to maximize economic benefits from the exploitation of this strategic mineral substance.
- Promoting new domestic resources (deposits with approved resources/reserves, mining residues in landfills, ponds, mine waters) for a maximum capitalization of the Romanian natural uranium ores.
- Reorganization and development measures for conservation, shut down, restoration, and environmental rehabilitation in premises where uranium mining activities ceased.
- Using a new mining perimeter located in the Eastern Carpathians, which is the Tulgheş-Grinţieş uranium deposit.
- Import and processing of technical uranium concentrates to obtain uranium dioxide powder as an option up to the exploitation of this new deposit.

- Construction of new processing and refining capacities with advanced technologies that provide increased uranium recovery and reduce production costs.
- Design, research and operation of a plant for processing and preparation of mining residues from waste dumps and tailings ponds.

We have identified several possible strategic options for achieving the targeted objectives in uranium ore mining in Romania by the 2035 time horizon:

- Ensuring raw material required to manufacture nuclear fuel for the operation of the Romanian nuclear power plants.
- Re-engineering/modernizing the processing/preparation and refining capacities by building (on the Feldioara industrial platform) two plants that provide the necessary production, under a high degree of recovery, by processing materials containing uranium from domestic sources and imports.
- Indentifying, outside Romania, the potential concentrated uranium suppliers and launching the award actions for the long-term procurement contract.
- Complying with the environmental rules and directives imposed at national and European levels.
- Improving both the radiological environmental and population protection system, and the radioactive waste management.
- Development of human resources through continuous training for adaptation to the economic conditions required by new production capacities.

So far, in Romania, the nuclear power capacities in operation and the activities associated with providing resources have shown competitive advantages (complete nuclear cycle; reduced impact of uranium price fluctuations in the price of nuclear fuel compared to other fossil fuel prices; safe technology, internationally recognized, low-carbon emissions; staff training programs consistent with best practice and international standards, etc.) and opportunities (significant contributor to energy security and reduction in carbon emissions; technological capacity to process tailings; optimizing production by relating the maintenance to the consumption curves; development of nuclear research programs, etc.).

Conclusions

In recent decades, oil has been a major factor in the international trade growth, being the preferred fuel due to availability, relatively easy transportation and applicability to many industrial processes. Consequently, the industrial sectors increased their production process efficiency, many companies locating their facilities near supply sources, transport corridors or coastal areas, which have not happened to the same extent to other industries such as coal mining and natural gas exploitation.

This economic flexibility resulting from the use of oil as a prevailing energy resource, along with improved communications and international flow of capital have allowed the internationalization of production. Consequently, companies have reduced production costs by relocation to areas where costs of labor, energy, capital, and knowledge were the lowest.

Natural gas will continue to play an important role in transition, too. Replacing coal (and oil) with gas in the short and medium terms, could help to reduce emissions by means of existing technologies until at least 2030 or 2035. The gas market requires more integration, more liquidity, more diversified supply sources, but also a larger storage capacity for gas to maintain its competitive advantages to generate electricity.

Despite the efforts to increase economic and energy efficiency in hydrocarbon extraction, specific environmental problems of the sector were, are and will be a critical issue, a challenge that cannot and must not be ignored, the more so as scarcity makes us forcefully address the issues and explain the policies for sustainable development of this industry.

Regarding coal, the EU documents are just one component of a diversified energy portfolio, contributing to security of supply. With the development of the CCS (carbon capture and storage) and other emerging clean exploitation technologies, coal can play an important role in a secure and sustainable future.

Regarding the long-term role of coal, most independent experts believe that coal-based energy provides security of supply, is available and sustainable, and is clearly an engine of economic growth. The future of coal in Europe depends both on the 20/20/20 EU Program, and on the challenge to natural gas in the energy mix. Natural gas is threatened by the price of instability, uncertainty in reserves growth, and increased exploitation of unconventional reserves. In the International Energy Agency (IEA) scenarios, coal consumption in the EU-27 will decrease by 2.5% annually until 2035, reflecting the Union's ambitious policies to reduce emissions. The share of coal in the EU energy mix will decrease from 16% in 2009 to just 8% in 2035. All projections and all major scenarios depend on nuclear energy, which will remain at the current level, will be reduced only marginally, or will grow.

In this respect, the Cernavodă Nuclear Power Plant nuclear project falls in the category of investment in technologies with low-carbon emissions, absolutely necessary for Romania in the context of the very ambitious de-carbonization at the European level, which means 40% reduction in emissions of greenhouse gases until 2030. At the same time, such large projects are characterized by major capital inflows during their construction, but providing secure and stable income during their operation (nuclear capabilities operate under the load curve for a period of 50 years, with a major contribution to ensuring the security of the National Power System).

So, we can conclude that the primary energy production in Romania based on both the exploitation of primary fossil energy reserves (coal and hydrocarbon) as well as the uranium ore ones, in the most optimistic case, will not grow in the next two to three decades. It follows that the coverage of primary energy demand growth in Romania will be possible by increasing the use of renewable energy sources and by imports of primary energy sources—gas, oil, coal, nuclear fuel. By the analyzed horizon, Romania will remain dependent on imports of primary energy sources. The dependence degree will be based on the discovery of new exploitable internal resources, the integration of renewable energy, and the successful measures to increase energy efficiency.

Finally, regarding mineral ores, further operations will be completely dependent both on the adoption of advanced methods of extracting the metal content so as to determine production efficiency, and on further geological research of the territory, geological and geophysical prospecting, and exploration by modern methods. To achieve these goals, we need: the capitalizing of over one century of geological expertise and study of the geological fund for database updating; release and declassification of geological information held by state-owned institutions; prioritizing what should reshape the mining industry in general and mining industry in particular, according to the new analysis regarding supply and demand for mining products.

Taking into account these major directions regarding the prospects for developing the extractive industry by the 2035 time horizon, we consider that among the above options identified in each extractive sector, the strategic options for the exploitation of mineral resources in Romania with the most significant impact are those shown in the following table (Table 1):

Table 1: Strategic options for exploiting mineral resources with the most significant impact in Romania

Extractive industry	**Strategic option with the most significant impact**
1. Hydrocarbon extraction	1.1. Increasing the reserve base by exploiting deposits in the Black Sea offshore and unconventional gas.
	1.2. Building interconnections of the national transport systems with neighboring countries.
2. Coal extraction	2.1. Fundraising and investments in the coal mining industry.
	2.2. Future orientation toward the production of liquid and gaseous fuels from coal.
3. Non-ferrous ore extraction	3.1. Fundraising and investments in the non-ferrous mining industry.
	3.2. Mitigating the impact of the mining industry upon the environment.
4. Uranium ore extraction	4.1. Increasing the energy capacity of the Cernavoda Nuclear Power Plant by two Nuclear Units.
	4.2. Ensuring the raw material required to manufacture nuclear fuel for the operation of the Romanian Nuclear power plants.

Source: Author's own proposals.

Scale benefits resulting from these strategic options will depend on the quality of the decisions made by the society as a political and administrative system, guarantor of security and welfare.

Endnotes

[1] Increasing security of energy supply can be achieved by: diversifying sources and routes of supply of crude oil and natural gas, and reducing dependence on energy imports; development of electricity and gas transport grids, and increasing the interconnection capacity with neighboring countries; increasing gas storage capacity (www.energie.gov.ro).

[2] Restricting the number of mineral and energy resources suppliers at the global level—in conditions of increased demands, caused by large consuming systems—determined that these resources be politically redefined as "geo-resources" (http://www.nato.int/lisbon2010/ strategic concept-2010-eng.pdf).

References

1. Dudău R. (2014). Oil and gas industry in Romania: Tradition and strategic opportunity, Employers' Federation Report for Oil and Gas, Energy Policy Group, Bucharest, December 2014.
2. Fodor, D. (2014). Coal industry again in actuality: The scientific path toward realistic solutions, Engineering Universe, No. 8/2014, www.agir.ro. 8/2014.
3. Ivănuş, Ghe. Ştefănescu, I., Antonescu, N. N., Mocuţa, Ş, Pascu Coloja, M. (2008). Industria de petrol şi gaze din România, Bucureşti, Editura AGIR, 2008/ Oil and gas industry in Romania, AGIR Publishing House, Bucharest.
4. Leca, A., Muşatescu, V., et. al. (2010). Strategii şi politici energie-mediu în România, Ed. AGIR, Bucureşti, 2010/ Energy-environment strategies and policies in Romania, AGIR Publishing House, Bucharest.
5. Neagu, C., Bulearcă, M., Sima, C., Mărguş, D. (2015). A SWOT analysis of Romanian Extractive Industry and Re-Industrialization Requirements of This Industry, in Procedia Economics and Finance 22:287–295.
6. ***Ministerul Economiei şi Comerţului (2012), Strategia Industriei Miniere pentru perioada 2012–2035, forma actualizată 31.05.2012, http://www.minind.ro /.Ministry of Economy: "The Mining Industry Strategy for the period 2012–2035", Updated 31.05.2012, http://www.minind.ro.
7. ***Ministerul Economiei, Comerţului şi Mediului de Afaceri, Strategia Companiei Naţionale a Uraniului 2015–2025, www.cnu.ro/Ministry of Economy, Trade and Business Environment: Strategy 2015–2025 of the National Uranium Company, www.cnu.ro.
8. ***Ministerul Energiei, Întreprinderilor Mici şi Mijlocii şi Mediului de Afaceri, Strategia Energetică Naţională 2011–2035, www.energie.gov.ro /Ministry of

Energy, "Small and Medium Enterprises and Business Environment": National Energy Strategy 2011–2035, www.energie.gov.ro.
9. ***Ministerul Mediului şi Dezvoltării Durabile şi Programul Naţiunilor Unite pentru Dezvoltare - Centrul Naţional pentru Dezvoltare Durabilă - Strategia Naţionala pentru Dezvoltare Durabila a României Orizonturi 2013–2020–2030, aprobată prin Hotărârea Guvernului României nr. 1460 of 12 November 2008, http://www.anpm.ro/ro/strategia-nationala-pentru-dezvoltare-durabila. / Ministry of Environment and Sustainable Development and the United Nations Development Programme – National Centre for Sustainable Development: National Strategy for Sustainable Development of Romania Horizons 2013–2020–2030 approved by the Romanian Government Decision no.1460 din 12 noiembrie 2008 http://www.anpm.ro/ro/strategia-nationala-pentru-dezvoltare-durabila.
10. http://ec.europa.eu/energy/2030_en.htm.
11. http://www.roadmap2050.eu/.
12. www.cnh.ro.
13. www.csnmeridian.ro, Evaluarea stării actuale şi perspectivele industriei miniere în România, CEIS şi Secţia de Ştiinţe Geonomice a Academiei Române, oct.www.csnmeridian.ro.
14. www.omvpetrom.com.
15. www.romgaz.ro.
16. www.snlo.ro.
17. www.transgaz.ro.
18. www.worldcoal.org, World Coal Association -- Energy for Sustainable Development.
19. www.worldcoal.org, World Coal Association – Sustainable mining practice policy statement.

Stelian STANCU

Informatics and Economic Cybernetics Department,
Bucharest University of Economic Studies, Centre for Industrial and
Services Economics, Romanian Academy,
email: stelian_stancu@yahoo.com

Constanţa Nicoleta BODEA

Informatics and Economic Cybernetics Department,
Bucharest University of Economic Studies, Centre for Industrial and
Services Economics, Romanian Academy, email: bodea@ase.ro

Mihai Sabin MUSCALU

Centre for Industrial and Services Economics, Romanian Academy,
email: msmuscalu@yahoo.com

Evaluation of Natural Resources of Fossil Fuels. Mathematical and Economic Models, Estimates and Predictions

Abstract: The domain of fossil fuels is appealing, mainly due to the strategic groups of the great powers, acting at the national and international level.

The paper presents the main concepts related to fossil fuels (coal, oil and natural gas) and develops the corresponding concepts of taxonomy. It also describes the past and current situation of the domain as a basis for the trend estimation in the medium and long term (70–80 years). The authors take into consideration the demand dynamics for primary energy (fossil fuels) at global and European levels and also for Romania. They reveal that the fossil fuel industry is facing major risks nowadays and the decisions regarding the usage of large quantities of fossil fuel reserves until 2090 to 2100 depend on the willingness to enforce the regulations on the limitation of carbon emissions and moral persuasion induced by the lobby made by non-governmental organizations.

The authors present original evolution scenarios for the production and consumption of fossil fuels by taking into consideration the natural resource reserves and ensuring continuous economic assessment. These scenarios were developed using specific mathematic models. The hypothesis for developing these scenarios is that fossil fuels represent an active factor for sustainable development when they are used efficiently and responsibly. Based on the empirical analyses for these scenarios, the authors made several quantitative judgments regarding the evolution of the fossil fuels' natural resources and economic assessments.

Keywords: fossil fuels, taxonomy, specific economic evaluation, mathematical models, evolution scenarios, sustainable development

1. Introduction

Natural resources include air, water in all its forms, sunlight, plant and animal biomass, soils, minerals in the soil and subsoil, natural rocks, fossil fuels, and ferrous and nonferrous ores. Over time, the evaluation of the natural resources of fossil fuels generated major controversies. In different analyses of the short, medium and long term, optimistic, pessimistic and possibly moderate approches (Sorrell, Speirs, Bentley, Brandt, Miller, 2010) were adopted. There were also methods and models of the prediction of crude oil production (Chen, Qu, 2013), crude oil production and consumption (Ma, Wu, 2010), forecasting natural gas consumption (Kaynar, Yilmaz, Demirkoparan, 2011 and Soldo, 2012), energy demand (Abdel-Aal, 2008), based on artificial neural networks (Fausett, 1994).

The application of neural networks in predicting the natural resources of fossil fuels paved the way to widespread use of evolutionary computation and computational intelligence in this area (Khoukhi, Oloso, Elshafei, Abdulrahefm, Al-Majed, 2011), genetic algorithms (Mitchell, 1996) and identifying elements for optimizing control parameters (Grefenstette, 1986).

Considering the high uncertainty of the research, the hybridization (the combination of two or more computational techniques) may lead to a better solution (Deng, Chen He, Liu Yin Guo, 2012). Hybridization helps to introduce techniques for information processing based on logic and fuzzy control (Chen, Tat, 2001), while ensuring the prediction of oil production by fuzzy techniques (Yu, Wang, Wen, 2008). The advance of hybridization allows for a wide usage of techniques based on support vector machines (Khashman, Nwulu, 2011a), and the symbiosis between neural networks and support vector machines (Khashman, Nwulu, 2011b). In this context, VaR models combined with neural networks became relevant for the crude oil market (Lai, He, Yen, 2007). RBF networks are used to forecast the reserves of fossil fuels (Qunli, Ge, Xiaodong, 2009 and Yu, Wang, Lai, 2005).

In the empirical analysis, the authors used, besides the mentioned methods, some of the screening techniques for dealing with the worldwide undiscovered resources (Wade, 2007), statistical data on the world's energy (BP, 2016), and also non linearity and effectiveness tests on future energy markets (Wang, Yang, 2010).

2. Natural resources vs. natural reserves of fossil fuel

The natural resources of fossil fuels (coal, oil and usable natural gas) can be divided into two categories: *uncertain fossil fuel resources* (RI), (Wade, 2007), representing the total amount of natural resources of fossil fuels known with certainty, the only assumptions being made on existing quantity, and *certain/almost certain fossil fuels resources* (RC), representing the total amount of natural fossil fuel resources found by geological survey and other rigorous scientific studies (Figure 1). The difference between RI and RC represents the remaining recoverable resource using current or future technologies. They include: *technically recoverable resources* (TRR) and *economically recoverable resources* (ERR).

The certain fossil fuel resources (RC) are part of the uncertain resources (RI), representing about 70–80%. The certain fossil fuel resources (RC) include: *immediately exploitable resources of fossil fuels* (REI), representing resources recoverable by current technologies and *exploitable fossil fuel resources with future science* (RESV), representing the remaining recoverable resources. These two sets show the following inclusion relationship: $RRE \subset RRT$ (*URR*). Whether we speak of immediately exploitable fossil fuels (REI) or exploitable fossil fuel resources with future science (RESV), they include: *technically recoverable fossil fuel resources* (RRT), i.e. resources that can be recovered using current/future technologies and *economically recoverable fossil fuel resources* (RRE), i.e. resources that can be recovered given the present/future economic efficiency.

Fig. 1: Natural fossil fuel resources structure

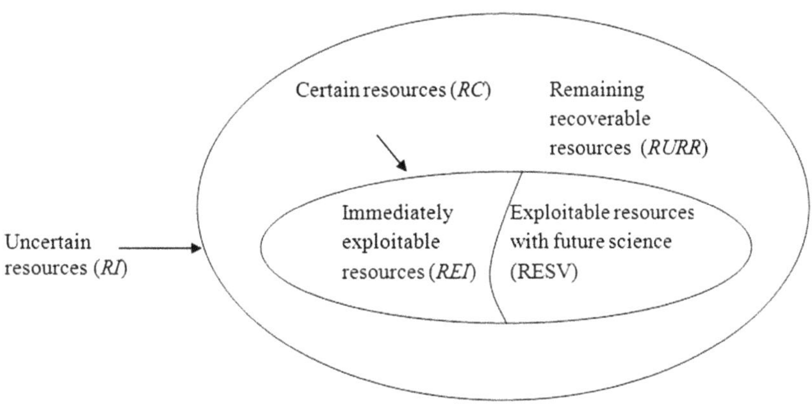

Natural reserves of fossil fuels (coal, oil and usable gas) represent a fraction of the certain resources (RC), that are expected to have a specified probability of being produced, calculated on the basis of the opportunity cost, admitting that a natural resource of fossil fuels will not be exploited/produced if the costs incurred are much higher than those of a similar imported resource.

One important approach to quantifying natural reserves is to model the process of discovery, to describe how the discovery process will develop over time, based on assumptions about growth stocks future (Sorrell, Speirs, 2009). These methods may differ from more widely used geological methods, which are generally used for areas that are relatively unexplored. However, there are errors and uncertainties in assessments (Hubbert, 1982).

The natural fossil fuel reserves contain: *proved reserves* (RD), i.e. resources whose existence is well identified; *proved and probable* (RDP), i.e. resources whose existence is well identified, but also those that are very likely to be identified in the near future; and *proved, probable and possible* (RDPP), i.e. resources whose existence is well identified, but also those that are very likely to be identified in the near future and may also be exploited economically. The following two inclusion relationships exist: $RD \subset RDR$ and $RDPPC \subset RDR$ (Figure 2).

Fig. 2: The structure of natural fossil fuel reserves with appropriate inclusions

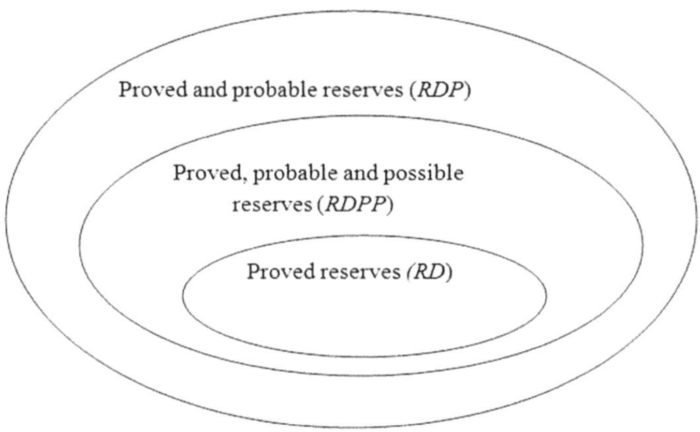

The increase of the natural reserve of fossil fuels (Thompson, Sorrell, Speirs, 2009) is the consequence of several factors, such as: changes in reserves in certain geographical areas, improvement of exploitation technologies, inclusion of new data or forecasts revision, better understanding of geological reserves and changes in the fossil fuel prices.

3. The methodology for estimating the reserves and the production of natural resources of fossil fuels. The classic model of Hubbert

Based on new deposits discovered and data on past fossil fuel production, the Hubbert curve helps to approximate data on previous discoveries in order to provide estimates for future production and reserves at each moment of the analysis. Hubbert developed a mathematical model to estimate fossil fuel production (Udochukwu, Ogbonnaya, 2011), which implies that the production of natural resources of fossil fuels follows a bell-shaped curve that rises rapidly to a peak and falls just as quickly. According to Hubbert's approach (Hubbert, 1982), the production of fossil fuels is a parable or a bell-shaped curve, given by:

$$P(t) = \alpha Q_1(t)\left[1 - \frac{Q_1(t)}{Q_{\max}}\right] = \alpha \frac{Q_1(t)}{Q_{\max}}\left[Q_{\max} - Q_1(t)\right] = \alpha \frac{Q_1(t)}{Q_{\max}} Q_2(t) \quad (1)$$

where:

$P(t)$ – the production over the time period t (usually, one year), expressed in number of the barrels of oil, with $P(t) \xrightarrow{t \to T} 0$, T being the moment when the resource/reserve runs out;

$Q_1(t)$ – the cumulative (total) amount of fossil fuels exploited from the moment when analysis started, t_0 and the present moment, t (it). If $t_0 \to 0$, then $Q_1(t)$ represents the area under the bell, until the moment t;

$Q_2(t)$ – the cumulative production that can be exploited from time t to time T, T representing the moment of depletion of the natural fossil fuel resources;

Q_{max} – the total amount of fossil fuels that will ever be recovered, i.e. the total available resource that is proved, probable and possible to be exploited economically (RDPP);

α – the logistics growth rate of annual production.

4. Prediction of the natural fossil fuel reserves using neural networks

4.1. Multi-layer perceptron (MLP) neural networks

A multi-layer perceptron (MLP) neural network has multiple layers of neurons, the signal propagation being in one direction, from inputs to outputs. The neurons process the inputs with sigmoid activation functions.

The prediction models based on neural networks are generally known as black boxes, due to the hidden layer(s), without an economic significance. These hidden layers are highly valued for their ability to store and approximate the nonlinear relationships. It is recommended that the initial number of neurons on each hidden layer should be around $\sqrt{mn}$, where m is the number of neurons on the input layer and n is the number of neurons on the output layer.

The steps required to make predictions by using MLPs are the following: (i) determining the structure of the network, i.e. the lags t-1, t-2, etc., which determine the number of inputs, the number of hidden layers, the number of neurons on each hidden layer and the number of network outputs. The number of network outputs is ussualy the same as the number of estimation intervals; (ii) segmentation of the database: one part for training (learning) network, and another one for validation; (iii) scaling the input variables to the range [0.1]; (iv) weights initialization. If the network has m entries, it is recommended that weights be within $[-\frac{2}{m}, \frac{2}{m}]$; (v) Weighting and summing up the input values; (vi) nonlinear transformation (using sigmoidal function) of the weighted input values, in order to obtain the outputs; (vii) calculaion of the estimation error, by comparing the predicted values with actual values; (viii) Weight adjustement based on the estimation error; (ix) repeating the steps (v)–(vii) until all training data has been used (the first period/epoch of the learning process has ended), in order to get an estimation error as small as possible, the learning process requires several epochs; (x) repeat the steps for another training epoch until a desired value of the estimation error has been calculated. If the results are not satisfactory, another network architecture should be designed.

4.2. Radial basis (RBF) neural networks

(a) Neural network with one RBF neuron. An RBF neuron has the vectorial difference norm $\|u-w\|$ as the net input and $z=\|u-w\|\cdot\tau$, as the summarization function. The activation function is $y=f(z)=e^{-z^2}$.

In fact, an RBF neural network is a perceptron with a radial function as an activation function, instead of linear or nonlinear one. For a network with a single neuron with Gaussian radial activation function, the weight of the input connection, ψ, and the signal applied to the input neuron, u, the output neuron is $f(u)=e^{-\frac{(u-\psi)^2}{2\sigma^2}}$. If the input of the neural network is the vector $U=(u_1,u_2,...,u_N)^T$ and the input weight vector is $\Psi=(\psi_1,\psi_2,...,\psi_N)^T$, then the neuron output is $f(U)=e^{-\frac{\|U-\Psi\|^2}{2\sigma^2}}$.

(b) Neural networks with many RBF neurons. RBF neural networks are made up of neurons arranged on three layers: the input or sensorial layer, which contains m input neurons, the hidden layer, containing p hidden neurons with radial activation functions and the output layer, consisting of output neurons. There is a nonlinear mapping of input space into the output space, while the mapping of hidden space into output space is linear.

The output of neuron k, with $k=\overline{1,n}$, considering the input signal $u=(u_1,u_2,...,u_m)$ is:

$$y_k=\sum_{j=1}^{p}\omega_{jk}f_j\left(\left\|u-w^j\right\|\right)-\omega_{0k}==\sum_{j=1}^{p}\omega_{jk}e^{-\frac{(u-w^j)'(u-w^j)}{\tau_j^2}}-\omega_{0k}=\sum_{j=1}^{p}\omega_{jk}e^{-\frac{\sum_{i=1}^{m}(u_i-w_{ij})^2}{\tau_j^2}}-\omega_{0k} \quad (2)$$

with $k=\overline{1,n}$, where: $u=(u_1,u_2,...,u_i,...,u_m)'\in R^m$ – input vector; $w_{i\bullet}=(w_{i1},w_{i2},...,w_{ij},...,w_{ip})'\in R^p$ – weight vector in the hidden neuron 1, 2, ..., p, starting from u_i, with $i=\overline{1,m}$; $\omega=(\omega_{jk})_{j=\overline{1,p},k=\overline{1,n}}$ - weight matrix for the connections between hidden and output layers; $\|\ \|$ - euclidian norm.

The RBF neural networks make local approximations, while multilayer feedforward networks provide global ones.

5. Empirical analysis

The estimations of natural fossil fuel reserves, at the worldwide level and per regions and leading countries, assuming a constant production rate (Lior, 2008) are shown in Table 1.

Table 1: Location of the world's main fossil fuel reserves in 2016

Region	Fossil fuel reserve (giga tonnes of oil) equivalent				Fossil fuel reserve (%)			
	Oil	Coal	Gas	Sum	Oil	Coal	Gas	Sum
North America		172.3	7.3	186.3	4.9	27.8	4.2	19.6
South America	16.3	14.2	7.1	35.3	9.3	2.3	4.1	3.7
Europe	2.4	41.4	6.1	48.2	1.3	6.6	3.5	5.2
Africa	17.2	35.2	14.3	64.5	9.8	5.6	8.3	6.8
Russia	19.3	153.6	53.8	224.1	11.1	24.8	31.3	23.6
Middle East	104.7	0	67.6	168.4	60.1	0	39.4	17.7
India	1.2	63.2	1.4	66.7	0.7	10.2	0.8	7.1
China	2.1	77.1	2.7	81.4	1.2	12.4	1.5	8.6
Australia and East Asia	2.2	61.4	11.1	73.2	1.2	9.9	6.4	7.7
Total	174.1	618.4	171.4	963.9	18.1	64.1	17.8	100.0

Source: Authors' computations.

Table 2: Fossil fuel reserve depletion times

Model	Hubbert's classical model			MLP neural model			RBF neural network		
	Oil	Coal	Gas	Oil	Coal	Gas	Oil	Coal	Gas
No. of years	36	108	75	35	114	68	38	112	64

Source: Authors' computations.

Table 2 illustrates the moment when fossil fuels will be depleted, determined by the classical model of Hubbert, MLP neural network and RBF neural network. As we can see in this table, 36, 108 and 75 years for oil, coal and natural gas depletion have been calculated by Hubbert's classical model, 35, 114 and 68 years by MLP and 38, 112 and 64 years by the RBF model. In all three models, the coal reserve is still greater than oil and gas reserves. This means that coal reserves will be available at least up to 2125, considering the underlying assumptions, and this will be the only fossil fuel in the world at that time, as shown in Table 2. Table 3 presents the estimated reserves of coal, oil and natural gas in the 2014–2100 period using the RNA-MLP model, in Romania, TW (Whole World), the EU and TEE. (Total Europe & Eurasia).

Table 3: Coal, oil and gas reserves estimation for 2014–2100

	Coal (Million tonnes)				Oil (thousands million barels)				Gas (Trillion cubic meters)			
	RDDP = Q2				RDDP = Q2				RDDP = Q2			
	Romania	TW (Total World)	EU	TEE (Europe and Eurasia)	Romania	TW (Total World)	EU	TEE (Europe and Eurasia)	Romania	TW (Total World)	EU	TEE (Europe and Eurasia)
2014	235,1338	740589,8	52863,33	260848,8	0,484812	1412,181	4,779560	130,1206	0,080802	155,3399	1,225390	47,87942
2015	221,1345	722948,2	47436,66	248172,0	0,472103	1369,883	4,641022	125,6164	0,075991	151,6395	1,099598	45,55257
2016	207,9687	705726,8	44362,06	236111,3	0,459728	1328,853	4,506500	121,2682	0,071467	148,0273	1,028328	43,33880
2017	195,5867	688915,6	41486,75	224636,7	0,447677	1289,052	4,375877	117,0704	0,067212	144,5011	0,961677	41,23262
...												
2025	119,6934	568069,3	24271,15	150797,0	0,361971	1010,688	3,458365	88,31820	0,041132	119,1534	0,562614	27,67916
...												
2050	25,79913	310911,5	4544,967	43400,31	0,186323	472,5538	1,657729	36,60661	0,008866	65,21416	0,105354	7,966231
...												
2075	5,560832	170165,8	851,0816	12490,87	0,095909	220,9456	0,794614	15,17291	0,001911	35,69253	0,019728	2,29273
...												
2100	1,1986	93133,86	159,3719	3594,95	0,049369	103,3045	0,38089	6,288951	0,000412	19,53497	0,003694	0,659862

Source: Authors' computations.

According to the results presented in Table 3, the reserves of coal, oil and natural gas in Romania will be extremely low, near collapse. In the EU, they will also be extremely low. In TEE (Total Europe & Eurasia), the situation is only relatively better while for TW (Total World) the situation is somewhat better only for coal and gas. Table 4 presents the predicted evolution of the oil reserves and production in the 2014–2100 period, by using an MLP neural network, for Romania, TW (Total World), the EU and TEE (Total Europe & Eurasia).

Table 4: Oil reserves and production estimation for 2014–2100

	Oil (thousands million barels)				Oil (thousands tones barels)			
	RDDP = Q2				P (Production			
	Romania	TW (Total World)	EU	TEE (Europe and Eurasia)	Romania	TW (Total World)	EU	TEE (Europe and Eurasia)
2014	0,484812	1412,181	5,278604	129,8624	-	-	-	-
2015	0,454136	1378,341	4,730730	0,454136	0,030070	33,63969	0,341873	6,311072
2016	0,425402	1345,702	4,429720	0,425402	0,028735	32,83836	0,307010	6,004365
2017	0,398485	1313,646	4,142609	0,398485	0,026917	32,05611	0,287111	5,712564
...								
2025	0,236219	1083,213	2,423566	75,07365	0,015956	26,43298	0,16797	3,834803
...								
2050	0,046093	592,856	0,453832	21,60666	0,003113	14,4671	0,031454	1,103680
...								
2075	0,008994	324,477	0,084984	6,218528	0,000608	7,918028	0,00589	0,317646
...								
2100	0,001755	177,591	0,015914	1,789730	0,000119	4,333636	0,001103	0,09142

Source: Authors' computations.

The results presented in Table 4 indicate that in Romania, the EU and TEE (Total Europe & Eurasia) the oil stocks will be lower than in the first scenario. At TW (Total World) level, the oil stocks situation is somewhat better than in the first scenario. As for the oil production to be achieved, it will follow a downward trend, because of the following factors: willingness to protect that resource as much as possible, the measures to reduce carbon emissions into the atmosphere and the usage of alternative energy resources.

6. Conclusions

Currently, the fossil fuels are covering around 85% of the world's energy needs, while 80% of primary energy used in the European Union comes from fossil fuels. After many consecutive years of dependence on fossil fuels, we can draw two firm conclusions: fossil fuels have a disastrous impact on health, the environment and the climate in general, and we will give up fossil fuels in about 80–85 years. Decreasing fossil fuel usage means less dependence on unreliable suppliers.

A significant proportion of the amount of fossil fuels needed at EU level is imported from outside the Union, hence the role of fossil fuels to create a centralized, hierarchical and inflexible energy distribution. Also, about 80% of the primary energy used in the European Union comes from fossil fuels, while the global climate is threatened by fossil fuels and our dependency on them. About forty percent of our emissions come from fossil fuels burned in power plants.

Regarding the energy sector, there is no project in the field of fossil fuels. We are still too dependent on fossil fuels instead of exploring alternative energy sources. This dependence can be reduced in the long term if we move from fossil fuels to renewable energy sources.

7. References

1. Abdel-Aal, R. E.: "Univariate modeling and forecasting of monthly energy demand time series using abductive and neural networks". *Comp. Ind. Eng.*, 54, 2008, pp. 903–917.
2. BP: "BP statistical review of world energy". URL: www.bp.com/statisticalreview, 2016.
3. Chen, X., Qu Y.: "A prediction method of crude oil output based on artificial neural networks", in: *Proc. of the IEEE Int. Conf. Comput.* Inf. Sci., 2013, pp. 702–704.
4. Chen, G., Tat, T.P.: *Introduction to fuzzy sets, fuzzy logic and fuzzy control system.* CRC Press: Boca Raton, 2001.
5. Deng, W., Chen, R., He, B., Liu, Y., Yin, L., Guo, J.: "A novel two-stage hybrid swarm intelligence optimization algorithm and application", *Soft Computing*, 6, 2012, pp. 1707–1722.
6. Fausett, L.V.: *Fundamentals of Neural Networks. Architectures, Algorithms, and Applications.* Prentice-Hall: Englewood Cliffs. 1994.

7. Grefenstette, J. J.: "Optimization of control parameters for genetic algorithms", *IEEE T. Syst. Man Cy.*, 16(1), 1986, pp. 122–128.
8. Hubbert, M. K.: "Techniques of prediction as applied to the production of oil and gas. Washington D.C, United States", in: *Oil and gas supply modelling; proceedings of a symposium; S. I. Glass*, Ed., vol. 631, 1982, pp. 16–141.
9. Kaynar, O., Yilmaz, I., Demirkoparan, F.: "Forecasting of natural gas consumption with neural networks and neuro fuzzy system", *Energ. Educ. Sci. Tech.*, 26(2), 2011, pp. 221–238.
10. Khashman, A., Nwulu, I. N.: "Intelligent prediction of crude oil using support vector machines". in: *9th IEEE Int Symposium Appll. Mach. Intell. Inform.*, Smolenice, Germany, 2011a, pp. 165–169.
11. Khashman, A., Nwulu, I.N.: "Support vector machine versus back propagation algorithms for oil prediction", *Lect. Notes Comput. Sci.*, 6677, 2011b, pp. 530–538.
12. Khoukhi, A., Oloso, M., Elshafei, M., Abdulrahefm, A., Al-Majed, A.: "Support vector regression and functional networks for viscocity and gas/oil ratio curves estimation", *Int. J. Comput. Intel. Appl.*, 3, 2011, pp. 269–293.
13. Lai, K.K., He, K., Yen, J.: "Modeling VaR in crude oil market: A multi scale non-linear ensemble approach incorporating wavelet analysis and ANN", *Lect. Notes Comput. Sci.*, 4487, 2007, pp. 554–561.
14. Lior, N.: "Energy resources and use the present situation and possible paths to the future", *Energy*, 33, 2008, pp. 842–857.
15. Ma, H., Wu, Y.: "A grey forecasting model based on BP neural network for crude oil production and consumption in China", in: *Proc. IEEE Comput. Society 3th Int. Symposium Inf.*, Qingdao, China, 2010, pp. 105–109.
16. Mitchell, M.: *An introduction to genetic algorithms*, MIT Press: Massachusetts. 1996.
17. Qunli, W., Ge, H., Xiaodong, C.: "Crude oil forecasting with an improved model based on wavelet transform and RBF neural network". *IEEE Int. Forum Inf. Technol. Appl.*, Chengdu, China, 2009, pp. 231–234.
18. Soldo, B.: "Forecasting natural gas consumption", *Appl. Energ.*, 92, 2012, pp. 26–37.
19. Sorrell, S., Speirs, J.: *Methods of estimating ultimately recoverable resources. Review of Evidence on Global Oil Depletion: Technical Report 5.* London, UK: UKERC, 2009.
20. Sorrell, S., Speirs, J., Bentley, R., Miller, R.: "Global oil depletion: a review of the evidence", *Energy Policy*, 38(9):5290e5. http://dx.doi.org/10.1016/j.enpol.2010.04.046. URL: http://www.sciencedirect.com/science/article/pii/S0301421510003204, 2010.
21. Stancu, S., Constantin, A.M.: *Reţele neuronale artificiale. Teorie şi aplicaţii*, Editura Academiei de Studii Economice, Bucureşti, 2014.
22. Thompson, E., Sorrell, S., Speirs, J.: *The nature and importance of reserve growth. Review of Evidence on Global Oil Depletion*: Technical Report 3. London, UK: UKERC. 2009.

23. Wade, P.: *Screening of global undiscovered resources.* Presentation; IHS London Symposium; London, UK, 2007.
24. Udochukwu, B.A., Ogbonnaya, I.O.: *A Prediction on Nigeria's Oil Depletion Based on Hubbert's Model and the Need for Renewable Energy*, International Scholarly Research Network ISRN Renewable Energy, Volume 2011, Article ID 285649, 6 pages, doi:10.5402/2011/285649, 2011, http://downloads.hindawi.com/journals/isrn/2011/285649.pdf.
25. Wang, T., Yang, J.: "Nonlinearity and intraday efficiency test on energy future markets", *Energ. Econ.*, 32, 2010, pp. 496–503.
26. Yu, L., Wang, S., Lai, K. K.: "A rough set refined text mining approach for crude oil market tendency forecasting", *Int. J. Knowl. Syst. Sci.*, 2(1), 2005, pp. 33–46.
27 Yu, L., Wang, S., Wen, B.: "An AI-agent trapezoidal fuzzy ensemble forecasting model for crude oil prediction", in: *Proc. of the IEEE 3rd Int. Conf. Innovative Comput. Inf. Control*, Dalian, China, 2008, p. 327.

Marius BULEARCĂ

Centre for Industry and Services Economics,
Romanian Academy, mariusbulearca@yahoo.com

Establishing a New System for Petroleum Royalties in Romania

Abstract: Nowadays, there are three major global systems of tax on hydrocarbon exploitation. Given these factors, the most important question is, in fact, what is the best tax system for the oil and gas industry? As a fundamental principle, such a system must be so as to maximize the return to the state and to attract and retain capital and technology investment. This article proposes a new system of taxation of hydrocarbons that could adopt a differentiated royalty model, with two pillars—for existing operations or for new ones. Moreover, we believe that the new system of taxation of hydrocarbons should provide different levels of royalties for operating onshore and offshore. Also, there should be differentiation between shallow and deep offshore deposits, because of differences in costs involved. The effects of the application of a new system are: increasing contribution to consolidated state budget; efficient management of the productive potential of existing deposits and sustainable use of internal oil and gas resources; and increasing foreign direct investment inflows in oil and gas extraction, particularly in the Black Sea continental shelf.

Keywords: oil and gas industry, royalties, sustainability

Introduction

The interests of investors and governments are not always convergent. This is true especially for taxation in the oil and gas sector, given the substantial contribution of this sector to the state budget revenues, but also for the strategic importance to the energy security of the country.

While the state seeks to maximize the budget revenues and collection of taxes as early as possible, at the beginning of the projects, investors seek to maximize the value for shareholders, financing mainly the investments and some payments to the state budget as late as possible, but only after cost recovery. Governments are interested in diversifying their resource portfolio, aiming to reduce risks and strengthen energy security, while investors are interested in preserving their market agility and ability to adapt to changing economic conditions.

It is clear, however, that a taxation system suitable for this sector must ensure a balance between the priorities of government and private investors, while meeting the requirements of civil society. Such a system should lead to a “win-win-win” situation for all stakeholders—governments, investors and civil society.

Oil and natural gas plays an important role in the Romanian economy. Romania currently produces over 100 million boe of oil and gas per year, a relatively significant production in relation to the internal needs of the country for these two resources. Production is dominated by two major companies representing over 95% of current annual production: OMV Petrom SA (oil and associated gas) and SNGN Romgaz SA (natural gas). In the past 30 years, the oil and natural gas production realized in Romania has steadily declined because of exhausting reserves from deposits in operation, many of these blocks being mature and in production for several decades. Compared to the oil exploitation peak period in Romania, between 1975 and 1989 (maximum production levels were recorded in 1976 for oil and in 1986 for gas), between 2011 and 2015 the oil and gas extracted quantities decreased significantly, by 70%, as development of oil and natural gas production is influenced by the maturity degree of the deposits.

Romania has the lowest well productivity in Europe and one of the lowest levels of deposit production in Europe, which indicates maturity of onshore deposits. To counteract this decline, significant investments have been made in recent years, a program of continuous investment being necessary, however, to improve the productivity of the existing oil and gas deposits.

From the perspective of the issues previously mentioned, comparing various countries is difficult because of many major differences, such as: the mix of production of oil and natural gas; the structure of onshore and offshore production; the average yield on the deposit; the average productivity of wells; the average production cost; the differences in the mechanism of imposing similar petroleum royalties and taxes, related to production and income on the one hand, or related to profit or a fixed percentage on the other.

At the same time, the national economic conditions vary across countries producing oil and natural gas. In addition, tax systems in some countries such as Britain, Poland, Croatia, Ireland, Lithuania, and Greece have recently changed or are changing, which will affect the current situation of similar royalties and taxes. Moreover, we found that similar observable royalties and taxes, as a percentage of revenue, differ compared to nominal rates for similar royalties and taxes because of differences in productivity and tax facilities in different countries.

1. The description of the problem and critical state-of-the-art

In Romania, according to the Oil Law, a company can explore natural resources by leasing a perimeter. Specifically, for a specified period of time, the Romanian state transmits to a Romanian or foreign legal entity the rights and obligations to perform, at its own risk and expense, oil and gas operations, and the rights to use goods of public property needed for these oil and gas operations, but in exchange for paying a royalty.

Therefore, the royalty is the amount payable by holders of concessions to the state budget to exploit a deposit or goods of public property. In other words, the royalty is the amount paid to the state budget by the companies that have leased natural resources for their exploitation

The difference between royalty and tax is that the royalty is charged only when using the good, while tax is paid regardless of whether the property is used or not. In general, the royalty is calculated based on the utilization degree of the good.

Usually, petroleum royalty is either a percentage of the gross extracted output value for oil and gas operations of oil and gas deposits, or a percentage of the gross income from oil and gas operations of oil and gas transport and transit. In the case of transit, there are taken into account the national systems of oil and gas transport and oil and gas operations carried out by state-owned oil and gas terminals.

The main companies paying royalties in the oil and gas industry in Romania are OMV Petrom SA, Rompetrol, Lukoil, MOL, Eni and SNGN Romgaz SA. In Romania, petroleum royalties are set as a percentage of the gross extracted output value.

The tax system base for hydrocarbon production is determined by the contractual form. It sets rights and obligations for investors and the state, for each hydrocarbon exploration, development and production project. Globally there are three main types of legal arrangements (three major tolling systems), with differences regarding property titles on the exploited resources and how taxes paid to the state are determined: (i) concession, (ii) production sharing contract, and (iii) service contract (some countries use a combination of these three basic systems).

The first system is the concessions system. The concessions system is the most widespread, being implemented in most OECD member states, particularly in Europe, Australia and North America, countries with tax systems and modern and stable legislation. Thus, subsoil resources belong to the state (and sometimes belong to private individuals) who grants exploration, development and operation rights to an investor for a payment.

Exploited hydrocarbons become the investor's property after their extraction, and the investor pays royalties to the state. The concession system is more flexible from the state point of view. This system, based on royalties, applied in Romania too, is used in countries like Russia, the United States, Canada, Brazil and Nigeria. Percentages are usually much higher, over 17%, and in some cases combined with other tolling arrangements.

The second option is the participation of the state in dividing the results. It refers either to delivering the state a part of the extracted oil, or compensating it in cash. The method is similar to that used in Romania in the 90s. Countries that apply it are generally African countries or in the Caspian Sea area.

The third option is the over taxation of the profit. It refers either to the difference between the market price and the production cost, or to exceeding a predetermined rate of return, varying from one country to another. Among the countries that apply this system the most important are Australia, Norway and the UK.

The fourth option, used in the Middle East, China or Algeria, is the exploitation of oil either by owned-state companies, or in partnership with the state.

The second system is based on production sharing, when the investor assumes the risk while the state receives a share of the oil production after the company recovers its investment. In the case of production-sharing contracts, resources belong to the state, but once exploited, hydrocarbon production is divided between the investor and the state.

In the first phase, the investor has the rights to a certain volume of the production required to recover the investment and the operating costs (the so-called "cost oil"), which sometimes includes a royalty payment to the state. Subsequently, additional production (the so-called "profit oil") is divided between the investor (who gains a profit) and the state, either in effective quantities, or at market value of that production volume.

This system is used mainly in Arab countries, in Asia and in some parts of the African continent, whose legislative stability is reduced, and the state may even take 70% of the deposit's production. Ukraine uses this system of taxation, too. In these circumstances, investors are looking for safety, and this type of contract offers it to a large extent because contractual terms are fixed and cannot be changed unilaterally by the government, unlike a law at national level applicable to all industries that can be amended unilaterally by the state (as in the case of concessions).

At the end of the contractual period, investments (equipment, infrastructure, etc.) remain in the state's ownership. At the same time, the state assumes any decontamination obligations, which can be expensive. The dispute of nearly two decades between the government of Ecuador and Texaco (later acquired by Chevron, in 2001) is a good example regarding the risks assumed by the state in connection with decontamination operations.

However, we should specify that this system is used especially for huge deposits in countries with considerable hydrocarbon reserves.

The third system is based on service contracts, when companies exploiting resources are committed to the state in its name and for its benefit (while hydrocarbons remain in state ownership), in exchange for a fee. Service contracts are used in countries such as Iran and Mexico, and the latter consider giving up this system because it does not provide sufficiently attractive prospects for the development of its hydrocarbon extraction sector.

2. Methodology and data

Given these elements, the most important question that arises is, in fact, which is the most suitable tolling system applicable to the oil and gas industry? Unfortunately, there is no unequivocal answer to this question, no "best" formula applicable to all producing countries. But, as a fundamental principle, such a system must maximize the gain of the state and draw and maintain capital and technology investments.

There are large geological, geographic, geopolitical and economic differences between oil and gas producing regions. The geological characteristics concern the existence of resources in one country's subsoil and the properties of those deposits, while the geographical characteristics concern their acessibility. Geopolitical characteristics concern the degrees of freedom policy and risk arising from the geographic proximity of a state, while economic characteristics concern factors such as the ratio between the resources demand and consumption, the industrial development profile, the market maturity, etc.

These characteristics determine the options and strategic constraints spectrum of a state. In this spectrum, resource exploitation management policies must be based on a national energy strategy that will provide development and long-term priorities and objectives. Very important for our analysis is that each deposit is different, the more each country is different.

Thus, depending on the deposits structure, Romania looks like Italy, both having a high degree of exhaustion of its deposits. Romania's hydrocarbon deposits are depleted in a proportion of 87%. According to a study by PwC, for an onshore deposit with a production up to 30,000 tons of oil per year, the average royalty rate is 3.3%, compared to 3.5% in Romania. Eni Group, the largest oil company in Italy, paid a royalty of 8% in 2012, while the average royalty in Romania was about 7–8%. The difference was because income tax is 27.5% in Italy, plus a regional tax of 3.9%. In Romania, there is a flat tax of 16%.

Depending on the operating costs level, Romania can be compared to the UK, where this cost is 23 dollars per barrel, compared to 17 dollars in our country. The average maturity of the deposits is similar, with 82% for British; the main difference is that in the UK, 99% of operations are offshore. Moreover, in our country, OMV Petrom SA, Exxon, Lukoil and other companies have plans to operate in the Black Sea continental shelf. The British state imposes a 50% tax on oil revenues, plus an overcharge of 32%. There is, however, a system of deductions that push the taxation down to 15%. However, in 2015, the UK government has reduced this surcharge, from the current 32% to 30%, hinting that further reductions could arise. In addition, the Executive in London will extend the deductibility tax for initial investments in new projects for oil and gas offshore exploitations in the North Sea, and will also increase tax incentives for companies that develop more offshore hydrocarbon deposits operating under difficult conditions, isolated, located deep underground, or requiring very expensive technologies.

Regarding the production level, Romania can be compared to Denmark, a country where a nominal tax of 52% is used, but is actually only 18%. In our country, the average is 7–8%, so there are European countries that collect at least double. Beyond the passions, especially among drivers and auto carriers, a glance at the royalties' level used in other European countries highlights the fiscal easing the Romanian state has promoted since 1990 and up today in this field. In combination with an income tax of just 16%, they make Romania one of the countries where it is most convenient to extract oil.

From these examples, it appears that through this analysis only it is very difficult to identify the best fiscal regime in the oil and gas industry as a result of comparison, because there are many risks when comparing fiscal and regulatory regimes, but also because there are European countries situated at different levels compared to Romania regarding economic and oil and gas sector maturity.

In our country, the current oil and gas royalties represent percentage shares of gross extracted output value, which were established in 2004 with the Oil Law.

For crude oil, royalties are 3.5% for deposits that produce less than 10,000 tons/quarter, 5% for deposits that produce between 10,000 and 20,000 tons/quarter, 7% for deposits that produce between 20,000 and 100,000 tons/quarter, and 13.5% for deposits producing more than 100,000 tons/quarter.

For natural gas royalties are 3.5% for deposits that produce less than one million cubic meters/quarter, 7.5% for deposits producing between one and five million cubic meters/quarter, 9% for deposits producing between five and 20 million cubic meters/quarter, and 13% for deposits producing more than 20 million cubic meters/quarter.

Hence, in Romania there is an average royalty of 7–8% of total revenues in the upstream sector, as previously mentioned.

Given the limitations mentioned above, which may affect the results, computing a simple arithmetic average for the European producing countries in 2014 resulted in 12.2%, while the average of most comparable European producing countries, based on well productivity, was 6.9%. In Romania, the average share of observable royalties and similar taxes, as a percentage of revenues, was 13.9%, represented especially by the contributions of the major companies, SNGN Romgaz SA and OMV Petrom SA, with 19.6% and 12.4 % respectively.

A similar calculation for European producing countries in 2015 resulted in 11.7%, while the average of most comparable European producing countries, based on well productivity, was 7.5%. In Romania, the average share of observable royalties and similar taxes, as a percentage of revenues, was 15.0%, represented especially by the contributions of the major companies, SNGN Romgaz SA and OMV Petrom SA, with 21.1% and 13.2% respectively.

Using similar calculations, by 30 June 2016, the average share of observable royalties and similar taxes, as a percentage of revenues, was 15.7%, represented especially by the contributions of the major companies, SNGN Romgaz SA and OMV Petrom SA with 19.3% and 14.1% respectively.

In Romania, this trend comes mainly from: the higher proportion of gas compared to oil; the overall production mix, gas being taxed with a supplementary tax of 60% on price increase resulting from the liberalization calendar, although oil prices declined in the second half of 2014, a trend that continued in 2015, too. The royalties charge formula uses a reference price of the average quotations from the previous three months (in a declining market this resulted in a higher percentage of royalties).

Under these conditions, total oil and mining royalties collected by the state in 2014 amounted to 1.64 billion lei, of which only those from oil and gas were 1.36 billion lei. Most of the royalties were paid by SNGN Romgaz SA and OMV Petrom SA. In 2015, the Romanian state received almost 10% less money from royalties compared to 2014. This fall was caused by drastic adjustments to the amounts paid by OMV Petrom SA mainly on the exploitation of oil reserves, in particular because of huge oil price decreases on international markets; on the other hand, compared to 2014, royalties on gas and mineral resources increased. Thus, in 2015, revenues from oil and gas royalties amounted to 990 million lei, while the mining royalties amounted to 230 million lei, giving a total of 1.22 billion lei received as royalties from extractive industries. Instead, for 2016, the National Agency for Mineral Resources (NAMR) estimated that it will collect taxes and royalties amounting to 1.5 billion lei from mining, and oil and gas.

We must emphasize that according to the discussions held at governmental level, the new tolling system of natural resources will be set for 20 years, compared to only ten years at this time, and taxes on oil and gas extraction activities will rise to 35%, with a 15% deduction for new investments. The tax on extractive activities will be called "oil tax", and will replace a number of temporary taxes the government introduced in 2013, namely the 60% tax on the liberalization of gas prices and 0.5% tax on extraction operations. Also, from 2017 the pole charge will be removed, which is 1% of the total assets, according to the new Fiscal Code. Thus, starting with 2017, oil and gas companies will pay the 16% tax on profits, like any other company operating in Romania, plus the 35% oil tax (mentioned above). Simultaneously, the government will eliminate a number of fiscal facilities introduced in 1999, enabling companies, in the present, to not pay taxes on oil and gas, and to not pay customs export commissions. Also, companies will still pay the royalties at today's percentage levels.

3. Results

From the analysis of previous elements, in our opinion, one can say that a new hydrocarbon tolling system could adopt a differentiated royalty system, based on two pillars—for the existing operations and for the new ones.

For oil and gas resources already in operation, charging might be to a level close to the EU average, through a system of fixed amount recognized costs, while the remaining so-called "super-profits" become public budget revenue. Such a policy would have as an effect increased revenues compared to the (ridiculous) level at present, on the one hand, and natural on-going calibration of oil and gas extracted volumes, on the other.

Thus, under the conditions of high oil prices on international markets, the wells would operate close to their maximum potential, providing some autonomy to external shocks; as the price falls, the wells with weaker potential and higher costs become unprofitable and automatically go into conservation so that resources are protected until the well's restarting proves to be necessary. As a result, a higher volatility is predictable for economic activities generated by OMV Petrom SA and SNGN Romgaz SA businesses, but this could be offset by increased explorations activity as supplementary tax incentives may be introduced.

For future oil and gas operations, where prospecting and exploration activities are needed, implying high costs and high risk, more suitable is a flexible structure that gives a better perspective for expenses depreciation to potential investors. Among the many existing accounting schemes, the simplest seems to be the complete exemption from paying royalties for a specified number of years, until the full recovery of the initial investment, following that just as the term expires to apply the tolling system available to resources exploitation, as mentioned above.

Moreover, we believe that the new hydrocarbon tolling system should also provide different levels of royalties from onshore and offshore exploitations, as investments in offshore oil extraction are significantly higher compared to those for onshore wells, the risks are higher, and the rate of return on investment is lower. Also, there should be differentiations between shallow and deep marine deposits, because of differences in costs involved. Simultaneously, besides royalties, an overcharge on profits from extraction activity of companies operating in the oil and gas industry might be introduced, and a series of deductions for investments in this segment.

However, the effects of the application of a new tolling system are: increasing contribution to consolidated state budget; efficient management of the productive potential of existing deposits and sustainable use of internal oil and gas resources; and increasing foreign direct investment inflows in oil and gas extraction, particularly in the Black Sea continental shelf.

Under these circumstances, the new tolling system would affect both OMV Petrom SA and SNGN Romgaz SA, and other blocks' concessionaires from Romania, such as ExxonMobil, Lukoil, NIS Petrol, Rompetrol, Stratum Energy, MOL or the Carlyle Group. At the same time, the shape of this future tolling system is vital for exploiting oil and gas deposits in the Black Sea continental shelf.

Conclusions and recommendations

In recent years several discussions dealt with raising the level of royalties, but so far, no decision has been taken. There were a number of projects that remained only on paper, while the companies that extract the natural resources of our country still pay a too small amount of money to the state budget.

The tolling system related to resource exploration had to be changed as of 2016, but the Ministry of Finance failed to establish, in 2015, the new method for computing the royalties that companies have to pay. Therefore, during 2016 the Ministry of Economy said that in the near future Romania will have a new bill on oil and gas royalties, which should be applied starting in 2017.

The decision taken in previous years not to apply new oil and gas royalties, was taken after the International Monetary Fund (IMF) warned the Romanian authorities to address this issue with cautious treatment. In a press release, dated October 2015, the IMF stressed that the new natural resource tolling regime should be calibrated carefully, to ensure a balance between stimulating investment, on the one hand, and the state obtaining the part that it deserves from such income, on the other.

Under these circumstances, Romania needs a tolling system for the oil and gas industry with effective moderate rates, close to countries with similar profiles (i.e., Italy's 8% of revenues, France's 4% of revenues), to attract investors in this field. Also, Romania should keep the concession system, applicable in all OECD countries.

Taxation of income in this sector is most appropriate for the country's economic development in the short, medium and long term, involving lower costs for tax administration, predictability both for investors and the state, and steady income to the public budget exactly from the start of operating the deposits. This system is transparent and easily understood by the public. Moreover, the system could be more flexible in order to accommodate production requirements for various deposits, possibly by granting tax deductions or other incentives for investment.

On the other hand, a tolling system based on profit is not suitable for conventional deposits currently in operation in Romania, given that the profitability level of a deposit is difficult to determine. This is caused by the existence of common installations and equipments that operate and service several deposits, by the challenges related to transfer prices between separate business units for vertically-integrated companies and by the difficulty in determining the precise costs recorded in the past with the deposits' development and operation.

It should be borne in mind that investments in the hydrocarbon extraction sector are long term, with a seven to ten year horizon for their recovery. Hence, Romania must ensure a legal, regulatory and fiscal framework, stable, transparent, predictable and competitive for the development of the oil and gas industry, while maintaining a high degree of energy independence.

The effects of any tolling system must be weighed against the impact on current production, whether it encourages or discourages the development of marginal deposits, how investors' willingness to continue or abandon their operations is affected, the sensitivity both to oil and gas prices, and to cost variations. There is no comprehensive system available. However, the need remains for a valid fiscal and regulatory environment, attractive, predictable and stable, regardless of the stage the hydrocarbon industry is at in any country.

References

1. Agalliu, I. (2011). Comparative Assessment of the Federal Oil and Gas Fiscal System: Final Report, 178–242, http://www.energy.senate.gov/public/index.cfm/files/serve?File_id=d174971 c-4682-4d96-b194-a85fa2b86774.
2. *Crude Oil Royalty Rates in Selected Countries*, The Law Library of Congress, Global Legal Research Center, January 2015, http://www.law.gov.
3. EY, "Global Oil and Tax Guide 2014", http://www.ey.com/Publication/vwLUAssets/EY-Global-oil-and-gas-tax-guide-2014/$FILE/EY-Global-oil-and-gas-tax-guide-2014.pdf.
4. Hogan, L., Goldsworthy, B. (2010). International Mineral Taxation: Experience and Issues, in *The Taxation of Petroleum and Minerals: Principles, Problems and Practice* 122, 131–32 (Philip Daniel, Michael Keen & Charles McPherson eds., 2010), http://lccn.loc.gov/2009047902.
5. Iuga, V. (2014). Petroleum Royalties from Romania between dubious arrangements and unconsciousness, PricewaterhouseCoopers Romania, September 02, 2014.
6. "Observation on royalties and similar taxes – An updated overview of Oil and gas upstream in Europe", Deloitte Romania, September 2015, https://www2.deloitte.com/content/dam/ Deloitte/ro/Documents/energy-resources/Deloitte-Royalties-upstream-September-2015.pdf.

7. *Oil Law*, No. 238 of June 15, 2004, Monitorul Oficial [Official Gazette] 2004, Part I, No. 535, art. 49.
8. www.omvpetrom.com, "Financial statements of OMV Petrom SA", 2014, 2015 and H1 2016.
9. www.romgaz.ro, "Financial statements of SNGN Romgaz SA", 2014, 2015 and H1 2016.

Georgeta-Madalina MEGHIŞAN

University of Craiova, Faculty of Economics and Business Administration, Craiova, Romania, Romanian Academy, National Institute of Economic Research "Costin C. Kiriţescu", Bucharest, Romania; email: madalina_meghisan@yahoo.com

Assessment of State-Owned Enterprises from Romania

Abstract: The research analyzes the activity of the state-owned companies from Romania and their place in the economic development of a country. Further attention will be paid to the analysis of the market as the place where the private enterprises and state-owned enterprises meet in particular branches of the economy. This research study is completed with an analysis of the current situation of state-owned companies from Romania in the contemporary economy, with conclusions that further underline their evolution. The results will reveal the importance of the management activity for these companies based on certified results and will represent a starting point for further research within this field.

Keywords: State-owned enterprises, Romania's economic branches, management activities, market perspectives

Introduction

"Emerging destinations are playing an increasingly important role in the competitive tourism market" (Claveria, 2016). This study aims to underline the evolution of the state-owned tourism companies on the Romanian market for the year 2015. Several research results "noted that one of the limitations of most tourism studies is the omission of economic indicators and the lack of attention paid to economic return" (Song et al., 2012).

This approach focuses on a regression model based on the following variables: Gross domestic product at market prices (GDP) and turnover in services (TURNO), put in a time series between 2006 and 2015. In a first step, we project these elements on maps representing the dynamics on the Romanian market during the 2006–2015 period. The second step of the research consists in constructing the regression model based on the above-mentioned variables.

1. Literature review

Several studies were conducted in tourism research, focusing on the analysis of groups of countries. Lozano and Gutierrez (2011) analyzed 25 European destinations using the Multidimensional Scaling (MDS) technique, summarizing the information of the following indicators: size of tourism industry and efficiency/weather.

Marcussen (2011) conducted a research to position 33 European destinations grouped by major language spheres, by combining MDS and factor analysis (FA). Claveria (2016) positioned and clustered 20 emerging markets, combining tourism and economic information.

From an economical point of view, other studies underline the importance of CDS's sovereign instrument for providing "important information about the evolution of a country risk as it is perceived by the financial markets" (Hurduzeu et al., 2015), especially by the credit market. For this point of view, Cristea and Dracea (2010) stated that a great influence on real GDP is given by the credit market. Acatrinei et al. (2013) conducted a study in order to "derive conclusions about investors' keenness to move capital to the Eastern Europe countries", with potential impact on the economy. The impact of the macroeconomic variables and the main results of pension funds, as an important component of the financial market, were also analyzed for privately managed pension funds (Cristea et al., 2011) and for voluntary ones (Cristea and Siminica, 2012). This demonstrated that knowing the impact of economic conjuncture on the results obtained in a field of the economy is very useful for fast and effective interventions. To reveal the connection between the insurance field and economic growth in Romania, using GDP as macroeconomic indicator Cristea et al. (2009, p. 135) demonstrated that "there is a strong correlation based on causality relation between the insurance market and economic growth". However, there is a "need for coordination the fiscal and budgetary policies in Romania" (Marcu and Meghisan, 2011) for the economic stability of a country. Moreover, for the Romanian economy, the financial sector has "a great importance for supporting economic growth". (Cristea et al., 2010).

On the other hand, some authors made research analyses on state-run companies. Marcu et al. (2016) conducted a research within the chemical industry, underlying the power of these state-run companies in this field. Tufan et al. (2007, p. 826) underline the importance of "Principal Component Analysis" when a field of economy is analyzed.

In this study, we analyze the connection between tourism and economic growth in Romania, with implications on state-run companies, using the regression model.

2. Data Description and Methodology

The study focuses on Romania's services market. First, we constructed the dataset using Eurostat as a source of information. Tourism indicator includes: Turnover in services (2010=100) (index); economic information includes: Gross domestic product at market prices in chain-linked volumes (2010) (million euro). All the data in the panel regression model is in annual frequency and takes into consideration the 2006–2015 period (Table 1).

Table 1: Variables definition

Variable	Definition of the variable	Time series
GDP	Gross domestic product at market prices in chain-linked volumes in Romania (2010) (million euro)	2006–2015
TURNO	Turnover in services in Romania (2010=100) (index)	2006–2015

Source: Own processed data

The next step in our research is to determine whether the data is stationary or seasonal. For the analysis of the seasonality of GDP during the 2006–2015 period, we designed the graphic in Figure 1. For the analysis of the seasonality of turnover in services during the 2006–2015 period, we designed the graphic in Figure 2. The results from both figures (1 and 2) show that there is a seasonality of the data series. We can suspect that the data is not stationary, it has an upward trend.

Thus, the next stage in our research of the seasonality of the data series consists in the analysis of the correlogram at the initial data level. If we analyze the results from Annex 1: Q-Stat, the figures are not zero, they are consistent. Thus, we can suspect that our varriable is not stationary; Prob- there is one value of 0.019 < 0.05. We can reject H0. The variable is stationary and accept H1. The variable is not stationary. The results from Annex show: Q-Stat figures are different from zero. We can suppose that our variable is not stationary; Prob- there is one value of 0.005 < 0.05. We can reject H0. The variable is stationary and we can accept H1; the variable is not stationary.

Fig. 1: The evolution of GDP in Romania, for the 2006–2015 period

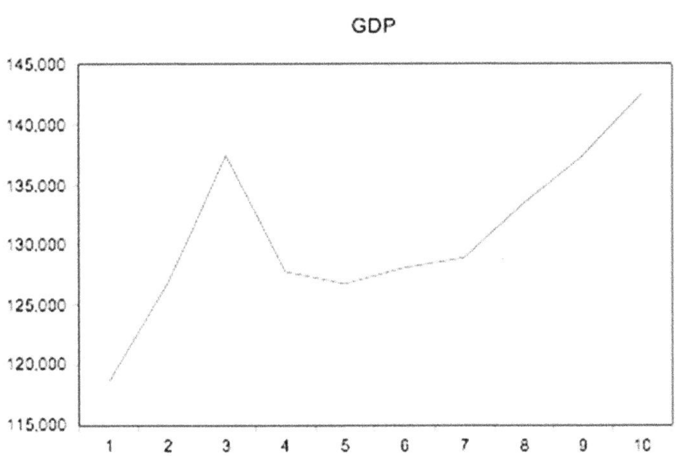

Source: *Own processed data, under those published on the website of Eurostat*

Fig. 2: The evolution of turnover in services in Romania, for the 2006–2015 period

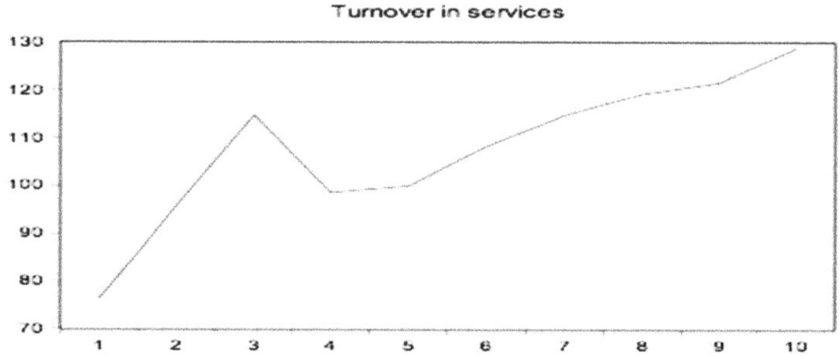

Source: *Own processed data, under those published on the website of Eurostat*

When converting the variable into first difference, the autocorrelation function (AC) becomes very small (Annex 3 and Annex 4). According to the Annex 3 results, AR (autocorrelation function) has become very small. Probably the variable has become stationary, there is almost no autocorrelation; P values are > 5%. We cannot reject H0. The variable is stationary, it has no trend. According to the Annex 4, AR (autocorrelation function) has become very small. Probably the variable has become stationary, there is almost no autocorrelation; P values are > 5%. We cannot reject H0. The variable is stationary, it has no trend.

The method used to estimate the parameters is Least Squares (NLS and ARIMA): the dependent variable D_GDP and the independent variable D_TURNO. The results of GDP estimation show (Table 2): R-squared > 60%. In the present analysis, R-squared is 86.44%. The variation of GDP can be explained by the variable turnover in services. The variable turnover in services has an influence of 86.44%; P value < 0.05. In the present example, P value = 0.0003. The variable (turnover in services) is significant and influences the dependent variable (GDP); Prob (F-statistic) <0.05. The independent variable should be significant to explain the dependent variable. In our case, P (F-Statistic) = 0.000282. The signs of the coefficients are following the economic theory. When the turnover in services undertakes a raise of a unity, the GDP increases with 520.77 unities.

Table 2: The results of GDP estimation

Dependent Variable: D_GDP				
Method: Least Squares				
Date: 10/04/16 Time: 02:06				
Sample (adjusted): 2 10				
Included observations: 9 after adjustments				
Variable	**Coefficient**	**Std. Error**	**t-Statistic**	**Prob.**
C	-383.2097	897.9699	-0.426751	0.6824
D_TURNO	520.7716	77.94074	6.681636	0.0003
R-squared	0.864457	Mean dependent var		2660.411
Adjusted R-squared	0.845094	S.D. dependent var		5898.570
S.E. of regression	2321.564	Akaike info criterion		18.53100
Sum squared resid	37727624	Schwarz criterion		18.57483
Log likelihood	-81.38950	Hannan-Quinn criter.		18.43642
F-statistic	44.64426	Durbin-Watson stat		1.037228
Prob(F-statistic)	0.000282			

Source: Own processed data under EViews program

The residual can be calculated as the actual GDP minus estimated GDP. Other variables that are not included in the model can influence the dependent variable (residus) (Annex 5).

For the residuals analysis, several rules should be obeyed (Tables 3 and 4, Figure 3). There should not be serial correlations in the residual. According to the Breusch-Godfrey Serial Correlation LM Test, Prob. Chi-Square = 0.1831 ($P > 0.05$). There is no serial correlation (Table 3).

Table 3: Breusch-Godfrey Serial Correlation LM Test

Breusch-Godfrey Serial Correlation LM Test:				
F-statistic	1.471272	Prob. F(1.6)		0.2707
Obs*R-squared	1.772315	Prob. Chi-Square(1)		0.1831
Test Equation:				
Dependent Variable: RESID				
Method: Least Squares				
Date: 10/04/16 Time: 02:23				
Sample: 2 10				
Included observations: 9				
Presample missing value lagged residuals set to zero.				
Variable	**Coefficient**	**Std. Error**	**t-Statistic**	**Prob.**
C	-67.09946	870.9462	-0.077042	0.9411
D_TURNO	28.05451	78.90833	0.355533	0.7344
RESID(-1)	0.487663	0.402044	1.212960	0.2707
R-squared	0.196924	Mean dependent var		-1.01E-13
Adjusted R-squared	-0.070768	S.D. dependent var		2171.625
S.E. of regression	2247.152	Akaike info criterion		18.53392
Sum squared resid	30298155	Schwarz criterion		18.59966
Log likelihood	-80.40262	Hannan-Quinn criter.		18.39205
F-statistic	0.735636	Durbin-Watson stat		1.634571
Prob(F-statistic)	0.517929			

Source: Own processed data under EViews program

There should not be heteroskedasticity in the residual. According to the Breusch-Pagan-Godfrey Heteroskedasticity Test, the Prob. Chi-Square is 0.8855 (P > 0.05) for Obs*R-Squared. We cannot reject H0. There is no heteroskedasticity in the results (Table 4).

Table 4: Heteroskedasticity Test

Heteroskedasticity Test: Breusch-Pagan-Godfrey				
F-statistic	0.016170	Prob. F(1.7)		0.9024
Obs*R-squared	0.020742	Prob. Chi-Square(1)		0.8855
Scaled explained SS	0.002744	Prob. Chi-Square(1)		0.9582
Test Equation:				
Dependent Variable: RESID^2				
Method: Least Squares				
Date: 10/04/16 Time: 02:24				
Sample: 2 10				
Included observations: 9				
Variable	**Coefficient**	**Std. Error**	**t-Statistic**	**Prob.**
C	4113616.	1214493.	3.387105	0.0116
D_TURNO	13404.57	105413.9	0.127161	0.9024
R-squared	0.002305	Mean dependent var		4191958.
Adjusted R-squared	-0.140223	S.D. dependent var		2940486.
S.E. of regression	3139887.	Akaike info criterion		32.95040
Sum squared resid	6.90E+13	Schwarz criterion		32.99423
Log likelihood	-146.2768	Hannan-Quinn criter.		32.85582
F-statistic	0.016170	Durbin-Watson stat		1.181900
Prob(F-statistic)	0.902388			

Source: Own processed data under EViews program

Residuals should be normally distributed. From the Histogram analysis, Probability = 0.6056 (P > 0.05) for Jarque-Bera test. We cannot reject H0. Residuals are normally distributed. (Figure 3).

Fig. 3: Histogram

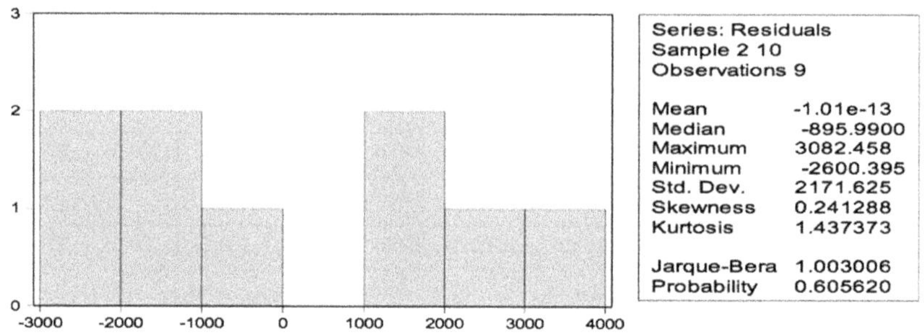

Source: *Own processed data under EViews program*

3. Results and discussion

According to the analysis made, the evolution of GDP in Romania is influenced by the independent variable: turnover in services. Regarding the services sector, we are interested in the tourism sector, especially the evolution of state-run companies in tourism, also influenced by consumers' cultural background. However, we have to underline the fact that "consumers from post-industrial economies evolved in a culture with omnipresent brands, in the market with companies continuously fighting to gain more visibility and attract consumers towards them" (Stancu and Meghisan, 2012), even though "choosing some services packages is sometimes very difficult due to the complexity of the offer" (Meghisan, 2012). Usually, the "selection of one brand over all other brands is a process of optimizing the consumers' utility" (Girboveanu et al., 2008). This concept can be successfully applied in the tourism industry, in the choice of hotels by the consumers. On the other hand, we have to underline the fact that "neuromarketing and the aggressive advertising have a contribution in altering the normal choice" (Meghisan and Meghisan, 2012) of the clients.

On the website of the Ministry of Economy, Commerce and Business Environment Relationships, there are 15 state-run companies (hotels) in its authority (Table 5).

Table 5: State-run companies in tourism in Romania

Nr. Crt.	State-run company name	Location in Romania	Available financial situation (year)
1.	SC IMOTRUST S.A.	Arad	2015
2.	S.C. BEGA TURISM S.A.	Timisoara	2015
3.	S.C. ROBINSON TURISM S.A.	Bucharest	2015
4.	S.C. LIDO S.A.	Bucharest	2015
5.	S.C. LITORAL S.A.	Mamaia (Constanta)	2015
6	S.C. MAMAIA S.A	Mamaia (Constanta)	2013
7.	S.C. NEPTUN-OLIMP S.A	Olimp (Constanta)	2015
8.	S.C. CARMEN SILVA S.A.	Eforie Sud (Constanta)	-
9.	S.C. ANCA-IRINA S.A.	Venus (Constanta)	2015
10.	S.C. CIUCAS S.A.	Baile Tusnad (Harghita)	2015
11.	S.C. HOTEL COTA 1400 S.A.	Sinaia (Prahova)	-
12.	S.C. GERMISARA S.A.	Geoagiu-Bai (Hunedoara)	2015
13.	S.C. T.H.R. MAREA NEAGRA S.A.	Mangalia (Constanta)	2015
14.	S.C. IEZERUL S.A.	Borsa (Maramures)	2015
15.	S.C. PREDEAL S.A.	Predeal (Brasov)	2015

Source: Own processed data, under those published on the website of www.mfinante.ro

Making the analysis of the turnover of these companies for the year 2015, we could observe that five of the twelve state-run companies had no activity during the year 2015: Lido Co., Litoral Co., Anca-Irina Co., Ciucas Co. and Predeal Co. (Annex 6).

If there was no economic performance in terms of turnover for five state-run companies within the tourism field in Romania, this fact implied the registration of loss for these companies. However, the top of the most profitable state-run companies from Romaina in tourism for the year 2015 is made of: Bega-Turism Co. (11,409,738 RON), Imotrust Co. (8,508,828 RON), T.H.R. Marea Neagra Co. (3,418,3784 RON), Robinson Turism Co. (144,643 RON), Germisara Co. (43,834 RON) and Cicas Co. (4,887 RON) (Annex 7).

When analyzing the total incomes and the total costs for the state-run companies in Romania's tourism field during the year 2015, we could observe that the total incomes exceeded the total costs for only six companies: Imotrust Co., Bega Turism Co., Robinson Turismn Co., Ciucas Co., Germisara Co. and T.H.R. Marea Neagra Co. (Annex 8).

Even though some state-run companies in Romania in the tourism field had incomes higher than costs, and their registered profit and turnover exceeded zero, during the year 2015, all of them had important amounts of debts during (Annex 9).

Making an analysis of the number of employees for the state-run companies, we can observe that it varies from zero to 354 persons (Annex 10).

4. Conclusions

According to the results of the research analysis, the evolution of GDP in Romania is influenced by the independent variable: turnover in services. The turnover in services can also be based on the turnover in tourism. Our further analysis underlined the profitability for the year 2015 of state-run companies in Romania that act in the tourism field. We could observe that only half of them are profitable. However, for three of them we could not find any published financial data. Romania is a country with perspectives in tourism and also with perspectives of growth for these state-run companies, with the condition that the persons that are put in the management position of these companies are specialists with certified results in the management of other companies. An important influence on the state-run companies' economic performances is made by the evolution of the labor market from Romania. "During the financial crisis of 2008–2009, the country's labor force suffered major changes and currently the country is trying to improve its macroeconomic situation" (Marcu et al., 2015). The employed residents of a country have a major contribution to the profitability of the tourism industry. This study can be enlarged by making forecasts regarding the evolutions of these state-run companies, based on the "bankruptcy prognosis model regarding Romanian companies" developed by Siminica et al. (2009). Another proposition for further study is the analysis of the "risk imperative", a concept developed by the authors Marcu and Sitnikov (2009).

References

1. Acatrinei, M., Gorun, A., Marcu, N. (2013). A DCC_GARCH Model to Estimate the Risk to the Capital Market in Romania, *Romanian Journal of Economic Forecasting*, 1/2013, pp. 136–149 http://www.ipe.ro/rjef/rjef1_13/rjef1_2013p136-148.pdf.
2. Buşe, L., Siminică, M., Cîrciumaru, D., Marcu, N. (2007). Analiza economico-financiară a firmei, Ed. Sitech, Craiova, Romania.
3. Cîrciumaru, D., Siminică, M., Marcu, N. (2010). A study on return on equity of Romanian industrial companies, *Annals of University of Craiova, Economic Sciences Series*, no.38/2010, pp. 38–46.
4. Claveria, O. (2016). Positioning emerging tourism markets using tourism and economic indicators, Journal of Hospitality and Tourism Management, 29:143–153.
5. Cristea, M., Dracea, R. (2010). Does credit market accelerate economic growth in Romania? Statistical approaches. *Finance - Challenges of the Future*, 11:184–190.

6. Cristea, M., Dracea, R., Marcu, N. (2010). The direction of Financial Sector Involvement in Overcoming Crisis: Case Study in Romania, *African Journal of Business Management,* 4 (15):3356–3365.
7. Cristea, M., Dracea, R., Tomescu, I. (2009). The economic significance of insurance market. Statistical study in Romania. *Metalurgia international,* XIV (16):131–137.
8. Cristea, M., Siminică, M. (2012). Study on the dynamics of voluntary private pension fund assets in Romania. *African Journal of Business Management, 6*(21):6347–6357. doi: 10.5897/AJBM11.309.
9. Cristea M. Siminică, M., Drăcea, R. (2011). Fluctuation in pension fund assets privately managed under the influence of certain factors. Statistical study in Romania. *Conference Proceedings "European Integration – New Challenges"*, Oradea, Romania, 2011, May 27–28, pp. 1086–1097.
10. Gîrboveanu, S-P., Craciun, L., Meghisan, G.M. (2008). The role of advertising in the purchase decision process, Analele Universității din Oradea (Annals of the University of Oradea), TOM XVII, vol. IV, 2008, pp. 897.
11. Hurduzeu, G., Musetescu, R. C., Meghisan, GM (2015). Financial market reaction to changes in the volatilities of CDS returns, Journal for Economic Forecasting, 3:152–165.
12. Lozano, S., Gutierrez, E. (2011). Efficiency analysis of EU-25 member states as tourist destinations, International Journal of Services Technology and Management, 15(1/2):69–88.
13. Marcu, N., Siminică, M., Cristea, M., Dascălu, D. (2016). The Analysis of the Correlation Regarding the Chemical Industry Main Results in Romania. Experimental Study, *Revista de Chimie,* 67(3):589–593.
14. Marcu, N. / Meghisan, G.M. (2015). Research on Romanian Labour Market Dynamics, *Revista de Chmie (Chemistry Journal),* 66 (9), 2015, pp. 1540–1544.
15. Marcu, N., Meghisan, M. (2011). The Need for Public Debt Management in the Context of Sustainable Development within the European Union, Conference *Proceedings "European Integration – New Challenges"*, 27–28 May 2011, Oradea, Romania, pp. 365–371.
16. Marcu, N., Sitnikov, C. (2009). The new risk imperative—an enterprise wide approach, *Revista Metalurgia International,* vol. XIV (2009), 2009, pp. 54–60.
17. Marcussen, C.H. (2011). Visualising groups of European destinations, *European Journal of Travel Research,* 4(2):180–190.
18. Meghisan, G-M. (2012). *Strategies on the mobile telecommunications market from Romania.* Aachen, Germany: Shaker Verlag Publishing House, 2012.
19. Meghisan, G-M., Meghisan, F. (2012). Marketing study regarding Romanian consumers' behavior towards fast-food products, *Procedia Economics and Finance,* 3:397–402.
20. Siminica, M., Marcu, N., Bandoi, A. (2009). The development of a bankruptcy prognosis model regarding Romanian companies between theory and practice. *Revista Metalurgia* International, vol. XIV, special issue no. 7:114–117.

21. Song, H., Dwyer, L., Li, G., Cao, Z. (2012). Tourism economics research: A review and assessment, *Annals of Tourism Research*, 39(3):1653–1682.
22. Stancu, I., Meghisan, G.M. (2012). Marketing study regarding consumers' behavior towards Auchan hypermarkets from Romania. *Procedia Economics and Finance* 3, 2012, pp. 502–508.
23. Tufan, E., Hamarat, B., Cristea, M., Giurcă-Vasilescu, L. (2007). Evaluation of Turkish domestic and foreign banks by using financial ratios. *The 11th International Conference on the Finance and Banking, "Future of the European Monetary Integration"*, Silesian University, School of Business Administration, Karvina, Czech Republic, 2007, Oct 17–18, pp. 814–829.

Annex 1: Correlogram of GDP

Date: 10/04/16 Time: 01:48						
Sample: 1 10						
Included observations: 10						
Autocorrelation	**Partial Correlation**		**AC**	**PAC**	**Q-Stat**	**Prob**
. |** . |	. |** . |	1	0.277	0.277	1.0255	0.311
. *| . |	. **| . |	2	-0.158	-0.255	1.4010	0.496
. | . |	. |* . |	3	-0.024	0.118	1.4106	0.703
. | . |	. *| . |	4	-0.044	-0.135	1.4497	0.836
. | . |	. | . |	5	-0.021	0.063	1.4605	0.918
. | . |	. | . |	6	0.048	0.004	1.5300	0.957
. | . |	. | . |	7	0.045	0.038	1.6125	0.978
. **| . |	.***| . |	8	-0.294	-0.372	6.8045	0.558
. **| . |	. *| . |	9	-0.329	-0.098	19.823	0.019

Source: Own processed data under EViews program

Annex 2: Correlogram of turnover in services

Date: 10/04/16 Time: 01:56						
Sample: 1 10						
Included observations: 10						
Autocorrelation	**Partial Correlation**		**AC**	**PAC**	**Q-Stat**	**Prob**
. |*** . |	. |*** . |	1	0.388	0.388	2.0054	0.157
. | . |	. *| . |	2	0.056	-0.111	2.0531	0.358
. |* . |	. |** . |	3	0.180	0.237	2.6109	0.456
. | . |	. *| . |	4	0.040	-0.155	2.6424	0.619
. *| . |	. *| . |	5	-0.145	-0.100	3.1466	0.677
. **| . |	. *| . |	6	-0.212	-0.183	4.4936	0.610
. *| . |	. | . |	7	-0.178	-0.040	5.7545	0.569
. **| . |	. **| . |	8	-0.321	-0.283	11.942	0.154
. **| . |	. | . |	9	-0.309	-0.043	23.385	0.005

Source: Own processed data under EViews program, according to Table 1 from Appendices

Annex 3: Correlogram of D(GDP)

Date: 10/04/16 Time: 01:51						
Sample: 1 10						
Included observations: 9						
Autocorrelation	**Partial Correlation**		**AC**	**PAC**	**Q-Stat**	**Prob**
. | . |	. | . |	1	-0.002	-0.002	5.E-05	0.994
. **| . |	. **| . |	2	-0.268	-0.268	1.0142	0.602
. *| . |	. *| . |	3	-0.077	-0.084	1.1110	0.774
. *| . |	. **| . |	4	-0.192	-0.289	1.8432	0.765
. *| . |	. *| . |	5	-0.072	-0.157	1.9704	0.853
. | . |	. **| . |	6	-0.036	-0.246	2.0139	0.918
. |* . |	. *| . |	7	0.098	-0.066	2.4854	0.928
. | . |	. *| . |	8	0.049	-0.166	2.7241	0.950

Source: Own processed data under EViews program, according to Table 1 from Appendices

Annex 4: Correlogram of D(TURNO)

<table>
<tr><td colspan="3">Date: 10/04/16 Time: 01:57</td><td></td><td></td><td></td><td></td></tr>
<tr><td colspan="3">Sample: 1 10</td><td></td><td></td><td></td><td></td></tr>
<tr><td colspan="3">Included observations: 9</td><td></td><td></td><td></td><td></td></tr>
<tr><th>Autocorrelation</th><th>Partial Correlation</th><th></th><th>AC</th><th>PAC</th><th>Q-Stat</th><th>Prob</th></tr>
<tr><td>. | .|</td><td>. | .|</td><td>1</td><td>-0.025</td><td>-0.025</td><td>0.0080</td><td>0.929</td></tr>
<tr><td>.****| .|</td><td>.****| .|</td><td>2</td><td>-0.478</td><td>-0.479</td><td>3.2369</td><td>0.198</td></tr>
<tr><td>. | .|</td><td>. *| .|</td><td>3</td><td>-0.050</td><td>-0.104</td><td>3.2783</td><td>0.351</td></tr>
<tr><td>. |* .|</td><td>. *| .|</td><td>4</td><td>0.102</td><td>-0.178</td><td>3.4840</td><td>0.480</td></tr>
<tr><td>. | .|</td><td>. | .|</td><td>5</td><td>0.069</td><td>-0.014</td><td>3.6016</td><td>0.608</td></tr>
<tr><td>. *| .|</td><td>. *| .|</td><td>6</td><td>-0.105</td><td>-0.180</td><td>3.9686</td><td>0.681</td></tr>
<tr><td>. | .|</td><td>. | .|</td><td>7</td><td>-0.033</td><td>-0.032</td><td>4.0222</td><td>0.777</td></tr>
<tr><td>. | .|</td><td>. *| .|</td><td>8</td><td>0.021</td><td>-0.136</td><td>4.0653</td><td>0.851</td></tr>
</table>

Source: Own processed data under EViews program, according to Table 1 from Appendices

Annex 5: Residuals

<table>
<tr><th>Obs</th><th>Actual</th><th>Fitted</th><th>Residual</th><th>Residual Plot</th></tr>
<tr><td>2</td><td>8141.60</td><td>9771.84</td><td>-1630.24</td><td>| . * | . |</td></tr>
<tr><td>3</td><td>10722.6</td><td>9511.45</td><td>1211.15</td><td>| . | * . |</td></tr>
<tr><td>4</td><td>-9715.70</td><td>-8819.71</td><td>-895.990</td><td>| . * | . |</td></tr>
<tr><td>5</td><td>-1020.10</td><td>345.871</td><td>-1365.97</td><td>| . * | . |</td></tr>
<tr><td>6</td><td>1338.80</td><td>3939.19</td><td>-2600.39</td><td>| *. | . |</td></tr>
<tr><td>7</td><td>821.000</td><td>3001.81</td><td>-2180.81</td><td>| .* | . |</td></tr>
<tr><td>8</td><td>4552.40</td><td>1960.26</td><td>2592.14</td><td>| . | .* |</td></tr>
<tr><td>9</td><td>3949.10</td><td>866.642</td><td>3082.46</td><td>| . | . *|</td></tr>
<tr><td>10</td><td>5154.00</td><td>3366.35</td><td>1787.65</td><td>| . | * . |</td></tr>
</table>

Source: Own processed data under EViews program, according to Table 1 from Appendices

Annex 6: Turnover analysis of the state-run companies in Romania's tourism field, for the year 2015

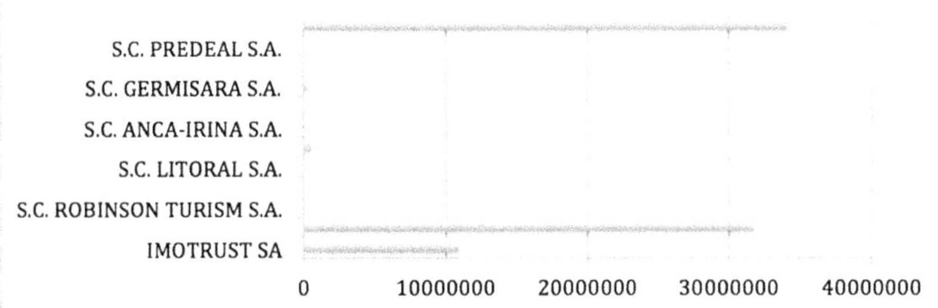

Source: Own processed data, under those published on the website of www.mfinante.ro

Annex 7: Profit and loss analysis of the state-run companies in Romania's tourism field, for the year 2015

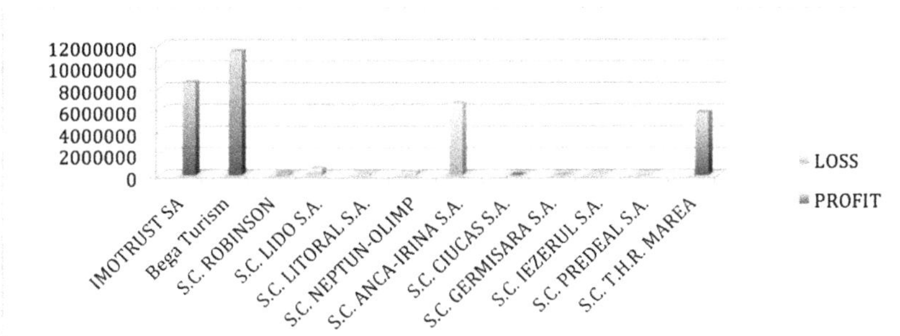

Source: Own processed data, under those published on the website of www.mfinante.ro

Annex 8: Incomes and costs analysis of the state-run companies in Romania's tourism field, for the year 2015

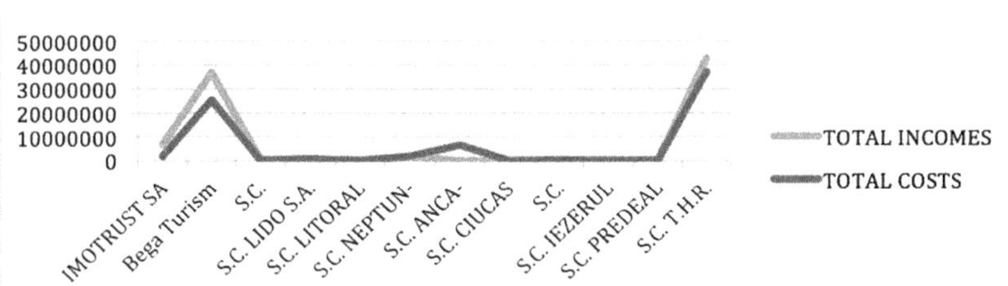

Source: Own processed data, under those published on the website of www.mfinante.ro

Annex 9: Debt analysis of the state-run companies in Romania's tourism field, for the year 2015

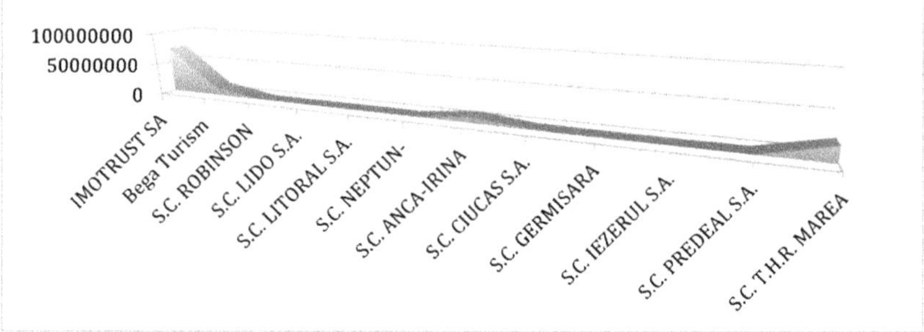

Source: *Own processed data, under those published on the website of www.mfinante.ro*

Annex 10: Number of employees analysis of the state-run companies in Romania's tourism field, for the year 2015

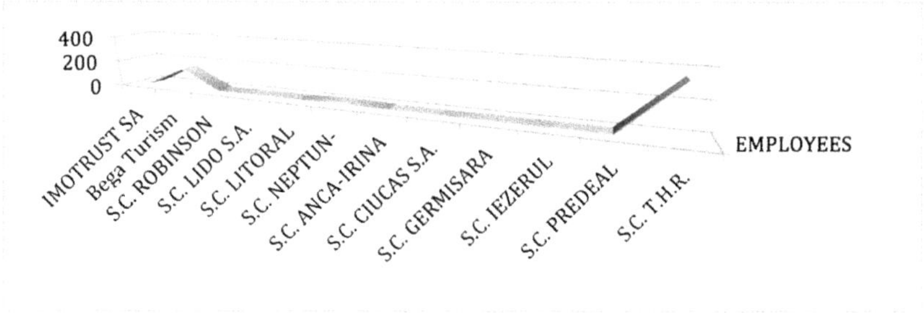

Source: Own processed data, under those published on the website of www.mfinante.ro

Victor PLATON

Institute of National Economy, Bucharest, Romanian Academy,
email: victor.platon54@gmail.com

Andreea CONSTANTINESCU

Institute of National Economy, Bucharest, Romanian Academy,
email: andreea_constantinescu07@yahoo.com

Side Effects of Subsidizing Renewable Energy Production in Romania

Abstract: This article analyzes the secondary/unintentional effects of subsidizing renewable energy production in Romania and other European countries, following the application of the European Union (EU) Climate and Energy 2020 legislative package. Economic instruments create incentives to promote environmental protection measures. In seeking to boost renewable energies, EU member states have chosen the method of subsidies granted to investors or a bonus for each MWh of electricity produced and uploaded to the network. Direct effects of renewable energy should be the elimination of polluting energy sources. This does not take place, at least in Romania, due to the nature of the installations producing renewable energy: they cannot provide energy twenty-four hours day, which requires the existence of backup equipment that comes into operation when it is not windy or at night. Therefore, technologies for producing renewable electricity cannot be considered mature after ten years of granting massive subsidy.

Keywords: renewable energy, subsidy, green certificate, side effects

Introduction

The Climate and Energy 2020 Package is a set of binding standards for the member states that aims to ensure that the European Union (EU) meets its climate and energy targets for 2020. The package sets out three main objectives:

- 20% reduction in greenhouse gas emissions (compared to 1990 levels);
- 20% of EU energy produced from renewable sources;
- 20% improvement in energy efficiency.

The objectives were formulated by EU leaders in 2007 and enforced through the 2009 legislation. At the same time, the above objectives are also included in the Europe 2020 Strategy for Smart, Sustainable and Inclusive Growth. In this paper, we discuss how to achieve Objective 2—i.e. 20% of the EU energy produced from renewable sources—in light of the developments in the 2004–2014 period.

1. The share of energy from renewable sources in gross final consumption, in Romania (2004–2014)

The main indicator for monitoring the 20/20/20 Strategy objectives is *share of energy from renewable energy sources (RES) in gross final consumption (%)*. As shown in Figure 1, in the analyzed period (2004–2014) there was a general increase in the share of RES. For example, the European average increased from 8% in 2004 to 16% in 2014.

In Romania, in 2004, the share of RES was around 17% and production was due almost entirely to the hydropower system built prior to 1990. Following the implementation of the package of measures created to achieve the goals/objectives for 2020, installations of hydro, solar, wind, biogas etc. plants increased from 17% to 24% of the total gross energy consumption, exceeding the target proposed by the EU for 2020. This unexpected situation is due, on the one hand, to the high share of existing hydro power facilities and, on the other hand, to the substantial subsidy granted to other types of renewable energy: wind, solar, small hydro and biomass.

Analyzing Figure 1 we notice that Romania is part of a group of countries (Sweden, Latvia, Finland, Austria, Denmark, Croatia, Portugal, Estonia, Lithuania and Slovenia) that exceeded the 20% target. These countries also benefit from a favorable geographical position that facilitated the development of the RES. Other countries that have a less favorable position and have no exploitable renewable resources were reluctant to make the investments needed to achieve the targets proposed by the EU ahead of schedule.

Fig. 1: Share of renewable energy in gross final consumption in EU (2004–2014)

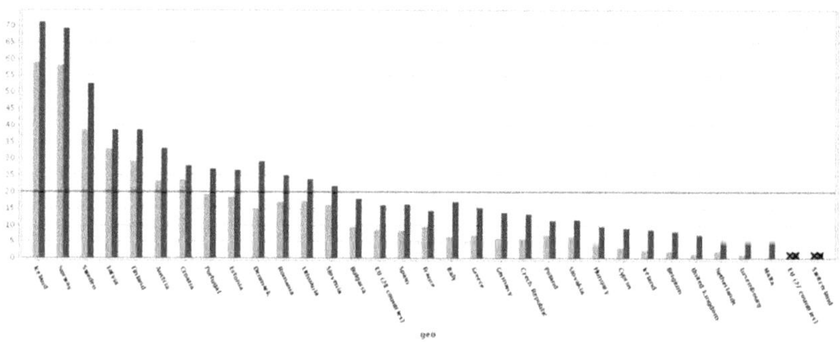

Source: Author, based on data from Eurostat, 2016, www.eurostat.org

We further analyze side effects of subsidies granted to producers of RES in Romania in order to achieve, ahead of schedule, the targets of the 20/20/20 Strategy.

2. Economic instruments to promote renewable energies in Romania

Economic instruments create incentives to promote environmental protection measures. In seeking to boost renewable energies, EU member states have chosen the method of subsidies granted to investors or a bonus for each MWh of electricity produced and uploaded to the network. The most representative field for the analysis of economic instruments for promoting renewable energy in Romania is the energy sector, which has the largest contribution to GHG emissions (Table 1).

Table 1: Economic instruments to promote renewable energy and reduce GHG in Romania

Sectors with high contribution to GHG emissions	**Share of total national GHG emissions (% in 2013)**	**Ways to answer / action**
Energy	58.1	RES subsidizing through green certificates
Transportation	11.8	Subsidies to promote biofuels, fuel cells, etc.
Agriculture	15.9	Control of livestock, rice crop control, etc.
Residential sector	3.7	Subsidies for thermal insulation of buildings, etc.

Source: Worked out by the authors.

According to Table 1, we can observe an extremely high share of the energy sector compared to other sectors considered as major emitters of GHG at the national level. In such circumstances, it is justified to examine the side effects of subsidies to the renewable energy sector through green certificates, for which the period under review is 2004–2014.

Thus, an economic analysis can be useful both for highlighting their effectiveness and to find possible alternatives for reducing GHG emissions in energy. The RES promotion system in Romania is based on subsidies called green certificates. This is a complex and intricate regulation through numerous laws, decisions, approvals and orders issued by the institutions involved. In principle, in Romania, the support scheme for green energy (solar, wind, micro-hydro, biogas) encourages investment in renewable energy and grants them green certificates. These green certificates are traded on a specific market. Essentially, green certificates, promoted by the National Energy Regulation Authority (NERA) and the Transelectrica SA operated by the Romanian Electricity and Natural Gas Operator (OPCOM), are a mechanism for subsidizing the RES production and its use through the intervention on the final price paid by consumers.

Green certificates can be used within 16 months and Romanian authorities estimated that the price attained the minimum level in 2016, when their number exceeded the threshold imposed by legislation. RES producers are required to offer on the market all the certificates they hold as long as, in one year, the offer is lower than the request, except for producers that are also suppliers and use their own green certificates in order to fulfill their mandatory annual quota.

To benefit from green certificate subsidies, a RES producer must be accredited by the NERA, in terms of rules of accreditation. The number of green certificates received by each producer varies depending on the type of installation. For example, wind farms are granted two green certificates for one MWh produced and solar energy receives six certificates for each MWh.

For the reason of granting generous subsidies, six years earlier Romania reached the assumed Strategy 20/20/20 target with the secondary effect of electricity price increase. Due to the fact that the initial allocation of green certificates was exaggerated (without any calculation), the number of green certificates that should go to each RES producer was reduced in 2014 as follows: from six to three certificates per MWh for solar plants, from two to 1.5 certificates per MWh for new wind capacity, from two to 1.3 per MWh for the pre-existing ones and from three to 2.3 certificates per MWh for hydropower plants below 10 MW capacity. By 2015, the average sale price of green certificates on the dedicated trading market was €29.36 per certificate, the minimum threshold value was preserved for 2016 (NERA, 2015).

3. The mechanism of subsidy; green certificates market in Romania

Green certificates are direct subsidies for RES producers, based on the energy production capacity (kWh) reported. In Romania, the green certificates are presented as electronic documents issued by the network operator, in this case, Transelectrica SA. Each RES producer receives a number of certificates, commensurate with the energy supplied in the system. They trade, distinctly from the certificates, the energy produced by them. Green certificates are traded on a market for green certificates, organized by a specialized operator in Romania, OPCOM. RES producers are those that sell the energy produced in this system and buyers are companies and households that pay a percentage set by law within their energy bill. Under this system, the grant is transmitted to producers by paying electricity bills by households and companies. To the value of green certificates is added the value-added tax (19% – VAT). That means an increase in the bill for electricity by 10–12% just for green certificates.

By law, the green certificates market has two separate components, which operate independently: a centralized market and one of bilateral contracts. The price of green certificates is set through a market mechanism, with legally binding terms for electricity producers. The green certificate market is centralized and provides the necessary transparency for a competitive environment. It works by registration of participants and monthly offers for sale or purchase. OPCOM takes these offers and validates them, setting the trading day, closing market price of green certificates (PIPGC) and the number of green certificates (GC) traded.

The onset of the green certificates market (PCBGC) was in February 2014 when the first centralized transaction was completed. By the end of 2014, they were traded by 467 active participants on the PCBGC, out of the 728 registered on the green certificate market, i.e. a total of 21,805,810 certificates. Their weighted average price was 134.21 lei/certificate (30.06 EUR/certificate).

Transactions established in 2014, cumulated on the two markets, comprised a number of 24,480,984 green certificates, representing obligations assumed by the contract partners for periods reaching 15 years, according to contract terms. For the energy produced from January to December 2014, a number of 12,328,894 green certificates were issued.

Table 2: Number of green certificates issued and subsidy value in Romania (2005–2015)

Year	Issued certificates	Average price		Subsidy value	
		RON/ GC	Euro/ GC	RON	Euro
2005	7.608	149.26	37.63	1,135,570	286.289
2006	23.497	168	42	3,947,496	986.874
2007	47.200	142.7	42	6,735,440	1,982,400
2008	141.068	301.5	45	42,532,002	6,348,060
2009	241.517	347.34	55	83,888,515	13,283,435
2010	693.463	232.36	55	161,133,063	38,140,465
2011	1,732,270	224.6	56.15	389,067,842	97,266,961
2012	5,547,302	229.928	56.08	1,275,480,054	311,092,696
2013	10,133,040	236.57	57.7	2,397,173,273	584,676,408
2014	12,650,486	161.6	36.07	2,044,318,538	456,303,030
2015	14,157,103	130.9	29.36	1,853,164,783	415,652,544
TOTAL	**45,374,554**			**8,258,576,576**	**1,926,019,162**

Source: Author, based on data from NERA Annual Reports, 2005–2015.

Table 2 presents the evolution of the total number of green certificates issued in Romania by the national authority during the 2005–2015 period and the average trading price of the certificates as well as the total amount recorded at the end of the year. We notice the number of green certificates grew at a steady pace until 2009, and since 2010, growth has been exponential, more than 14 million in 2015.

Fig. 2: Evolution of issued green certificates in Romania (2005–2015)

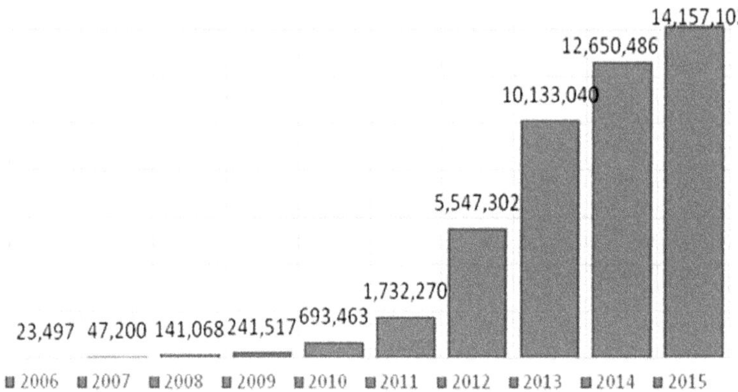

Source: Author, based on data from NERA Annual Reports, 2005–2015.

During the period under review, it is clear that the granted subsidy amounted to 8.26 billion lei or the equivalent of nearly two billion euro. Through this mechanism, in ten years, the RES share grew by 7% in total gross energy consumption (from 17% to 24.5%), exceeding the target of green energy proposed by the EU for 2020, as of 2014. The graphic situation of the green certificate market evolution is illustrated in Figure 2.

Regarding Romania, the described mechanism for the RES development support system based on a compulsory quota of electricity, combined with trading a number of green certificates, transfers all costs to final consumers (firms and households). The fact that a large number of investors accessed this support system even after subsidy was reduced by 50% means that this system granted an over-compensation to investors and created an unreasonable burden on consumers.

At the national level, the most significant increase was registered by wind power plants, which, in 2012, recorded a plus of 665% over the previous year.

Fig. 3: Evolution of subsidies granted for RES and coal mining sectors

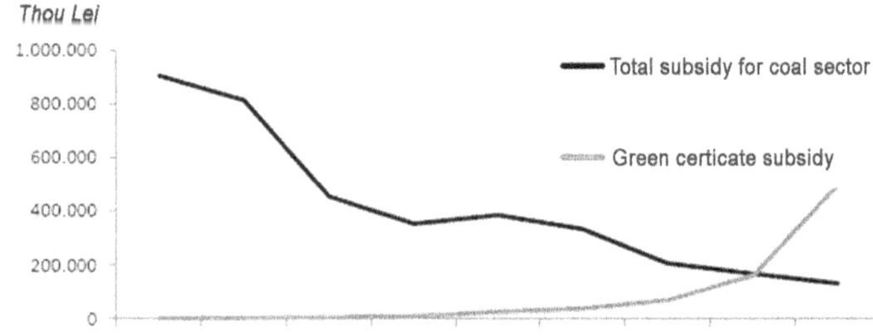

Source: Annual Report OPCOM, 2015.

By comparing the amounts received for subsidizing coal with those for subsidizing renewable energy, as submitted by the responsible authorities, covering the 2005–2013 period, we notice that, by 2010, the amounts received by RES producers were insignificant, as the coal industry received grants five times higher (see Figure3). In 2012 the trend reversed.

Fig. 4: Evolution of RES capacities that benefited from subsidies in relation to the system operating days (2005–2015)

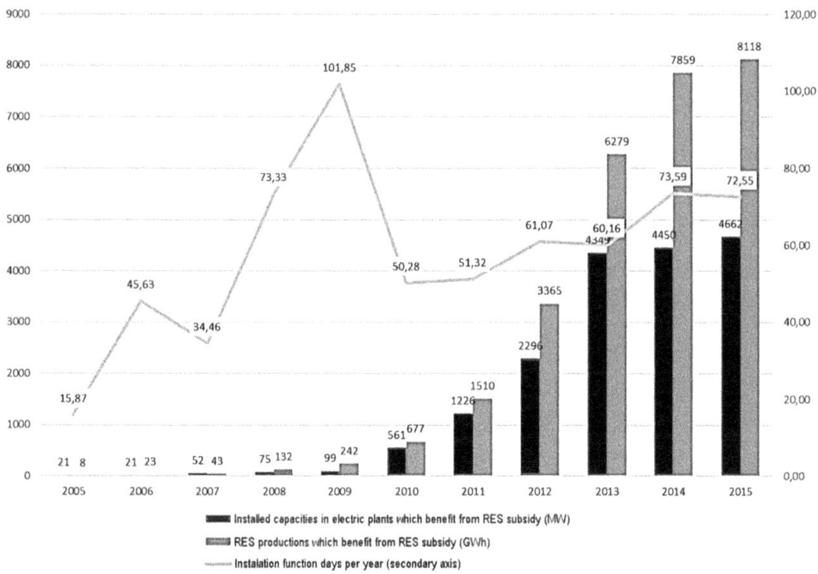

Source: NERA Annual Report, 2016.

Figure 4 presents the evolution of a significant indicator belonging to this sector: installed electricity capacity for plants that are part of the RES subsidy system. It can be seen that since the launch of green certificates until now, this indicator grew steadily, and in 2009–2013, it almost doubled every year (NERA, 2016).

Calculating by installed capacity and the number of operating days during a year, it appears that the average is about 58 days a year. Given that the minimum is 15.8 and the maximum is 101.8 days per year, it may be concluded that the facilities currently existing in Romania alone cannot provide the energy needed for 24 hours a day, 365 days per year. Due to specific climate conditions, wind and solar power are randomly distributed throughout the year so the installations that produce energy are less reliable than other power sources.

4. Side effects resulting from subsidizing renewable energy

The direct effect of subsidizing renewable energy is supposed to produce the reduction of greenhouse gas emissions. According to the theory, this type of energy is clean and virtually endless, in the medium and long term. As well, it is alleged that costs are much lower, especially if the price of oil products were to increase rapidly. Hypothetically, renewable energy provides improved security of energy supply and limits the import of energy.

So far there has been no audit done to show or to prove which is the contribution of subsidies to GHG reduction. Industry decline caused by the electricity price increase cannot stand for a policy to reduce GHG emissions (Platon, Turdeanu, 2006).

It is certain that investments in renewable energies also produce unexpected effects. For example, in Germany, after investments of billions in renewable energy installations, all in order to reduce GHG emissions, in 2013 they found that lowering CO_2 emissions was only temporary, and currently the trend is rising again (Porter E., 2016). This happens because renewables do not usually have a constant flow of energy as they are dependent on environmental conditions (sunlight, wind), and when the sun or wind are not present, thermo plants using classical methods (coal, natural gas) must be operated fast to cover energy demand. Practically every KW of renewable energy capacity installed must be doubled by gas or coal capacity production, which is started when there is no wind or sun.

Thus, substantial investments made in Germany in order to achieve GHG emission reduction targets proposed by the European Horizon 2020 strategy prove to be unsuccessful or at least substantially below the forecast efficiency, because CO_2 emissions did not decrease. Maintaining the function of thermo power plants is expensive, but necessary in this context. For example, Germany now covers 40% of domestic consumption from energy produced by thermo power plants (Neubacher A., 2013). Given that power plants are increasingly used for backup capacity, the question is whether there are investors in coal plants or gas, when they cannot be operated constantly but only on a transitory basis, with high GHG emissions.

4.1. Overgeneration and replacing other sources of energy in the network

Oversupply of energy occurs when all the energy generated, including that from renewable energy sources, exceeds the demand in real time. This phenomenon is also aggravated as more renewable energy is added to the network but the demand for electricity does not increase. This phenomenon is also aggravated by the fact that plants producing energy from renewable energy are producing expensive energy, and the authorities are forced to purchase through long-term contracts concluded in previous years. This is a matter of concern because if the market cannot automatically handle the oversupply, this can lead to overgeneration, requiring government intervention to maintain balance on the market. In periods of overgeneration, the wholesale price of energy can be very low and even negative (energy suppliers must pay the electricity network to take their generated energy, especially if the power plants cannot be closed frequently, the nuclear plants).

Thus, a first very visible side effect of developing renewable energy is replacing other electricity generators. In Germany, renewable energies have replaced energy produced by nuclear power plants that were deliberately closed (but did not replace thermo energy).

In the US, specifically in California, nuclear energy sources are threatened with bankruptcy because they cannot provide energy at times of high consumption, i.e. during the day. Figure 5 (Goose Curve) presents the situation of energy consumption throughout the day (in California). Starting at 6 am, the solar capacities become operational and are given priority in consumption. Because solar capacities are growing in the US, they are expected to eliminate other producers during the sunny period (6 am–6 pm). At the end of this period, the supply of solar energy falls sharply just when consumption increases suddenly and requires an additional capacity of 13,000 MWh for the next three to four hours to cover this demand. The issue raised by this pattern appears more significant in the case of renewable energy, mainly solar, which can provide large amounts of energy for the periods of time when there is sunlight, between 6 am and 6 pm and, between the hours of 5 pm to 8 pm, which is the end of the day. When daylight decreases, their production stops and other sources must provide electricity to cover the high demand for energy.

Fig. 5: Evolution and forecast of energy demand throughout a day in California ("goose" curve)

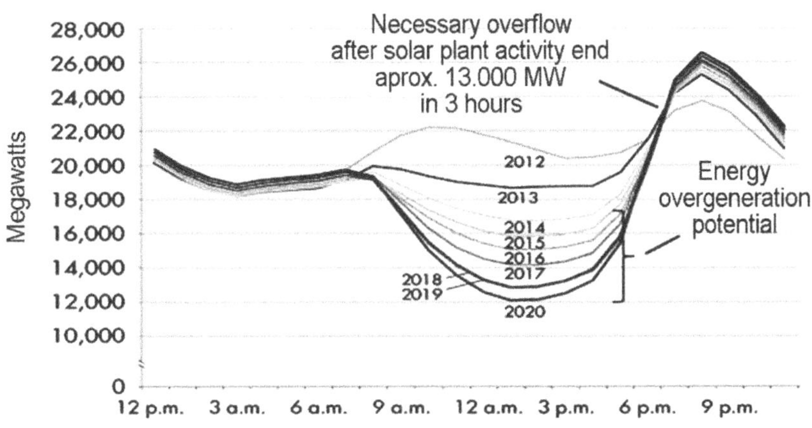

Source: Author, based on data from Loutan C., 2015, CAISO.

As nuclear capacities are in danger of bankruptcy because they no longer have access to the power network, the question is how to cover this big demand in the in the evening. It is forecasted that in 2020 no producer will be able to cover the demand. One solution is to limit solar capacities and enable coexistence of other energy sources.

Another solution could be the shutdown of nuclear power plants, like in Germany, but then gas power units should be built to stand in reserve. With this solution, an analysis recently conducted by Bloomberg New Energy Finance showed that nuclear reactors that provide 56% of the US energy come to operate at a loss in more than three years. If they were replaced with central gas—a cheap and available resource, it would increase CO_2 emissions by 200 million tons annually (Porter E., 2016).

This is actually the paradox of energy from renewable sources: with increased production capacity of clean energy, nuclear energy is eliminated and thermoelectric capacity is installed, to ensure flexibility and continuity of electricity supply, but increasing GHG emissions.

4.2. Electricity price increase and effects on industrial structure

As mentioned above, the price of electricity increases by 10–12% due to subsidies (Green Certificates or GC) and VAT for GC. As a result of the increase in electricity price, the social efficiency of the subsidy is negative because it reduces the low-income population's access to electricity. The second effect of increasing the electricity price is the loss of jobs in industry. During 2005 to 2014, the Romanian industry lost more than 350,000 jobs.

Table 3 presents the dynamic of employment in metallurgy and chemical industries for the period of granting of subsidies for renewable energies (2005–2014). As one can see, 27,000 jobs were lost in metallurgy while the chemical industry lost 23,000 jobs.

Below we test the hypothesis that there is a direct link between the increase in electricity prices, the main cause of which was a subsidy for renewable energy and job losses in some industry sectors (we chose two industries highly dependent on electricity consumption).

Table 3: Evolution of jobs in two industrial sectors in Romania (2005–2014) (thou employees)

	Metallurgical Industry	Chemical Industry
2005	57	49
2006	55	46
2007	50	47
2008	48	45
2009	37	31
2010	36	30
2011	35	29
2012	33	30
2013	30	27
2014	30	26
Difference 2014–2005	**-27.00**	**-23.00**

Source: Author, based on data from Statistical Yearbook of Romania, INS, 2016.

For this, we used a regression analysis in which the independent variable was the GC value (Ln (GC)) while the dependent variable was the number of employees in the metallurgical (Figure 6) and chemical (Figure 7) industries. The results are discussed below; they reiterate the theory that links between various economic indicators can be confirmed by the usual statistical analysis (Platon, Constantinescu, 2014).

4.3. The link between employees in the metallurgical industry and green certificates

In order to analyze the link between employees in the metallurgical industry and GC value, a semi-logarithmic plot model has been used. The resulting equation and R^2 are:

Metallurgical Industry Employees = 90.61 -3.813* Ln (Green Certificate Value)

$$R^2 = 0.924$$

Statistical parameters of the equation are as follows:

	Coefficients	*Standard Error*	*t Stat*	*P-value*	*Confidence interval (99%)*
Intercept	90.613	5.110312	17.731	1.047E-07	[73.466 ; 107.761]
Ln (GC Value)	-3.813	0.386609	-9.863	9.40362E-06	[-5.110;- 2.516]

The table above shows that the two parameters of the equation are statistically significant (the probability of accepting the null hypothesis is by far lower than the threshold proposed, 0.01).

Fig. 6: The link between the number of jobs in the metallurgical industry and the green certificate subsidy granted, in Romania (2005–2014)

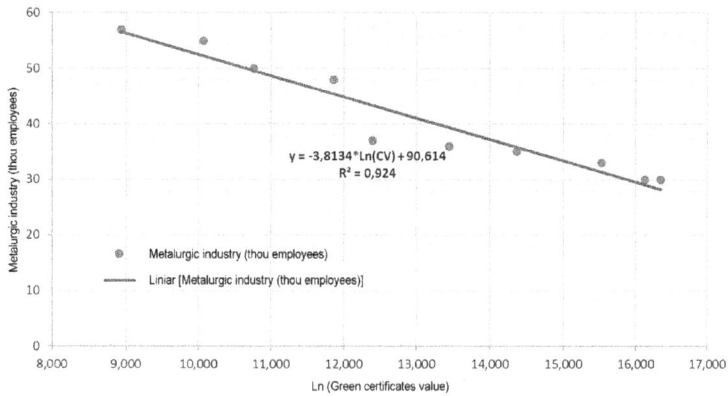

Source: Author, based on data from the Statistical Yearbook of Romania, 2014 and ANRE Annual Report, 2006–2014.

The calculation reveals that the confidence intervals do not include the zero value, which indicates a significant relationship between the two variables analyzed. We consider that the independent variable influences the dependent variable by 92.4%.

4.4. The link between employees in the chemical industry and green certificates

To examine this link, we used a semi-logarithmic plot model. The resulting equation and R^2 are detailed below.

Chemical Industry Employees = 79.03 -3.314* Ln (Green Certificate Value)

$$R^2 = 0.8438$$

Statistical parameters of the equation are as follows:

	Coefficients	*Standard Error*	*t Stat*	*P-value*	*Confidence interval (99%)*
Intercept	79.029	6.663	11.860	2.34314E-06	[56.672; 101.387]
Ln (GC Value)	-3.313	0.504	-6.574	0.0001739	[-5.005; -1.622]

From the above table, we see that the two parameters of the equation are statistically significant with a probability higher than the threshold of 0.01.

We notice that the confidence intervals do not include the value of zero, which indicates a significant relationship between the two variables analyzed. We consider that the independent variable influences the dependent variable by 84.3%.

Fig. 7: The link between jobs in the chemical industry and subsidy granted by Green Certificates, in Romania (2005–2014)

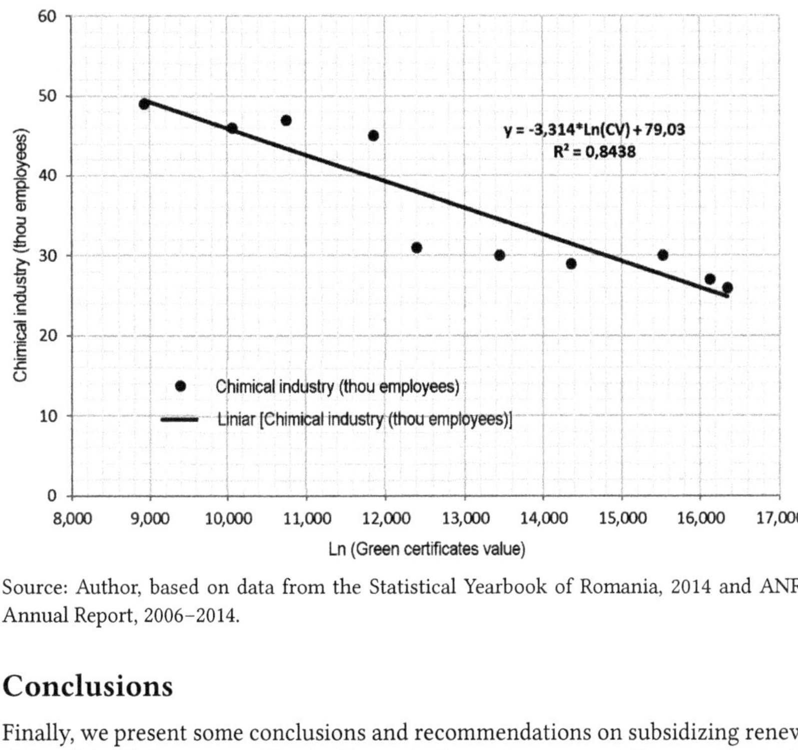

Source: Author, based on data from the Statistical Yearbook of Romania, 2014 and ANRE Annual Report, 2006–2014.

Conclusions

Finally, we present some conclusions and recommendations on subsidizing renewables. Subsidizing renewables in Romania through green certificates attracted a large number of investors, which resulted in a share of renewable energy in final consumption of 24.5% in 2014 (from this value, 17% were pre-existing hydro capacities, and only 7% of output is the energy produced by wind, solar, small hydro, and biogas). The target of 24% was expected to be reached in 2020, but because the subsidy was extremely high (virtually no economic justification for the value of green certificates granted), there was an effect specific to pyramid schemes. Many investors rushed to install wind, solar, small hydro generators to benefit from the money available because it was clear that the initial level of subsidy was not sustainable.

There was a hypertrophic development of facilities producing renewable energy without taking into account technological efficiency criteria, the meteorological factors etc. As for small hydropower, over 500 plants under ten MW are in operation, under construction or endorsement (Macri D., 2014). Although the Water Framework Directive requires a good water quality, few mountain rivers in Romania remained in their natural state; water from mountain rivers was diverted into underground pipes destroying entire mountain river ecosystems.

Direct effects of renewable energy should be the elimination of polluting energy sources and the reduction of CO_2 emissions. This does not take place due to the nature of installations producing renewable energy: they cannot provide energy throughout the day, which requires the existence of backup capacities that come into operation when it is not windy, at night or when there is drought. This reserve capacity can only be thermo plants that can be turned on or off relatively quickly. Nuclear plants cannot play this role. For this reason, some countries such as Germany, which made great efforts for "green revolution", faced increases in CO_2 emissions, not decreases as planned. Thus, renewable energies cannot be considered zero emission technologies. For these technologies, one should allocate CO_2 emitted by heating plants in stand-by to be turned on when there are adverse weather phenomena.

At the national level, although the value of green certificates was reduced by half in 2014, the interest in the subsidies remained just as high, especially since bank interests are close to zero. Such investments in renewables have high returns of 12–15% per year, which will put pressure on new solar/wind farms, although the side effects are significant. By providing a subsidy of about two billion euro in ten years, an over-capacity of renewables occurred six years before the 2020 deadline. The awarded grant is not derived from the consolidated state budget but is paid directly through the electricity bill by households and firms. Consequently, there was an electricity price rise that consequently eroded Romania's industrial competitiveness. Many firms in industries with high added value, such as the metallurgical or chemical, lost in this last decade 27,000 and 23,000 jobs respectively. The causal link between the number of green certificates issued and decreasing employment in industry is statistically significant.

The phenomenon of electricity networks' oversaturation occurs when renewable energy production is high (favorable climatic factors) and demand is low. Although renewable energy is more expensive due to long-term contracts, it is highly purchased, while other types of energy no longer have buyers. A phenomenon of dislocation from the network of other energy producers appeared, especially during favorable daytime (abundant sunshine, wind, etc.). This dislocation creates great difficulties for the electricity supply after sunset, when energy demand is growing sharply.

Therefore, technologies of producing renewable electricity cannot be considered mature in ten years of granting this subsidy. Economic efficiency is negative, because they cannot operate without subsidies and social efficiency is also negative because, by increasing the price of electricity, it limits the access of the vulnerable population groups to electricity. Also, environmental efficiency is not positive because, as shown, in some countries CO_2 emissions are increasing. It is true that the energy price increase has caused elimination by bankruptcy and insolvency of some industries but this course of action is not useful as a tool for environmental policy. To eliminate excesses made in promoting green certificate subsidy, a series of measures should be taken:

a) Audit of the current scheme of subsidizing renewable energies to determine environmental effectiveness.
b) Development of transparent grant schemes that provide investors with income equal to the average industrial sector; this would mean calculation methods that take into account the amounts invested and the technologies used and profit limiting in correlation with average interest rates of amounts deposited in banks.
c) Maintaining an elastic structure of energy supply that prevents hypertrophic growth of renewables because it eliminates other energy producers (nuclear power); it is possible that 10% green energy, without taking into account the hydro power, could be a maximum value.
d) Removal of VAT payment at green certificate subsidy would limit electricity price increase and ease pressure on the jobs in industry.
e) Reduction in subsidy for solar energy because it is the most expensive, and the sunny period in Romania is on average 2,000 hours/year compared to other areas with more than 4,000 hours/year.

References

1. Loutan, C. (2015). Briefing on the duck curve and current system conditions, http://www.caiso.com/Documents/Briefing_DuckCurve_CurrentSystemConditions-ISOPresentation-July2015.pdf.
2. Macri, D. (2014). Microhidrocentrale – Macroprobleme, National Geographic., nr. 127, https://www.natgeo.ro/romania/natura-ro/10086-microhidrocentrale-macroprobleme.
3. Neubacher, A. (2013). Reality check – Germany's defective green energy game plan, Der Spiegel, http://www.spiegel.de/international/germany/commentary-why-germany-is-waging-its-green-revolution-wrong-a-929693.html.
4. Osborn, L. (2016). Sunniest Places and Countries in the World, https://www.currentresults.com/Weather-Extremes/sunniest-places-countries-world.php.
5. Platon V., Turdeanu A. (2006). The Sustainable Development in the EU and Romania: Comparative Analysis, Romanian Journal of Economics, nr.23/2006, http://www.revecon.ro/content/volume-23-2006.
6. Platon V., Constantinescu A. (2014). Monte Carlo method in risk analysis for investment projects, Procedia Economics and Finance, vol. 15/2014, http://www.sciencedirect.com/science/article/pii/S2212567114004638.
7. Porter E. (2016). How Renewable Energy Is Blowing Climate Change Efforts off Course, http://www.nytimes.com/2016/07/20/business/energy-environment/

how-renewable-energy-is-blowing-climate-change-efforts-off-course.html?_r=0.
8. Anuarul Statistic al României, 2006–2015, http://www.insse.ro/cms/ro/content/indicatori-de-dezvoltare-durabila.
9. Raport anual ANRE, 2006–2014, http://www.anre.ro/ro/despre-anre/rapoarte-anuale.
10. Raport anual OPCOM, 2016, http://www.opcom.ro/tranzactii_rezultate...
11. http://ec.europa.eu/eurostat/data/database.
12. Legea nr. 220/ 2008, pentru stabilirea sistemului de promovare a producerii energiei din surse regenerabile de energie, publicat în: Monitorul Oficial nr. 577 din 13 august 2010.
13. OUG 57/2013 privind modificarea şi completarea Legii nr. 220/2008 pentru stabilirea sistemului de promovare a producerii energiei din surse regenerabile de energie. Publicat în Monitorul Oficial, Partea I nr. 335 din 7 iunie 2013.
14. http://www.agerpres.ro/externe/2013/04/04/corespondenta-bulgaria-criza-fara-precedent-in-sectorul-de-energie-productia-depaseste-cu-mult-consumul-presa--11-03-41.

www.ingramcontent.com/pod-product-compliance
Ingram Content Group UK Ltd.
Pitfield, Milton Keynes, MK11 3LW, UK
UKHW021830100926
8556IPUK00004B/263

9 783631 673317